Matthew 16-20

Commentary

by

Stephen Manley

Upward Flight Books™

Matthew 16-20 Commentary

Copyright © Stephen Manley, 2009

Edited by Delphine Manley

ISBN: 978-0-578-02355-7

Additional copies may be ordered from:

Stephen Manley Evangelistic Association, Inc.
PO Box 2089
Lebanon, TN 37088-2089

www.crossstyle.org

CONTENTS

Part Three: Matthew 17

Faith in the Cross :: *Confirmation of the Cross Style*

Part Four: Matthew 18

Self or the Cross :: *Confessions of the Cross Style*

Part Five: Matthew 19

Living the Cross :: *Configuration of the Cross Style*

Part Six: Matthew 20

Reviewing the Cross :: *Conclusions of the Cross Style*

PART ONE

Matthew 16:1-12

A Sign or a Cross

Considerations of the Cross Style

Matthew 16-20

Introduction

To study a passage properly, you must see that passage through the writer's purpose. To take the passage out of its context is to abuse and misuse the Word of God. The purpose of Matthew's writing is to convert the Jews to the truth and experience that Jesus Christ is the Kingly Messiah. His focus is on this one major thrust. He is like a lawyer, stacking evidence upon evidence, building a strong case. Each chapter, paragraph, verse, and word has significance in the fulfilling of this purpose. By the time you arrive at chapter sixteen, you have seen Jesus as authoritative over all elements of life (chapter 8). He even has authority over sin (chapter 9). The resource He contains for this ministry is so powerful, that He can give it to others (chapter 10). His ministry strategy is to win the world for the Kingdom (chapter 11). We see Him as King of the Kingdom over the Sabbath and in the thrust of the parables (chapters 12 and 13). All of this focuses on His power and rulership. It is a convincing argument.

Chapters fourteen and fifteen set the stage for a powerful truth. It is not a new truth, but Matthew highlights it now. Jesus takes His disciples from the ministry in Judea into Gentile territory. They travel up into Tyre and Sidon (15:21), and then, over the northern tip of Galilee, to Ceasarea Philippi (16:33). It won't be long before He will begin His last trip to Jerusalem for the Passion Week. There is a definite purpose for this move. He wants to focus on His disciples. Jesus has an important task to accomplish with them. Jesus must get them ready for the coming events. They need to grasp the fundamental of the Kingdom of God - the Cross. Jesus needs to be alone with His disciples to train them in this great truth. They must become people of the cross and its style.

Consideration of the Cross Style
Matthew 16

Jesus begins in chapter sixteen with the introduction of the subject. He approaches His disciples with a fundamental question. ***"But who do you say that I am?"*** (16:15). The response of the disciples encourages Jesus. It was a high moment for they are confessing Him as ***"the Christ, the Son of the living God,"*** (16:16). Jesus tells them He is going to build His church on this kind of confession. He is going to give the keys to the Kingdom of Heaven to the people who believe.

Jesus quickly moves into an area that strikes a nerve. Once the disciples really believe He is the Messiah, He moves into the discussion of "what kind of Messiah He is!" He begins to show them that He is a bleeding, suffering, dying Messiah, who is going to give His live for His world. Jesus gives His first prediction of His death and resurrection (16:21). The disciples respond to this violently. Peter takes Jesus aside and begins to rebuke Him (16:22). Again the discussion is not on whether Jesus is the Messiah, but upon the content of His Messiahship. The disciples are not responding well to the idea of a bleeding, dying, suffering Messiah. They want the miracle worker, ruler, who puts people in their place, a take charge kind of guy. They have this in mind because they want to derive the benefits of this kind of Messiah. The disciples have visions of thrones, for they had already been into the miracle work.

Jesus strongly resists their comments (16:23). He even says that they might think about how the disciples of that kind of Messiah would also experience bleeding, suffering, and dying. He is calling them to do exactly that. ***"If anyone desires to come after Me, let him deny himself, and take up his cross, and follow me,"*** (16:24). In this Kingdom He is establishing, no one can live for his or her self. The style of the Kingdom is that of King Jesus, which is to give yourself away.

Confirmation of the Cross Style
Matthew 17

"Now after six days" (17:1), is the way Matthew begins chapter seventeen. What had happened in the last days? Obviously, it is the argument and rebuking that have been taking place over the content of Jesus' Messiahship. Whether He is the Messiah is not the issue of the discussion. But there is heated argument about the context of a suffering Messiah. No doubt for six days Jesus has tried to show them Old Testament Scriptures, but they reported "that is not what our Sunday School teachers taught us." Their traditions, the way they have always done it, and what they have always believed, cause the disciples to resist the vital new truth presented to them by Jesus.

He must have thrown His hands in the air and said, "I do not know what to do with you. You are not listening to me. Your minds are already set. You, you and you (Peter, James and John), come with me. We are going to have a prayer meeting." So He takes three of the most influential disciples to the mountain to pray (17:1).

Jesus is transfigured right before their very eyes. His clothes begin to glisten from a light within. Moses and Elijah come down from heaven and begin to carry on a conversation with Jesus. What is the topic of discussion? It is the subject of the cross and its style (Luke 9:30-31). They must be telling Him not to give in to the rebuke of the disciples. They know that the cross is the only chance there is for righteousness. Moses had been the instrument of the law, but he knew the law had never produced righteous, Kingdom people. Elijah had done miracles and preached with power and passion, but he knew it had not produced righteous, Kingdom people. There is only one possibility for this to happen - Jesus has to go to the cross.

Before the scene is completed, the Father God descends upon the mount. What He has to say is powerful. ***"This is My beloved Son, in whom I am well pleased. Hear Him!"*** (17:5). Don't listen to your traditions or your prejudices. Don't listen to what you have always believed. Listen to the new truth that Jesus is telling you. It is the truth. He is a bleeding, suffering, dying Messiah, and if you are going to be a disciple in this Kingdom, you must embrace the cross and its style.

Jesus has now gathered the three disciples together and has started down the mountain to join the other nine disciples in the valley. The first subject He mentions in their conversation, after the Mount of

Transfiguration, is about His cross (17:9). He has again verified that He is a bleeding, suffering, and dying Messiah. This is His style.

Meanwhile, in the valley, nine disciples are in a dilemma. It should not have been a problem for them. In Matthew chapter ten, Jesus had given them His power and sent them out to minister. They came back from that experience excited that the very miracles' Jesus did, they were now able to accomplish. Even the demons came under their control these nine disciples have ministered in deliverance of demons. A father has come with his son who has a demon. He is seeking their help. There is only one demon; this will be no problem for the disciples with such vast experience as these nine. They move right in to handle the situation. After doing all the things they have always done, the demon laughs at them. The disciples find themselves powerless. Of course, when Jesus arrives in the valley, He immediately solves the problem. The nine disciples come to Him privately, and with some embarrassment, ask Him about their lack of power. Oh, the answer is plain! ***"Because of your unbelief,' He says, "***(17:20). He is telling His disciples that they do not trust Him. They must have looked at each other in amazement. When had they not trusted Him? They believed He was the Messiah. But they have argued with the new truth He has given them about the content of His Messiahship. You cannot argue with Jesus and have power for ministry.

You can easily see this is a chapter of great confirmation that Jesus is a bleeding, suffering, dying Messiah. If you are going to be His disciple, get ready for this style. On the Mount of Transfiguration, Moses and Elijah verify this great truth. The conversation of Jesus, as they descend the mountain, adds to the focus. The disciples in their lack of power tell us that this truth is vital.

Confessions of the Cross Style
Matthew 18

This chapter is a powerful theological statement. Jesus responds to a question being asked by the disciples (18:1). The entire chapter is a private discourse given only to the disciples (18:3-35). It again shows us how important it was in the mind of Jesus for the disciples to grasp the cross style.

To grasp the tone of the passage, there are certain things you need to keep in mind. The extent of the effort, thus far, has been to convey the truth to the disciples. Remember that the moment the disciples testified of His Messiahship, He began to tell them about this cross style content. This discussion went on for six days as they argued with Him. Jesus took three disciples to the Mount of transfiguration to pray about it. Moses and Elijah came down from heaven and verified the truth of the cross style. The Father spoke in confirmation. They discussed all of this on the descent from the mountain. The weakness of the nine disciples in the valley testified to the fact that they must embrace this bleeding, suffering, dying Messiah. Surely these disciples have gotten the message and will embrace the style of this Christ.

There is definitely a disruption taking place among the disciples. Their faces are a bit red for they have been in heated debate. Several of them won't stand next to certain others. They come to Jesus for a solution to their argument. It must be an important subject to create such an upheaval in the group. Here is the question they ask, ***"Which*** *one of us gets to be number one in the coming Kingdom?"* (18:1). Self-seeking, self-centeredness, and self-promotion fill these men. They have not gleaned the truth of the cross.

Jesus asks the disciples to sit, and they begin to discuss the content of His Messiahship in terms of a child. He calls a child over to sit on His lap. As the two of them hug each other, Jesus must have grinned at the disciples. He said, "See! This is what it is all about. All this child wants is me. This is all about love and not self-seeking." When will the disciples learn the great lesson of losing their lives? The cross style is the heart of the Kingdom.

Before His theological statement is over, Peter has interrupted Him (18:21). With an additional response Jesus ends His statements with a parable about forgiveness. At the heart of the cross style is forgiveness. It would be impossible to pour your life out for others without living in a constant state of forgiveness. Unforgiveness is a focus on oneself. Unforgiveness only sees the hurt it has experienced. Forgiveness dies to its own needs. Forgiveness thinks in terms of the other person and how to pour out its life. It is a powerful lesson!

Configuration of the Cross Style
Matthew 19

To study and discuss this theology is great; but it is not worth much unless we apply it. What does the theology of chapter eighteen mean in everyday life? Matthew takes the great theology and applies it to three main areas of life. It is interesting that these areas hit every one of us right at the core of our lives. These are not areas that would be of interest to the senior adults, but not the teenagers. These areas cut across all age brackets, cultural differences, and custom barriers. Here is how the cross and its style apply to everyday life.

The first area of application is **Marriage and Divorce** (19:1-2). Should not we see cross style in the home first? Jesus presents marriage from the original intent of God by quoting the Old Testament (19:4-5). The husband is to lose his life to his wife. He is not to live for himself, but for her. The wife is to lose her life to her husband. Thus, they become one flesh. This is the union of marriage. But the Pharisees reported that Moses "commanded" that they get a divorce (19:7). Jesus would not let them get by. The reason for divorce was not Moses, but the "hardness of your hearts." Moses simply "permitted" them to do what they had already decided to do (19:8). "Hardness of your hearts" has to do with an unforgiving spirit. That is what Jesus talked about in the theology section of chapter eighteen. Filled with themselves, the disciples state, ***"If such is the case of the man with his wife, it is better not to marry"*** (19:10). They miss the application of the cross and its style to the home life.

The second area of practical application is **Mothers and Dependents** (19:13-15). You see the power of this application forcibly when you look carefully at chapter eighteen and see how Matthew uses the words, child or little one. There is significance in each usage. When Jesus spoke of death to self-centeredness, His focus was on those who are less than you are. Soon after you see the disciples rebuking the children and they keep them from coming to Jesus as if they were unimportant. This cross and its style must apply to how we treat those who are not on our level. The only way you can pour out your life, for those who cannot give back to you, is to come to the cross.

Materialism and the Depressed is the third area of application (19:16-20). This is the story of the Rich Young Ruler, who comes running to Jesus in search of life. In His last statement to the young man, Jesus gives the answer to climax his search (19:21). ***"If you want to be perfect, go, sell what you have and give to the poor, and you will have treasure in heaven; and come, follow me."*** A key part to the statement is "you have." It is an ownership issue that is all about control. When we own, we control and demand. This is a call to the surrender of ownership that is the cross in its essence. Live the cross style in the materialistic realm of life.

Conclusion of the Cross Style
Matthew 20

It becomes very evident in this chapter that the disciples have not grasped the cross and its style. Two of the disciples, cousins to Christ, have brought their mother (Jesus' aunt) to ask Him a key question (20:20). They are asking about the possibility of these two disciples getting the right and left-hand positions in the coming Kingdom. Of course, when the other ten disciples hear about it, they are angry. There is an immediate power struggle. This is a repeat of chapter eighteen. The disciples have not learned the lesson about the cross style.

Jesus realized that His time with the disciples, in this type of intimate setting, is just about finished. He gives them a discourse that summarizes and gives the conclusions of the cross style message (20:25-28). He gives a strong call to servanthood (19:26), and even uses the symbol of "slave" (19:27). The highlight of His conclusion is that He is only asking them to do what He has already done (20:28). He is the pattern of the cross.

What a powerful section this is! We must interpret every paragraph of chapters sixteen through twenty, considering the total theme. We are anxious to begin a more detailed study of these chapters.

Matthew 16

Making of a God

There is a hideous disease that has infected humanity at a startling depth. It is cancerous in its nature, for it literally eats away the essence of living. When you know the truth about this disease, you are swept away by the terribleness of its destruction. You find yourself unable to think about anything else. You immediately want to go on television and have a telethon to raise enough money to do something about it. You find yourself unable to sleep at night. Everyone you see leaves a question in your mind, "Do they have it?" It is the worst of all plagues. It is not a matter of fact that one out of every four people experience this disease, as it is with cancer. Everyone has, or has had, this disease. I am talking about the terrible disease of the carnal mind.

The Apostle Paul spends much time in his writings exposing this mind. It is the opposite of the mind of Christ. It is enmity against God. This mind is in constant war against the Divine will. Every one of us has been born with it. This mind wells up within us and expresses itself in self-centeredness, pride, and self-sufficiency. You can see it in the attitude that wants to do its own thing. The focus of this mind is self.

A single ounce of this carnal mind is like an ounce of cancer. If you allow it to remain, it will eat its way to your vital organs. It will destroy you in total damnation. Death is inevitable if you tolerate one bit of self-centeredness. Some have thought to train this mind into submission. This is like bringing a wild cat into your home. You may have the best of intentions. You may have the best ability in animal training, but sometime your guard will be down and the wild cat, running freely in your home, will destroy you. It is a no win situation. So it is with the carnal mind. You cannot tolerate, train, or ignore it. The carnal mind must come to a cross and die!

This is the dynamic of the message Jesus is giving to His disciples. He has called His disciples to a special six months training where He will challenge them with His cross and its style. The title of chapter sixteen is "The Consideration of the Cross Style." Jesus introduces this subject as the theme of the training; it is His focus. He is building an entire Kingdom with the cross style as its foundation. Everyone in the Kingdom will live this way. The disciples must grasp it if they are to lead the world into the Kingdom.

You quickly see in chapter sixteen, that the disciples have a difficult time accepting the cross as the style of Jesus. They have no problem accepting Him as the Messiah, but He keeps breaking the Messiah rules. The Pharisees also have this problem. Jesus did not come as a Messiah from God should come. He did not fit their desires for what they wanted a Messiah to be. However, the basic problem with all these groups is not in their training or prejudices, but in the carnal mind.

A key expression of the carnal mind is that it needs to build and shape its god after its own image. Unless you realize this, the carnal becomes very difficult to identify. It can easily express itself in so many different ways. The carnal mind so attaches itself to the human personality, and interweaves itself throughout, that it is a natural expression of that person. It becomes difficult to distinguish what is carnal and what is human. The carnal mind expresses itself in drug addiction or in singing in the choir. It wears the garb of the street prostitute, but also can commit spiritual adultery while serving on the church board. Both are an expression of the self-centeredness within the heart.

However, there is a basic expression of the carnal mind in everyone's life. The carnal mind always builds its god according to its own self-serving ends. The carnal nature is not against God as such; it is only against the God it cannot control. The process is simple; you will recognize it, having done it yourself. This carnal mind constructs god according to the desires of the self. Having built a god with his own heart, man now asks, "What do you require of me, god?" Since I build my own god, how could he require anything except what I want him to require? So this god establishes the standards of my life, which are really my own requirements. I easily achieve them with a great sense of satisfaction. God says that I am okay. What god? The god who is a product of my own desires is approving me. This is really an approval of myself. It is all a product of carnal self-centeredness, the opposite of cross style.

You need to understand this for your own life, but also to understand chapter sixteen. This is the dynamic that is taking place. Here it is as a proposition: The god you build and/or serve will determine your entire life style. As we look at the complete view of this chapter we can see three examples of this truth.

HEAVENLY SIGNS VERSUS EARTHLY SIGNS
The Pharisees
Matthew 16:1-4

Verse one gives you the setting of the scene. ***"Then the Pharisees and Sadducees came, and testing Him asked that He would show them a sign from heaven."*** This is not the first time the Pharisees have engaged Jesus in this kind of demand (see Matthew 12:38-42). On that occasion, Jesus gave them such a powerful answer, and they went slinking away. Now they have finally regained courage with the help of reinforcements - the Sadducees. This is an interesting linkage, since these two groups are at the opposite ends of the theological poles. They are the conservatives (Pharisees) and the liberals (Sadducees) of the theological world. Now they have joined arms together against a common enemy - Jesus. Here is their demand, "Show us a sign from Heaven."

Let's look at the **Heavenly versus Earthly.** Understand that the demand as seen in verse one is a sign "from heaven." The word "from" literally means "out of." The Pharisees and Sadducees are asking for a sign out of heaven. My reaction to this is to ask, "What is your problem? Look all around you. What on earth do you think this Jesus has been doing?" He had been doing an abundance of miracles from raising the dead to healing the lepers. He had conquered nature my calming the seas and controlled the spiritual world by casting out demons. Every area of life has been touched with His tremendous miracle power. What other sign could He give than what He has already given? Their reaction is, "those don't count!" The Pharisees and Sadducees considered the miracles of Jesus as earthly signs. They wanted a demonstration from heaven. They wanted Jesus to do something similar to the Old Testament days. For instance, Elijah is on Mount Carmel with a great sacrifice altar he has drenched with water. He prays a five-second prayer and fire falls from heaven. Lightning bolts burn the sacrifice, the rocks melt, and the water evaporates. In another instance, Joshua and the Israelites were engaged in a great battle and they were winning. They were running out of time; it would soon be the Sabbath Day. The Israelites would have to lay down their weapons. It would be wholesale murder as the enemy destroyed them. Joshua prayed and raised his hands. The sun stood still for thirty-six hours as Israel won the battle. That is a powerful heavenly sign. The Pharisees and Sadducees are demanding this kind of sign again.

I used to do the same thing. However, I was a child when I demanded a sign from heaven. I am not saying that the Pharisees and Sadducees are childish, or am I? Before I would go to bed at night, I would place paper and pencil on my night stand. On my knees I would pray, "God, if you really hear my prayer, write me a note." There is no end to the problem of sign seeking. If God had written me a note saying, "Hi, Manley," and signed it, "God," I would have thought my mother did it. I would have put the paper out again and asked for a longer note. All the time I was demanding a sign, God must have been saying to me, "Look around you, son. I gave you Christian parents who love and pray for you. I gave you the opportunity of hearing the Gospel Sunday after Sunday. I have healed your body a dozen times when you did not even know it. I have saved you from accidents a multitude of times. I have given you the Word of God in your hands and a heart that hungers for it. What more do you want? You have your eyes on the clouds. You want some kind of lightning bolts flashing from the sky, when I have been intimately pouring my life all over you. How can you have the nerve to ask for a note?" I have discovered, if you cannot see Him in your day in and day out life, you will not see Him in the lightning bolts either.

Now notice with me, **Faith versus Sight.** Maybe this is the key factor to the whole matter. It is simply a matter of choice concerning what you believe. God has given each person, through prevenient grace, the ability to believe, but we decide the focus of that faith. Faith is not a mystical force that grips my heart and makes me believe in Christ. I choose to believe, or I choose not to believe. All of the signs in the world are not going to do that for me.

An example is the issue of creation by God or by evolution. What do you choose to believe? Prove to me the creation story as given in the Book of Genesis. It cannot be done. By scientific analysis and methodology, I cannot, without dispute, lay out evidence that God created exactly as the Book of Genesis says He did. If you are going to believe it, you must choose to do so. On the other hand, please prove creation by evolution. By scientific analysis and methodology, establish the evidence. You cannot! There are many missing links. If you are going to believe in evolution, you must choose to believe. However, I propose to you that it requires a greater leap of faith to believe in evolution than it does to believe in the Creator Christ.

Hundreds of people saw the miracles of Jesus and believed that He was the Messiah. The Pharisees and Sadducees looked at the same miracles and did not believe. It was a matter of their own choice! You have the same choice.

Now, please notice, **Spectator versus Participator.** The Pharisees and Sadducees have demanded a sign out of heaven. All of the miracles Jesus did have not convinced them He is the Messiah, because they choose not to believe. Why would they choose not to believe? Let us go back to the proposition of chapter sixteen. The god you build and/or serve will determine your entire life style.

The Pharisees and Sadducees have constructed god the way they want him. He is a god who does heavenly signs. He dwells in the temple and gives forth a lot of rules. Every now and then he spits out lightning bolts and startles everyone. We come on Sunday morning and applaud the god who performs his great heavenly feats for us. We can witness the activities of our god without getting involved.

Can you imagine having a God who does earthly signs? If you have a God who heals the sick, gets involved with the poor, and feeds the hungry, He might ask you to deliver the food He has multiplied. He might ask you to follow Him and get involved. We are much more comfortable with a god who juggles lightning bolts than a Jesus of the streets who calls us to join Him. No wonder we want a God who gives forth rules, then we can be legalistic and judge others. But the Christ of the cross will demand our lives poured out in His style - the cross style. We must deny ourselves and lose our lives. This is the struggle of chapter sixteen and the crisis of our personal lives.

MILITARY COMMANDER VERSUS SUFFERING SERVANT
The Disciples
Matthew 16:13-23

For nearly three years Jesus has been ministering to, and with His disciples. His disciples have seen, felt, and known the impact of His ministry. It has been on the job training. Do they understand what has been happening? Through all the demonstration, have they understood who He really is? After all of this training, it is time for the test. It is a bit risky. What if they did not get it? Jesus takes courage and starts out easy. **"Who do men say that I, the Son of Man, am?"** (16:13). In other words, what are the rumors from downtown? But that is not the real question on the heart of Jesus. **"What I really want to know is who do you say that I am?"** (16:15). Jesus must have held His breath waiting for their answer.

Peter came through victoriously as he jumped to his feet and shouted, **"You are the Christ, the Son of the living God"** (16:16). Jesus must have wiped the sweat from his brow. He responded by giving a blessing to Peter and the disciples. He told them that they had received the revelation from the very mind of God. He knew they really did believe He was the Messiah.

However, the major issue here was not just His position as Messiah, but the content of His Messiahship. Now He starts the training for which He has gathered his disciples together (16:21). Jesus is heading for the cross. He is a bleeding, suffering, dying Messiah. He is going to lose His life for the sake of His world. He is establishing a Kingdom upon the cross and its style. Everyone in the Kingdom is going to live by this fundamental principle. It is opposite of the Kingdom of the world.

The way to win is to lose! The way to live is to die! Jesus was going to set the pattern and establish it firmly through His cross.

The disciples responded immediately to this kind of Messiahship. Peter led the way by rebuking Jesus (16:22). This was not what the teachers had taught Peter concerning the actions of a Messiah. A Messiah did miracles, walked in power, conquered nations, and established thrones. The disciples just would not bend from this idea. They did not want a bleeding, suffering, dying Messiah. It was contrary to their teachings and everything they wanted.

Let me give you something of a background. The children of Israel had been in captivity in Babylon. In the Book of Nehemiah, we have the story of their return to Jerusalem. This took place under the leadership of Nehemiah, the prophet, and Ezra, the scribe. Their goal was to rebuild the temple and the city. These great leaders knew they would also need to retrain the people in the ways of Jehovah. They brought the people back to the law of God. They built a wooden platform from which they could read to the people every morning. However, there was a slight problem. The Old Testament law was in the Hebrew language. The Israelites had spoken Hebrew until the Babylonian captivity. Those who were born and raised in Babylon had learned Aramaic and did not understand Hebrew. It was necessary that a translation be made of the Old Testament books from Hebrew to Aramaic.

Dr. Dennis Kinlaw, of Asbury College, tells of being asked to teach a class on the Aramaic language. He decided to have the students translate the familiar Old Testament passage in Isaiah, chapter fifty-three. This passage concerns the Messiah, and the students were to translate from the Aramaic to English. In preparation for the class, he also did this translation. He reports that when he finished, he was a bit startled by his translation and decided to do it again. He discovered that when they had translated Isaiah fifty-three from Hebrew to Aramaic, they had changed all of the pronouns. They had altered the entire meaning. Instead of the passage reading, "But He was wounded for their transgressions, He was bruised for our iniquities: the chastisement of our peace was upon Him, and by His stripes we are healed." The Aramaic read, "But they were wounded for their transgressions, they were bruised for their iniquities; the chastisement of their peace was upon them, and by their stripes they were healed." The translators had changed the concept of the Messiah from a suffering servant to a military commander. The Messiah was not going to bleed and suffer for His people; He was going to come and make all bad people suffer and protect the chosen people of God. This is what Peter and the disciples had learned every Sunday morning in Sunday School class.

They believed Jesus was the Messiah. Therefore, He would be a military commander who would lead the way to military victory. How could it be that He would continually talk about dying on a cross? He spoke of throwing His life away and getting involved in the sins of those around Him. He was always doing non-Messiah type things. He washed disciples' feet and embraced lepers. This was a very hard thing for the disciples to understand, and was it any wonder? Who wants a Messiah who has the cross style?

Let me remind you of our basic proposition. The god you build and/or serve will determine your life style. A God of the military style would make all bad people suffer, but he would reward all good people, and that comforts us. If you have a suffering servant who gets involved in the hurts of the sinful world, He may ask you to join him. A military commander has a throne and would probably give us one. A suffering servant has a cross and would require us to bear one also. The disciples were not interested in this cross style. They argue about who would get the right and left-hand positions in the coming Kingdom (20:20-28).

Let us review. The Pharisees and Sadducees had built a god of rules and heavenly signs. They wanted spectacular activities from the sky. With this kind of god they could feel comfortable isolating themselves from the needs of their community. They did not have to get involved in the pain of their brother. It was a religion of spectators. Based upon their structuring of God, they dismissed Jesus as the Messiah. He simply did not qualify.

The disciples did believe that Jesus was the Messiah. However, they were like the Pharisees and Sadducees in that they wanted to shape the Messiah as they wanted. They pictured a military commander who would give them opportunity for power and position. This would not involve a cross, but would feed their own desire for prestige.

WINNER VERSUS LOSER
Jesus
Matthew 16:24-28

Jesus was the perfect demonstration of His Father. It is through Jesus we learn how the Father feels, acts, and thinks. He is the very insides of God, pulled out and dumped on the streets for us to view. Paul said, ***"He is the image of the invisible God,"***(Colossians 1:15). The invisible God stepped out of His hiding place to become known.

The God of Mt. Sinai has come from fiery law giving and has walked in our town. Now the God of the burning bush has become the visible Christ of the cross. We know God because of Jesus. Jesus expressed Him to us.

We have been operating on the premise that the god you build and/or serve will determine your entire life style. If this is true, it must be true for Jesus. Jesus knew the Father. He came from the very bosom of the Father. The intimacy that Jesus had with the Father reached out and shaped the life style of Jesus. Jesus lived as He did because of the intimacy He had with His Father. Thus, if you want to know what kind of god Jesus had, you can look at His life style and you see the true God.

Notice the **MOTIVE** of Jesus. We see it in verse twenty-four as Jesus calls His disciples to His life style. ***"If anyone desires to come after Me, let him deny himself. . ."*** To get next to Jesus is to be close to One who denies Himself. You cannot get near Jesus, even for a passing moment, without being aware that He is One who does not care about Himself, but cares for others. He is not pulling for Himself, but for others. He is not possessed with what He can get, but with what He can give. Jesus breaks the entire pattern of self-centered activity. When Jesus said, "This is the way God is," there was a ring of reality about it. Jesus did not just talk the theology of how God is; He lived a life proving the reality of it. Jesus was so deeply involved in the heart of God that it shaped His entire living experience. Now we know the heart motive of God because we have seen it shaping Jesus. But this was not just some good gesture. It played itself out in reality.

Notice the **METHOD** of Jesus. We see His method in verse twenty-four. ***"If anyone desires to come after Me, let him deny*** *himself, and take up his cross. . ."* It is not clear that the method was the cross and its style? I love the theology of the cross. I love to sing the great songs about the cross. I love to place the cross at the front of the church and wear a gold plated cross around my neck. But don't remove it from the hymn books. Don't take it from the front of the church. And please don't make it a living reality in my life. When the cross is not on a necklace around my neck, but is placed on my back, it consumes my life. This was Christ and His cross. It was reality. It was the actual shedding of blood. He took on the needs of His world. Do you know what He said about it? He said, *"Whatever the Father does, the Son also does in like manner"* (John 5:19). Why is Jesus embracing the cross and its style? Because He is intimate with His Father whose whole inward being flows with this style.

Notice the **MISSION** of Jesus. What was Jesus wanting to accomplish? We see it in verse twenty-four. *"If anyone desires to come after Me, let him deny himself, and take up his cross, and follow Me."* Jesus calls us to follow Him as He has been following the Father. Jesus has given Himself to the Father and, thus, has become a demonstration of the Father. We will display Jesus as He has displayed the Father. We will become the reproduction of the life of Christ in our world! If you will lose your life to Jesus as Jesus lost His life to His Father, you will prove Jesus as Jesus proved His Father.

Here is the supreme test. Can we tell that you belong to Jesus by your life style? You say you believe in Jesus, Who washed dirty feet, yet I see no bowl and towel in your hand. You say you believe in a Christ Who threw His life away for His world, yet I see you constantly saving and protecting yourself. You say you believe in a Christ of the cross, yet

I see you lounging in comfort. Please tell me how I can believe your testimony when your life style tells me it is not true? Your life style is shaped by the god you build and/or serve. Could it be we have been like the Pharisees, the Sadducees, and the disciples? We have built our own god. Could it be we have never embraced the real Christ and seen Him as He is? We have sung the song **OH, TO BE LIKE THEE**, but we never intended the real Christ to have His way in our lives.

This chapter is a call to the cross and its style. Who will risk his or her entire life and let the real Christ of the cross do the shaping? I want to be the one. It is the deepest motive of my heart to cease to shape Christ like I want Him, and allow Him to reveal Himself to me as He is. I know when I see Him as He is, I will be like Him. The god you build and/or serve will determine your entire life style.

Matthew 16:1-4

Denials of the Heart

As far as I can remember, no one ever asked me if I wanted to be born. No one came knocking on my door saying, "You should sign up now or you will miss it." I did not have any choice in the matter. I simply woke up one day and I was here. I found myself thrust into this world with all of its pressures, trials, tribulations, and overwhelming circumstances. No one ever asked me!

Now that I am here, it seems like I ought to have some rights in this whole scene of my living. Doesn't the fact that I was born give me some innate rights? Don't I have a right to my opinion? Don't I have a right to my own life style, to go, to do, and to be as I see fit? After all, I did not choose to be here. Doesn't that give me some definite rights upon which I can stand and make claims for myself?

Even when it comes to relationship with God, don't I have some rights? God can sit in His sky and make fantastic decisions about the universes, and I do not care. When He comes down here and sticks His fingers into the middle of my life experience, don't I have some rights?

Don't I have a right to make some demands of God? Don't I have a right to give God some advise? He is messing with my life. Should I not have some say into what effects my life?

There is a man called Jesus, who is walking the streets of our town. He is another budding Messiah. They come and they go, these Messiah types. We have had dozens of them come through here. They have done their miracles and pulled off their magic tricks. So what is so miraculous about one more budding Messiah, even if His name is Jesus? Am I so out of line when I come to Jesus and say, "You are going to have to prove it to me." After all, I should not be gullible and accept everybody who comes along claiming to be a Messiah. It is going to take a little more than a few articles in the tabloids to get me to accept His claims. This Jesus wants me to surrender my life to Him and follow Him as my Messiah. Then He is going to have to come up with some really convincing proof. After all, isn't this my right?

"Then the Pharisees and the Sadducees came, and testing Him asked that He would show them a sign from heaven," (16:1). The word "testing" is a very strong word. It literally means "to tempt Him." After all, isn't that within the realm of my rights? Shouldn't I press Jesus against the wall and test Him out? Aren't we supposed to try the spirits? We should not be blown about with every whim of doctrine or new idea that comes along. Would you not agree that we have a right and an obligation to do that? The word "asked" is very, very strong. It literally means "to demand or to insist." Here is a group of men who are leaders of their day. They are the intellectuals of their hour. They had the religious responsibility of leading the people of God. Don't they have the right to come and demand that Jesus must produce some very convincing proof? Who could say they are out of line? Wouldn't you and I join them?

Before you answer, or pass any judgments, or make any decisions, think it through. There is a little bit of this in all of us! Which one of us hasn't come into the face of God making our demands? After all, don't we know best? It is our life? Hasn't each of us told God how to heal us? Which one of us hasn't told God what to do about our circumstances? We have been full of advice, making our demands upon God.

Is it wrong to make demands upon God? The Word of God tells us that it is not wrong to make demands upon God, but it is very, very dangerous. When you make demands upon God, you literally open yourself and reveal your inward heart; when you reveal your heart, you risk relationship (the last phrase of verse four). When you demand from God, you reveal some qualities that exist in your heart. There are certain qualities inside us that cause us to make demands upon God. The life that makes demands is a life full of denials. It is difficult to come to grips with our denials because it requires total honesty. Perhaps we can look into the lives of the Pharisees and Sadducees and glean some insight into the denials that are present in our own lives.

Denial of Divine Purpose
Matthew 16:1

Perhaps you cannot accept this kind of truth at first glance. You may need to chew on this for a time before you find the ability to swallow it. I have discovered from the Word, when a person comes and makes a demand upon God, there is a denial of the Divine purpose deep in their heart. God has definite, distinct plans that are unfolding. God is not confused. He is not scratching His head wondering what His next move will be. He has it all laid out. Everything is under His sovereign thumb. He has it all down pat, and He understands the next move. When I come and make demands upon God, telling Him what to do, I am literally denying the Divine purpose.

For instance, when I make demands upon God, I deny the **Direction of Divine Purpose.** God is going in a definite direction. He is pouring his purpose out in one direction. He has one thing He wants to get done. It is one focus, one concentration, one desire. We call it the cross style. In the language of this passage it is earthly as compared to the heavenly sign the Pharisees and Sadducees are demanding. This Divine God of ours is pouring His life out for others. This Divine God of ours reveals His purpose in His Word, ***"For God so loved the world. . . . "*** (John 3:16). This is what He is after - the world. God has focused His presence on the streets. He heals a man here and helps a woman there. He then moves to aid the disabled person over there, and He feeds a hungry person here. Some one has a fever over there. This earthly business of pouring Himself out in cross style has consumed God. The Divine purpose of God is flowing in the direction of this world.

The Pharisees and Sadducees, of all people, should have understood this. They had the Old Testament at their finger tips. They knew the prophecies that illustrated exactly what Christ would do and in what direction the Divine purpose would move. Jesus went to the synagogue one day. He got the Scripture as He sat in Moses' seat. He began to read one of those prophecies about Himself. It was

Isaiah 61:1-2. He began to describe Himself as He read, ***"The Spirit of the Lord is upon Me; because the Lord has anointed Me to preach good tidings to the poor*** (the focus is on the earthly). ***He has sent me to heal the broken hearted*** (that is the cross style), ***to proclaim liberty to the captive and the opening of the prisons to those who are bound and to proclaim the acceptable year of the Lord."*** These leaders of Israel should have grasped the truth. The Old Testament said it; Jesus displayed it. The whole direction of the Divine purpose is the cross and its earthly style.

Now look at the demands of the Pharisees and Sadducees. ***"They "asked that He would show them a sign from heaven,"*** (16:1). The word "from" literally means "out of." They are demanding a sign out of heaven. What did they think had been going on all around them? The cross style was touching their earth, and they did not want it. Embracing a leper, feeding poor people, and getting involved with the needy was not their idea of a great Sunday afternoon. They wanted lightning bolts flashing from the sky at His command, or the raising of His hands so time would stand still (as done by Elijah and Joshua). These are heavenly signs not earthly, cross style signs. I wish we were just talking about them, but I fear we have entered the picture, and we are guilty. We have denied the direction of the Divine purpose, but it does not stop here.

For instance, when I make demands on God, I deny the **Determiner of Divine Purpose.** Look carefully again at verse one. ***"Then the Pharisees and Sadducees came, and testing Him asked that HE. . . . "*** They came to Jesus expecting Him to give them signs from heaven. Their problem was they came to the wrong person. There is someone who is an expert at giving heavenly signs. It is his whole direction and manifestation. He would have loved to accommodate them. I am speaking of the Devil. His program has always been the flash, the big deal, the spectacular.

Jesus spent forty days and forty nights in the wilderness without food (Matthew 4:1+). The Devil appears in all of his cunning ability. He approaches Jesus with great temptation from three different directions. One of them was all about heavenly signs. Jesus was into the business of redemption. Satan offered to help Him. He proposed a great plan to win the world overnight. He wanted Jesus to jump from the pinnacle of the temple. He would plunge down to the earth with the multitudes watching Him headed for His death. Just before He reaches the ground, angels would swoop in to catch Him, and Jesus would experience no physical damage. God had promised this protection in Psalms 91:11-12. People would marvel at His great importance. It would be a great Hollywood stunt. He could follow it up with an evangelistic message and multitudes would thunder into the Kingdom. There is no need to get focused on this cross and its style. It is so earthly. Bleeding, suffering, and dying is so drab and unappealing. Lightning bolts and Hollywood stunts from the sky are definitely the way to go. This was the Devil's program.

The Book of Revelation tells us the anti-Christ is coming. You know all the facts about him. He will be an individual who will rise and attempt to replace Christ. He will be anti or opposite of what Jesus is. His description says, ***"He performs great signs, so that he even makes fire come down from heaven on earth in the sight of men,"***

(Revelation 13:13). His program is to flash some lightning bolts, stir up a great multitude, and pull off some spectacular Hollywood stunts.

This is not our Christ. Jesus has a Divine purpose. The direction of Divine purpose is the earthly, cross style. He is choosing the route of a bleeding back and a crown of thorns. He is producing a Kingdom where the fundamental principle is death transformed into life. If you have His style you will pour out your life, get involved in the hurt of your world, and play the role of Jesus to those around you. His style was born out of His heart. He is the determiner of Divine purpose. When I come making demands on God, I always deny this Jesus as He is.

When I make demands upon God, I deny the **Distribution of Divine Purpose.** Look carefully again at verse one. *"Then the Pharisees and Sadducees came, and testing Him asked that He would SHOW THEM . . ."* Come on and show us, Jesus. We want to sit back in our Lazy Boy recliners while you get up on the stage and show us. You pull off your big spectacular stunts, and we will hang in the back ground selling tickets and making a profit for the church. They wanted to watch! They did not want to get involved; they wanted to view. Every time I make demands upon God, I am telling Him to perform the big feat, and I will stand back and watch.

One great fear we have for this generation is that we are creating a spectator mind set. We love to watch television, see adultery take place in our living room, experience murder before our eyes, but never get involved. We love to watch the ball game, but we never sweat or get bruised. We just watch. We amble into the church and expect Jesus to pull off a big one tonight, at least He better if He wants us to stay awake. He can juggle a few lightning bolts and create a three-ring circus, but don't ask me to take up the cross and its style. Don't ask me to lose my life and let God use me to bear the hurts of my neighbor. Don't ask me to set aside my second job and have a lower standard of living. That might mean I can get aggressively involved in the redemptive process of those around me, and I am not sure I want that. I just want to stand around and watch.

No more demands! No more giving God advise! I just want to fall at His feet and pray that the Divine Determiner will work His Divine purpose through me. The distribution of the Divine purpose is to be through me. God wants to captivate my life, so I will be His hands, His face, and His lips. He is not going to move through this generation except that He moves through me. As surely as He had His own flesh two thousand years ago, now He wants mine. I am to be His body in this day to distribute His Divine purpose.

Denial of Divine Productions
Matthew 16:2-4

I understand this is a bit strong. You may want to dwell with it for a time before you accept it as family. But I have discovered every time I make demands on God, I strip Him of His deity. I come telling Him what I want from Him, which obviously means I know better than He does. Since I am smarter than God is, what does that make me? It makes me a god. My demands dethrone God and enthrone me. They deny the Divine productions that are going on all around me. I have not even noticed them.

The Pharisees and Sadducees have come to Jesus demanding a heavenly sign. They are literally ignoring the thousands of Divine activities that have been taking place on their streets. Their demands are a denial of the Divine productions that are already happening. When I make demands on God, I deny the **Direction of the Divine Productions.** In the passage, Jesus gives an answer to the demands of the Pharisees and Sadducees. *"When it is evening you say, 'It will be fair weather, for the sky is red;' and in the morning, 'It will be foul weather today, for the sky is red and thundering.' Hypocrites! You know how to discern the face of the sky, but you cannot discern the signs of the times,"* (16:2-3). Here is a good discussion on the weather. We speak of the weather regularly. It is idle conversation for us. It is a "taken for granted" factor of our lives. It controls our schedules. I mow the yard today because it is going to rain tomorrow. The weather dips its fingers into our day in and day out living experiences.

Jesus turns to the Pharisees and Sadducees and says, "You big hypocrites!" They had no problem identifying the signs of the weather and letting that control their day in and day out living. However, when it came to the signs of the times, they have no discernment at all. Their lives were untouched by the signs of eternal things. The eternal things God was doing right in their midst did not effect these men. Jesus is saying that the Divine direction of Divine productions is daily living experience. If God gets involved in my daily life, He is likely to come down to my temple and tip over my profiting tables. He might upset my worship experience and call me to service. For when God gets involved in the day in and day out life style, He begins to dictate His purpose and productions through that schedule. So when I come making my demands upon God, I am saying that I do not want Him to interfere with my daily living. That is when I deny the direction of the Divine productions. But it is bigger than that.

When I make demands on God, I deny the **Determiner of Divine Productions.** You see the direction of the Divine productions is my daily living, while the Determiner is a moment by moment Divine God who wants intimacy in my life. He is not in show business. He is not interested in a yearly firecracker event, where we utter admiration over His brilliancy. He is not into an annual event called "revival" where we all come together and get really spiritual. We feel His presence for a week and look forward to next year. He does not hang behind the clouds waiting for us to get into a real mess so He can come with sirens blaring. He rescues us while we applaud Him as He rides away shouting, "Hi, 0 Silver, away!"

This Jesus is One who wants to be, moment by moment, intimately involved in my life as it is lived. Twenty-four hours a day, day after day, He wants to put His fingers deep into my business life, my school life, my recreational life, my sexual life, my resting, and my eating. There is no area you can name of which He does not want to be a part. He is a moment by moment God who gets involved in my total life and produces Divine activity through me. When I make demands upon this God, I deny Him the right to act through me. He is no longer the Determiner of those productions in and through me.

When I make demands on God, I deny the **Distribution of the Divine Productions.** When Jesus finished His conversation with the Pharisees and Sadducees, Matthew writes, ***"And He left them and departed,"*** (16:4). How do you respond to that? When I read that, I want to get on my face before God and weep. Do you realize the tragedy of those words? When He leaves there are no Divine productions. They cease!

However, it is even more tragic than you might think. Jesus established a new pattern that the Pharisees and Sadducees had not recognized at all. This pattern had been happening between Jesus and His disciples. The direction of Divine productions has been the day in and day out life style. The Determiner of this life style is a moment by moment God who wants intimacy in our lives. By that, He wants to use our lives as the instrument of distribution for these Divine productions. He wants to live His life through us. He had done this with His disciples. He had taken the Spirit and power of God within Himself and transferred it to His disciples, (Matthew 10). Jesus sent the disciples out to duplicate His ministry. They became the Divine production to their world.

The Pharisees and Sadducees wanted God to come down and do the Hollywood stunts while they watched and applauded. Jesus is saying that He wants intimate involvement in every cell of your being, your very mind, every attitude of your heart, on a moment by moment basis. God involved in the total function of our lives will, through us, begin to produce His life. We will be the distributions of Divine productions.

If it does not happen through us, it will not happen. You and I are the keys to the Divine activity of God in our day. Did you ever see God drive a van and pick up boys and girls? I have. He did it through someone like you. Did you ever see God get involved with the hateful man down the street and break his heart with love? I have. And He did it through someone like you. You are the flesh of the distribution of Divine productions.

Denial of Divine Presence
Matthew 16:1-4

I realize this is very severe. You may want to think it through carefully before you adopt it as a part of your thought pattern. I have discovered every time I make demands on God, I deny Him. It is a direct reproach to His person. When I make demands on God, I deny the **Direction of the Divine Presence.** Let us view verse one again. *"Then the Pharisees and Sadducees came., and testing Him asked that He would show them a sign from heaven."* Here is the impact of that verse. The Pharisees and Sadducees always flow with the crowd. They never do anything without the big group to see their spectacular performances. They want to be impressive, which gives them self-esteem and control. We do not know what kind of crowd was present at this scene. We do know that the Pharisees did not want to come alone, but enlisted the help of the Sadducees for reinforcements. We also know that time after time, when the Pharisees confronted Jesus, it was always in front of a large crowd. So here is the challenge - Jesus, show us a sign in front of the big crowd.

The Divine Presence never chose the direction of big crowds. The Divine attention always chose "one to one." Did He not deal with large groups? Yes, but even then He was not after the crowds. He had compassion over the individuals who desperately needed help. I have discovered from the Scriptures that the focus of His direction was on the individual. How can I help YOU? He does not come to display Himself before hundreds of people; He comes to embrace me! I do not need a God who appears Sunday morning and impresses the thousands. I need a God who will get underneath my skin, wrap His arms around my inward soul, and weep with me when I hurt. I don't need a God who wants to move the multitudes, but I need a God who will infiltrate my mind and help me with my confusion. I need a God who will get inside my fingers and help me with my temptations. A God who is interested in one on one is what I need. I have found Him. It is Jesus. But when I come making demands on Him, I deny the very direction of this Divine Presence.

When I make demands on God, I deny the **Determiner of Divine Presence.** Jesus makes a closing statement to the Pharisees and Sadducees. *"A wicked and adulterous generation seeks after a sign, and no sign shall be given to it except the sign of the prophet Jonah"* (16:4). You remember this is not the first time this very same confrontation has happened between Jesus and the Pharisees. This closing statement of Jesus is a duplication of Matthew chapter twelve, verse thirty-eight. He gave them the same answer both times.

The language structure of this verse is very significant. The key statement is "the sign of the prophet Jonah." It is not saying that God gave Jonah a sign, and that He will give the same sign to the wicked and adulterous generation. It does not say that Jonah gave a sign. Jonah WAS the sign. Jonah, himself, standing in front of the people of Nineveh, was the actual, literal sign of God. Jesus is saying to the Pharisees, "You have been looking for lightning bolts from the sky and Hollywood stunts while all of the time the very sign of God has been standing right in front of you. I am it!" Do you see the tragedy of it all? They had sought for the spectacular, when they should have sought Him. They wanted fantastic feats of convincing elements, when they should have surrendered to Him. When they should have gone after Him, they had sought for mystical experiences. They had gone after solutions, when they should have sought Him. They had looked for a way out, when they should have looked for Him. They had been like the little boy who waited for days on his father to come home from a business trip. The lad jumped into his father's arms and asked him, "What did you bring me?" The mere presence of his father was not enough to satisfy him. It is time to push everything aside and seek Christ alone! Everything else is chaff. It is junk. Nothings else matters except the Divine person Himself. Embrace Him! Every time I make demands on God, I deny the Determiner of the Divine presence who has come to my life.

When I make demands on God, I deny the **Distribution of the Divine Presence.** The secret is found again in verse four. Here He tells us that Jonah was the sign to the people of Nineveh. The sign was God, through Jonah, to the people of Nineveh. When Jesus walked the streets of Galilee, the sign was God, through Jesus, to the people. Guess what the sign is on our streets? It is Christ, through you, to your next door neighbor.

One night a man had a dream as he slept. He saw into the heart of a sick world that desperately needed love, purity, joy, peace, happiness, rest, love, kindness, and all of the fruits of the Spirit. He also saw a stairway to the sky that he immediately ascended. He came to a heavenly supply counter. Quickly he hit the bell and an angel appeared. He cried, "I have just come from a world that desperately needs all of the fruits of the Spirit. Give me all you have so I can take it back. I will make as many trips as is necessary." But the angel simply smiled and said, "We do not have any of those things here. We only have SEEDS!"

I don't mind taking an evening out of my life to run up to heaven and get a supply of what my neighbor needs. I can deliver it to him. But to surrender by life, so Christ can be planted deep within me to flow through me to my neighbor, is the call of the cross and its style. Christ implanting Himself deep inside me, so He can flow the needs of the world through me, is cross style. I don't mind coming to prayer meeting and asking for my world to have a sign sent to them so they can believe. But to give the control of my life to Christ, so through me, He will be the sign to this world, is a call that takes my all. It is the cross. No more demands, just surrender. No more giving advise, just yielding. Just being available, instead of telling God what He should do. It is choosing death instead of seeking signs. It is the call of the cross and its style.

Matthew 16:1-4

Sign Seeking Mentality

We all agree with the fact that we live in an amazing time. I would imagine this is the most exciting of all the historical settings in which to live. There are so many radical changes taking place. Each aspect of life has so much development. It is impossible to maintain proper knowledge about all of them. Everywhere I turn there are great new insights, radical inventions, and scientific discoveries. It is a significant, important generation in which to live.

The great concern for us who are spiritual is that we have not kept pace in spiritual development. While we have made tremendous advances in all realms of the physical life, we have remained spiritually immature. In the field of medicine we have discovered how to operate on an unborn baby who is still in his mother's womb. However, in the room next door we are committing wholesale murder as unborn babies are aborted. Over 4,000 abortions are committed in our country each day. The moral and ethical values have slipped through our fingers in the midst of the advances. This is an appeal for a new focus on spiritual experience. It will take a raw honesty and an openness to change, which we have never had before. It is essential if we are going to survive. We can no longer travel in the vehicle of our spiritual traditions. This is an hour where we cannot possibly tolerate laziness. If there has ever been an hour when God calls us to the depth of spiritual knowledge and insight, it is now.

In days gone by, a man could live in the wilderness. He could experience the room, space, and privacy needed. However, this is not true in our day. There is no privacy. The doctor has pictures of my insides. The school system has measured my brain capacity and knows what I can achieve. The psychologist has tested and knows what I will do before I do it. There is no privacy. For sure, the Pharisees and Sadducees who come seeking a sign, hide nothing. Just as a psychologist does a series of tests and knows about me, so verses one through four expose the deep spiritual insides of these individuals. The sign seeking mentality quickly reveals the person. There are characteristics always present in the lives of those who seek signs. Will you take the test?

Characteristic of Substitution
Matthew 16:4

The concluding remarks of Jesus to the Pharisees and Sadducees as He is departing is very revealing. He gives them a title that is not one you would want to put on your name tag. He called them, *"A wicked and adulterous generation . . . "* Don't misunderstand what He is saying! An adulterous generation is not an accusation that they have been having a sexual affair on the side. The Pharisees are the legalist of their day. How could Jesus make such a statement about them?

We understand Jesus borrowed this idea from an Old Testament day. These Pharisees and Sadducees are exactly like their ancestors. Constantly, throughout the Old Testament the Israelites had been unfaithful to Jehovah. He was to be their God and they were to be His people. He kept His part of the agreement perfectly, but Israel did not stay true. Jehovah spoke of this in terms of harlotry and adultery, (Jeremiah 3:9, 13:27). They had committed spiritual adultery. It was a process of substituting someone or something for the proper and right. Every time we do that, it is adultery whether in the relationship of marriage or relationship with God.

The Pharisee had all of the characteristics of adultery in his life. He would wear a great religious face, and he kept all the laws of God. He participated in the programs of the church and observed all of the prayer times. His voice had just the right inflection when he read the Scriptures, but behind the religious face, he was playing the game. Behind the religious mask, there was religious adultery taking place. He was substituting something for the very God to Whom he claimed to belong.

The Pharisee was substituting **The Senses for the Supernatural.** You see it plainly as you read these four verses. Let us illustrate it in terms of marriage. Jesus would give to the Pharisees the Biblical picture of marriage (19:4-6). God had made male and female in the beginning of time. He instructed that a man should leave his father and mother and be joined to his wife. The result would be one flesh. The "one flesh" idea is a powerful concept. It comes through two individuals being joined or "cleaving" together. Thus, they have become a unit. They cease to be separate or independent, and they become one. It is all about bone of bone and flesh of flesh. Two individuals have so given their lives to each other that they operate with one will, function with one purpose, live with one thrust, and are going in one direction. Paul described this picture as Christ and the Church. He laid down His life for the Church. It would be well for you to analyze your marriage with this idea as your guide.

There is nothing more tragic than to see a young couple, just married, who don't experience this one flesh. One member of the marriage takes the resources of the couple and lavishes it upon his or herself and what they want. They take all of their energy and use it for their own sensual pleasures. The focus is not on intimacy, relationship, and oneness, but upon self, sense and pleasure. Anyone seeing this situation, would feel sorry for such a couple. This is a picture of the actions of the Pharisees and Sadducees.

They came to Jesus and demanded that He show them a sign. Did they want intimacy with God? No! They wanted Jesus to appease their senses. They wanted a juggling of lightning bolts that would satisfy their senses. The thrills and the spectacular would give them satisfaction. God was moving all around them. Supernatural Divine activities were taking place everywhere because of Jesus. He had raised the dead and cast out demons. However, these men were not interested in the needs of others, but in the satisfying of their own senses. It was a substitution.

Wouldn't it be tragic if we fell into the same trap? We ask the Kingdom of God to satisfy our five senses rather than to redeem our world. We use Jesus to appease our emotional needs and give us highs, but we never experience Divine activity through us. Divine activity does not appease or satisfy. It changes. It alters our life. Are you open to it?

The Pharisee was substituting **Spectator for Surrender.** Let us go back to the view of the marriage relationship. We would all think it a bit strange if one member of the family would hang back in the shadows and simply watch. Other members participate in the family activities, but one only observes. Can you imagine this? The wife prepares the family meal, and when it is ready, calls all family members. Everyone is enjoying the great feast, except the husband. He is standing against the wall watching the others eat. He has met all of the requirements for marriage. The man gave his blood for the test, attended premarital counseling, went through the ceremony, but has never really participated in the marriage relationship. What foolishness for an individual to read all of the marriage manuals, attend the preparation seminars, complete all of the legal requirements, but never enter the marriage relationship. You would think there was definitely something wrong with such an individual. He is watching, but not surrendering.

This is a picture of the Pharisees and Sadducees. They have all the legal requirements of religion. No one can criticize the Pharisees regarding law keeping. They made the right sacrifices, kept the feast days, and operated the right programs. Then the true Messiah came from God, and they would not get involved because He was on the streets touching the lives of needy people. They would not surrender to a Messiah who introduced the Kingdom of God to the streets.

Do we dare apply this to ourselves? Who would question the legal aspects of religion? Haven't we kept them all? Don't we tithe, keep the Sabbath day holy, and go through the right patterns? In the final analysis, the real issue is not the legal aspect of religion. Has the Messiah of the Kingdom filled us and taken us to our streets? Does the Kingdom of God flow through us, touching the needy of our world? Isn't that what He is calling us to? The second and third generation evangelicals of our day know all the religious routines, but know nothing about the flow of a living God through their lives. They never participate in the intimate service to men and women in their neighborhoods. They run the church with effective business principles, but never get involved in moving their society for Christ. What good is the legal routine, if we do not impact our world with the life of God flowing through us?

The Pharisee was substituting the **Superficial for the Spiritual.** Isn't it tragic to see a marriage that has nothing but superficial relationship? The members of the marriage go their own ways, operate their own programs, have their own finances, and never develop the intimacy of one flesh. Everything is superficial. This is exactly what the Pharisees and Sadducees were doing. The whole thrust of the Kingdom of God was flowing through Jesus and calling them to intimacy with God and their neighbor, while the superficial satisfied them.

We see this plainly when we view their lives. They have come from Jerusalem to confront Jesus about the biggest issue they can find, (15:1-9). It is the issue of unwashed hands, or ceremonial cleansing before they eat their meals. Don't we have to admit this is extremely superficial? Jesus spoke to them about spiritual depth and heart purity. Wash your hands or don't wash your hands, but be sure and embrace the living God.

The Pharisees willingly accepted blindness (15:13-14). They did not have to get involved when they were blind. It was an excuse for their superficial activities. If understanding, or light, ever came to their lives, it would drive them deep into relationship and demand changes within.

Often I have wished I could get confused. Confusion does not require in-depth participation. After all, you simply do not understand. But when the light of God comes and strikes the inward heart, superficial darkness gives no satisfaction. When light comes, you see truth. When you see truth, you must do something about it. If you do not want to operate in the light of truth, then superficial scratching will satisfy you. Then you can remain in your blindness.

The Pharisees willingly accepted ceremonies. Matthew contrasts this with a woman of Canaan (15:21-28). She had nothing going for her but faith in God. This faith drove her to intimate relationship. The Pharisees had everything going for them, but their ceremonies satisfied, and they bypassed intimacy with a living God.

What about us? Wouldn't it be tragic if we stayed close to the program of the church, but superficial religious experience was enough to satisfy us? Often we want religious experiences but do not want to embrace the fullness of the Spirit. Many of us want to experience the movement of God in revival for the church, but we do not want the movement of God deep within. That might call us to depth change. We speak of an awakening! It is God moving upon our hearts in conviction until we see new truth and repent. At altars of prayer we have sought relief. Perhaps emotional release has satisfied us instead of the deep movements of God. We have dealt with side issues, but we have not been willing to let God do all He wants to do. It is spiritual adultery as we substitute the superficial for the true surrender of God.

Characteristic of Scrupulous Without
Matthew 16:4

Jesus, speaking to the Pharisees and Sadducees, says, ***"A wicked and adulterous generation seeks after a sign. . ."*** The word "wicked" is right up front in His statement. Its true meaning in this passage is "morally corrupt or evil." You must understand the context of the situation. Jesus looks right into the eyes of the Pharisees and Sadducees as He speaks these words. He accuses them of being wicked. They respond with a look of shock on their faces. How could Jesus possibly be speaking about them? There is no possibility they could fit into this category. In their minds, they are not wicked. If we are going to comprehend what Jesus is saying, we must discover the kind of wickedness about which Jesus is speaking.

The wickedness of the Pharisee is **Standard Procedure.** ***"A wicked and adulterous generation seeks. . ."*** (16:4). The word "seeks" is in the present tense, which shows it is a standard procedure for those who don't believe. When you do not have faith in Christ, there are only two alternatives. First, you rely on the logic of your own mind. This is a trust in yourself and your own senses. The Pharisees and Sadducees were trusting more in their senses than in logic. They came to Jesus offering a test. They demanded a passing of their standard if He were to be the Messiah. Their test was senses, so Jesus would have to do some heavenly, spectacular sign that would satisfy their senses. This puts this group in judgment over whether Jesus is going to be God or not. How easy it is for us to do the same. We become the judge and jury over whether God is going to be God. If He does not act like we want Him to, we simply dethrone Him.

The question "why?" fits into our discussion now. If God is really the God of the New Testament, then why did He let this happen? I sit in judgment on the God who is not acting like I want Him to act. I put God in a box, and I limit Him to my desires and wishes. But God is bigger than our boxes and he is not limited to our plans. There are some real issues in our generation. Why is their poverty, homelessness, and suffering? If He is a God of love and compassion, why does He let it continue? Am I going to be the judge of God? The New Testament is calling us to a commitment to Christ that goes beyond our little tests and analysis. It is surrender to total, absolute yielding of control so God can be God in our lives. Isn't the peak of wickedness, not drunkenness, but man parading himself as the judge of God, thus, making himself god?

The wickedness of the Pharisee is **Sincerity Lacking.** *"Then the Pharisees and Sadducees came, and testing Him . . ."* (16:1). The actual word "testing" has to do with tempting Him or tricking Him. Let us suppose Jesus would have gone along with them. Suppose He would have reached up and snatched a couple of lightning bolts from the sky, juggled them for a minute or two, and then jarred the Pharisees and Sadducees with an electrical charge. That would have attracted their attention, but they still would not have believed. They had already made up their minds about Him. They staged the whole scene. It was a trick. They had already reached the conclusion about Jesus back in chapter eleven. They did not really want a sign. These men would not have believed if He had given them one. There was no sincerity. They had already closed the case. Their decision was final. They had reached the zenith of wickedness, which is closed mindedness.

I am praying daily for a renewal of spiritual hunger. I want God to do something inside each of us until we would hunger and thirst for righteousness. What we know now, or what we have experienced until now, can no longer satisfy us. We cannot stand it until we have more. It amazes me that people are so relaxed in the middle of the spiritual dynamics of revival, as if it does not matter. We can relax to the point that we sleep comfortably in the services. It is as if we do not have any hunger to know. We are not seeking. We have boxed ourselves into our tradition and do not want to get out of the present rut. Thus, we have placed a lid on the ever expanding revelation of truth. If He gave us new truth and we grasped it, we would have to change our living. This closed mindedness could be the peak of wickedness.

The wickedness of the Pharisee is **Selected Foolishly.** The entire passage revolves around the desire of the Pharisees and the Sadducees for a sign to help them believe. Jesus reminds them that He had already given them a sign and they would not accept it. He called it *". . . the sign of the prophet Jonah,"* (16:4). A detailed study of the sign will reveal that the sign of Jonah was the actual person, Jonah, himself. It was not what Jonah did, nor what he preached. It was Jonah. Jesus is relating this to Himself. He is telling the Pharisees and Sadducees that He is the sign for which they have been looking.

The Pharisees and Sadducees definitely had a problem with that. They didn't want to embrace Jesus. They wanted lightning bolts. Call down fire from heaven, Jesus, and do some big trick that will bring the crowds. Jesus is not adequate for them. Isn't that the essence of wickedness? They did not want the person of God. They wanted what He could do for them. They wanted the benefits, but not the person.

Perhaps we need to see how this relates to us. We want lightning bolts, but Jesus wants relationship. We want miracles, but Jesus wants us. We want experiences, but Jesus wants intimacy. We want to watch, but He wants us to get involved. We want to belong to ourselves, but Jesus wants our hands, our face, and our energy to belong to Him. He wants to move through us until the world sees His demonstration.

Characteristic of Sanctimonious
Matthew 16:2-3

The Pharisees and Sadducees have demanded a sign. Jesus begins His answer to them by saying, ***"When it is evening you say, 'It will be fair weather, for the sky is red;' and in the morning, 'It will be foul weather today, for the sky is red and threatening;' Hypocrites! You know how to discern the face of the sky, but you cannot discern the signs of the times,"*** (16:2-3).

In the midst of a spiritual discussion, Jesus begins to talk about the weather. Weather is a superficial, surface, conversation piece. It is neutral ground. It is not wrong for Jesus to talk to them about the weather, but in the discussion He says to them, "You big hypocrites!" What does that have to do with the weather?

They were hypocritical because of **Spiritual Appearances.** The Pharisees and Sadducees are the elite of the religious people. Israel is a religiously oriented society and these individuals are the upper class of that society. They are the experts, the leaders, the ones who decide political policies. When they speak, every one listens. The Pharisees are the experts on the law of God. They have the final word on the matter.

If you have any kind of question regarding right and wrong, you come to them for the answer. This is the area of their expertise.

These leaders of Israel do not claim to be experts on the weather. How is it then that they can predict the weather with great accuracy? They can discern the signs of the sky regarding weather. However, the realm where they claim expertise, they have no ability in discerning the signs of the time. The area in which they are not experts, they do well, but in the area they claim expertise, they are very, very poor. How could this be? They have missed it! They should forget religious things and stick with predicting the weather. They are hypocritical. They parade themselves as experts and yet have no expertise.

I believe this is our hour. If there ever was a time for us to rise to the occasion, it is now. We, in the holiness movement, have claimed to have the answers to the problems of a world, yet we have spent our time predicting the weather. It is time to focus! We cannot allow any more games. We must shift our priority system and allow first things to be first. We must lose our lives with a new sense of abandonment. We must become a stage upon which He can do His activity. Hypocrisy must cease. We must be experts on the holiness we say we experience and believe.

The Pharisees and Sadducees were hypocritical because of **Selected Relations.** This is the first time in the Book of Matthew that we see the Pharisees and Sadducees linked together in a cause (16:1). They have been separate groups because of their theological positions. They are in one constant argument about a variety of issues. They can hardly tolerate each other in the church services. If one says, "Amen," the other knows it must not be true. There is total and absolute disagreement between these two groups. In Acts 23:6-8, the Apostle Paul is standing before the Sanhedrin. The ruling body has equal division of the Pharisees and Sadducees. Paul uses that to his advantage by announcing he is a Pharisee who believes in the resurrection from the dead. Immediately, there is an argument over that theological issue, and they dismiss the case against Paul. But here in this scene, the Pharisees and Sadducees have chosen to link themselves.

If you did not know them you would think the old walls had come down and there was a new unity in the church. Probably they all knelt at the altar in a great prayer meeting and forgave each other. Here they are in oneness, taking a stand. But don't be fooled! They are simply using each other. Hypocrisy fills their linkage. The Pharisee has the constant pattern of using. They use the law for their own ends. They use the church for their own needs. They use the organization to line their own financial pockets, and now they are even using God.

I wonder about our own Christian experience. Is it a using experience? We use God instead of being available for Him to use us. The amazing thing about Jesus is, He did not come to use, but to give. He did not come to be served, but He came to serve. It is the cross style. He has called us to the same. It would be tragic if we simply used God to ease our conscience, or used God for a free ticket to the sky. What if we only used God to solve our problems, give us financial prosperity, and make us look good? What if we used Him for what we want, but we never come to the cross and lose our lives to Him? Our tragedy would be that we never allow Him to use us. We are so prone to take God and put Him into our time schedules and our prejudices. He adjusts so well to our desires. God forgive us!

The Pharisees and Sadducees were hypocritical because of **Seclusion from Christ.** The conclusion of the story is startling. ***"And He left them and departed,"*** (16:4). The grammar structure is very abrupt. Jesus looked them square in the eye. He gave them the great statements of verses two, three, and four, and abruptly walked away. There is no need for further discussion, no need for extended truth. It is over. When the Pharisees confronted Jesus with the woman caught in adultery, He had no condemnation for her. When He came to the tax collector who had been cheating the public, He called him to be His disciple. When He came to the fishermen who were concerned about their living, He called them to be fishers of men. When He came to sinners, He called them to repentance. But when He came to the sanctimonious Pharisee, He left.

"Jesus, please don't leave us. Change us!"

Matthew 16:5-12

Human Limitations

The most delicate area in the realm of Christianity is "human limitations." It is the most important area for Christian growth and maturity, and the greatest area for defeat. In Christian experience and the outliving of holiness, this area of "human limitation" is a difficult area for all of us.

Most of us find it very difficult to talk about our human limitations, lest we should admit to ourselves and others that we have them. Yet, in our most honest moments we all have to admit they are a daily part of our lives. The Apostle Paul told us that "earthen vessels" hold the great treasure of the fullness of Christ (II Corinthians 4:7). The holiness people have no problem talking about the great treasure! It is the power of God impacting a world through us. The wonder of the fullness of the Holy Spirit is indwelling man and producing a holy life. This is only half the truth Paul was sharing with us. "Earthen vessels" contain the great treasure. A "cracked pot" is the best description of this vessel. The perfect love of God expressed has come to indwell and shine through a cracked pot that has frailties. Often, the perfect love, shined through this earthen vessel, does not come forth as we would want.

In Christian experience, we must all deal with this issue. I realize it is dangerous to speak openly about human limitations. We could use this subject as an excuse for every conceivable wrong doing and sin. But this is true only for those who have an insincere heart. We are not discussing voluntary disobedience against God. That is what we call "sin proper so called." Those actions spill forth from a rebellious heart. We want to discuss those actions rooted in human limitations.

The cross style Jesus is calling us to is the style of death. Jesus has cleansed us of carnal mindedness. He has filled the heart (source of the being) with the motive of perfect love. Yet, when one examines the expression of that love, it is seen filtered through an earthen vessel. We have an abundance of illustrations, used in the past, to show us this truth. For instance, a family built a new house that cost more than they had planned. They did not have resources to complete the landscaping and many other outside projects. Many of those projects did not matter. However, one important one was left undone. There was a steep drop off at the back edge of their property, and there was no fence for protection. The father and his toddler were in the front yard of their new home, planting some flowers. The father, busy planting, forgot his little daughter. Suddenly he realized that she was not with him. She was missing. His first thought was the deep drop off in the backyard. He bolted to the back of the property, and saw his daughter standing right on the edge of the cliff. He ran to save her, but tripped over a rock, and literally pushed his daughter to her death. No one accused him of murder. The pain on his face told you of the sorrow in his heart. His heart motive was perfect, but his outward expression was lacking. We can identify with this. All of us find ourselves living daily with these same human limitations. We have been to the cross and experienced the crucifixion with Christ. Our heart longs to be all we ought to be, but we realize the tremendous limitations of the "cracked pot" in which we live.

These human limitations include such a large variety of aspects. There are the past experiences and training that need adjustment and retraining of the Holy Spirit. Our nerves need rest, having been stretched beyond limits. There is patience that is in the process of being developed. Heritage from my ancestors influences my thinking and needs correction. I am pleading with you to recognize these things in your life. We are not stuck with them. We are not without the possibility of change. God wants us to grow, but we need to recognize they are present in our lives. Maybe the disciples could help us, for they were just like we are.

The Problem Verbalized

We realize that any problem must be out in the open before it can be solved. The state of denial never resolves the issues. The first step to healing is openly admitting one's need. It is true, also, in the area of human limitations. If we are covering, excusing, or rationalizing our human frailties, there is no change or growth in our lives. This is true for the disciples.

There is an interesting progression in this story, especially concerning the revelation of the problem. First, there is **Concentration**. *"And when His disciples had come to the other side, they had forgotten to take bread."* (16:5). Now that sounds exactly like something I would have done. They tell us that forgetfulness is the first sign of old age, which proves that it is simply a human limitation. The disciples have climbed into the boat and set sail in a hurry. They have reached the other side of the Sea of Galilee, only to realize they had not come prepared.

Memory is often based upon concentration. These disciples had not been concentrating on the subject of bread; they left without adequately preparing for their physical needs. This area of concentration, or focus, is a problem for many of us. Some people concentrate on the negative, forgetting the positive. Some of us concentrate so strongly on the cobweb in the corner of the church, that we forget the sermon. There is a parallel between memory and concentration.

I suppose one could simply slap their hand and tell themselves not to do it again. But the forgetfulness of the disciples has happened repeatedly. Just three to six months before this very event, Jesus had fed five thousand men, besides women and children, in a tremendous miracle (14:14-20). It was a miracle of creation - a miniature form of what He had done in the creation of the worlds. The disciples did not have the resources to take care of such a great crowd, but Jesus never seemed to lack resource. The disciples participated in the whole activity. Would you ever have forgotten such a dynamic occasion?

Just a few hours ago another miracle had taken place. There is a congregation of four thousand men, besides women and children (15:32-39). Most of the people are disabled with tremendous needs. They have been with Jesus for three days in concentrated ministry. No one has thought about eating. The disciples are again totally helpless in ability to meet the needs. Jesus takes what little they have, and a multiplication miracle takes place. The time between the two miracles was three to six months. They had forgotten how Jesus handled the problem the first time, but don't you think this second miracle would have planted it on their minds so they would never forget?

Now they are in a boat with only twelve disciples. There are not five thousand men, besides women and children; there aren't even four thousand men, besides women and children. The disciples forgot to bring bread, and they are worried. Perhaps the real issue is not the physical, but the spiritual. The real tragedy is they have forgotten, not the bread, but that Jesus can solve their problem. The adequate resource of Christ has slipped from them again. They are men who have left all to follow Jesus, but their human limitations are still a part of their lives. They have forgotten!

The disciples had human limitations, and you have them too. What is the human limitation you are battling? You want to be all that God wants you to be, but you have limitations that constantly hinder you. I have prayed with those who wept over their physical weight, over their impatience, over their nerves, and over scars of the past. What is your human limitation?

There is a second step in the preparation of this story. It is **Consternation.** ***"And they reasoned among themselves, saying, 'It is because we have taken no bread,"*** (16:7). It is a common pattern of life. Where ever there is human failure, anxiety follows. The disciples have forgotten to take bread and now they have anxiety over their failure. It is the failure-anxiety syndrome. It is a terrible circle. When I experience human limitations, I experience failure. Failure causes anxiety. Anxiety causes worry. Worry causes frustration and stress; stress causes me to fail more. The circle then begins to repeat itself. It is a trap! It all has to do with this subject of human limitations.

The third step in this progression is **Condemnation.** The disciples started with the realization that they had forgotten to take bread (16:5). Jesus turns to them and attempts to teach them some great spiritual truth. He says, ***"Take heed and beware of the leaven of the Pharisees and the Sadducees,"***(16:6). However, the disciples miss the whole truth because of their human limitation. They think Jesus is condemning them for not bringing bread. This is the area where Satan attacks the spiritually right with God. He creates guilt over our human limitation, and builds walls in our relationship with God. We begin to imagine that God is upset with us. But it is NOT true. There is only one thing that brings condemning guilt in our lives - it is voluntary disobedience against God. This has to do with rebellion in the heart motive. God understands our human limitation. In love and kindness He wants to help us. The condemnation is false guilt. Again, it is a terrible patter. We fail because of our human limitations. We have anxiety over our failure, and we feel condemnation, which causes us to fail more.

It is important to know that God is not condemning us. He wants to help us. Guilt boxes us into defeat. Openness allows God's instruction to expand our lives in growth. Listen for the instruction of His voice. He wants to teach you discipline in the area of your problem. He is using the area of human limitations to bring you back to Him. He is teaching you that you cannot possibly make it without Him. He is not condemning you, but reaching out to you. Bring your body drives under His control. Learn to lean in your spirit upon His resources. He is adequate, even in the reality of human limitations. The cross and its style works most effectively in this area.

The Pitfalls Recognized

The Bible teaches us that there is only one reason anyone goes to hell. God does not want anyone to perish. He died an adequate death to provide full salvation for every person. People do go to hell, but it is against what God wants. It is voluntary disobedience that destroys relationship with God. God will work with an individual in all areas of human limitation, but we stop all progress when we shake our fist in His face in rebellion. We must live in brokenness before Him.

It is through this brokenness (cross style) that God will create within us the guards necessary for our spiritual safety and growth. While human limitation is not voluntary disobedience against God, it does present tremendous pitfalls into which we can fall and commit voluntary disobedience. This is a crucial area. It is in this story that the Scripture reveals the pitfalls to us.

The first pitfall is **Confinement.** *"But when Jesus perceived it, He said to them, 'Oh you of little faith . . ."* (16:8). We need to understand this statement. The disciples do have faith. Jesus teaches us that the issue of faith is not how much do you have, but what is the object of your faith. It does not matter how much you have, but where do you focus the faith you possess. "Little faith" is not a statement regarding size. Its lesson concerns focus. The disciples had faith to leave all and follow Jesus. They have been His disciples for over two years. Others had ceased to follow Jesus in times past, but not these twelve disciples. They have had faith to stick with their commitment.

The problem is not that the disciples do not have faith. They have taken the faith they have and confined it to certain areas of their lives. Surely you and I can see ourselves in this picture. For instance, Peter stands tall and straight while making a great confession of Christ being the Son of the living God (16:16). He had faith to step out on the water and walk for a few feet (14:29). Peter and the other disciples had been duplicating the miracles of Jesus in their own ministry. Yet, when it comes to the teaching on bread, which effects their personal daily lives, they are not able to grasp it with faith.

I have found this true in my own life. I amaze myself at how smart I am in some areas of my life, but so absolutely dumb in many other areas. My faith seems to operate greatly in many areas, but it is so weak in others. I can preach strongly regarding some truths, but there are other truths that do not grip me. Those are the areas where my faith has a hard time being applied. I can look at my brother and see how blind he is in his life, yet could it be I have blind spots also? Could there be areas in our lives where our faith is weak and God wants to build it? We have confined our faith, and God wants His presence, through faith, to possess our total lives. Are you open to this?

The second pitfall is **Carnality.** ***"But when Jesus perceived it He said to them, 'O you of little faith, why do you reason among yourselves. . ."*** (16:8). We understand that carnality is self-centeredness. It is pride! You think that human limitations would simply defeat all pride in our lives. We are so limited, we have nothing about which to be proud. Yet, carnality will raise its head and deny human limitations. Carnality will rely on our own reasoning and mental ability.

The disciples have forgotten to bring bread. Jesus has tried to teach them a great spiritual truth, but they think He is condemning them. Now they are relying on their own thinking to solve this problem. They are plotting to set things right. Doesn't this sound just like us? We have questioned the balance between the experience of entire sanctification and the daily process of dying to ourselves. If Jesus has cleansed my carnal nature, why do I find it raising its head repeatedly in my daily life? Entire sanctification is a crisis experience dealing with internal heart purity. The problem is that when Jesus cleanses the carnal mind from my heart, there is a residue that remains in my system. I have taught my hand to be self-centered. It does it automatically. I have trained the very nerve fibers to reach out and grab for me. While the heart is pure, I need retraining for my hand. I need the old patterns uprooted and the new cross style established. This is a daily process of bringing my life style under the control of Christ, Who now is supreme in my heart. We are not discussing hatred or bitterness, which are sins of the heart. We are speaking of human limitations that need to come under the training of Jesus, Who is Lord of my life.

The third pitfall is **Concealment.** Jesus says to His disciples, ***"Do you not yet understand, or remember the five loaves of the five thousand and how many baskets you took up?"*** (16:9). We can read this same passage in the Gospel of Mark. However, Mark gives us the answer the disciples gave to the question Jesus just asked them (Mark 8:19). They answer, "Twelve." In other words, the disciples tried to cover up the fact that they had forgotten about this great miracle. Isn't that just like us?

Again we see the established pattern. The confinement of their faith was to certain areas in which it was easier for them to believe. This confinement caused the carnal patterns, allowing them to gain control, which caused them to conceal their mistake. They then denied their human limitations and missed the opportunity of growth. The concealment becomes the worst of all, because it blocks the possibility of growth. God is calling us to total honesty! It is in this kind of openness that God can use us to minister to the body of Christ. Otherwise, we develop a group of people filled with hypocrisy, who cover their human limitations, and stagnate in their spiritual lives.

The Power Realized

The third step in this process is great news for all! Jesus has come to indwell this earthen vessel. We need not falter in the middle of suffering with our frailties and human limitations. We need not live in the bad news, but we place our trust in Jesus, Who promises to live in us. He is in the middle of my human limitation with His Divine power. In fact, He uses it to display His greatness to my world.

In relationship to the disciples, and to you, notice **Confrontation.** *"But when Jesus had perceived it . . ."* (16:8). The disciples had forgotten to take bread (16:5). Jesus gives them a spiritual message about the leaven of the Pharisees and Sadducees (16:6). They think He is condemning them for their forgetfulness (16:7). But when Jesus perceives their human limitations, He sets about to correct them.

Jesus knows what is taking place in our lives. God is omniscient, and therefore, knows everything. However, that is not the kind of knowledge we are discussing here. This is not simply a sovereign God of the sky, but a God Who has leaped off His throne to take on our flesh. He has experienced our human limitation. He knows because He has been here. Satan tempted Him just as Satan tempts us. When Jesus was in the flesh, He experienced exactly what we experience in the way of temptation. He is one of us! He is not out to get you or to put you down. He is not condemning, but is sympathetic of your frailties. You can be open with Him; He understands a heart that burns to be right, but a body that does not always respond. He understands the ignorance of our thinking, the body drives of our flesh, the nerves that get frazzled. He knows what it is to be in doubt concerning the direction to take, and have to pray all night. Jesus knows your human limitations.

This is also a **Confirmation.** Jesus said to His disciples, ***"Do you not yet understand or remember the five loaves of the five thousand and how many baskets you took up? Nor the seven loaves of the four thousand and how many large baskets you took up?*** (16:9-10). These are not statements of condemnation, but of confirmation. He is not wagging a finger of shame in their faces, but He is reminding them of some great victories of the past. He is building their faith by reminding them of what He has done for them in the past. If He had fed all these other people on two great occasions in the past, could He not take care of twelve hungry disciples. This is a loving Christ, sharing Himself with His disciples, who have human limitations. He wants to be involved and share His resource with us to make us adequate for His purpose.

Perhaps the climax of it all is that this is also a **Construction.** Jesus ends His statement to them saying, ***"How is it you do not understand that I did not speak to you concerning bread? But you***

should beware of the leaven of the Pharisees and Sadducees" (16:11). This expresses His main purpose. He is instructing and constructing to build strong disciples. He is teaching and training these men. He has gone over these truths repeatedly, but is willing to do it again, though they continually forget. He is aware of their distractions and their human limitations, but He continues to teach them until they grasp it.

You have an inward heart that beats to serve God, yet you are deeply aware of your personal, human limitations. Do not conceal them! Do not ignore them as if they do not exist! You can deal with it honestly; because you have a Jesus who knows. He is loving you, and is instructing you in that area of limitation, until you are all He has dreamed you can be. What has been a limitation can become an asset to you, through His grace.

Matthew 16:5-12

Escaping From

Isn't it interesting that within the dynamics of relationship there are such a variety of perspectives? Two people may have intimate relationship with each other, and yet, come from totally different backgrounds. They view things from different perspectives. We understand that communication within those relationships has to deal with those perspectives.

I returned home after an extended absence from my family. I found each member, one after the other, quoting a phrase. Each time one quoted the phrase, they would all break out in laughter. It was a meaningless statement to me. I investigated to discover they had picked up this phrase from a television program they had watched. There were a variety of comedy scenes that revolved around this statement. Each time they gave the quotation, those scenes came to their minds, causing their laughter. I had missed the television program, so I found no humor in the quotation. I was outside their perspective.

We have all had the experience of being accused of stating something, which, in reality we did not say. It is not that the person who accuses us is lying. They simply took what we said, and filtered it through their perspective. When that process was completed, the result was a statement that was different from what we said from our perspective.

This is the same thing that is going on in Matthew 16:5-12. The disciples are coming from one perspective, while Jesus comes from another. There are problems in communication and understanding for the disciples. Jesus says, **"Take heed and beware of the leaven of the Pharisees and the Sadducees,"** (16:6). Note how the disciples respond, **"It is because we have taken no bread,"** (16:7). These disciples were thinking in terms of their stomachs. Isn't that just like a disciple, always wondering when the next potluck will be?

They thought Jesus was upset with them because they had forgotten to buy bread for this trip. They were coming from the western coast of the Sea of Galilee, which is Jewish territory. This territory is densely populated. There were all kinds of bakeries where they could have bought the type of bread a Jew may eat. Now they have crossed the Sea of Galilee to the eastern coast, and this territory is scarcely populated. It is Gentile territory, and there is no bread that a Jew can eat. They think Jesus is upset with them because they missed the opportunity to buy bread before they make the trip.

Jesus must have simply shaken His head, and then questioned them concerning their memory. **"Do you not yet understand, or remember the five loaves of the five thousand and how many baskets you took up? Nor the seven loaves of the four thousand and how many large baskets you took up?"** (16:9-10). The indication is this. Considering the powerful miracles they had witnessed, how could they even consider that Jesus would be upset by the lack of supply to feed twelve men. Five thousand men, besides women and children, four thousand men, besides women and children were no problem for Jesus. Obviously, feeding twelve men would not even be a consideration. Why would Jesus be upset with them over this issue? He was not talking to them about bread. He was coming from another perspective.

It is the perspective of the Kingdom of God. Jesus has been intimately involved in the thought process of the Kingdom of God. He has been building and structuring this Kingdom. He is going to take this Kingdom and give its responsibility into the hands of these twelve disciples. They must get His perspective and think like He thinks. They must see what He sees. It is time for them to quit thinking about bread.

Jesus has just come from a raging conflict with the Pharisees. It has not been a cold war, but a heated battle. This has been taking place in several chapters before sixteen. The Pharisees have come the long distance from Jerusalem to present to Jesus the issue of the tradition of the elders (15:1ff). The battle is over philosophy, ideas, and theology. It has to do with the way they think, compared to the way Jesus thinks. This continues as they gather to demand a sign from Him (16:1).

Jesus gets into a boat to make the journey to the other side of the Sea of Galilee. As the boat sails across the water, He is thinking about the conflict He has had with the Pharisees and Sadducees. He sees clearly the influence of the Pharisees over the disciples concerning the eating process. It is like the leaven in the bread. It permeates, controls, and dominates the soul. It destroys the mind. They look so good on the surface, but underneath they are nothing but dead men's bones. This influence, in its camouflaged state, degrades and tears down the very soul. His disciples are so weak in their faith, and He is placing the Kingdom in their hands. There is, within Jesus, a great desire to warn His disciples as He says, ***"Take heed and beware of the leaven of the Pharisees and the Sadducees,"***(16:6).

Matthew helps clarify the intent of Jesus' message. ***"They understood that He did not tell them to beware of the leaven of bread, but of the doctrine of the Pharisees and Sadducees,"*** (16:12). Jesus was concerned about doctrine, ideas, concepts, and the philosophy of the Pharisees and Sadducees. It had to do with their mind set.

What is the doctrine of the Pharisees and Sadducees? If you go to a Bible dictionary you will find valuable information concerning the Pharisees. The very word, Pharisee, means "to separate from." The heart of the Pharisee is separation. This is not all negative. We believe in separation from a world. A definition of sanctification is "to be set apart." However, there is a difference between being "separated" from and "escaping" from. The Pharisees were attempting to be separated from, by escaping. It was isolation they emphasized. Their religion was a wall of self-righteousness, barriers that removed them, and laws that isolated them from their world. However, the focus of Jesus was on bringing His message into a world. ***"For God so loved the world that He gave His only begotten Son, . . . "*** (John 3:16). He was embracing the world in love and redemptive caring. Pharisees build walls to keep people away; Jesus was tearing down walls to get people in! Pharisees were escaping from, while Jesus was running to embrace.

It will not be very many days before Jesus will be placing the responsibility of this message into the hands of these disciples. Will they be influenced by the leaven of the Pharisees? Will the escape methods of these isolationists dominate the minds and shape the thinking of the disciples? Will they fall into this pitfall that looks so good - keep rules, build walls, keep people out? Or will they experience the heart of God - embrace, bleed, suffer and die? Will they experience the cross and its style? What are the escape methods of the Pharisees? You can see them easily in the encounters between Jesus and the Pharisees.

Escaping from Reality

"Let them alone. They are blind leaders of the blind. And if the blind leads the blind, both will fall into a ditch," (15:14). This is an interesting statement. Jesus has had a conflict with the Pharisees, who have come from Jerusalem (15:1-9). He seems to have a concern for the multitudes who were listening to the verbal exchange during this conflict (15:10). So Jesus tells the multitude a parable (15:11). The disciples then come to Jesus and suggest that He was offensive in His statement (15:12). Jesus then gives His reply (15:13-14).

The Pharisees wear dark suits, have beards, stand a bit removed from others, and fold their arms. They look scary. They hold the political strings of the nation in their hands. You do not cross them. But something happened. The Pharisees have unfolded their arms and come from their removed position. They have joined the disciples for some moments of fellowship. They have asked them to go to the local burger shop, and have even offered to buy. With mustard in their beards, these Pharisees do not look as fierce as they did before. The disciples quickly discover that these Pharisees are just real people like themselves. They have feelings, families and dreams. They have religious convictions that are admirable. These Pharisees really are nice guys.

The disciples come to Jesus after their meeting with the Pharisees. They are upset with Jesus. After all, He has been very hard nosed about all of this. So they say to Him, **"Do You not know that the Pharisees were offended when they heard this saying?"** (16:12). The Pharisees are real people too, and they have feelings. The disciples say that Jesus said some rather sharp things. Perhaps He was a little harsh, and it would not hurt a thing if He would apologize to the Pharisees. But Jesus looked into the eyes of His disciples and said, **"Let them alone. They are blind leaders of the blind,"** (15:14). He warned them not to get sucked into the escape methods of the Pharisees. Watch what you are doing, disciples, lest the leaven of the Pharisees permeate your lives!

"Leaven of the Pharisees" is equated with "blindness of the Pharisees." If they had a physical disability, we would be sympathetic and understanding. It is not a physical disability, but it is a slow eating process of spiritual blindness. Notice several things about this leaven - spiritual blindness.

First, it is **Self-Inflicted**. This is not a physical disability about which they have no choice. They know better! This is a deliberate act of their will to escape from the reality of truth. Perhaps I have had a misunderstanding about the Pharisees. I thought they were the students of the law, the scholars of the hour. I thought because they knew the law so well, they felt free to interpret it and apply it to everyday living. But I have discovered the Scribes were the students of the law. The Pharisees have some Scribes who are a part of their group. They pick up a little truth from them in bits and pieces. They put it together the way they want it. What they have is hearsay. They build their little structure the way they want it. They can adjust it, or twist it, to meet their own needs. God has not spoken to them through His word. They have simply adopted what is comfortable for them.

I am concerned about a Christian movement in our hour that wants to hang around the television set and pick up a little here and a little there. Play a tape here and sing a song over there. Get this idea from Sunday School. Read a new book. Select the truth that you want and build a structure of religion that fits your personal needs. It is so comfortable. You have got it all settled, but you have never come to the Word of God on a daily basis, to allow God to speak to you. You have never been broken and exposed before God and His Word, until He can shape you into what He wants. It is the need of this hour.

We must not play the game of the Pharisees - escaping from reality. *"And this is the condemnation, that the light has come into the world, and men loved darkness rather than light, because their deeds were evil,"* (John 3:19). Could it be this is not just a reference to the gross sins (darkness) of a world? Could it be the blindness of the Pharisees? The Pharisees who love bits and pieces of truth, giving a parade of righteousness, but never submit to the power of His Word for changed lives. It is self-inflicted blindness.

There is a continued progression. The second step in self-inflicted blindness is **Self-Diluting.** Jesus told the disciples, *"Let them alone. They are blind leaders . . ."* (15:14). Anyone who is blind, but is determined to lead, must think he can see. Indeed, the Pharisees think they can see. They have taken light and perceived it as darkness; they have taken darkness and perceived it as light. Because of this delusion of seeing, they think they have the capacity of being leaders of men. Jesus said something permeating to them, **"If you were blind, you would have no sin; but now you say, 'We see.' Therefore your sin remains,"** (John 9:14). If they really were blind, we would all understand and want to help them. If they are truly blind they are not responsible; there would be no sin involved. But the Pharisees had seen the truth and refused it; yet they acted as if they could see even in their blindness. Bits and pieces, second hand information, and structure it like I want it, are all characteristics of the blind leaders of the blind. They never come to grips with the reality of truth. We must apply this to ourselves. I am concerned about individuals who are in the church but have become unreachable. They have picked up bits and pieces, got their structure put together, and locked in. If God wanted to do something new, He would have to fight against them, because they have it all down in a neat package. How long has it been since God gave you a brand new idea out of His Book? Would you not die inwardly, if, week after week, God didn't give you new revelation? Wouldn't you feel terrible inside if you have diluted yourself into thinking you see, when the truth is, it is an escape method from reality.

This blindness is not only self-inflicted, self-diluting, but it is also **Self-Destructive.** Jesus said, **"Let them alone. They are blind leaders of the blind. And if the blind leads the blind, both will fall into a ditch,"** (15:14). We all feel terrible about a Pharisee who ends up in the ditch. No one rejoices over the demotion of an individual, even if it is a result of self-inflicted, self-diluting blindness. But what really stirs us is the truth that you never go to the ditch alone. You always take a parade with you.

A father can say to his children that he does not want to influence them. He can tell them he gives them the right to choose for themselves. But the truth is, what he does so over rides what he says, that the children do not hear his words. The influence we have is startling. We never go to the ditch alone; we never walk into the Kingdom alone. Blindness is not only self-destructive for us, but for those who have come under our influence. I beg you, if you have picked up bits and pieces, hung around the church and listened, built your personal structure of belief, leveled off in growth experience, and settled in your comfortableness, beware of the leaven (the escape methods) of the Pharisees.

Escaping from Royalty

You can see this depicted in the scene at the beginning of chapter fifteen. The leaders have come from Jerusalem to confront Jesus, which tells you how important this is to them. They want to discuss, what is to them, a BIG issue. It is the "tradition of the elders." They have narrowed the discussion to one facet of that tradition. It is about ceremonial cleansing. The disciples do not wash their hands before they eat their food (15:2). The issue is not about dirty hands in the physical sense. They believed the Gentiles were unclean and could defile them spiritually. If dust should blow from a Gentile, through the air, and land on the hands of a Jew, he would have unclean hands. He would pick up a glass to drink, but the glass is unclean because of his hands. This makes the contents of the glass unclean. He drinks the contents and becomes unclean inside. There must be a ceremonial cleansing before any eating or drinking is done. He would pour clean water over the wrist, down the fingers, and onto the ground. If he really meant business, he would do this several times. This is their big issue. Why don't your disciples do this, Jesus?

Jesus takes this opportunity to speak about the heart as the source of life and about the commands of God. There is a progression in what He says to them. First, the Pharisees are **Negating His Lordship.** It is easy to understand. They have approached Jesus about unwashed hands. If He had solved that problem for them, they would have brought up the issue of picking grain on the Sabbath Day. If He had solved that problem, they would have turned to the subject of healing on the Sabbath Day. They were not going to quit. This was not really about the issues of the law, but it was a power struggle. It was a power struggle between the Lordship (royalty) of Jesus and the self-centered carnal pride of the Pharisee. It expresses itself in the life style of each. Jesus was living the cross style, but the Pharisees were living the self-style.

Often in the church we squabble over the most insignificant issues. Any issue that won't matter one hundred years from this moment, is an insignificant issue. A world is dying and going to hell, and we argue about the color of the carpet. The organ, the pulpit furniture, the parking lot, the length of the service, and the offerings, are all major issues to many of us. But the truth is, they are not the issues at all. We could solve each of those small issues, but we would not stop our arguing. The real issue is His Lordship over against self-centered carnality.

Notice, by negating His Lordship they **Nullify His Commands.** This is always a sign that you are having trouble with His Lordship. Jesus says to the Pharisees, ***"Thus you have made the commandment of God of no effect by your tradition,"*** (15:6). The Pharisees have not shaken their fists in the face of God in open rebellion. They have dedicated themselves to keeping the laws of God. But that is why this truth is so important. They don't openly rebel; they simply nullify and make the law of God of no effect. They stand tall, and straight, and fight over the issue of unwashed hands, but regarding the commandment of God about honoring your parents, they find a way around (15:5-6). They are not in rebellion, but they are distracted. They have so given themselves to the things that don't count, that the major issues have slipped through their fingers. When I am arguing at church about the color of the carpet, the commandment about loving my neighbor seems to slip away. My distraction keeps me from pouring my life out in cross style. When my focus is keeping the rules of the church, the internal heart passion of love for Christ, that causes me to spill out my life, is absent. I focus on things instead of on Him. I negate His Lordship, and, thus, nullify His commandments.

This brings us to a third step. We **Neglect Our Hearts.** Jesus said, ***"Hypocrites! Well did Isaiah prophesy about you, saying, 'These people draw near to Me with their mouth. and honor Me with their lips, But their heart is far from Me. And in vain they worship Me, Teaching as doctrines the commandments of men,"*** (15:7-9). The Pharisees had fulfilled the prophesy of Isaiah. Jesus calls for hearts to be ablaze. He wants heart passion to fill us. When the heart grows cold, the rules increase. When all that matters to us are the traditions of men, and the good deeds we do, we have nullified His commands. If our focus centers on keeping the rules and we are without a burning heart that loves God and counts nothing as sacrifice, we have negated His Lordship. Beware of the leaven of the Pharisees.

Escaping from Responsibility

The Pharisees knew if they came to grips with reality (truth), they would have to come under the Lordship of truth (royalty). Then they would be responsible for carrying out that truth. They did not want that kind of responsibility, so they established escape methods. It is plain to see how they escaped from responsibility.

First, they enlisted in **Perpetual Searching**. The Pharisee is always looking, but never finds (16:1-4). It is very comfortable to never find. If I never find, you cannot expect anything from me. What if I remain confused? You cannot expect any accomplishments from me in my confusion. If I understand, then I will have to do something. If I know what the next step is, I will be responsible for taking it. I have talked to parents who referred to their children as perpetual students. These students are always going to school, but never getting into the real world and fulfilling the call of God. They are always preparing to do, but never doing. Jesus called the Pharisees, ***"Children in the marketplace,"*** (11:16-17). These men acted like children who were always looking for something new and exciting, but never wanting to give their lives for the importance of it. We thought you wanted to dance, so we played the flute for you. But you did not want to dance. We thought you were sad, so we wept with you, but our weeping did not satisfy you. John the Baptist came, not eating; you said that he had a devil. Jesus came eating;

you said that He was a winebibber and a gluttonous man. We came giving you earthly signs and you wanted heavenly signs (16:1). Jesus came, giving Himself, and you wanted lightning bolts from the sky. He came walking and talking with sinners, and you wanted Him to segregate Himself. He came dealing with the heart cry of men, and then you wanted Him to keep little ceremonies at the church. What do you want? You are always searching, but never satisfied with what He has given you.

I have become suspicious of the word "potential." It is a word used often in relationship to the church. A pastor will say, "We have much potential here." I am wondering when we are going to give ourselves to Christ, and let Him do, through us, what He wants to do. I am tired of speaking about revival; I want to have one. I don't want to go to any more seminars; I want to surrender my life to Christ, and let Him do, through me, what He has already called me to. Are you walking in all the light God has given to you? Are you simply absorbing more, or are you giving more?

They were also escaping by **Profitless Searching.**. Jesus told them, ***"A wicked and adulterous generation seeks after a sign, and no sign shall be given to it except the sign of the prophet Jonah,"*** (16:4). The great tragedy with their lives was that they were seeking that which they would never find. We must not seek after that which God has not promised. He did not promise you prosperity or good health. He did not promise to solve all of your problems, or to wave a magic wand and make you patient. His promise was not to lift you out of your humanity, or to remove your trial, but He did promise to give you victory in the midst of it. What has He promised? He has promised to give you Himself. Is He alone not enough to satisfy you?

They were also escaping by **Predetermined Searching**. *"Then the Pharisees and Sadducees came, and testing Him. . . ."* (16:1). The word "testing" literally means "to tempt Him." They were not sincere. It was a trap. They were not going to follow Him, even if He did give them the so-called sign from heaven. They had already made up their minds. They were closed.

I wonder about your mind. You have read book after book, heard tape after tape, and gone to revival after revival. No one could say or do anything, you haven't already experienced. Beware of the leaven of the Pharisees. Could you be escaping? What if God wants to do a new thing in your life? Would you give Him the right to do as He sees fit, no matter what it changes? The decision is yours.

PART TWO

Matthew 16:13-28

A Rebuke or a Response

Considerations of the Cross Style

Matthew 16:13-17

Mystery of His Person

To walk with Jesus is to walk with an amazing mystery. You never feel like you have conquered Jesus. All that He is, is just beyond what you know. I have studied about Him, and I have experienced life in Him. I know a lot concerning Jesus, and yet I am keenly aware that I have hardly scratched the surface in knowing the mystery of His being. What a fantastic person this Jesus is!

This does not mean we do not know something about Jesus, but it does mean we are far from knowing everything about Him. We are far from any accomplishment in this mystery. C.S. Lewis stated it well in his series, **THE CHRONICLES OF NARNIA.** In the book entitled *PRINCE CASPIAN*, the children had been in Narnia for sometime, but had not encountered the great Lion, Aslan. They are resting in the forest for the night. They are exhausted after escaping from battle. Lucy hears her name being called. At first it sounds like her father, but then she thinks it is Peter, her brother. Finally, she realizes it is neither and she stirs from her sleep. She follows the sound of the voice, and then she sees Him. If it had not been for the movement of His tail, He might have been a stone lion. It has been several years since Lucy has seen Him. She feels as if her heart will break if she waits another moment. Rushing to Him, she buries her face in the rich silkiness of His mane.

As she sobs, Aslan says, "Welcome, child."

"Aslan," cried Lucy, "You're bigger."

"That is because you are older, little one," He answered.

"Not because you are?" Lucy asked.

"I am not, but every year you grow, you will find me bigger," Aslan said.

I have found it so with Jesus. As I investigate Him and grow older in Him, He becomes bigger to me. He never shrinks; I never know it all. I am investigating the mystery of His person. What a magnificent God He is!

The disciples have been studying under their Tutor, Jesus, for nearly three years. Jesus has been teaching them powerful truths. They have had on-the-job training. The display of miracles has been more than adequate to validate His Messiahship. They have experienced His preaching and the warm and intimate moments around the camp fire at night. He has adequately informed them.

Jesus has not tested them before now. After three years of study without a test, it will be a bit overwhelming. Jesus eases into it with a question. He asks it after they arrive in the region of Caesarea Philippi. This was Gentile territory, located on the east coast of the Sea of Galilee. The population of this area was sparse which would give Him time to deal directly with His disciples. ***He asked His disciples, saying, "Who do men say that I, the Son of Man, am?"*** (16:13).

Jesus already knew what the rumblings were regarding His person. Some of the Pharisees thought He was in league with Beelzebub, the prince of demons (12:24). The mother of Jesus and His half brothers had come to get Him because they felt He was out of His mind and needed help (12:46). Herod Antipas had feared that Jesus was John the Baptist, raised from the dead (14:1). The hometown folks of Nazareth had accused Him of being an illegitimate child (13:54). They thought He had nothing to offer to them because they knew His history. There were other followers who thought He was Elijah, the forerunner to the real Messiah. Some said that He was Jeremiah. The legend was that Jeremiah had hidden the Ark of the Covenant just before he died. One day he would arise from the dead and present the Ark to Jerusalem in power and might. Oh, the list goes on and on.

Jesus is deeply aware He is without any reliable following. He only has this group of twelve disciples who are before Him. If anyone is going to sincerely believe in His Messiahship, it will have to start with this group of twelve. He is going to place the entire responsibility of the Kingdom of God upon their shoulders. They have to be firm in their belief. It is scary, but it is time to put them to the test.

"He said to them, 'But who do you say that I am?" (16:15). Jesus braces Himself for the answer. Will these disciples give the right answer? Do they comprehend? Are they ready for the staggering responsibility of leadership and world evangelism? Have they gotten sidetracked? It is a crucial moment.

Peter jumps to his feet; he will be the spokesperson for the entire disciple group. His states with great conviction, *"You are the Christ, the Son of the living God,"* (16:16). Jesus must have cried, "Good for you Peter! You see it! After two and one half years of training you do get it. You have lived with the influence of my person for all these days and it has not been in vain."

Peter did not know all there was to know about Jesus. There was plenty of room for growth, but he did know something about this Christ. In fact, his confession established a pattern for you and me to follow. The ingredients found in Peter's confession is the kind of material (solid, rock, foundational) that you and I need. Would you be willing to follow his confession? Let's look at the content of his confession.

THE MESSIANIC MYSTERY
Matthew 16:16

"And Simon Peter answered and said, 'You are the Christ, the Son of the living God," (16:16). Peter has been walking with a mystery for over two years. This Messianic mystery has grabbed his attention and will not allow him to go back as he has been. It is true, he does not know the depth of confession. He does not know all the details contained within the concepts he was proposing, but he has grasped something of the mystery. Oh, that this mystery could capture us!

One great aspect of the mystery in Peter's confession is **DEATHLESS**. He said, *"You are ..., the Son of the living God."* The word "living" leaps out at you! It smacks of all that is going on in the eternal life of the person of Jesus Christ. He was living, and Peter had felt and experienced this fact. Peter took what he had learned about God in the Old Testament, and he applied it to this mystery he has been touching in present days.

The Old Testament is a contrast between the Living God and the stone faced gods who are dead. Peter had heard the stories. The fact that Jehovah was a God of action was the proof He was living. The stone faced gods did not act because they had no life. The living God displayed Himself in the midnight hours as a pillar of fire. He could safely lead the children of Israel through the wilderness. In the day time He appeared as a pillar of cloud, but always He was there acting, guiding, and protecting. He was a living God who had been there at the crisis hour and parted the Red Sea. When all was lost, His power brought total deliverance. He had descended upon Mt. Sinai and thundered out the moral code by which man was to live. This living God wanted direct participation into each person's daily life.

Peter knew all these stories and more about the living God, but as he walked with this Messianic Mystery, these stories came to life. Through Divine revelation he became deeply aware that there was an intimate connection between the living God and this Mystery. The living God had leaped out of the pages of the Old Testament and had become alive in the person of the Messiah.

Matthew is setting the stage for the statement Jesus will make in verse eighteen of this chapter. Jesus says, ***"And I also say to you that you are Peter, and on this rock I will build My church, and the gates of Hades shall not prevail against it,"*** (16:18). The actual word for ***Hades*** means death. All the powers of death cannot stop this living God. The last enemy of man will not conquer in this situation. Death has encountered a living God. At the heart of this Messiah is a living God who has leaped out of the eternities and dipped His finger into our time. When you are rubbing shoulders with this Christ, you are rubbing shoulders with an Eternal One. He is from the beginning to the end and always will be! He has never started, but always is; He cannot end for He is deathless. This is a tremendous mystery.

A second great aspect of the mystery in Peter's Confession is **DEMONSTRATION.** He said, ***"You are the Christ, the Son of the living God," (16:16).*** Mark the words "Son of" as significant in the statement. Each of us has an understanding of what those words mean. If you are a son of, you are a product of, or you come from, the seed of an individual. You call the one from whom you come, Father.

However, Jesus was not a son of in the normal sense. Jesus had prior existence before His birth in Bethlehem. He is eternal; He is a deathless Christ. "Son of" has an additional meaning in the New Testament. It was often used to identify an individual as having certain characteristics. If you refer to a person as the son of peace, it means he has peaceful mannerisms. When this person is present, peace fills the atmosphere. Peace is the characteristic of his life. If a person is referred to as a son of love, he has loving ways. There is flowing through his life, the essence of love. Love is the characteristic that spills from his life.

Let us take that idea and place it into Peter's confession. ***"You are the Christ, the Son of the living God,"*** (16:16). Jesus is the "Son of" in that He has the very characteristics of God. All that I hope to see in the person of God is flowing out of Jesus. The person of Christ proves every living, dynamic, eternal quality of God. The living demonstration of Jesus reveals everything that I want to know about God. I suddenly see and know God in the Christ I have been worshiping all my life.

Paul forcibly tells us that Jesus is the image of the invisible God (Colossians 1:15). What a mystery that is! Who has seen the face of God? What does He look like? **"No one has seen God at any time,"** (I John 4:12). What a marvel! God has taken on a face; He has revealed Himself. He has leaped into our time and walked on our streets. We have seen the person of God! His name is Jesus. Everything we need to know about God, we have embraced in Jesus. Jesus is the secret of the ages gone by, now revealed to us. Man can experience in Jesus the entire unfolding revelation of God. We have seen the Messianic mystery unfolded before us.

Peter had walked with Jesus for several years and had begun to grasp something of the mystery revealed in Christ. Jesus was deathless; He was a demonstration. At the close of his great confession, Peter is going to climax the great mystery with the fact that Jesus is a great **DELIVERER**. Consider the confession again, **"You are the Christ, . . ."** (16:16). The word *Christ* or the word *Jesus*, used so often by us in prayers, hymns, and sermons, has become common. Would you consider it again?

Christ literally means, *Anointed One*. The Old Testament Hebrew word, *Messiah*, brought into the New Testament Greek, is translated *Christ*. Peter was saying in his confession, "You are the Anointed Messiah." All that I have wanted in a Messiah, as taught from the Old Testament, I have seen flowing through Jesus. Christ fulfills the hopes and dreams for the King of Israel. He is the *Anointed Messiah*.

Think carefully through this great confession. The person of Christ powerfully displays all the resource of the living God. The deathless One has walked into our history to bring pressure to bear upon the essence of sin. All of the demonstration of the deathless, eternal God is flowing through Christ to bring deliverance to us. Deliverance is here! It was common practice in the Jewish home to start the day with the father asking the question, "Could this be the day?" He was referring to the Messiah coming to bring deliverance to Israel. They dreamed about it and longed for it to happen. Peter must have been shouting as he stated, "This is the day!" Jesus is the fulfillment of all the prophecies of the Old Testament. We no longer look for the Messiah to come. He is here.

You cannot be casual about this. It is not the average message of religion. This is not another social reformation movement. It is not one more cause trying to get your attention. The eternal, deathless, God has shown Himself in our world to focus the power of His person in deliverance for every man. You can be free. What a Messianic mystery!

HISTORICAL HERITAGE
Matthew 16:13

What we have discussed so far is great theology. You could go to any one of our theological schools and learn these facts in the class room. However, I have a deep desire to express to you that this Messianic mystery is not a theological fantasy. This is not a *pie in the sky* idea. We are not dealing with a vision or a dream that has no connection with reality. The revelation of God is rooted in our historical heritage.

Christ is **RELATED TO MAN.** All that we have discussed so far presses us to the fact that He is a part of us. Jesus and His disciples had come to the region of Caesarea Philippi. He turned to them and asked, ***"Who do men say that I, the Son of Man, am?"*** (16:13). The discovery of what the people of the streets are saying about Jesus is always interesting. It gives you insight into His ministry to them. It is great to consider Peter's confession concerning Christ. Here are those who have spent the most time with Him. It is also very valuable to find out what Jesus has to say about Himself. In His own confession, He calls Himself *"the Son of man."* In other words, you are My relation. I am one of you. I am not One who is far off; I am here. I am not One who is strange; I am of your kind. I am not One who does not know you; I have worn your shoes and your flesh, and have walked where you walk. I have experienced your trials and temptations, and felt your pain. I am one of you!

Christ is not master over against slave. He is not high human over against low animal. He is not sovereign God over against millions of specks of insignificant people. The eternal, deathless God has injected Himself into our flesh and has become one of us. This is an out spill of Genesis chapter three. There it is written that God turned to Adam and Eve to make the first Messianic promise. God told them that the seed of the serpent would bruise the heel of the seed of woman. But God also promised that the seed of the woman, Son of man, would bruise the head of the serpent (Genesis 3:15). God would not pass redemption out from the sky. We would experience redemption here, where we are. Salvation would not be from above, but from below. It would come from one of us. He is one of us. One from our ranks has become the Redeemer. Is it not an overwhelming thought that someone has reached the heart of the Father and has the total attention of God? That Someone is one of us.

Christ is **RELATED TO HISTORY.** Perhaps you have studied other great world religions. There are tremendous similarities between the concepts and stories of these world religions. Most all world religions have some basic story about the flood that covered the earth. The account of a virgin birth is not unique to Biblical Christianity. There is such a story in relationship to Buddha. A beautiful young maiden was in a lovely garden. God took on the form of man and visited this young lady. He had sexual relations with her and from that Buddha was born. It is an attempt to establish Buddha as born of god through a virgin. There are other interesting stories among the religions. White salamanders come down from the heavens to visit a man in a trance. A world religion is born with the delivery of great tablets.

However, you must understand, the only religion on the face of the earth that does not have its roots in mythology is Christianity. The basis of Christianity is not visions, dreams, and mystical stories, but the very histories of humankind. The roots of Christianity are in the events of people. We are not spreading some message that comes from theologians who dwelt in a class room and had a vivid imagination. We are talking about time - a moment in time. Our message spills out of a place - an isolated country, with an isolated town, with an isolated stable, with an isolated manger. It was in the fullness of time that Christ was born. Christ roots Himself in our histories, not our visions. He calls us to come face to face with the facts of history.

This is the call of decision. It is not a decision about great theology or dreams that you think might be true or not true. You must come face to face with historical facts and your reactions regarding them. This is not a matter of opinion, but a matter of history; you cannot escape dealing with it. Historical heritage! It is a magnificent mystery.

Christ is **RELATED TO TRADITION.** In discovering His relationship to man and then to history, a question quickly appears. Is this some kind of lark? Did it just happen? Was it a freak accident? This is not the story of a god who accidentally was traveling in space and fell through a trap door into our time zone. Christ is a distinct result of a long range plan designed by the Divine God. It is not by chance that you are reading this writing about the amazing impact of Christ upon this world. It is the result of our sovereign God. Year after year, generation after generation, He has dipped His fingers into our histories. He manipulated peoples and nations. Pharaohs came under His control and contributed to the plan. He blockaded some plans and promoted others. He saved a remnant that would not have been if He had not acted. He moved through prophets to unfold His revelation. It is the revelation of God moving in our histories. He caused the fullness of time, and He injected Christ into our world. What we are viewing is the overwhelming fulfillment of the dream of God. It is startling, indeed!

I suppose you could respond to this by reflecting that this is good information or great theology, but this is far beyond that kind of reflection. This is a Messianic mystery spilling out of a historical heritage demanding response. The response demanded is explained in the following.

COMPELLED CONFESSION
Matthew 16:15-17

Let us join the disciples as they are sitting before Jesus. He has brought them to the place where they are forced to make a confession. They are not people of the streets, nor are they of the world. They have attended Sunday School class and heard the teachings of Jesus. They have done miracles themselves as Christ has trained them. They have been faithful to prayer meeting. They are the ones from which He is compelling a confession. This is not an evangelistic message for the unconverted. He is calling His disciples. He wants them, from deep within, to come to grips with the amazing confession of who He is. Will you join them?

It is an **INDIVIDUAL CONFESSION**. Jesus is speaking directly to His disciples, *"But who do you say that I am?"* (15:15). This is not - let us come together, quote the creed and all believe. You and your God are face to face, honest, person to person. You are facing Him, and you must confess individually. Another translation states this verse as saying, *"But what about you?" He asks. "Who do you say that I am?" (NIV)* Even another translation quotes the verses like this, *"But you," He asks, "Who do you say that I am?"* When you investigate the grammar structure of this verse, you discover the personal pronoun *you* is dominate. It stands at the beginning of the verse. It stands out, bold, and up-front! It is an individual confrontation between you and your God. We want information from others. What they think can be of some value to us. However, the ultimate need is, what do you think?

It is important to notice in this passage that Peter is a representative of the disciples. He is speaking for them. Jesus is asking the question as He looks at twelve men, but He is asking each of them individually. What about you? Have you come to grips with who I am? I know you have good theology; you have learned the proper lessons in Sunday School. I know you have been to the altar several time, and testified. I want to know what is in your heart. Has the truth mastered your life?

It is an **INSPIRED CONFESSION.** Jesus responded to this confession by saying, *"Blessed are you, Simon Bar-Jonah, for flesh and blood has not revealed this to you but My Father who is in heaven,"* (16:17). This is a startling Scripture. Peter has been in all of the training sessions. He has gleaned the facts. He had learned the Old Testament with its Messianic concepts. He knows something of the traditions of his fathers. He has now been under the influence of Jesus for several years. The miracles and the teachings have impressed him. He is trying to put all of the pieces together. Something is going on here that is bigger than just another idea. This is not just another fact logged into the computer. Something supernatural is happening. There is a Divine God who has come to Peter's mind. He has taken all of the facts and put them together. The lights have come on in Peter's thinking. He sees something He has never seen before. Jesus is the Christ!

How about you? You have been around the church. You have prayed with people at an altar of prayer. You have learned the lessons and gleaned the information. You can quote the theology and give the facts. Oh, would not it be something if a Divine God would move upon the scene? He could take all the theology with its facts and information about Himself and turn on the lights for you. Suddenly it ceases to be an intellectual belief and becomes an internal heart passion. God confronts you in this hour. You come face to face with the living Person in the internal heart of your own being. Is He going to be Lord? Will the truth which is beyond your personal analysis master you? It is no longer facts that you can believe or not believe. You are experiencing a personal encounter with a Divine God. He is taking all the facts and giving them life. This forms a confession that must be spoken with your heart. It is an inspired confession.

It is an **INFLUENTIAL CONFESSION.** Again think about verse seventeen. ***"Blessed are you, Simon Bar-Jonah, . . ."*** The grammar structure of the verse becomes important to us. There is no article before the name in this verse in the original language, as would normally be found. This bespeaks the fact that Simon Peter is a representative. He is speaking as a representative for the entire disciple group. In other words, what Peter says in confession affects eleven men. Tremendous influence surrounds this confession.

Think of a father sitting at his kitchen table. He turns to his family and says, "I do not want to influence you. You are free to do as you want, but I am not going to get involved with Jesus and the Church." What a ridiculous statement. Does he think for one moment that his sons are not going to be influenced by him? The confession he makes, for Christ or against Christ, will stand as a wall over which his family must crawl. There is no way to make this kind of confession without influence. A mother is thinking foolishly if she thinks she will let her children make up their own minds when they get old enough. When you do or do not confess Christ, your decision is never isolated by itself. There is always a tremendous impact of influence. Every teenager needs to understand that kneeling at an altar of prayer will never be hidden or kept separate from the high school halls. A confession of Christ must spill out and aggressively influence the very atmosphere in the high school. If they do not want to get involved there, the altar is not the place to kneel. You cannot confess Christ without that confession influencing multitudes.

The Messianic mystery is confronting you. You have handled it; you have tasted it. It has bombarded you in Sunday School class, Sunday morning worship, and revivals. This mystery has dipped into our history. This historical Christ, now present, is confronting you. Not just facts, or theology, but the Holy Spirit bringing all that knowledge together in the person of Jesus. He wants to be Lord of your life. He wants you! No more games or half-heartedness. He is compelling you to let Him be your personal Lord.

Let us pray. "Dear Jesus! We treat truth like watching television. When will there be another commercial? I will get something to drink. We are not experiencing that superficial activity. Somehow all we have known about you has become the person before us. It is no longer knowing about You, but embracing You. Such an embrace will demand my entire life. Oh, deathless Jesus, live in me! I surrender to You. In the style of Your cross, I give my life to You. Amen!"

Matthew 16:17-19

Mystery of His Project

"Lord, you have insisted that we tell everyone. We have heard the news; we have seen the reality; we have known the demonstration; we have found the design and the plan; we have felt; we have experienced You. Now You give us the responsibility of telling everyone. Make us the Church! In Jesus' name we pray, Amen."

The flow of history bends itself to the Divine redemptive activity. When you view the events of history, you see the fingers of God in the middle of those events. They are not isolated scenes. They did not just happen. God has become a part of the moving of the history of humanity. He has a plan, a direction. He knows where He is going, and what He wants to get done. He has a distinct design, and He reveals it in the pages of history.

The Old Testament is the history of a great people. However, it is much more than that. It is the movement of God traced within the lives of people everywhere. God has literally manipulated nations and generations of time to cause His dreams. He is a sovereign God and can capably do that. He has a project.

There is an enemy. We all understand that fact. The enemy is out to thwart and complicate the movement of God. He wants to blockade all of God's plans, but you and I know nothing can stop a sovereign God. He moves around the Satanic force; He gets done what He designs to accomplish. In the end, He will carry out His plan. He has a project.

It is true in the life of Jesus Christ. As you come thundering into the New Testament, you see the unfolding life of Jesus. You quickly sense that things are not taking place by accident. The events in the life of Christ are not happen chance. Somebody is in charge of this scene. God has stuck His fingers in the middle of this Life. Jesus' life is an unfolding of the Divine redemptive plan. The Old Testament as it unfolds flows directly into the life of Christ. What is taking place in Christ is a climax of everything God has been doing in the past. All history flows into Christ; all future flows out of Christ. He stands at the pinnacle, the climax of everything that is taking place. History revolves around the person of Jesus Christ. He knows where He is going. He has plugged into the Sovereign plan. He has a project.

Listen to His words, ***"And I also say to you that you are Peter, and on this rock I will build MY church,"*** (16:18). This is His project - ***build MY church.*** Notice the emphasis on the word ***MY.*** When you view verse eighteen in the original language of the Bible, you notice that this word is completely out of order. This means that heavy emphasis is placed upon ownership, the possessiveness, which Christ has concerning the church. This is His church. He is the owner, the architect. The church is safe. You do not need to worry about the church; it belongs to Jesus. Everything is okay. He has a project.

Where does Peter fit into all of this? Is he some kind of star, a great performer in the activity of the building? Does he have one up on the rest of us? Does he possess a position that we do not have? At first glance you might think this verse suggests that fact, but you must look deeper. In the original language of the Bible, each time Peter's name appears in this passage, Matthew has eliminated the definite article before it. This tells us that Peter is only a representative of all the other disciples. When Jesus addresses Peter, He is really speaking to all of the disciples. Jesus is not just speaking to Peter or to the other eleven disciples, but He is talking to every disciple who will exist in the future. This includes you and me! Jesus is addressing all of us in this passage.

For instance, you can see this plainly in Peter's confession (v16). Jesus has asked the pointed question, ***"But who do you say that I am?"*** (16:15). Peter's response is, ***"You are the Christ, the Son of the living God."*** Understand clearly, this is not Peter's confession alone, as if eleven other disciples were not involved. Eleven other disciples are not stumbling in the dark, not understanding who Jesus is. All twelve disciples have had discussions about this. They have come to this conclusion together. Peter is the representative; he is representing the entire disciple group. We see this pattern repeatedly in the Gospels.

This is also true as you continue into verses eighteen and nineteen. It is here that Peter is given the keys of the Kingdom. The Bible calls him a *Christian scribe,* which is the undercurrent of the meaning of the keys. Peter has not been selected for elevation over the other disciples, but he is a representative. Jesus is giving this position to all the disciples. This affects you!

You play a key role in the building of the mysterious project. What role do you play? Within these verses of the passage there is a distinct progression unfolding.

FORTUNATE TO SEE
Matthew 16:17

Jesus is addressing Peter, *"Blessed are you, Simon Bar-Jonah, for flesh and blood has not revealed this to you, but My Father who is in heaven,"* (16:17). Now remember, it is not Peter alone to whom Jesus is speaking. Peter is representing you in this passage. Jesus has something powerful to say to you.

Note how Jesus starts. *"Blessed are you, . . ."* You may not have any idea how great these words are. If you can catch the significance of these words you will find your life challenged forever. You will remember, this is not the first time Jesus used these words. You can discover them in the Beatitudes (Matthew 5). *"Blessed are the poor in spirit. Blessed are the peace makers. Blessed are those who hunger and thirst after righteousness."* Now Jesus is giving a repeat of these same identical words.

The word *blessed* literally means *happy*. The problem with the English word *happiness* is its root. It comes from the word *chance*. This teaches us that happiness is a result of fate. If good circumstances happen to come my way, then I am happy. If poor circumstances come my way, then I am miserable. It is all a matter of chance, but this is not the basis of the word Jesus is using.

This word *blessed* has a basic understanding in the Greek language. It relates to a place, an island. They called it "Happiness Island." If you could ever arrive on this island, you would never want to leave. It was a place of total contentment. There was an abundance of fruits and vegetables. The weather was always ideal. It was blessedness, happiness. It is the idea of arriving. This is the undercurrent of what Jesus is saying. He is telling you that you have arrived, and that everything you need is at the end of your fingertips. All the resources and power for total living are yours. Blessed are you! It is all yours.

Remember the statement is in the present tense. ***"Blessed ARE you, . . ."*** You have it right now. This is not a dream for the future. You are not working toward it. This is what has been placed into your hands this moment. Blessed are you. It is all yours in the present!

You need to be aware of another strong undercurrent which the word has. It has the idea of congratulations. It is a slap on the back. Congratulations! You have made it. You have got it. It is all yours right now. So Jesus, through Peter, has come up to you. He has slapped you on the back and said, "Congratulations, you have received it!" What is it you have received?

You have received **REVELATION.** ***"Blessed are you, Simon Bar-Jonah, for flesh and blood has not revealed this to you, but My Father Who is in heaven,"*** (16:17). You have moved to a place where you cease to listen to your own inward humanism, your own resource, your own knowledge. You have ceased to operate out of the flesh; you are experiencing the mind of the Father, and you are living in the flow of the Divine. Congratulations! It has taken nearly three years, but you have made it. You see it! You have come out of yourself into Him.

There is a strong contrast contained in this verse. It is between "flesh and blood" and "My Father Who is in heaven." This contrast is the call of the Gospel. Cease to listen to flesh and blood. It has the connotation of tradition, cultural, education, appearances. These all have the smell of the flesh or self-centeredness. You have stepped out of that and tapped into My Father. This is the fullness of the Spirit of God. You have ceased to live out of yourself and are now living out of Him. It is no longer what you can do; it is what He wants to do through you. You are not doing for God; you are now relaxed in His presence and He is flowing through you. Oh, congratulations!

You understand with Peter this was not some moment of vision in the midnight hour. It was not some mystical scene where God took some truths and implanted them in Peter's brain. This was a result of three years. Others had watched Christ, but had not grasped it. What did they think of Him? They thought He was John the Baptist, Elijah, Jeremiah (v14). They did not get it. But the disciples had walked with Jesus intimately for nearly three years. They had begun to see the truth. It came because they saw God revealed through the person of Jesus. The disciples had finally grasped it. Congratulations!

It was **PARTICIPATION.** *"Blessed are you, Simon Bar-Jonah, . . ."* (16:17). There is a slight problem with this statement. There is no problem with calling Peter by the name of Simon. We understand that the name Simon is another way of saying Peter. The difficulty is with *Bar-Jonah.* "Bar" means "son of." So this is referring to Simon who is the son of Jonah. This is where the problem appears. The New Testament relates that the father of Peter was John, not Jonah.

Why would Jesus address Peter as Simon, Son of Jonah? Where did Jonah come from? We see the answer in the climax to which Matthew is flowing this entire section. Jesus has linked what is going to happen in the life of Peter with Jonah, the prophet. This should not surprise us. Jesus has already referred to Jonah in this very same chapter (16:4). The scribes and Pharisees have demanded a sign out of heaven. Jesus' reply was, ***"A wicked and adulterous generation seeks after a sign, and no sign shall be given to it except the sign of the prophet Jonah."*** Now in this context Peter has made this great confession and Jesus links him with the sign of the Prophet Jonah. This scene takes place in another section in Matthew (12:38). The Pharisees have demanded a sign. Jesus gave them the same answer in chapter twelve as in chapter sixteen. However, He does give an additional explanation about the sign of the Prophet Jonah. He says, ***"For as Jonah was three days and three nights in the belly of a great fish, so will the Son of Man be three days and three nights in the heart of the earth,"*** (12:40). The sign was the death, the suffering, the blood process - the cross of Jesus. So Jesus links the sign of Jonah with the cross and its style. Peter has said that Jesus is the Christ. Jesus responds by congratulating Peter as a representative of all the disciples. Peter is to be congratulated because He is going to have the privilege of participating in the cross style. In fact, this becomes the theme of the rest of chapter sixteen.

What is true about Peter is true about you. Jesus has linked you with the cross through Himself. How long has it been since you praised Him for the fact He called you to share in His cross? Have you looked Him in the eye and thanked Him for calling you to share in His sufferings? He has slapped you on the back in congratulations. You have had revelation from the Father so you are no longer living out of yourself. The mind of the Father can spill through you as it did through Jesus. Congratulations on your calling! You are fortunate to see!

FORMING HIS BODY
Matthew 16:18

Jesus continues to speak to Peter, *"And I also say to you, that you are Peter, and on this rock I will build My church, and the gates of Hades shall not prevail against it,"* (16:18). Remember, what Jesus says about Peter is also true about you. Peter is a representative of all disciples. You are fortunate; you have received the revelation and have become a participant in the cross and its style. The result of this is that you are going to form His Body.

As you look at verse eighteen, it appears again that the emphasis is upon Peter. Peter seems to capture our attention as he is addressed at the beginning of the verse. However, if you look carefully, you will see that the emphasis is not upon Peter at all but on Jesus who is speaking. The first few words of verse eighteen are revealing when you see them as Jesus spoke them. A proper translation would be, "In fact to you, I am saying." The emphasis in this verse is upon Christ, Who is speaking.

Who is the Christ Who is speaking in this verse? What is the content of His person? The answer is found in the phrase, *"I will build My Church."* He is the builder, the constructor, shaper, molder. He is putting this whole thing together. He is the authoritative Christ. He has a right to build the church. He is the One Who is speaking to you. Will you listen? What does He have to say?

He speaks about the **FOUNDATION OF HIS BODY.** *"I also say to you that you are Peter, and on this rock I will build My church,"* (16:18). We understand there is much confusion clustered around this verse. Verses seventeen through nineteen are only found in the Book of Matthew. All three of these verses seem to foster controversy. The confusion is found among the various translations you can read. The controversy is found among ourselves in the very concepts we have concerning the church. There is such a variety of opinions held. I am absolutely convinced there need be no confusion with them at all over the Word of God. We must get into the flow of the whole context instead of just seeking a proof text. You have no right to take these verses out of their context and do as you please. These verses are in the progression of the Book of Matthew and are climaxing in great truth. What is that truth?

The confusion seems to cluster around a play on words. Peter is the word "Petros" (v18). The word for rock is "petra" (v18). The actual statement by Jesus is, *". . . you are Peter (Petros), and on this rock (petra) I will build My church."* Both words come from the same root word. Petros is masculine. Petra is feminine. Petros means "detached little stone." Petra means "solid, huge bedrock." So the statement of Jesus would read, "And I also say to you that you are Peter, a little stone, and on this petra, the solid bedrock, I will build My church." Peter is not the foundation of the church; he is a little stone. The bedrock, the solid foundation, upon which He is going to build His church will be unshakable. What is it?

The answer is found in the flow of the entire Book of Matthew. Chapters five, six and seven contain the Sermon on the Mount. It is the powerful words of the authoritative Christ Who is speaking. He reaches back into the Old Testament law structure and presents it to the people. He pulls it apart. He puts it back together. He did things with it that no one had ever had the courage to do. He acted like He wrote it! Chapter six is a contrast between "the ole timers said" but "I say to you." As He thunders to a climax, He presents a parable (7:24-27). Again He presents a contrast. It is between two men who build houses. One built his house upon the sand. But when the storms came, it collapsed. What a foolish man! The wise man built his house upon a "petra" - a bedrock. The same storm came, but this house was immovable. Jesus gave His own interpretation of this parable. He told us that the man who built his house upon the rock is a picture of the man who hears His sayings and does them. He is obviously telling us that the bedrock, the solid foundation is "these sayings of Mine." This is the petra upon which He is going to build His church. The authoritative Words of Christ are the solid foundation of the church.

Chapter eight of Matthew is just as revealing. He takes the preaching to the streets and lives it. One scene is Jesus' encounter with a Roman centurion. The centurion has a servant who needs healing but is some distance away. Jesus simply speaks the authoritative Word -the Petra- the Bedrock, and the servant is healed. In this chapter, Jesus **"cast out demons with a word,"** (8:16). The Petra, Bedrock of the Word controls demons. He is going to build His church upon it.

In chapter thirteen, Jesus tells seven parables that explain something of the mysteries of the Kingdom. He turns to His disciples to express that He is handing to them these mysteries, these words, these understandings, these concepts, these principles, this powerful Word. He was placing into their hands the Bedrock, the foundation upon which He was going to build His church.

If you approach me and slap me in the face, I would ask you the reason you did such a thing. You might quickly deny that you did anything at all. You try to explain that it was your hand, not you, that did the slapping. I would not accept that explanation. There is no difference between you and your hand. So it is with the authoritative spoken Word and the living Word of God. How can you separate what Jesus says from the Jesus Who said it? These Words are an extension of Jesus as your hand is an extension of you. So the Bedrock foundation is the Words that spill from Christ. It is intimate with Who He is! Jesus said, ***"I am the Truth."*** These are not isolated ideas or simple principles, somehow they are the very mind of Christ. The living Word and the written Word are so solid that the church can be built on that solid foundation. He is the foundation!

He speaks of **FORMATION OF HIS BODY**. Let us go back to where Peter fits into all of this. Remember that Peter is simply a representative of all the disciples. What is true about Peter in this passage is also true about you. Who is Peter in this Scripture? He is a little detached stone. What is the value of a little detached stone? Not much, unless it gets into a sling that causes it to hit a giant between the eyes. What good is a little stone? Not much, unless two, three, or four little stones get together. Out of that you can build a superstructure, that could become the church.

Immediately I recognize my desperate need for you. I am worthless without you. I am a detached little stone rolling around doing nothing, unless you and I can get together in the dynamic of Who He is.

Upon the solidness of the One who is the Rock, we become a superstructure called the church, that can shake a world. Come on! All the little stones really need to get together!

You can see that we really need to be together. We are being threatened. *"And I also say to you that you are Peter, and on this rock I will build My church, and the gates of Hades shall not prevail against it,"* (16:18). To what does the last word of the verse refer? It does not refer to the rock - the foundation of His Words. It refers to the church - the superstructure of little detached stones who have come together. The gates of Hades is not threatening this Christ, the foundational Rock. He is secure; you cannot shake Him! The gates of Hades are threatening the superstructure, the church, the little stones. It is threatening you and me. Our security is in Him. He links us together. He is putting us together in Him as His body. Why has He gone to all of this trouble for us?

FLOW HIS LIFE
Matthew 16:19

Jesus said, *"And I will give you the keys of the kingdom of heaven, and whatever you bind on earth will be bound in heaven, and whatever you loose on earth will be loosed in heaven,"* (16:19). This is all about flowing His life. Why would Satan spend the energy to go after the little stones who make up the superstructure? Why would he have one bit of concern about the church? Why would he go after you, the little stone?

God has given you tremendous **RESPONSIBILITY.** *"And I will give you the keys of the kingdom of heaven, . . ."* (16:19). The responsibility of the keys of the kingdom of heaven is yours. Do not forget that Peter is a representative of all disciples. He is not some special, super saint. What is true about him is true about you. Look into your hands, disciple. You will see the keys!

What does it mean? Remember the Bedrock of the church is the Words of this powerful Christ that cannot be separated from His person. So the figure of the keys of the kingdom of heaven relates to what we have been calling "a Christian scribe." Let's go back to chapter thirteen where Jesus told seven parables relating the mysteries of the kingdom of heaven. When He finished, He decided to ask His disciples how much they understood of what He said.

When the disciples convinced Him that they understood the mysteries, He slapped them on the back and congratulated them for becoming "Christian scribes." The role of the scribe was to handle the Word of God. In the Christian sense, you and I have become an authentic, authoritative, interpreter of the Word of God. I am giving you the keys of understanding, of knowing, of grasping, of explaining the Word. You have the responsibility of this powerful Word.

The responsibility is not one of preaching or teaching. This is a constant responsibility. Every attitude and action, (speaking, listening, and seeing,) all reflect upon this Word. It has been committed to your hands. The person on the street will never read the Bible, except what he reads in you. You can yell from a Sunday School class that God is love. But the person on the street shakes his head in disbelief, until he sees this love of God being interpreted by the Christian scribe. This love is through you. This is the responsibility. Forgiveness, spoken of in testimony at the church, is not as valuable as the next door neighbor sensing forgiveness from you. You have become an authentic, authoritative, interpreter of the Word of forgiveness to the world. You are a Christian scribe who has the keys of the kingdom of heaven. God wants to unlock the mysteries of the kingdom to the world through you.

But it goes deeper than that! Notice, it is also **REFLECTION.** *"And I will give you the keys of the kingdom of heaven, and whatever you bind on earth will be bound in heaven, and whatever you loose on earth will be loosed in heaven,"* (16:19). We are given tremendous promises in this verse. I am afraid there is some confusion about these statements. The confusion has to do with the verb tense. As the verse reads in the above translation, it appears He gives us the keys that enable us to do down here. Once it is done down here, heaven is required to follow suit. In other words, heaven becomes a reflection of what we are doing here. If this is true, I have little desire to go to heaven!

The above translation states "will be." In the original language of the New Testament we learn the proper translation is "will have been." Here is the promise Jesus has given, *". . . and whatever you bind on earth will have been bound in heaven, and whatever you loose on earth will have been loosed in heaven."* What the Christian scribe does down here should be a duplication of what is being done in heaven. We are to discover what is taking place in the spiritual realm of the kingdom of heaven and allow Jesus to reflect through us in our day. You are to be the flow of what is happening in heaven to this present world. You are to be the channel through which the heavens can reach this society.

You will reflect the heavenly on this earth. You are an extension of Divine activity. You are to be the reproduction of His life. People anywhere, in all circumstances, can look at you and see what God is all about. The flesh of humanity reflects the holiness of God.

How long has it been since someone mistook you for Jesus? Do you confuse people about who you are? You look like Him; you act like Him; you love like Him; you live like Him. Yet, you are not Jesus. He is doing something through you. You are a reflection of Him. Martin Luther called the Christian a "little Christ."

"Jesus, we are just little stones, but we have been placed on the Bedrock. Somehow You have seen fit to take what is going on in the heavens and flow it through our lives. Through us and out of us, would You project Your life? We would be the church, the reflection of Who You are. We would be the caring love of the Father. Make us the church! Thank You for including us. In Jesus name, I pray. Amen!"

Matthew 16:21-23

Mystery of His Program

A penetrating question has been gripping me! I would like to propose this question to you. How surprised will you be when you get to see Jesus face to face in His second coming manifestation? I am not talking about the surprise of discovering who is the anti-Christ, or the surprise of seeing who actually made it into heaven. Some will make it that you were sure did not have a chance; others will not make it and you will wonder why. I am sure the experience of the trip into the heavenly realm will be a surprise, as will our mode of transportation. But these are not the surprises I want to highlight.

I want to confront us with how surprised you will be over the actual person of Jesus Christ. You are now seeing Him in all of His majesty. Is He like you thought He would be? Do you recognize Him? Does the atmosphere of His person coincide with what you have been experiencing? When you finally see the depth of His personality, will it surprise you? I have a goal for my life! I desperately want to keep the surprise to a minimum. I want to know Jesus so well now, through intimacy, saturation, and experience, that when He comes in His person, there will be few surprises.

This is something of the dynamics that are taking place in the New Testament. It was difficult for the people of Israel to accept Jesus in His first appearance. He was an absolute total surprise to them. They just could not seem to buy into His revelation. They had the Old Testament in their hands. They came daily to make their sacrifices and perform their ceremonies. They knew all about the temple structure; it had become common place to them. They knew the Messianic promises; the hope still burned within them. But it is startling when He finally appears. He totally surprises them. They do not even recognize Him! He has qualities about Him, methods He uses, duties and activities in which He is involved that are a total surprise to them. He did not come as they expected Him to be.

It was not much better for the disciples who accepted His Messiahship. They have lived with Him for nearly three years, and they still were not seeing it. Three years of Divine activity, miracles, and the flow of God through the life of Jesus, left them with big questions. They were so unready for His death that they did not know where to find the empty tomb. If it had not been for the women of the church, they would not have even looked.

Jesus is taking His disciples aside for six months of special focus. He wants to reduce the surprises. He is going to give them the insight into what is going to take place. He wants them to see what He is really like! He wants to reveal the subject of the cross and its style. The disciples must grasp how Jesus will build the Kingdom. The entire future of this Kingdom seems to rest in the hands of these twelve disciples.

They must see the cross revealed. This stuns them, and they do not seem to grasp it. But Jesus was not going to give up. This was too important to attempt only once. Matthew writes, **"From that time Jesus began to show to His disciples that. . . ."** (16:21). Jesus would have no other subject about which to speak. Every activity, miracle, and parable would all point toward one thing. What is it Jesus wants to show to His disciples? As you search these three verses (21-23), you discover there are three basic elements He wants to reveal to them.

HIS IMPACT - THE PLAN
Matthew 16:21

This must have been really important for Jesus. He has taken the last six months of His ministry to focus on His disciples, to say just one thing to them. He knew these were the closing days of His time on this earth. Surely He would carefully give His time to the most valuable need. It was communication to His disciples.

Peter has made his great confession about the Messiahship of Jesus (16:16). Peter thinks he has arrived at a high knowledge, knows what there is to know. But Jesus begins to speak of His crucifixion. He is going to die on a cross; He will identify with the sins of men. It is very negative. Oh, He ends with a positive note about His resurrection, but the idea of the cross so stuns them, they did not hear it. How could they believe a Jewish Messiah would accept the curse of the law? The worst that could happen to any Jewish man, any place, or under any circumstances would be to receive the curse of the law - a cross. The disciples cannot imagine; it is mind boggling! They have grasped something of the mystery of His person. They believe He is the Messiah who has come to build the Kingdom. But this information of a bleeding, dying, cross bearing Messiah violates their traditional teachings concerning how He is going to build the Kingdom. What makes it worse, He does not leave any room for adjustment.

Jesus relates to them **ITS NECESSARY QUALITY.** *"From that time Jesus began to show to His disciples that He must go. . ."* (16:21). Notice the powerful statement, *He must go.* Jesus has not called His disciples together to vote on this new idea of the cross and its style. He is not even asking their opinion concerning how they think it might work. There is an internal Divine compulsion. *He must go.* Certainly He is not asking for their approval. *He must go.*

In this passage, the word *must* is very significant. The New Testament uses this word five ways. The context that follows the word decides its use. First, the necessity, or *must*, lies in the nature of the circumstance. An example is the Parable of the Prodigal Son. At the close of the parable, He speaks of the elder brother and the Father. They are having a conversation in the story. The closing verse of that parable shows the Father passionately attempting to explain to the elder brother what he should have already known (Luke 15:32). The Father says that it was necessary; it was right. They should give the prodigal a party. Celebration just has to be. It is the nature of the case. Your brother has come home! What else could we do?

A second usage of the word is that the circumstances cause the necessity, or what some one else has done. The Apostle Paul relates this for us. He writes, *"If I must boast, I will boast in the things which concern my infirmity,"* (II Corinthians 11:30). It is a foolish thing to boast, but He is forced to do it. There have been a variety of people who have been undermining his ministry. The Gospel, as it has flowed through him, is at stake. He feels this pressure to boast, due to the circumstances. However, He decides to boast in his weakness and the display of the power of God through that weakness.

In the New Testament, you discover a third usage of the word *must*. The passage uses a must (necessity) when a circumstance requires a certain end. John gives us this in his description of the Samaritan women - the woman at the well. In her conversation with Jesus she tries to get Him side tracked because He is getting very close to her personal life. He begins to talk about the proper place to worship. She relates that they worship in the mountains around them, but the Jews say that all must worship in Jerusalem (John 4:20). The Jews believed that to be close to God one must go to Jerusalem, where He is. This is a necessity to reach the goal of closeness to God.

The fourth usage of the word *must* is the command of the law or of duty. Jesus was speaking to the Pharisees. In this conversation He spoke of the minor points of the law. He agreed with the Pharisees and said, **"You must do them,"** (Luke 11:42). The minor points of the law are necessary to accomplish, but the Pharisees left undone the major items. They ignored things like love and mercy.

The fifth usage of the word *must* is found in this passage in where Jesus is sharing with His disciples. It is not in the nature of the case. It is just the right thing to do. It is not because circumstances have trapped Him. It is not just to reach a certain end, such as redeeming a world, that He must do this. It is not a law or command and, if He wants to be right, He ought to do it. The decree and the council of an almighty, sovereign God establishes the necessity that lies at the heart of the cross and its style. Jesus is going to a cross. He will establish a kingdom based upon this style. Matthew is telling us that the primary motivation behind this style and what drives it, is the Sovereign Plan. This is not up for debate or vote. It is an absolute necessity, burning in the heart of Christ. He has heard the decree of His Father.

We need to clarify one aspect of this. There is a fine line between God's sovereign decree and man's responsibility. The fact God has decreed it, does not excuse the sin of man. It is a *must*. For instance, Judas does not have an excuse for his betrayal. This does not mean the Pharisees are not held accountable. You have also played a part in this, and you are responsible. While man maintains his responsibility, the undercurrent of this cross and its style is the sovereign decree of God.

Jesus relates to them **ITS NEVER ENDING QUALITY.** *"From that time Jesus began to show. . ."* (16:21). The verb is present tense with continual action. There is a point in time when He began. It is followed with a continual unfolding. This unfolding is the revelation of what He wants to bring to the minds and hearts of the disciples. They have to get into the heart of this reality. He is starting something, and He will continue to do it. It is not going to stop today or tomorrow. It is going to flow through the rest of His time on this earth. It will flow through the resurrection and into the Day of Pentecost. It will resound through two thousand years of Church history. It is a never ending, unfolding revelation of the Divine decree to redeem the lives of men. It is a cross and its style.

Can you believe the attitude of Peter? He has had one little speck of revelation. He was able, at a moment in time, to receive from the Father one aspect of an important truth. That truth being, Jesus Christ is the Messiah. Because of this moment of revelation, he thinks he knows it all. He feels qualified to grab Jesus by the shoulders, pull Him aside, and tell Him He is wrong concerning the cross and its style (16:22). Perhaps we should be careful in condemning Peter. We have aggressively played this role. God was so gracious to us and allowed the revelation of one truth. We immediately begin to act as if we know it all; we have a corner on the market of truth. We box God into our little framework of thinking as if there is nothing beyond what we have seen. But God is always far beyond our thinking and the limitations we place on Him. This is not finished; revelation is going to continue.

Jesus relates to them **ITS NEGATIVE QUALITY.** This is a distasteful approach to make. ***"From that time Jesus began to show to His disciples that He must go to Jerusalem, and suffer many things from the elders and chief priests and scribes, and be killed, and be raised the third day,"*** (16:21). This will all take place in "Jerusalem." It is astounding? God will establish the cross as the style of the Kingdom, and the scene of all the activity is Jerusalem. The grammar structure of the list of those involved is important. You will notice there is an article before the word *elders,* but none before *chief priests* or *scribes.* Matthew has lumped them together in one group. These are the individuals who make up the Sanhedrin, the ruling body of Israel in Jerusalem. This whole scene that Jesus is describing is going to take place in Jerusalem, under the control and leadership of the Jewish denomination.

It is in the holy place, the sacred place, the place where you feel like taking off your shoes. That is the location of the crucifixion. It is the heart of religious activity. In Jerusalem, they say and do all the right things. The scholars live here. The thinking people, who decide what the rest of Israel will know and understand, abide in Jerusalem. This is the atmosphere that creates the crucifixion.

I am not interested in criticizing the leadership of any church. I am not critical of those who have studied and know truth. But somehow I want to cry for a new openness to the will of God. May God prevent us from slipping into this kind of box. May we, who are a part of the church, who have all the established traditions, have a new freshness to the will of God. We do not want to end up crucifying Him.

It is sometimes sad to have a revival. The Spirit of God moves upon the lives of people. Some receive salvation and others receive a new fire. Then, when the meeting is over, the leaders of the church meet together in a board meeting and crucify the new movement of God by their self-centeredness. Somehow we are back in Jerusalem; the whole scene of the crucifixion is being acted out again. God has to do something anew in those of us who are at the heart of Jerusalem.

OUR IGNORANCE - THE PLOT
Matthew 16:22

"Then Peter took Him aside and began to rebuke Him saying, 'Far be it from You, Lord; this shall not happen to You," (16:22). This is a great statement of ignorance. You see this unfolding pattern everywhere in the Word of God. In the middle of our stupidity, God is so loving. In the middle of our blundering, God is so over-shadowing in His Divine love. This passage is no exception. The Divine necessity that has planned for the redemption of a world through a cross has run into the ignorance of humanity. If you feel like I do, you want to

give Peter a swift kick and yell at him. The problem with that is, it would be like kicking and yelling at yourself. We find ourselves identifying with Peter in this passage.

Matthew relates **PETER'S CONFESSION.** I do not want to paint too bad of a picture of Peter. Contained with Peter's rebuke is a great confession. He has not lost the insight he gained earlier (16:16). He has taken Jesus aside to rebuke Him, but pay close attention to what he says, *"Far be it from You, Lord, this shall not happen to You,"* (16:22). A literal translation would sound something like this, "God will have mercy on You, Lord. This shall not happen to You." Peter's training has convinced him that Jesus, the Messiah, will not die on a cross because the sovereign God would not allow it to take place. Peter really believes Jesus is the Messiah, but he also believes that a Messiah will not suffer as Jesus is describing. At the heart of Peter's rebuke is his confession.

It is interesting to compare the same Scripture with Mark's account. You know that Mark wrote his Gospel account under the influence of Peter. Mark just writes a blunt statement about Peter's rebuke with no attempt to explain it (Mark 8:32). Mark presents Peter as very foolish; it is a harsh statement. We now see Peter in the worst of light. But Matthew attempts to color Peter's rebuke with this undercurrent of Peter's strong belief that Jesus is the Messiah. Peter may be ignorant, no question, but he has this strong motive and love for Jesus as the Messiah. He has a good heart; he wants to protect the Christ.

Matthew relates **PETER'S MISCONFESSION.** *"Far be it from You, Lord, this shall not happen to You,"* (16:21). Oh, what a misconfession it is. Peter is saying that there is no way Jesus is going to a cross. It is so ignorant of him to say this; the cross is a Divine decree. I was going to illustrate this for you, but I am not sure I need to. When I see this blundering man in all of his ignorance, a hundred illustrations from my own life leap to mind. They all remind me that I have consistently done the same identical thing.

The major problem here is not the ignorance of Peter. We could tolerate his ignorance, except it is lined with overwhelming arrogance. He grabs Jesus by the shoulders and in great arrogance acts as if he knows better than the sovereign God. Immediately sides have been chosen! Jesus says that it is a Divine decree and the cross is the style of the Kingdom; while Peter is saying that this is foolishness because the Divine decree would not allow the Messiah to suffer. The division spills out of the ignorance, lined with arrogance. Peter really thinks he is right. What if we are so right we are wrong? We are so arrogant about what we think we know. All the time our knowledge is ignorance, lined with arrogance. We are so right we hurt our brother, split our churches, cannot tolerate each other. While we are right we are blockading the flow of redemption that comes from the cross and its style. In all of our rightness our altars are barren. Could it be that our arrogance lines our ignorance? God save us from ourselves!

Matthew relates **PETER'S CONFESSIONAL.** You remember the sequence of events in Peter's life. In his ignorance, he goes on in his arrogance. He stomps into a Garden of Gethsemane as if he can handle anything that comes. Peter does not need to pray; he can sleep in the crisis hour. Before he gets done, he has grabbed his sword and cut off the ear of the servant of the high priest. Jesus has to intervene and protect him repeatedly. After many dark hours, there is a crisis. *"Peter* remembered the words of Jesus who had said to him, 'Before the rooster crows, you will deny Me three times.' Then he went out and wept bitterly," (26:75). Is it not tragic that we have to come to this? Dark hours have to come before our ignorance, lined with our arrogance, becomes visible to us. We experience repentance in these moments. Why do we have to follow afar off? Why do we have to come to stressful moments when even a servant girl, pointing a finger at us, shakes the foundation of our life? God, save us from ignorance that is lined with arrogance. God save us from ourselves.

SATAN'S INFLUENCE - THE PERSECUTOR
Matthew 16:23

Jesus is now turning to Peter and speaking, **"Get behind Me, Satan! You are an offense to Me, for you are not mindful of the things of God, but the things of men,"** (16:23). I want us to be careful how we view Peter. We must not put him in the same class as Judas. Satan had entered the very heart of Judas; he has entered into the plot of carrying out the crucifixion. This is not true with Peter. However, in the middle of his self-centered ignorance, Peter has come under the influence of Satan; Satan is using him. It is not that Peter is just out to save himself. He comes to a Garden of Gethsemane and risks his life to protect Jesus against six hundred to a thousand armed men. He is sincere; he intends to do the right thing. His self-centered carnality has produced a handle for Satan to reach out and grab. Satan is using Peter in ways that will crush him in days to come.

This is why holiness is our message. This is why we are constantly proclaiming the message of the cross and its style. This is why we plead with you! Do not tolerate one ounce of self-centered carnality. Do not put up with the alien principle of self-sufficiency. Weep and pray until God has given to you total deliverance. It will be that one ounce of carnality the Devil will use as a hold to manipulate you. He will blockade the flow of the Spirit of God, damn souls, and ruin churches through your self-centeredness. You cannot afford it. You must come clean.

Now we see Peter in one of his finest moments (16:16). It is a moment of great confession as he stands leading the disciples in the direction of commitment. In just a few moments, we will see him in one of his lowest moments. He is under Satanic influence, creating a blockade to Christ Himself (16:22). One moment Jesus is praising him because he has been an instrument to deliver God's revelation (16:17). Peter has seen and known the truth! The next moment he is under Satanic attack and is losing (16:22). He ends delivering Satan's message.

A great contrast in this passage is the contrast between Peter's reaction and Jesus' reaction. One contrast is **DISCRIMINATION or THE SENSES.** Jesus turned to Peter and said, ***"Get behind Me, Satan! You are an offense to Me, for you are not mindful of the things of God, but the things of men,"*** (16:23). Is it not significant that the minute anything was out of line with the will of God, Jesus was totally sensitive to it? He spotted it immediately. There was no hesitation or question in His mind. If something showed up that detoured one degree from the Divine decree, Jesus would not tolerate it. He was constantly in tune with the Spirit of God.

But look at Peter. He was just as sensitive to the flesh. The moment something ran contrary to his own pleasure, schedule, political advantages, or his own materialism, he immediately stepped into action.

Everything he wanted or desired was the constant focus of his attention. Peter was sensitive to the flesh; Jesus was sensitive to the Spirit.

This is dangerous to talk about because it gets very close to home. We are quick to respond when something gets out of line with the flesh. We quickly speak out if something appears to threaten our comfort, but when something runs contrary to the Spirit of God, we respond with dullness. In our normal self-centered way we say, "Well, I know what the Bible says, but if you do that it will just cause trouble." Well, then under God, let us cause trouble. Let us get back to surrender and Spirit sensitivity. Let us flee from the flesh, humanism, our own manipulation, and let us cling to the Divine activity. Let us leave the rut of least resistance, ease, and comfortableness. Let us flow with the ruggedness of the cross and its style, let us get back to bleeding, suffering, and dying. Let us focus again on losing our lives.

Another contrast between Peter and Jesus is **DETER-MINATION or THE STUDY.** Jesus turned to Peter and said, *"Get behind Me, Satan! You are an offense to Me, for you are not mindful of the things of God, but the things of men,"* (16:23). What are things of which you are mindful? When we mention "study" here, we are not speaking of education, rather, our focus is on your mind time. On what do you spend your time thinking? What thought patterns flow in your mind?

Jesus had an amazing thought pattern. His total mindset was "redemption." Everything Jesus Christ did was redemptive. He never thought a thought, moved a finger, had an attitude, but what it was redemptive. He was always lifting! He was always boosting. His whole mind process automatically flowed in cross style. It is no wonder it constantly spilled into His actions, because it was constantly in His mind.

Peter had the thought pattern of safety, materialism, schedules, and inconvenience. He thought about his future political positions. How could he get the right or left-hand position? He needed to maintain his leadership in the disciple group. He thought in terms of his personal power.

What about your thought patterns? What is your mindset? On the street when things do not go the way you want, what is the avenue of your thought process? What do you automatically begin to think? Is your first thought, "Things are falling apart!" Do you immediately fall into redemptive mode, asking, "How can I help? What can God do through me to redeem and touch these people?" At the board meeting when people are all upset, do you immediately begin flowing the Spirit of God to save the scene? Holiness is radical; it calls us to think like God.

A third contrast between Jesus and Peter is **DIRECTION or SEEING.** Jesus is amazing. His great concern was not this passion week and the suffering He would have to experience. His concern was not how He was going to make it through this immediate crisis. He was desperately concerned about the long range establishment of the cross. The style of the cross is at the heart of the Kingdom. He was seeing with eternal perspective. He saw a world that needed redemption. Jesus saw beyond the present into the future. He saw you.

Peter's focus was "right now." The temporal had mastered him. We must break with the now. By the grace of God we must pick our brain up off the floor and see above our knees. We must view the insult, the hypocrite, the temporal crisis in light of eternity. We must live big. I fear some of us identify strongly with Peter. We are so ignorant; our ignorance is lined with arrogance. We strut in our fleshly thought process, protecting ourselves. The immediate is our focus. We have the mind of the flesh, instead of the mind of God. ***"Let this mind be in you which was also in Christ Jesus,"*** (Philippians 2:5).

"Dear Jesus, make us big. Will You save us from the narrowness of the flesh, the grip of the immediate, and the plight of the temporal? Give us the mind of Christ, the sensitivity of the Spirit, and the heart of the Father. We give You the right to move into our lives and do whatever needs to be done to accomplish this. In Your name, we pray, Amen."

Matthew 16:24-28

Mystery of His Projection

"Jesus, please allow us to grasp the truth. Do not allow Satan to misguide us. Do not let us misunderstand. Save us from confusion. We promise! If you share with us the truth, we will respond. In Jesus' name, Amen."

I am very concerned about having proper perspective in understanding the Word of God. I desperately want to interpret it correctly. I have no desire at all to take my bias and impose it upon the Word of God. One thing that is a constant corrective to keep me from doing that is to stay in the flow of this Book. In other words, the Scripture must be kept in its context. It is true that you discover more about a verse from its context than you do from the actual words of the verse. You must not take verses out of context and do with them as you want. You must interpret them, considering the context.

As we view the passage here, there are two basic approaches we could make. The verses themselves would lend support to either one.

The only way to tell which approach is right is to look at the entire context. To act as if either approach would be all right is foolishness. The approach you make can alter your entire idea of Christianity. What you do in your day in and day out life style, will be affected by the approach you make to this passage.

One approach you might make to this Scripture is to consider Jesus as proposing some conditions you must achieve if you are going to be in the Kingdom of God. In verse twenty-four He calls us to *"deny ourselves."* Is this a condition or requirement we must have if we are going to be disciples of Christ? Another idea in the same verse is *"take up your cross and follow Me."* He then gives us a great summary by stating, *"For whoever desires to save his life will lose it, and whoever loses his life for My sake will find it,"* (16:25). Are these conditions or standards for the Kingdom of God? We must try really hard, struggling until we achieve these conditions; then we can be disciples of Christ.

There is another approach that I believe to be the correct one. These are not standards or requirements to meet in order to make entrance into the Kingdom, but they are natural results of being in the Kingdom. You do not do them and arrive in the Kingdom; you must get in the Kingdom and these things will appear in your life. These things begin to flow from the deep internal heart of your being. You can see these are two vastly different approaches; they will effect your life at its very core.

If these are simply conditions Jesus is establishing, we could call them **Requests of the Master.** A tyrant, called God, is dictating out of His own whims. He is dictating what He wants me to do. He is a hard taskmaster and I must attempt to please Him. However, if these are not conditions, but are attitudes that come from being in intimacy with Christ, then these are **Results of Mutual Oneness.** They are the spontaneous, natural results springing from relationship with God.

If these are standards I must meet, then they are the **Requirements of the Law.** I must bite my lip, slap my hand, and try harder to do my duty. If these are not conditions, but are internal qualities flowing from the life of God within, then they are a **Resource of Love.** I just love Jesus with all of my heart and out of me pours these natural results. Love knows nothing about denial or sacrifice. Love gives itself up and delights in the giving.

If these are requirements I must achieve, then they are **Responsibilities of Duty.** I must meet up to my obligations. I must do my part. At the church I am trying to fulfill my role, however boring it may be. If these are not requirements established by God, but are attitudes resulting from Him, then it is **Relax in Delight.** It is a flow from within that you cannot manufacture. I can simply relax in all that He is and it will happen through me. The strain is gone.

Would you be willing to analyze your spiritual experience upon this basis? Do you have high standards you keep attempting to reach? Do you keep slapping your hands, attempting to build control or discipline? Or do you have a burning passion in the depths of your soul? Does this passion come through intimacy with God? Has love been shed abroad in your heart and do you live with a spontaneous flow of delight to serve Him?

If these are conditions God has established for me to achieve, then when I meet them I can have **Pride in my Accomplishment.** I can strut my stuff and say, "Aren't I something?" If these are not conditions, but inward attitudes that flow because I have Jesus, then I must spend my time **Pondering His Assets.** I realize it is not me; it is Him. I am doing what I cannot do and living like I cannot live. The Divine God is doing something through me that is bigger than I am!

If these are requirements I must accomplish, then I must **Push my Desires.** I keep struggling, striving, aching, and trying. Any time I might happen to reach the requirements, it is a product of my superior ability that produces pride in myself. If these are not requirements established by God, but are attitudes flowing from intimacy with God, then I simply **Pull on His Direction.** I constantly focus on His will and allow Him to make me into what He wants.

If these are standards set up for me, then I can **Parade my Discipline.** People stand in awe of self-control and how I have achieved the high standards of sainthood. If these are the natural, spontaneous results of Christ being in me, then I simply **Propose my Denial.** This is not of me. I deny that I have produced this. It is of Him. All that is happening in my life has come because of His Divine Presence. This is what He is doing in me.

I admit that I tremble over this kind of truth. It is because I am thrust into a deep spiritual analysis. What has been the essence of Christian for me? Has it been a high standard, a ball and chain, a challenge of self-achievement, or a task to accomplish? Or have I found an intimate relationship with God that produces a spontaneous quality of the life of Christ? Is Christianity simply past training or a flow of His Divine life? I believe with all my heart this is the intent of the cross style. I am to die to my own achievement and allow Him to bring to my life

His own qualities. Therefore, you can test your experience with God by discovering the source of these qualities. Are they spontaneous in your life? Do you have them, not do you do them? Jesus gives us powerful insight into this attitude or these qualities.

STATEMENT OF ATTITUDE
Matthew 16:24

Jesus turned and said to His disciples, ***"If anyone desires to come after Me, let him deny himself, and take up his cross, and follow Me,"*** (16:24). In my imagination I can clearly see the faces of the disciples. They are in total shock. They have never heard anyone talk like this. This is foreign language to them. Jesus is acting like everyone who is in the Kingdom is going to be like this. What if I do not measure up?

If these are conditions to achieve, I can report, "I am trying. I am working hard at it, but remember that no one is perfect. God is not done with me, you know! I do make mistakes." If these are qualities that come from intimacy with God, then I do not strive harder, or work more, or seek to attain. I must die; I need His cross in my life. The very thing that keeps me from having this flow is my trying. I must give it up. God is calling the very basis of my spiritual experience into check.

Maybe Jesus just gave these statements in a casual manner. He really did not think through the ramifications of what He was saying. It was just a chit chat time with His disciples, and He was not really intending to give some radical spiritual statement. Each of the three statements in this verse start with an imperative. This gives you something of the inflection of the voice of Jesus as He spoke these words. This is not a light statement, but a stern call with a command to be obeyed. These are not optional. It is not good if you want to, but do not worry about it if you do not want to. It is not a call for a few saints who want to be radical. This is for every man and woman who is going to walk with God.

The first call is **THE IMPERATIVE OF PURPOSEFUL DENIAL.** Jesus says to His disciples, *"If anyone desires to come after Me, let him deny himself, . . ."* (16:24). The denial He is calling us to strikes at the very core of the heart of man himself. This is not about cutting down on the amount of ice cream you eat before going to bed. That is a surface level. His call to denial deals with the inner heart core of self-sufficiency. He wants us to give up all reliance on what we are by our own nature, resources, and self-centered ability. We must cling exclusively to Him alone. You cannot cling to self and to Him simultaneously. This is a strong blow to the carnal nature that is enmity against God.

If there is something you do not understand in the Scriptures, there is a commentary I strongly recommend. It always has the answer! It is the Bible. The Bible is the best commentary on the Bible that I have ever found. If there is a verse you do not understand, keep on reading. You will find an explanation in the rest of the Scriptures. The most powerful commentary on this verse is Galatians chapter two verse twenty. Paul states, *"I have been crucified with Christ;* (nevertheless I am still alive, yet) *it is no longer I who live but Christ lives in me;* (so it is me, yet it is not me; I am under new management) *and the life which I now live in the flesh I live by faith in the Son of God, who*

loved me and gave Himself for me." That strikes a death blow to the very heart of self-centered carnality residing at the core of humanity.

This is our only problem! The heart of sin is S **I** N. Some one said, "Everywhere I go, I go too, and spoil everything." I would like to go some place without myself. I have some great advice for you. Take a vacation - not a two-week vacation. Take a five-second vacation from yourself. Tomorrow morning, eat your breakfast at the breakfast table. When you are finished, run into the living room, leaving yourself at the breakfast table. It will do you a tremendous amount of good. It would be a break from your biggest problem - you.

Pogo, in the cartoons, came bounding out, ready to fight. He had all the equipment for conflict. The helmet was on his head; the shield was in his hand. He had on the breastplate and was swinging the sword. He was yelling at the top of his lungs, "Hey, gang! I have found the enemy - and it is US!"

Carlyle wrote about a great monster who stood ten feet tall. He had great broad shoulders. No one could identify him, for he had a veil over his face. Everywhere Carlyle went, this monster followed him. It was ruining his life. He had such fright. He could not adequately do his work. When Carlyle was in the living room, the monster would wait for him at the door. One day Carlyle was going downtown. The monster followed about ten paces behind him. He slowed his stride and the monster grew closer. When Carlyle thought he could do it, he whirled around and grabbed the monster by the throat. He yanked the veil from his face. His great discovery was that the monster was HIMSELF. He was the monster who had been haunting his own life. He was his own biggest problem. He had blamed everyone else for his problems, but he was responsible.

Jesus says, *"Deny yourself!"* (16:24). If this is a condition I must achieve, then I will put a lid on my pride. I will simply slap my hand and try to do better. I will get my self-centeredness under control so it does not show as much. But if this is not a condition of denial to achieve, all my self attempts will be useless. Self-control just will not work. Putting on religious garments by increasing my activities at the church will not compensate enough. I must experience a crisis moment with God when He does something in me that I cannot do for myself. He must cleanse me of the principle of carnality - self-centeredness. I must have something take place in me that I cannot do for myself. When He comes and does His work, it will result in "denying myself."

The second call is **THE IMPERATIVE OF PECULIAR UPLIFT.** Jesus said, *"If anyone desires to come after Me, let him deny himself, and take up his cross, . . ."* (16:24). In this passage Jesus is asking His disciples concerning His person. They confess Him as the Christ, the Son of the living God. There is no question about His Messiahship in their minds. The problem comes when Jesus describes for them the content of His Messiahship (16:21). He is going to be a cross style Messiah. Peter explodes over the very idea. He takes Jesus aside and proceeds to rebuke Him (16:22). But now Jesus has added to the dilemma. Not only is Jesus going to the cross, but the disciples must take up their crosses also. Peter could not tolerate the idea of Jesus having a cross, but now he suddenly realizes he has one also. What a reaction must have appeared on his face!

"Take up your cross" was not a new phrase to the disciples. It was a part of their culture which experienced crucifixions on a consistent basis. The phrase literally meant that you took up the horizontal bar of the cross. You carry this bar from the place of judgment to the place of execution. People would line the streets and cast insults at you. They would throw things at you and laugh. This is what Jesus calls us to!

If this is a requirement I must accomplish, it is repulsive. I must go against peer pressure. I do not want to be ridiculed, the object of laughter and mockery. It conflicts with my comfortableness. It simply is not what I want to do. Since it is a requirement to go to heaven, I will make the sacrifice. I will do it, but do not ask me to be happy about it. I drag myself through the painful task of being Christian. It is no wonder I do not win anyone else to Christ. It is repulsive to be a Christian. The cost is too high.

If this is not a requirement, then the whole picture changes. If Christianity is an intimate experience with God, then love is at the heart. He has captivated me. I have seen Him in all of His glory. In experiencing Him I have found all I could ever want. My heart has one passion - to be like Him. The cross is not repulsive, but I glory in the cross. It is my crown, my desire, my passion. I consider it a privilege to join Jesus on the cross in redemptive process for my world. The cross style has become great delight.

The third call is **THE IMPERATIVE OF PROGRESSIVE FOLLOWING.** Jesus states, *"If anyone desires to come after Me, let him deny himself, and take up his cross, and follow Me,"* (16:24). The first two imperatives are in the aorist tense. This has to do with beginning at a point in time and ending in a completed action. But in this last imperative, the bold statement is in the present tense. It is the present tense with continual action. Immediately the whole picture changes.

If this is a standard Jesus is establishing for all who want to become Christians, then I must bite my lip and go through it. I must go to the altar twice and get it over. It is like a surgical operation. It is something to get over and place in my past. It is simply a memory I wish I did not have. Of course, it is an accomplishment. I did what many other people did not get done. I met my obligation.

This is not a standard Jesus is establishing. This is a burning attitude of the heart, resulting from the indwelt presence of God. Denying yourself and taking up your cross is not an experience of the past. These are the daily, progressive, and unfolding experiences of your life. We are going to be exactly like Christ. We are going to embrace Christ and live off the cross. Redemptive process is going to flow daily through us. This is not a one time experience to accomplish, but a style to live. Yet the style is totally impossible in myself. So He must do through me, His style.

The question is not "will you do it?" I must ask, "Is this present reality in your life?" Are these qualities flowing spontaneously through your heart and are they a result of His presence? Are these qualities a natural result of all that He is in all that you are? This is the statement of the attitude (16:24). We should consider why it is this way.

SENSE OF THE ATTITUDE
Matthew 16:25

Jesus says, *"For whoever desires to save his life will lose it, and whoever loses his life for My sake will find it,"* (16:25). He has already stated the absolute essentials resulting from intimacy with Him (16:24). Now He proceeds to tell us why these are essentials and why they are a natural result (16:25).

Jesus describes the **CERTITUDE OF THE ATTITUDE.** There are two distinct statements made in this verse. *"Whoever desires to save his life will lose it. Whoever loses his life for my sake will find it,"* (16:25). He begins both statements with an element of doubt. He then thunders to the end of each statement with a definite certainty.

He begins with *"whoever desires to save his life. . . ."* He is not sure anyone will desire to save himself. This is uncertain. But the absolute certainty of the case is this, if he does want to save his life, he will absolutely, without question, lose it. That is an irreversible principle. The second statement is in the same pattern. *"Whoever loses his life for my sake. . . ."* It is not certain that anyone will want to lose their life for Christ's sake. If there should be someone who does, it is an absolute certainty he will be a winner. This is not a questionable principle. This does not work sometimes with certain people, but you cannot count on it all of the time. It is an absolute certainty.

Jesus describes the **CLARITY OF THE ATTITUDE.** What is the principle itself? It is the "save-lose/lose-find" principle. If you try to save, you will lose. If you will lose, you will find. There must be, at the very core of my living, one principle. One principle alone must influence everything I say, everywhere I go, everything that I do. There must be no compromise at this level. We are not talking about levels of growth or improvement. We are not referring to *practice makes perfect*. This is about a deep heart change in perspective. In everything I am, I must lose my life for His sake.

This is not a religious standard that I must accomplish and maintain. If it were, I could just try to achieve it. I could simply isolate it to the religious area of my life. After all, in a religious sense I have lost my life for Christ. But in my business practices I can continue to operate on the "dog eat dog" principle. Jesus is referring to a natural, spontaneous flow that comes because I have intimacy with Him and it spills into a "lose-find" principle. Therefore the "lose-find" attitude in my religious life spills into my business life and controls all of my business practices. A business man came to a great theologian. He was apologizing for his living by saying, "I know it is wrong, but I have to live, don't I?" The theologian quickly answered, "You do?" We have forgotten there are other alternatives to living. You can die. You can join Jesus on His cross and live its style.

If this principle is a condition I must match, then I can simply isolate it to my relationship with Christ. I have lost my life to Christ, but my relationship to Him is only one of many relationships in my life. Losing my life is simply what I do to Jesus. Meanwhile down at my home I can dominate my wife, and cut her to pieces in public with jokes. However, if this is not just a condition, but is an attitude flow from the core of my life, then I cannot isolate it to my relationship with Christ. My relationship with Christ is so deep within my life that all relationships are effected by Him. He radically changes my home life. I must treat my wife and Jesus the same way. For the way I treat my wife is the way I treat Jesus. My whole life is now dominated by the "lose-find" attitude.

The question for us is not will you do it, but is it flowing? In every section of your living are you losing your life? Have you found an attitude change at the core of your living that flows to every aspect of life? Do you find a perspective within that calls every area to adjust to its "lose-find" attitude?

Jesus describes the **CHOICE OF THE ATTITUDE.** This must be very clear to us by now. For this is not a choice I make to be in the Kingdom of God. This is a choice I consistently make through out my life, because I am in the Kingdom. This choice is at the core of the nature He has now given to me because I am a son of the Kingdom. At a crisis moment with God, change was effected deep within me. Can I explain it? Did I earn it? Is this something I finally accomplished? The answer to each question is "No!" This is not about me, but about Him. He has done something beyond words in my life. It is now flowing throughout my life. I find myself delightfully choosing to lose my life in every aspect.

I am concerned about an Evangelical Christianity that seems to live in constant struggle. Living the Christian life is such a battle. Each issue of life is such a major crisis in choice. Will we, or will we not, do what Christ calls us to do? It is no wonder we never reach our world for Christ. Our energy is constantly drained with the battles of merely maintaining some meager level of Christianity for ourselves. We are so focused on making it ourselves that we can not intercede for others. We spend all of our time fighting over our own problems. Can we really get into the Kingdom of God? Better than that, can the Kingdom of God really get into us? Can we know the fullness of the Spirit of God within? Could we live in the flow of all that He is? Instead of making Christianity happen, could Christianity begin to be spontaneous in its outflow? Would this not cause an evangelistic spill of spontaneous love for the people around us? It would not be a new program, but a natural result of Christ in you, the hope of glory.

SECURITY OF THE ATTITUDE
Matthew 16:26-28

It amazes me that Christ's approach to the security of this attitude is not an emotional approach. This is not a negative statement concerning emotions. We could tolerate more emotional expression. But I need more than a little emotion when I have a headache or discover my tire is flat. I need a deep internal reality with God that makes sense. His approach in the security area is logical. It is almost as if He is saying, "Do the right thing because it makes sense." You must not forget the reason it makes sense. You are in the Kingdom and Jesus has changed your perspective. You are now understanding the reality of truth as you never did before. Before you memorized rules and did them because it was demanded. Now truth is flowing from your internal being. You cannot help yourself. It simply makes sense.

Jesus begins with the **COST BENEFIT ANALYSIS.** *"For what is a man profited if he gains the whole world, and loses his own soul? Or what will a man give in exchange for his soul?"* (16:26). The words *whole world* have to do with the wealth in the materialistic world. Then Jesus suggests the idea of the *soul* that bespeaks the eternal destiny and value of the person. On the one hand is all of the junk and the temporal stuff of the world. Over against this is the eternal value of the never dying soul. Materialism is not wrong, but it is not our focus. We hold materialistic things loosely because we see with eternal eyes. We have a perspective beyond junk. We do not give our lives for that which does not matter. We do not spill tears over that which does not count. We weep over the things that are eternal. Do not have a heart attack over junk, those things that will not matter one hundred years from now! Work yourself to death for that which will last forever. Do not live for the puny that rots in your hand. Live for that which is big; wear yourself out for that which is important.

How do you get this perspective? This is not a condition that I match. It is not discipline or self-control that bring me to this level. I have had an internal experience with God. This has changed my perspective. My eyes have been opened! This is not a matter of hearing more sermons. People set in our congregations for years and still go on grabbing for their materialism. Something has to happen inside us that changes our value structure.

Jesus continues with the **PUNISH REWARD ANALYSIS.** *"For the Son of Man will come in the glory of His Father with His angels, and then He will reward each according to his works,"* (16:27). There are rewards involved. When most of us think about rewards, it is always about right over against wrong. You have not done the wrong things. But you have been taught that the more right things you do, the more rewards you will get. God has this gigantic brownie point chart in the sky. You get a check mark for each good thing you do. I must really work hard for the church. If I teach a Sunday School class, sing in the choir, give money, then I will have a big mansion in heaven.

But If I am lazy and slack off, then I will have a little cabin on the back forty somewhere, with an out house. This is how we seem to view the whole reward system. This violates the very context of this passage.

Jesus is speaking about works which spill out of the resource of His person. They are not self-works, but God doing through you. The whole issue of works is, where do they come from? What is their source? Works are not good or bad in themselves. Everything that comes from you is illegitimate. The only thing that counts in the Kingdom is what He does through you. You could work your fingers to the bone for the church and never get one reward.

Christian service is not what I do for God as He watches me. The essence of Christian service is what He is doing through me. He fills me with Himself. He is flowing through my life. He produces the works that come from me. You can easily see the difference. I have learned through the church that I have to love everyone. It is very hard to love everyone, especially you. You are so difficult. Yet I am obligated to love everyone, including you. It is a condition; if I do not live up to the condition, I will not get the reward. Therefore I develop a "grit your teeth" love. The amazing thing about gritting your teeth is the moment you do it you automatically grin. So here we are hanging around the church, greeting each other in love through our gnashed teeth. It is all an attempt to meet up to the condition of loving everyone. This is not the work that receives rewards. Reward comes for the spontaneous love of God that flows out of me because He has cleansed me of all my self efforts. The work is not a result of me, but of Him. I find myself unable to keep from loving you.

Let me give you another example in the realm of worship. I know I am supposed to worship God. I realize this takes place at the church, but it is so boring. So I come Sunday morning and lean my cold dead body against a pew back. They count me as a number on their board. I worship; I never miss on Sunday morning. I do my little works, hoping God is keeping a record of my faithfulness. He will one day give me my reward. But this is not the true picture. God does not give rewards for this. The real issue is not whether you come Sunday morning or whether you do not. The issue is whether you set on the edge of your pew. During the song service do you worship? Do you pour your life into the moving of God during the worship service? During the prayer do you lock your mind into God, pleading before Him? Do you endure preaching, or do you hang on every word as the truth? Worship is not a standard I must achieve, it is a burning, passionate, love for Jesus deep within the heart because I have met Him face to face.

Jesus closes with the **SEEING BELIEVING ANALYSIS.** *"Assuredly, I say to you, there are some standing here who shall not taste death till they see the Son of Man coming in His Kingdom,"* (16:28). Jesus is not speaking concerning His second coming manifestation. He is relating the dynamics of His cross and its style. There will be men who have seen with their eyes, but there will be many who have not seen with their eyes. Those who have not seen are walking in the Kingdom by faith. You disciples will see and believe. The belief I am calling you to is not that which is caused by seeing. If it is caused by seeing, it becomes a condition that we must all meet. I am calling you to that which spills from deep within because He has done something inside you. Out of the revelation of His presence within you, faith comes.

Faith is never that which you do and then God comes to your life. Faith is a response to the Christ who has revealed Himself to you. Will you let your heart respond?

"Dear Jesus, have You given us conditions to achieve? We slap our hands and try to do better. An evangelist comes and makes us feel bad; we are different for a few weeks. You have convinced us that You have not given us conditions but spontaneous attitudes that flow out of our relationship with You. It is a hard analysis. If I do not have these things flowing out of my life, then I am not in proper relationship with You. I give You the right to do in me what You need to do. Thank You. In Jesus' name, we pray. Amen."

Matthew 16:24-28

The Spirit of Martyrdom

As you walk down a long corridor, the clanging of the iron doors reminds you of where you are. The sounds of the guard's hollow heeled boots striking the marble floor fill the air. These guards are escorting you. The handcuffs that hold your hands behind your back are hurting your wrists. You are on a journey. It will probably be your last. The corridor is short, but it seems to go on forever. The sternness upon the faces of those who are guarding you tells the whole story.

Your captors usher you into a room. It is rather bare except for a chair. It does not look as if the builder had comfort in mind when he constructed this chair. It has a straight back, and there are electrical wires extending from it. They will fasten you in this chair. It will only take a moment. They will pull a switch; a surge of electricity will pulsate through your body. You will be dead. It is the electric death chair.

Can you imagine starting a new religious movement with the electric death chair as the symbol of faith? Men and women would gather to listen to this message. "Come and take up your electric death chair and follow the One who did so before you!" As you look beyond the one who is speaking you would see a life size electric death chair hanging with lights focused on it so all could see. On a table outside the front doors of the sanctuary there would be small, gold-plated electric death chairs on necklace chains for sale. This new religious movement would revolve around a call to the electric death chair.

Who would want to join such a strange religious movement? There might be a few neurotics, a few misfits. Surely this twisted idea would not attract decent people. But think about this. Is this not familiar? It is like the echo of a man called Jesus who preached, "Come and take up your cross and follow me!" It is the strange Gospel to which we are committed; is it not? The heart of the message of this redemption is that which is for criminals; it is the curse of the law. Can you imagine people gathering to hear the message? "Come and take up your electric death chair, your cross, and follow me. Come and give yourself away; lose your life. Come and live the living death. Abandon yourself. Come and live off a cross. Come and be possessed with the spirit of martyrdom."

Martyrs seem to attract us, and we have deep admiration for them. Yet there are so few volunteers for martyrdom. It is a dead idea for us. We have not grasped it in our cultural setting. It is a mere memory of some strange people in days gone by who were so possessed, but the philosophy is weird to our minds. The spirit of martyrdom runs cross grain to our very thought process, our self-centeredness, our defense for our rights. Our comfortableness, our control finds no room for the spirit of martyrdom. I would like to invite you to take a new look at this spirit of martyrdom. There have been more martyrs from the year 1900 to 1985 than all of the previous years of church history. There are predictions by many that there will be more martyrs from the year 1985 to the year 2000 than all of the previous years. There is a good chance that some of you considering these facts may be martyred for the sake of the Gospel.

The subject of martyrdom is closely associated with the end of the age. The Book of Revelation consistently approaches the subject. "The Cry of the Martyrs" (Revelation 6:9-11), is the title of the fifth seal. The Bible tells, ***"And they overcame him by the blood of the Lamb and the word of their testimony, and they did not love their lives to the death,"*** (Revelations 12:11). Their testimonies were powerful because they enforced what they said by not loving their lives. They cared not for themselves. Life or death did not matter. What mattered was their testimony and their faith. According to the Scriptures, the ultimate weapon God has against Satan is a person who is possessed with the spirit of martyrdom. They are constantly risking their lives for the sake of the Kingdom of God. Satan has no defense against such a person; it is the ultimate weapon. The times in history when the church is the most powerful is when the blood of the martyrs is flowing. The Greek word for "witness" is the root word for martyrdom.

It is easy to sit in a soft chair after a good meal and read about the spirit of martyrdom. We can debate in our minds whether we will, or will not, be martyred. We can project how we would act if someone threatens our life for the sake of the Gospel. But it is a meaningless exercise. What we are being called to in this moment is to be possessed by the spirit of martyrdom. In the Book of Matthew, from the Sermon on the Mount to chapter sixteen, we see Jesus flowing with the spirit of martyrdom. He did not care for His own life, but constantly gave

Himself away for others. He was always calling His disciples to join Him in this spirit.

Surely you can see the verses we are studying (16:24-28) as a summary of all that has happened? The proposition is Christ has called everyone to possess the spirit of martyrdom! If this is true we must be clear on the content of the spirit of martyrdom. What is it?

THE DESIROUS ATTITUDE DISPLAYED
Matthew 16:24-25

Jesus was constantly displaying one attitude. Everywhere He went, all of His reactions, the very flow of His life was all focused in the spirit of martyrdom. Everything came from one driving fundamental motivation from within. He cared not for His own life. He lost His life for the Father's sake. He settled that issue when He leaped off His throne and took on flesh to walk among us. He was the constant picture of the attitude - the spirit of martyrdom. He forcibly talks about it to His disciples.

He presents them with the **FOUNDATION OF THE ATTITUDE.** *"For whoever desires to save his life will lose it, and whoever loses his life for My sake will find it,"* (16:25). Here is the abiding principle that is at the heart of the spirit of martyrdom. It is the principle of losing your life. This is not about legalistic rules. This is not the performance of certain ceremonies. It has nothing to do with rites of activities done. This is not about obligations you must adhere to. This was the supreme clash between Jesus and the Pharisees. The Pharisees' focus was on laws and obligations. Jesus irritated them by pointing them back to their inward heart and focusing on their motive. The duties accomplished are all nullified unless you have lost your life inwardly. It is the spirit of martyrdom.

Would you be willing to face this issue? Most of your concerns spring from the fact that you love your own life. Your love for your own life prompts the tears dropping from your eyes. What upsets you, causes you to worry, and frustrates you, seems to revolve around the fact you love your own life. Self-protection fills us, preserving our lives. We spend our time simply looking out for ourselves. This is the principle that has gripped us. Yet Jesus came to strike a death blow to this principle. It is the carnal mind (self-centeredness). The spirit of martyrdom is the opposite and is the call of Christ. We must take up the cross.

She was the first foreign woman to be admitted to the Belgrade underground movement. It was an organization formed to harass Hitler's forces if they crossed the Yugoslavia frontier. She knew she was to go out the front door and down the street to the right. After some distance and many turns she arrived at a very plain office building. Climbing several flights of stairs, she arrived at an office door. She knocked timidly. A muffled voice said, "Come in." Stepping inside, she surveyed the one room office. There were no pictures on the wall and only a desk with two straight backed chairs. A man, engrossed in shuffling papers, motioned with his hand for her to be seated in the other chair. She sat there for what seemed like hours while he finished his work. Finally he looked up at her. He reached over and pulled out the top desk drawer. He offered to her the capsule retrieved from the drawer. As she held it in her hand, she heard him state, "You will keep this with you always. It is a capsule of poison. Not one of our members has ever been captured alive!" He rummaged through the papers on his desk and located a list.

Her name was at the top of the list. With a pencil he struck several lines through her name reporting as he did, "I just crossed your name off the list. You just died. You are a dead woman. When you join our group, you value your life as nothing!"

What do you think happened when you knelt at an altar of prayer and accepted the name and person of Christ? Was this some kind of escape from problems, bad feelings, or a quick fix? Did you not know you joined the cross and its style? You joined the group that values their lives as nothing. Your name has been crossed off the list. You died. The spirit of martyrdom, that demands the spilling out of your life, has gripped you. You have joined the group that lives the cross style. Risking your life daily is now your style. It is the attitude of the spirit of martyrdom. The foundation of this attitude is the loss of your life.

He presents them with the **FOCUS OF THE ATTITUDE.** *"For whoever desires to save his life will lose it, and whoever loses his life for My sake shall find it,"* (16:25). The phrase *"for My sake"* is a powerful statement. *"Take up your cross and follow Me,"* (16:24), makes a strong impact. The focus of the spirit of martyrdom is not a twisted psychological state of neurosis, but a burning passionate love for Him. He is the focus of our total attention.

The spirit of martyrdom is not setting around the church comparing our sacrifices with others. Parading the various examples of our cross style living is not contained in it. A total focus on Jesus has brought us to the place where we are unaware of any sacrifice. Love knows no limit; it delights in giving itself away. He now consumes us.

I am deeply concerned about a Christianity with cheap faith. Is it not time to fear when the church stoops to promotion instead of prayer, to self-doing instead of Spirit empowered, to men's applause instead of the Master's approval? The church must not present three easy steps to Christianity and hide the Lordship of Christ Who commands all. We must boldly proclaim Jesus as our total focus from the very beginning. The spirit of martyrdom is not optional, but is the fire of the soul that comes from our focus on Him. This is the only kind of Christianity there is. For without the cross and its style, there is no Christianity. He who is Lord is the focus of the attitude of the spirit of martyrdom.

He presents the **FORMATION OF THE ATTITUDE.** *"If any one desires to come after Me, let him deny himself, and take up his cross, and follow Me,"* (16:24). The closing phrase of the verse is again important for us. It would be proper to put the word "after" into the phrase. It would read "follow after Me." Do you realize He has done it first? Is it not amazing? He never asks us to do anything He hasn't already done. He has set the pattern; He is the example. There is no question concerning what the spirit of martyrdom is, for we have seen it in the life style of Jesus - the style of the cross. What He is in His inward spirit is now captivating me. His attitude is going to form me after His style. It is more than just doing the things He did. He is beyond imitation; it is participating with Him in His cross style. He is inviting us to join Him. The desirous attitude displayed is to fill us. It is the spirit of martyrdom.

THE DECISIVE ACTIONS DEMANDED
Matthew 16:25-26

The importance of attitudes cannot be over stated. They form the inward motivation, the heat of the passion, the focus of the being.

But attitude must flow to action. It is one thing to set in the sanctuary and feel the passion of losing our lives to Christ, it is another to have that attitude produce decisive action. Faith without works is dead.

There is **LOVE ACTION.** *"If anyone desires to comes after Me, let him deny himself, and take up his cross, and follow Me,"* (16:24). *"Take up"* is a voluntary love action. No one thrusts this upon you. This is the spirit of martyrdom moving from within to without. This is love compelling us. We can afford to risk ourselves in light of all we have received.

He gives us a distinct contrast in these verses. It is a contrast between love action for yourself and love actions for others. We understand through personal experience love action for self. Loving self promotes fighting for self, protecting self, grabbing for self. Jesus is proposing love actions spilling forth from love for Him. Love for Him now acts in aggressively fighting for Him even to the risking of your life. This naturally shapes you in love action for others.

This truth draws us into analysis of our own individual lives and the body of Christ. Do we not have to question the fleshly promotions used to manipulate people into evangelism efforts? We appeal to their love for themselves rather than pointing them to the high calling of death to self. We turn the church into the common marketplace where we shop for the best deal - the best music, the best teen program, and the shortest sermons. The self view is what will the church do to help me? The spirit of martyrdom calls me to pour my life out. How does God want to use me to help the church? He demands decisive love action.

There is **LOSE ACTION.** *". . . and whoever loses his life for My sake will find it,"* (16:25). The word *loses* has the element of risk about it. In fact, you might translate it, risk. He is inviting us to go after it! The time for counting the cost is over. We are to launch out without any hesitation. Such action is very risky. However, it is not so for the person who has died. When the spirit of martyrdom possesses an individual, that person knows no risk. The person who has died has nothing.

Where is the threat to the one who has already resolved deep inside to abandon his life for the sake of Christ? Satan comes to the Apostle Paul and states, "Paul, you are a real pain to my program. If you don't quit it, I will have you killed!" What is Paul's response to this - ***"I have been crucified with Christ; it is no longer I who live, but Christ lives in me; and the life which I now live in the flesh I live by faith in the Son of God, who loved me and gave Himself for me,"*** (Galatians 2:20). How can you threaten a man with death who has already been nailed to a tree? He has resolved in his heart to lay his life down. He has already settled the issue!

Satan comes to the Apostle Paul and says, "Paul, you are a real pain to my program. If you do not stop it, I will have you beaten." Paul turns to him and whispers, ***"I am always carrying about in the body the dying of the Lord Jesus, that the life of Jesus also may be manifested in my body," (II Corinthians 4:10).*** Pain cannot threaten Paul; he has already experienced the pain of the cross. He has already died; the spirit of martyrdom has become his heart. Paul is free; he has settled in the deep resolve of his heart the issue of life and death at the cross.

One of our problems is we have never come to the place of total surrender of our lives. We are not free. We have surrendered things, issues, habits, but not ourselves. We don't dare risk embarrassment, our families, our materialism. The spirit of our own self-care has captured us, not the spirit of martyrdom.

There is **LONG RANGE ACTION.** *"For what is a man profited if he gains the whole world, and loses his own soul? Or what will a man give in exchange for his soul?"* (16:26). The word for *soul* has the connotation of eternity. There is a contrast given by Jesus between the temporal and the eternal. He speaks of gaining the whole world which has to do with materialism, and that is temporal. It is the junk. It is stuff you handle day after day. The soul is of eternal significance.

I need to spend no time arguing with you concerning the eternity that is before us. But there may be something we have missed. From a Biblical perspective, eternity is not a state of time over there. It is not just the future or something to which we look forward. Somehow eternity has dipped its fingers into our time. The concept from the Gospel of John is that eternity has started now. We have already crossed the line into the essence of its reality. Eternal life now throbs through our veins. We do not live in this life for the temporal. We handle all materialism loosely. It has no attachment to us. We are giving our lives for that which matters forever and ever. We live with the new perspective of eternity. We have already died. The spirit of martyrdom has gripped us. It is a cross.

Let us summarize for a moment. There is the **Desirous Attitude Displayed.** We see it in the life of Christ. Can I see it in your life - the spirit of martyrdom? There is the **Decisive Action Demanded.** Has the spirit of martyrdom gripped you within until there is spilling through your life the actions that tells me it is so?   But there is another to consider.

DELIGHTFUL AWARDED DEED
Matthew 16:27-28

"For the Son of Man will come in the glory of His Father with His angels, and then He will reward each according to his works. Assuredly, I say to you, there are some standing here who shall not taste death till they see the Son of Man coming in His kingdom," (16:27-28).   This gives us news of rewards. I am not sure what reaction that produces within me. It is the opposite of what we have been discussing. To the individual who has lost their life, to the one to whom love for Christ is the total motivation rather than love for self, there is no interest in rewards. The moment an individual demands rewards it s a sign they have not lost their life. If our motivation is reward, then the spirit of martyrdom has not gripped us. Yet, Jesus presents us with the subject of rewards.

There is the **DISTRIBUTION OF THE DEEDS.** At the end of verse twenty seven, Jesus says, *". . . . and then He will reward each according to his works."* It is important to note what works He is discussing here.   He is not speaking of good deeds over against bad deeds. In other words, this is not a list of all the good things I have done for Jesus that can now be presented for rewards. The deeds referred to are those that come because of losing your life. Deeds coming from self-centered carnality, from performance of self-displayed, or from self-righteousness, mean nothing. All you can accomplish through self-centered ability or talent is negative. The only deeds rewarded are those coming from the source of Christ flowing through the loss of your life.

Such a person finds himself in heaven, totally amazed. He is receiving rewards, yet deeply knows his unworthiness. He forgot rewards, for he has focused on Christ. What you do for Jesus does not count. He rewards what He does through you. The one who wants rewards does not get them; the one who does not want them is the one who receives them.

In the Sermon on the Mount Jesus instructed us not to be like the Pharisees who stand on the street corner. They loudly proclaim their glorious prayers so all can hear. He called us to go into our closets and hide. It is in the solitude of intimacy with God that your Father sees and answers. When you fast, wash your face. Do not tell anyone. If you parade it, it becomes self-centered and you already have your reward from those who applaud you. But the individual who pours out his heart on his knees in secret, moves the Father's hand. These are the deeds that come from the source of the loss of your life - the spirit of martyrdom.

There is the **DIRECTION OF THE DEEDS.** Did you understand that the emphasis is all on the future? We pride ourselves on being the "now" generation. We want our rewards in the present. Jesus states, ***"For the Son of Man will come in the glory of His Father with His angels, then He will reward . . . ."*** (16:27). We do not live for this world; we live for the world to come.

A young man took a position at a Christian college to teach Greek. He was a brilliant professor; he taught the students well. His reputation began to build until those at other colleges began to hear about him. A prestigious, well-to-do college contacted the young man to offer him a position. It was a definite promotion in the eyes of the world. The salary increase was very attractive. After prayer, the professor rejected the offer. This rejection astonished the representative of the prestigious school. He responded, "Young man, don't you want to get ahead in the world?" The immediate answer of the young professor was, "Sir, which world?"

There is the **DETERMINER OF THE DEEDS.** Jesus clearly states, *". . . and then He will reward each according to his works,"* (16:27). Did you notice the word *"each?"* This is an individual rewarding. We all believe in the corporate action of the Body of Christ. As the Body of Christ in unity, we can do something in the world that cannot be done individually. We desperately need each other to accomplish the dreams of God for our day. We also understand that in the final hour, when the final line is drawn, individual activity is the focus. Your accomplishments will not be the basis for my rewards or judgment. I cannot hide behind the corporate action of the Body of Christ. The Father will view what has been spilling forth from my personal life.

I can make a statement without any kind of embarrassment. I have decided to lose my life to Christ. I want to experience the cross and its style. I want the spirit of martyrdom to flow through my life. Despite what the corporate Church does or does not do, I must experience death in Jesus. There will be no place for me to hide behind what others have done. I will be held accountable before Christ as an individual.

The Roman Empire conquered the world. There were multitudes of cultures, nationalities, and customs among the people they conquered. They had no common denominator to link them together in oneness.

Caesar decided to establish emperor worship that would give everyone one thing in common. He built a huge statue of himself in all of the major cities of the world. Every citizen was required to buy incense and offer it to the statue with the statement, "Caesar is Lord." Upon doing this the citizen would receive a certificate of proof that was valid for one year. Soldiers would stop you on the street and demand the certificate. Not to have one was in direct violation of Caesar's command and considered treason.

For most people in Rome, this did not matter. One more god added on to the many already worshiped was insignificant. But for the Christian, it proposed a real problem. Immediately within the early Church, there arose three groups of people. There were those who gave up their Christian faith. They decided not to risk their lives for Christ. A second group was the martyrs. They could not state "Caesar is Lord," therefore, they had no certificates. They risked their lives for Christ.

Then there was a third group we need to look at closely. They decided there ought to be a way around this dilemma. They could not get a certificate by saying "Caesar is Lord" but there was a friend who worked at the court house who handled those certificates. For a slight bribe, he would give a certificate to them. They were not backsliders from the faith. They had not said, "Caesar is Lord." They came to church faithfully and worshiped the same as always.

Several years went by. They changed the policy of the government, and certificates were no longer required. The officials released those who had been punished for not having a certificate. They came back to the local church. Can you imagine the scene? It is Sunday morning worship. Sitting in the pew is a man who has comfortably, without risk, made it through those years; he had a certificate purchased with a bribe. Sitting next to him is a man with scars on his face because of his loyalty to Christ. There is a man who has had his tongue cut off so he could never speak the Gospel again. There is a man who cannot lift his hands in praise. He lost his hands when they chopped them off so he could no longer serve Christ with loving deeds. Friends carried one man into the worship service, for his legs had been cut off so he would never carry the Gospel to his world.

In the colonial days of the United States the churches came to a conclusion. They established a "halfway covenant." It was for those who were not fully committed but still wanted to experience the benefits of Christianity. It was an interesting picture. A certificate being seen in your pocket as you raise your hands in worship to Christ. It is a halfway covenant given to you on Sunday morning as you join the fellowship of the church. But the Kingdom of God has never tolerated such an idea. The heart of our faith is still a rugged cross. It calls us to the loss of our lives. There is only one possibility in Christianity, it is the spirit of martyrdom. The cross is the style of the Kingdom.

"Jesus, we have treated Christianity lightly. Forgive us. You have called us to lose our lives. Bring us back to a cross! Shake us loose from all that holds us to this world; bring us into Your world, the Kingdom. Give us Your style. Possess us with the spirit of martyrdom. One moment we have spoken of Your death; another moment we have loved ourselves. You have been a god of convenience for us. Forgive us. Call us again to the loss of our lives for Your sake. In Your name, I pray. Amen."

PART THREE

Matthew 17

Faith in the Cross

Confirmation of the Cross Style

Matthew 17

Introduction

Revelation When It Is Needed

"Jesus, we would like to see You! We want to see You on our streets. We have had mountain top experiences, yet that is not our dwelling place. We must see you in the scenes of hurt and pain, in our everyday living. We desperately need revelation from You. In Your name, we pray, Amen."

The printing press is a great and forceful invention in the history of humankind. Man can accumulate knowledge. One generation passes its learning experience down to another, through the means of books. The average person can go to the library and find the entire wealth of knowledge learned through the generations. It gives us an advanced beginning place. The total knowledge of man is ours.

However, if I were to be honest with you, I would tell you bluntly that I am weary with what man knows. This was the conflict we experienced in chapter sixteen of Matthew's Gospel. The heart of this chapter asks, "Who knows what about the Messiah?" This heart is expressed in two questions asked by Jesus of His disciples. The first is, ***"Who do men say that I, the Son of man, am?"*** (16:13), and the second is, ***"But who do you say that I am?"*** (16:15). Both of these questions center on the knowledge of man about the Messiah.

A mixture of ideas arises from this probing. There are the curious followers of Jesus who think He is Elijah or Jeremiah, who has come back from the dead. He must be an old prophet. God reveals Himself through the mind of man, but Satanic influence quickly clouds it as darkness settles upon the scene again. There is an intermixing of brilliant light and knowledge with shadows that complicate and bring despair. It so easy to get confused when you focus on what man knows.

HALLELUJAH! Chapter seventeen quickly comes to the rescue. What man knows about the Messiah is the focus of most of chapter sixteen. What God knows and thinks about the Messiah is the focus of chapter seventeen. What God thinks immediately elevates the discussion. It is on the level of eternal thought process. This is knowledge beyond the accumulation of man. All that man knows is truth discovered. What God knows has been invented by Him. He is the Truth.

It is almost one week after Peter has given his great confession at Caesarea Philippi (16:16). Chapter seventeen begins, ***"Now after six days Jesus took Peter, James, and John his brother,"*** (17:1). Jesus has taken these influential disciples to a mountain top nearby. It was probably Mt. Hermon, which is a very high mountain. If you would stand on the Dead Sea on a clear day, and look one hundred miles off in the distance, you could see this mountain. It was nine thousand feet in elevation. It was massive, huge, and rugged. Somewhere on the slopes, between the minor peaks of this great mountain, Jesus gathered with these three disciples.

This is a scene of distinct, desperately needed, revelation from the Father, concerning the Messiah. A great cloud descends and the voice of God begins to speak. It is a clear statement, from the mind of God, concerning Jesus. This revelation comes at a crisis hour, declaring itself at this time, for all time. This brings us to the proposition of this chapter. We see it in every event recorded here by Matthew. The **PROPOSITION** - When we need revelation, God will always give it. When there is a desperate need for revelation, you can expect God to split the sky open. In the darkest moments of life you can count on the light of God appearing. God will expose His wisdom when overwhelming confusion fills your mind. When we seek direction, but do not know it, we can expect God to display His will.

When is revelation needed? This is what this chapter is all about. There are three distinct scenes in Matthew's account that display the need for revelation. It will be extremely necessary for you to come from where you are. You must enter these scenes as if you are there. You must begin to think like the disciples.

The Renewed Revelation of The Ruler
Matthew 17:1-13

This is the powerful description of the Mount of Transfiguration. Again let me urge you to become a disciple on the slopes of this Mount.

If you are to understand what is taking place, you must view it through their eyes. You will need to know their culture, feelings, and mind.

The first thing you feel as you experience their setting is **THE ARGUMENT BELOW.** *"Now after six days, Jesus took Peter, James, and John, his brother, and brought them up on a high mountain by themselves,"* (17:1). Keep in mind, this was almost one week from the time of Peter's great confession at Caesarea Philippi. He had stood to his feet and said, *"You are the Christ, the Son of the living God!"* (16:16). It is now six days later, on the slope of a mountain. Luke's account of the Mount of Transfiguration begins with this **phrase**, *"And it came to pass, . . . after these sayings,"* (Luke 9:28). Both Matthew and Luke have connected the Mount of Transfiguration with what happened in this six-day interlude. The mountain experience seems to spill out of, or is necessary because of, these six days.

What were the events of these six days that would demand a revelation of verification from God, the Father? The answer is found in one word - argument. Does this sound familiar? Everywhere you turn you experience argument. It permeates our homes. Disciples of every generation seem to have a common characteristic. This characteristic is argument. The disciples of Jesus have had one focus for six days, and it is argument.

"From that time Jesus began to show to His disciples that He must go to Jerusalem, and suffer many things" (16:21). Make special note of the word *began* as a description of what *Jesus* is doing. *"Then Peter took Him aside and began to rebuke Him,"* (16:22). Make special note of the word *began* as a description of what *Peter* is doing. Here is a parallel phrase or description. The word *began* is in the

aorist tense, which shows an action that starts in a point of time. Both Jesus and Peter began to do something they had not done previously. ***Jesus began*** to show His disciples the fact of His coming cross. ***Peter began*** to rebuke Jesus concerning the fact of His coming cross.

Notice also in both verses (16:21 and 16:22), the words ***to show*** and ***to rebuke***. This is present tense, with continual action. Jesus began, in a point of time, to reveal the fact of His cross, and He is still doing it. Peter began, in a point of time, to rebuke Jesus about the fact of His cross, and he continued to do so for at least six days. Jesus is attempting to unveil the mysteries of the cross that was to come, and the powerful resurrection that is going to take place. The death, blood process is going to be the foundation of the Kingdom He is establishing. It is the very style of Christianity. All this time the disciples, under the leadership of Peter, are rebelling. They are arguing.

The word ***rebuke,*** as used by Matthew, is a very strong word. It is the same word Matthew uses when he records Jesus rebuking the demons. This is not a light, casual discussion, for a brief period. For almost one week Jesus unfolds the wonders of the revelation of the cross, and the disciples hold tight to their traditions. They argue with Jesus day after day. No doubt, from what we know about the disciples, it is often a heated debate. Jesus attempts to reveal the Old Testament Scripture to them while they quote their Sunday School teachers.

No one ever wins an argument. Jesus could not convince them. They were not seeking truth, but wanted to win. A wall began to build itself between Jesus and His disciples. He was losing them. They had been following and seeking His wisdom; now, they were clinging to their traditions and old framework of thought. Have you put yourself in the middle of the scene? Do you feel the heat of the argument? This is a terrible place to dwell.

But we cannot stop here. There is not only an **Argument From Below**, but there is an **ANNOUNCEMENT FROM ABOVE.** *"While he was still speaking, behold, a bright cloud overshadowed them; and suddenly a voice came out of the cloud saying, 'This is my beloved Son, in whom I am well pleased,"* (17:5). It is definitely an announcement from above. Are you still back in that day as a member of the disciples? For almost one week, you have joined with the other disciples in an argument with Jesus. It is over the issue of what His Messiahship means. You have acted like you knew better and more than He did. He just did not have it together, and you must straighten Him out. Now Jesus has taken three of you to the Mount.

This has become a time of separation between Jesus and His disciples. There is a wedge between them that has not been there before. Jesus is giving them new revelation, but they are rebelling. A gulf has been building between them. He realizes He is losing them. The focus of the disciples is not the focus of Jesus. Do you realize how tragic this is? There is great pressure upon this hour. These are the last days of the earthly ministry of Jesus. He does not have ample time to retrain them. He is not dealing with superficial issues, but the very heart of the Kingdom of God is at stake. The disciples are further away from grasping the reality of truth then when He started training them three years ago. When Jesus really needs them, they are the furthest removed from Him. The entire responsibility of the Kingdom is going to rest in their hands. He is going to turn it over to them. The future of the

Church is here. Jesus is without any reliable following outside this small group. They have to grasp the truth!

What is He to do with them? Luke gives us some tremendous insight. He tells us, ***"He took Peter, John, and James and went up on the mountain to pray,"*** (Luke 9:28). You can understand this, can you not? What do you suppose He is praying about? Is He not crying to the Father concerning the blindness of His disciples? They are not ignorant of His Messiahship. It is the content, or kind of Messiah, that is the problem. They are blinded because of their tradition. If they are to understand, the Father is going to have to bring revelation to them. The Father had revealed to them that Jesus was the Messiah (16:17); could He not reveal to them the cross content of His Messiahship? Luke tells us, ***"And as He prayed, the appearance of His face was altered, and His robe became white and glistening,"*** (Luke 9:29). The message was a call to the disciples to cease argument and listen to Jesus. There was an **Announcement From Above.**

My heart cries out, "Do it again!" We have heard all of the arguments. The Word has charted out the logic for us to see. The best we can produce has been done. We need to come back and see Him. The Father needs to split the sky open again and bring an announcement from above.

The result to all of this is the **AWARENESS FROM WITHIN**. ***"And they were exceedingly sorrowful,"*** (17:23). Jesus and the three come down from the Mount of Transfiguration. Jesus deals with the demon-possessed boy, and immediately takes His disciples back to the beginning. He covers the same subject that prompted the argument in the first place (16:21). He turns to them and forcibly states, ***"The Son of*** *man is about to be betrayed into the hands of men,"* (17:22). He is going to go to a cross! He is going to identify with the sins of men, and this will require His blood. Now He is calling them to blood process. It is right back to what He has been telling them for almost one entire week. But there is no more argument from the disciples. Their mouths are shut and they turn exceedingly sorrowful.

Now remember, you are putting yourself in the middle of the disciples. You are there as the disciples argued with Jesus. What role are you playing? Do you identify with the disciples at all? How easy it is for us to argue with the Divine voice. It is tragic for us to raise our self-centered arguments in the middle of Divine revelation. God wants to unfold His Divine plan, but we seem to know better. A young person sees the Divine plan for his or her life, but decides they can do better in their own wisdom. As if God does not know the future, where the ages are going, or what ought to be done.

A part of the great tragedy is the wasted time. Jesus spent nearly one week in argument with His disciples. That week could have been used in such valuable ways. He only had thirty-three years of life, with only three years of ministry. There was no time to waste. What a tremendous ministry could have flowed through Jesus and His disciples during those six days, but they were isolated together in argument. They could have changed hundreds of lives and fed the multitudes. Eternal destinies were at stake. Still the disciples were arguing.

I will not argue, but obey! It is such a privilege to have the revelation of God in my life. I will listen, with no more argument. In the middle of the argument, revelation will come from Him, when I desperately need it. It is the **Renewed Revelation of the Ruler.**

The Needed News of Our Neglect
Matthew 17:14-21

In the second scene Matthew relates to us almost the opposite of argument. It is neglect. But both scenes need the revelation of God. The Bible gives the truth, but personal experience can also give it. Most of us can go back in our experiences and relate that there is an awful price to pay for arguing with the Divine revelation. It is way too expensive, and you cannot afford it. There is not enough resource at your disposal to pay the price.

In the following scene, you must place yourself in the middle of the disciples, and think like they think. The disciples pay the price of **FORM WITHOUT POWER**. *"So I brought him to Your disciples, but they could not cure him,"* (17:16). This is the report of the father of the demon-possessed boy. We find the disciples in total shock.

Jesus had taken the power He contained within Himself and transferred it to His disciples (Matthew 10). He gave them specific instructions on how to minister this power to others. He then sent them out in pairs to reproduce His ministry among the people. The disciples were doing all the miracles Jesus had been doing. They were healing the sick, delivering the captives, conquering nature, and even raising of the dead. They ministered for some time and then returned to report to Jesus what had been taking place. When they returned they were in a joyful state because they had such great power.

A small boy, with one demon, is brought to nine of disciples. These disciples move into this scene with great confidence. They must have related to each other how they had cast out hundreds of demons through the ministry Jesus had given them. One demon would be no problem at all. They had total confidence. As they moved into the scene, they began to do what they had always done when casting out demons. They knew how to make the prayers. These disciples knew the proper time to stand and the proper time to sit. They had all the right patterns memorized. They had learned all of the choruses from memory. The religious phrases and forms were known by them. To their astonishment, this time, it did not work. What were they doing wrong? They had followed the procedures of successful. What is the problem? What is the missing element?

Someone described the church as a referee who has swallowed his whistle. He knows all the rules of the game. He runs up and down the playing field, making all of the motions. But without his whistle he cannot direct the game, or bring it to an end! He has all of the right forms, but no power or authority.

This is the tragedy of our hour. We are aching for revival, from the leadership of the church down to the grass roots level. We are screaming from the bottom of our lungs and the depths of our hearts, "Oh God, give us revival!" We have established the organization with all the right programs and standards in place. The best buildings belong to us, and money is available. We have the educational centers for training. Our music is the best in the world, but have we swallowed the whistle? Are we looking at each other like the disciples in astonishment? Is there something missing?

The disciples have the right form, but they have no power. From where did this powerless state come? It was the price they paid for arguing with the Divine revelation. It is an expensive price. They cannot afford it.

FAITH WITHOUT PROGRESSION is the second price of this scene. Be sure you have identified with the disciples. You are a part of their group. Jesus takes His power and places it inside you (Matthew 10). You have received the instructions and He is sending you out to minister. There was no argument from the disciples in this situation. They were not questioning His instructions. Jesus told them where to go, and they followed His directions. The result was that the power flowed through them to minister to their world.

Now they have returned from that ministry. Somehow in the middle of their success, they have an elevated view of their own knowledge. They have a sense that they have arrived. After all, when demons obey you, nature comes under your control and you dispel sickness by your word. What more is there to accomplish? They think they have arrived at the top level.

New light has come to them (16:21). Jesus has been speaking to them of an expansion of the light. He has been talking about death, suffering, the cross and its style. This is all new material. The disciples were willing to walk in the old light, but this new light presents a problem for them. They argue with Jesus and resist the expansion of their light. Now a small boy with a demon presents himself. They revert to the old light, but find it no longer works. There is no rebellion against the old light; they just refuse to progress into the new. Out of that refusal comes argument (16:22). As a result, they have abundance of faith in the old light, but they are helpless in the middle of overwhelming need.

"Bless God! This is the way we have always done it." There is nothing wrong with the old light. What God has done through days gone by is tremendous. It built our courage and strengthened our faith.

He is the same God as He has always been, and it is the old fashioned way. Glory Hallelujah!

But we are in a new scene. There are brand new pressures we have never before faced. There is new revelation. We have a new thought pattern in our generation that is different from days of old. This is a new hour. The light of days gone by is great, and you must walk in it, but God is expanding that light in your life. Truth is coming alive in new ways and for new areas. Will you progress in your life and follow moment by moment, or will you miss out? The disciples missed the flow of the Divine power for their time of crisis. Will we? The disciples had form without power and faith without progression. Will we follow their example?

They also paid the price of **FUTURE WITHOUT POSSIBILITIES**. *"So Jesus said to them, 'Because of your unbelief; for assuredly, I say to you, if you have faith as a mustard seed, you will say to this mountain, 'Move from here to there,' and it will move; and nothing will be impossible for you,"* (17:20). The disciples are powerless in the face of one demon. Jesus arrives and rescues the situation. The disciples then seek out Jesus in private to question Him concerning their failure (17:19). Jesus' reply was so simple! It was because of their unbelief.

Do you not find this strange? The disciples were believers in Christ. They had left all to follow Him. They had joined in the great confession at Caesarea Philippi. They had been involved in a powerful ministry. They had cast out hundreds of demons in their evangelistic campaigns. One demon in a small boy confronts them, and they believe with all their hearts that they can handle the situation. There is no doubt at all concerning the power of God to cast out demons. Now Jesus tells them the reason they cannot bring deliverance is unbelief.

What did they not believe? It was the new light of the cross style (16:22)! They had refused to walk in this light. They had belief in the power to cast out demons, but they had not trusted Jesus in the new revelation as He called them to the cross. Unbelief in the new light carried over into lack of power to minister.

I have been trying to apply this to the area of the miraculous miracles of healing and deliverance. We want to slip out of our seat and kneel at an altar of prayer. We want to put a blinder on and just believe. We refuse to doubt and talk ourselves into a positive thinking mode. By this means, we force God into action and receive the healing we want. But when He does not come through as we expect, we explain it by hidden doubts. Would you make another approach? Could it be that God has been attempting to teach you something new? Has your mind and heart received new light and have you followed it? The problem is not in your belief in God's miracle. The problem is your responsiveness to the light of God as he does a new thing in your life. Life has convinced me that there are no miracles outside of our response to the revelation of God. He is taking us on a great journey.

The disciples have pushed aside their new revelation. Neglect and defeat have caused them to miss the revelation God has sent to point them in the right direction. There is no progress beyond light given and the failure to respond to it. We must go back to our point of neglect.

The Instant Instruction of His Identification
Matthew 17:5

Revelation from God always comes when we need it. In the argument, there was a need for **The Renewed Revelation of the Ruler**. Also, a **The Needed News of Our Neglect** came in the revelation. When they were failing, Jesus came to the disciples with His revelation. As God reveals His instructions to them, there is **The Instant Instruction of His Identification**. *"While he was still speaking, behold, a bright cloud overshadowed them; and suddenly a voice came out of the cloud, saying, 'This is My beloved Son, in whom I am well pleased. Hear Him!'"* (17:5). Oh I like that - *"Hear Him!"* I can hear the booming voice of God in my mind saying, *"Hear Him!"* You are with the disciples. You must identify with them in their personal setting. You have argued with Jesus for nearly one week. No one is accepting the content of His Messiahship. You cannot stand to think about the cross style being the style of the coming Kingdom. You have forcibly stated to Jesus that He is wrong. You believe He has clouded thinking. He has worked too hard and needs some rest. Now here you are on the side of the mountain, where you behold His transfiguration. Moses and Elijah are speaking with Him. Suddenly, a great cloud descends, and the booming voice of God begins to speak, *"Hear Him!"* It is a call to come out of your own thought process into His. Give up your humanistic patterns and *Hear Him!* You are trapped in your traditions and how you think it ought to be. *Hear Him!* Come out of form without power, and *Hear Him!*

Hear Him in **THE QUESTIONS OF LIFE**. *"And His disciples asked Him, saying, 'Why then do the scribes say that*

Matthew 17 – Introduction

Elijah must come first?" (17:10). We have little trouble with the Mount of Transfiguration. It is a mountain top experience where great revelation takes place. The problem is, we do not dwell on the mountain, but on the streets. It is here we have overwhelming questions. It is not on the mountain where we need to hear Him, but in the cries of life. We must listen closely when great questions bombard our minds.

The disciples want to know how they fit into all of this? The scribes have told them about Elijah. There was to be a time sequence, and the patterns of Jesus did not seem to fit. What did Jesus expect out of the disciples? The disciples had great questions. Does this sound familiar?

Jesus says, "Let me explain it to you." He continues by saying that the scribes are correct. Elijah does have to come, but he has already been here. He was John, the Baptist. You know what happened to him, do you not? Herod had him beheaded. John suffered and bled in the style of the cross. He was the forerunner of Jesus, and He acted in the style of Jesus. That style includes suffering and bleeding. It is the style of the cross. Now the disciples are to join Jesus and John in suffering and bleeding. They are to join in the style of the cross. This is where they fit into the plan. John the Baptist suffered - blood process, the style of the cross. Jesus, the Messiah, suffers - blood process, the style of the cross. Disciples suffer - blood process, the style of the cross. This is all tied together. The disciples will be a part of the flow of the style that will redeem an entire world. But do not forget, Jesus will be with you. Christ will be in the middle of the entire suffering scene. Disciples will have no pressure or persecution where Jesus is not. No tragedy or pain will come to life, but what He joins in the suffering. He comes in the great

185

questions of life; so hear Him. Focus on Him! You can hear Him in **THE INEQUALITIES OF LIFE.** There is no problem with the great revelation of the mountain, but we live in the valley, where things are not fair. Life just does not treat us right. Jesus has come with the three disciples from the mountain to the valley. There is a boy who is demon-possessed; it is not fair. No boy should have this kind of complication in his life. This should not be; but it is.

This promotes the age-old question, "Why?" Why did this happen to me? Why do the best people in the world get cancer? Did you realize that in asking why, there is blame. If I could find out why, then I would know who to blame for this condition. I need someone to blame. The issue is not why! It is Jesus. He joins us in the inequalities of life. He did not stay on the Mount of Transfiguration, but has come to the valley, where we are. In the inequalities of life do not shrivel up in your spirit - hear Him! As you experience that which is not fair, hear Him! He has come to join you. Focus on Him.

In **THE QUEST OF LIFE,** hear Him. *"And when they came to Capernaum, those who received the temple tax came to Peter and said, 'Does your Teacher not pay the temple tax?' He said, 'Yes,"* (17:24-25). We do not have a problem with the great revelation on the mountain. We love the emotional high of a great experience. Our problem centers in how to pay our taxes. Is it not significant that closely following the story of the Mount of Transfiguration, is this account of paying your taxes?

Paying taxes bespeaks the whole daily function of life. Jesus is not isolated to the mountain side. He has come to the ordinary routine of our life. He wants no more arguments from us. He wants our response. He has brought the revelation of Himself to our daily lives. It will be here in daily living, He will manifest Himself, through us, to our world. Are you available?

"Dear Jesus, how easily we argue with you. We have discovered our arguments cost us severely. Without argument, we come! You know best. We trust You. Bring your revelation to us. We embrace the style of the cross. Thank you for including us. In Jesus' name, we pray, Amen."

Matthew 17:1-8

Let's Talk About Jesus

God has convinced me that He never does anything just to be doing it. He never operates on a whim. The Apostle Paul tells us that God did things for His good pleasure. However, this does not mean He did things just for fun. He always has a long range plan in mind. He knows where He is going, and a distinct purpose governs His actions. If you examine the great thing, or the seemingly insignificant item, both have great destiny at their foundation.

We dare not view Christianity as if it was just for our pleasure. We do have exceedingly abundant good times in Christianity. It is tremendously fun to walk with Jesus. The relationship is great. The changes He has brought into our lives are a constant thrill, which brings rejoicing. But it is foundational to say that God never does anything, even in our personal lives, just to have a good time. He has a distinct purpose in mind. When He touches you, it is for overwhelming destiny. He never "messes around." His touch is never the whim of the moment.

He is going some place. God has that which He wants to accomplish - a great purpose.

When we approach the Mount of Transfiguration, this factor becomes clear. The mountain top experience is not just for the fun of it. Jesus is transfigured; Moses and Elijah descend; the Father speaks of His pleasure. None of this is done without a purpose. It becomes very important, in a study of this experience, to discover the purpose.

Some have thought that Matthew's purpose for telling of the Mount of Transfiguration, relates to Jesus. The conflict has been going on between Jesus and His disciples for six days. They are arguing over the content of His Messiahship. Jesus has been revealing the cross and its style. He has linked Himself with the sin of humanity; it is a Divine redemptive process. The fundamental is the loss of your life. The disciples have rebuked Him severely (16:22). Peter led the way, and the rest of the disciples joined him. Feel what Jesus must be feeling. Discouragement and frustration press in upon Him. Could it be that Jesus is questioning whether the disciples might be right? Was there some kind of hesitation in His mind about whether He might be going in the wrong direction? Maybe the cross style was not God's will? Jesus often went to the mountain to get new direction. Could it be that Jesus has taken three of the most influential disciples to this mountain to seek verification of the cross and its style?

There are several problems with this purpose. When we read the close of chapter sixteen, Jesus is so definite. Jesus is One who is steeped in a single idea. He is committed to one great fundamental principle - cross style. He has given Himself to this style throughout His ministry.

It is the thread that ties everything He does together. Jesus, going to the Mount of Transfiguration, is not a questioning individual.

What is the purpose of the Mount of Transfiguration? We get a beginning revelation of the purpose in verse two. It says, *"and was transfigured before them."* Matthew is referring to the disciples. The purpose of this great experience focuses on the need of the disciples. Disciples are so needy. These followers have been arguing. They must have new vision. This arguing has built walls between the disciples and Jesus, and there is a need to tear the walls down. It is here we find the great purpose of the Transfiguration. The three disciples on the mountain represent the nine disciples who have remained in the valley. The nine disciples in the valley represent you. Therefore, the Mount of Transfiguration is for you. How does it apply?

TRANSLOCATION

Let's Move Along

"Now after six days, Jesus took Peter, James, and John his brother, and brought them up on a high mountain by themselves," (17:1). Probably the greatest hindrance to our Christian life is that we are not open to new truth at our present position. It is tragic that we get so bogged down in comfortable routines, common patterns, and established traditions. We miss new revelation when it comes. New truth seems to threaten our established system. It seems that God has to relocate us to get through to us.

We see this in the lives of the disciples. Jesus begins to unfold the revelation of the cross and its content of redemption. He tells them how He is going to suffer and die. This is the simple style He has been living before them for nearly three years. This cross style is to be the foundation of the Kingdom. It is not isolated in Him to establish the Kingdom of God, but is the life style of the Kingdom of God. Everyone in the Kingdom will live like this. The disciples violently reject this new revelation. Almost one week goes by as they argue. The disciples do not want to follow a Messiah with this pattern. The arguing has built walls between Jesus and His disciples. He cannot convince them. Jesus is without any reliable following, outside this small group. The future of the Kingdom of God rests on their ability to grasp this new truth.

It is bigger than the disciples following their Master to a cross, joining in His suffering. Everything Jesus is telling them is contrary to what their traditions have taught them. They believe the Messiah will be a military conqueror. What Jesus is saying is radical in content. It is unbelievable! Jesus must take them out of themselves and their past, if they are to accept this new revelation. It will take a radical relocation.

We must understand the application of this to our lives. Relocation for us could mean several things. It could mean a geographical change. Depression can relocate a person emotionally. Sickness or tragedy shakes us at the very core of our lives. Such calamities cause us to question, and they shake our confidence. We are then open for God to speak to us in a new way. The students of church growth tell us that an individual's openness to change raises significantly when negative things happen to them.

The danger of this is to begin to relate these tragedies to God. We view God as the cause of these negative happenings. God gives people cancer to shake up their lives. God pushes little children in front of moving trucks to awaken their parents. We do **NOT** believe this. On the other hand, we have an amazing God. In His great wisdom, He uses the circumstances of our lives. He relocates us in a desperate attempt to bring the necessary changes that might cause us to grasp the truth He wants us to see.

Would it not be productive to take a new look at the pressures recently pressing your life? Perhaps they are excellent opportunities for God to tell to you something you would have never learned without them. Would it not be helpful if you approached sickness, tragedy, family problems, or even unemployment, with a new challenge? Do not rebel at that which strikes you at the heart level. Do not argue as the disciples did. Could you be open to a new revelation that comes through relocation? It is through the relocations of life that God expresses His truth to you. How will this relocation take place in your life? The disciples are good examples for us. They were **CAPTURED BY HIS PERSON.** *"Now after six days, Jesus took Peter, James, and John. . . ."* (17:1). The word *took* is not used casually. Jesus did not stretch and say, "Let's go to McDonalds." The force of the word *took* literally means "captured." It is the idea of taking someone into custody, to arrest. You can see that in the circumstances of the passage. They have been experiencing a six-day argument of hot proportions. They have given all the arguments; the debate has ended. There is nothing left to say. No one is listening. Jesus has been revealing; they have been resisting. A great wall has built between Jesus and His disciples. Jesus knows this is a desperate moment. He captures three disciples and arrests them by His presence. He draws them close to Himself for revelation.

I marvel at how far Jesus will go to get through to us. There is no end to it. I would have ceased to argue with those ignorant disciples and left them to themselves. I would have packed my gear and sought a new disciple group that would listen to what I have to say. For three years they had on the job training, experienced great miracles, and heard powerful preaching. Now for six months He has focused His entire attention on getting them ready for their coming responsibility. For nearly one week He has given them details concerning the revelation of the cross style. It has spilled from His heart. They are arguing with Him as if they are the masters and He is the disciple. The response of Jesus is not impatience, but a drawing closer. He goes to three of them, and He arrests them for distinct revelation. That is just like Him, is it not?

Would we dare look at our own stubbornness? How many times has He tried to get through to you and me? Our humanistic tendencies have dominated us, and we have focused on our careers. Pride of our own knowledge fills us. Lest we admit that our mate is smarter than we are, we cannot even be open to their correction. How will we ever yield to Jesus? Yet, to draw us close for radical revelation, He comes and arrests us. We just would not listen when He gave us this revelation before. How far is He willing to go to get through to us? He is not going to turn us loose.

He has not only captured three of the most influential disciples to draw them to Himself, but notice, they are **RAPTURED BY HIS PURPOSE.** *"Now after six days, Jesus took* (captured by His person) *Peter, James and John his brother, brought them up* (raptured by His purpose) *on a high mountain by themselves,"* (17:1). We might think this verse is redundant. Why did He repeat the idea twice? He ***took*** and ***brought up***. The two verbs are so similar. It is like a double statement. When you get at the heart of these verbs, they are radically different. ***Took*** means to capture and bring close to His person. ***Brought up,*** in the New Testament sense, is always used to show offering up spiritual sacrifices to God, but with two exceptions. One exception is found in the ascension of Jesus. Luke tells us, at the close of his gospel account, ***"that He was parted from them and carried up into heaven,"*** (24:51). As I look at this passage, immediately I want to shout, "But this is not an exception to the meaning of the word!" The author of the Book of Hebrews teaches us that Jesus is the great High Priest. He enters the tabernacle, not made with hands, to offer up spiritual sacrifices to God. This High Priest is not only the one offering up the sacrifices, He is the sacrifice. So, is this an exception to the use of the word?

The other usage, which is viewed as an exception, is this passage in Matthew (17:1). Again I am not so sure this is an exception either. Jesus has been talking to His disciples about the cross and its style. His theme has been the denial and sacrifice of oneself. He has strongly called His disciples to participate in this style. It is not significant that Jesus brings these three disciples to Himself, to bring them up to the mountain top. Is He not offering them up as a living sacrifice? They are dedicated to the purpose of the cross and all the Father wants to do through them.

Could this be applied to your life? The trials you have been going through may be the very process God is using to bring you close to Himself. Their purpose is to prepare you for the revelation of new truth. You cannot discover this revelation any other way. Could the pressures you are experiencing be the means by which Jesus is offering you up to the heavenly Father? You are a spiritual offering, and you are intimately connected to the blood process God needs to win your community.

How does this work? Let me give you an example. John the Baptist has a pulpit one hundred feet long, and he uses every bit of it. He is a fiery preacher who rants and raves as he powerfully tells the truth of God. Suddenly, Herod's men yank him from the banks of the Jordan river, and they slam him into a dungeon cell. The walls begin to close in on him. The ceiling begins to come down. Depression and confusion begin to torment him. Jesus sends him a message saying, "What is your problem? Don't you know that in a dungeon cell you are being offered up as a sacrifice? You are forerunning a cross!" What a privilege. They were going to cut off his head, and he would go through blood process. It would provide the foundation upon which Christ would march to cause a world redemption. Christ was going to plant the cross right in the middle of the back of John the Baptist. John had a piece of the cross. God allowed his relocation, and he was to be offered up as a part of redemptive process.

Could it be that instead of complaining, rebelling, resisting, or wondering, we should see our circumstances for what they are? They are a wonderful opportunity for God to teach us what we could not know otherwise? God can drip His blood through our lives to touch our world. This will radically change our living.

TRANSFERENCE
Let's Change Within

"And was transfigured before them. His face shone like the sun, and His clothes became as white as the light," (17:2). Change

constantly pressures our lives. Our job, transportation, and communication are all changing. Occasionally we are thrilled with this kind of change, but most of us resist change with all we have. There is something very frightening about personal change. This is a picture of the disciples. It is great for Jesus to come and change the world. He can alter the entire structure of Rome. The disciples would be thrilled with that, but they are strongly resisting personal change.

The disciples like what has been happening. They are in the middle of miracles and crowds. There is a touch of glamour in the whole scene. They are not only famous because of their attachment to Jesus, but each of them has a ministry of there own. These men have been discussing the future establishment of the Kingdom. Position is important to them. They have it all planned, but Jesus is upsetting their plans. He is not talking about power positions, but about bleeding and dying. The idea of the cross enamors Him. He is calling them to sacrifice, not stardom. His lesson is about learning to embrace pain, not fame. The cross style is a frightening idea to these disciples.

You and I can identify with this. We kneel at an altar of prayer. God gives us His glorious presence in a salvation experience. We find peace and joy. It is a brand new experience. Enjoyment is found in kicking off our shoes and leaning back in our padded pews. The new benefits of Christianity are wonderful. The preacher tells good jokes, the singers are entertaining, and we love the fellowship and good food at the potluck. Then something unexpected happens! Suddenly the truth of the Gospel begins to come clear. Jesus calls us to put our shoes back on and go to a cross. He calls us to die to ourselves. He wants us out of the padded pew and beyond the ten dollars in the offering. We are going to be involved in the blood process that redeems a world. This is scary! But my discovery is that there is no way out of this with Jesus. The cross and its style are not optional. The cross is inevitable. There is no way to stay in the pew and be His. There must be radical inward change.

This is what is happening on the Mount of Transfiguration. What kind of change is this cross going to mean? There are only three places in the New Testament where the word *transfigured* is used. This makes this word very significant. It appears this word has been reserved for something special. As you study the three usages of this word, it is as if they are tied together.

The first usage of this word is right here in the passage we are attempting to study. ***"And was transfigured before them,"*** (17:2). This is the **PREVIEW CONCEIVABILITY**. What Jesus gives the disciples, here on the Mount of Transfiguration, is something of a preview. He wants to show them the kind of change needed within them. Jesus is the pattern of what is going to happen. The disciples have no conception of what the cross is going to mean. Jesus is giving them a physical view of the kind of change He is proposing. The word *transfigured* gives us the word "metamorphose." It literally means to change form. The worm inside the cocoon changes to a beautiful butterfly. This is the type of process about which He is speaking. This is what Jesus desperately wanted for His disciples. A.T. Robertson reminds us that this word presents the essence of a thing as separated from the fashion, the outward accident. In other words, Jesus is being stripped of His outwardness. From deep within, you are seeing the flow of what He is really like. The Mount of Transfiguration is not a light shining upon Jesus, and He reflects it. Rather you see a light from within, shining through Him, until even His clothes glisten. You are receiving a preview of what the fullness of the Spirit of God is to be within the believer. It is a visible view of an invisible happening within the life. A cross will cause this happening.

This is the reason Jesus is going to a cross. It will take a cross to cause this kind of experience. The disciples are going to possess the same kind of resource and power as displayed on the Mount. The same Holy Spirit, Who filled Jesus, is going to fill them. They will also radiate the life of God to a world as Jesus is doing. It is no wonder that He is calling His disciples to die to themselves. The arguments must cease. There is only one possibility to experience the truth of the Mount of Transfiguration. It is the cross.

The second place we find the word **transfigured** is in Romans 12:2. We call this **RENEWED CONSCIOUSLY.** *"I beseech you therefore, brethren, by the mercies of God, that you present your bodies a living sacrifice, holy, acceptable to God, which is your reasonable service. And do not be conformed to this world, but be transformed by the renewing of your mind, that you may prove what is that good and acceptable and perfect will of God,"* (Romans 12:1,2). The verb **transformed** is in the imperative sense. This is a command. It must be like this - **transformed by the renewing of your mind.**

To properly understand the word's usage, we must see it in light of the two worlds. On one hand you have "this world." This world contains all the junk, human tendencies, sinful depravity, and self-centeredness (carnality). All of this shapes you into an individual God never intended you to be. It molds your life style. Paul is calling you out of this world. You can only *be transformed,* by God, into this other world. It is the world of righteousness, the Kingdom and resource of the Spirit. Paul is calling us to open our minds to the resource of this kind of world. Let this world *transform*, shape, mold, build, and structure you, through a renewed mind. What happened to Jesus on the Mount of Transfiguration as the flow of the Spirit moved through His being? That is exactly what Paul is talking about in Romans. God is going to fill us with His Spirit. The Spirit will, through us, mold, shape, and glisten, until our lives radiate Him from within. We will be in the image of Him!

Disciples, do not argue anymore. You must give up yourself and your little traditional views. God has dreamed so much more for you. He wants you to come to a cross. In your embrace of that cross the transformation will take place. This will not happen through a Messiah who does miracles. This can only take place through one process - the cross style.

There is a third usage of this word. It is **REVIEWING CONTINUALLY.** It is found in II Corinthians 3:18. *"But we all, with unveiled face, beholding as in a mirror the glory of the Lord, are being transformed into the same image from glory to glory, just as by the Spirit of the Lord."* The contrast between the Jewish world and the Christian world permeates the context of this verse. In the Jewish world, God had veiled His glory, and they could not see it. In the Christian world, God ripped the veil from top to bottom, revealing the brilliancy of His glory. In the Jewish world, God hid Himself. He dwelt in the Holy of Holies and was hidden from the people. In the Christian world, God removed the veil, and we get to stare into the visible image of the invisible God. We have seen God face to face, through the Spirit.

The Jewish tradition focuses on duties and performance; but Christianity focuses on intimate relationship with the Divine God, until we know Him. The Jews resist change. They focus on their tradition that depends upon everything staying the same. This is how the leaders of Israel maintained their positions. But Christianity throbs with change. The Holy of Holies has been exposed. Nothing can ever be the same again. The face of God has been seen. We are now walking in intimacy with a Divine God, Who is constantly unfolding new revelation, bringing change. He is transforming us into His image, from glory to glory. He is flowing through us and is revealing Himself. We are becoming a little Christ.

So, disciple, quit your arguing! Give up your spiritual resistance. Do not be frightened anymore. Disciple, embrace a cross! Let us leap to the occasion, willingly and aggressively. You must die to yourself. In the fullness of the Holy Spirit, you can see the same kind of transformation in yourself that is seen in Jesus on the Mount of Transfiguration. The light of God indwelt Him, and it shone through Him, until everything about Him radiated that light. It will take a cross to get this done. Your traditional view of the Messiah will not accomplish it. The military commander Messiah will not bring this about. It only comes through the suffering, cross style, Messiah, Who will make it possible? Embrace the cross!

This is the great need of our hour. We need a reproduction of the life of Jesus on our streets. We do not need a renewal in theological understanding, or a better plan for Church structures. Our programs are quite adequate. We need a Mount of Transfiguration transformation, until Jesus can flow His life through us.

Let us now review what we have said. How does the Mount of Transfiguration apply to our lives? There is **Translocation - Let Us Move Along.** Will you see the relocations He allows in your life as opportunities? You can flow with His blood in redemption. New revelation will allow God to offer you up as a sacrifice for your world. Then there is **Transference - Let Us Change Within.** Will you allow the Holy Spirit to transfer to you? Then through you, Christ will reveal the greatness of His life. A third great application awaits us now.

TRANSLATION
Let's Minister Again

Mountain top experiences are always thrilling. They produce great memories and cause us to speak of the good old days. So what? I am trying to make a living in a business that may not survive. My teenager is rebelling, and my marriage is not good. How does the great Mount of Transfiguration translate into my Monday living experience? I do not live on top of the mountain. Great spiritual highs are not worth the moment it takes to experience them, if they do not translate into my home and job.

Let us begin with the **STALWART IN HEART.** *"But Jesus came and touched them and said, 'Arise, and do not be afraid,"* (17:7). When the Mount of Transfiguration is translated into everyday life, it flows with new courage and vitality. It is terrible to live, day after day, in paralyzing fear. Many of us are possessed with the spirit of fear. In one way or another, fear blocks the fullness of life. All that Jesus has been telling the disciples about the cross has frightened them. As they visualize the cross, and the change it would make in them, they tremble.

Now they have come to a Mount of Transfiguration. Heavenly beings are present. God speaks, and they are flat on their faces in fright. But this is not the end. Christ has come and placed His hand on them. He has told them that they do not need to be afraid.

Contained within the flow of the fullness of God, as visualized on the Mount, is all you need to make it in your world. There is no circumstance or pressure that this indwelt Presence is not adequate to handle. You can walk courageously into every situation. We have been timid about arresting our world with the Gospel. If we would get into the flow, as visualized in Jesus, we would march as He did. We would also become an extension of the blood process - the cross style.

Now let us continue with **SINGLE IN VISION**. *"And when they had lifted up their eyes, they saw no one but Jesus only,"* (17:8). Jesus only? Yes, they saw Jesus only! How does the Mount of Transfiguration translate into your daily world? It ends division. You can no longer use manipulation to get your own way. It stops your limited self resource and self doing. You no longer use your influence to get what you want. It is now Jesus only. One purpose of a great spiritual experience like the Mount is to clear out all the junk cluttering our lives. Then we can focus on Him. Come back to Him, until in your daily living He is your life, resource, strength, answer, delight, relaxation, power, happiness, breath, and love. He is all there is! It is in focusing upon Him that you experience new courage.

There is one more aspect regarding the Mount of Transfiguration translating into our world. It is **STABLE IN MESSAGE**. *"Now as they came down from the mountain, Jesus commanded them, saying, 'Tell the vision to no one until the Son of Man is risen from*

the dead," (17:9). Jesus and the disciples were making their way back to the valley. They had just witnessed the powerful revelation of what the cross was going to provide. Jesus told them, "Do not tell anyone!" Is that not strange? I would have supposed Jesus would want them to tell everyone. The complete instructions were that they were not to tell until after the resurrection. Then the ascension would take place and the Spirit would impart His fullness. Their lives would reveal the reality of the Spirit. The cross would provide it all. Then they were to tell everyone.

Do you realize we are living in that time? Jesus is not instructing us to keep still. We are in the very hour when everyone can see and share it. This is our moment in history! This is the time to pour out our lives. Now is the time to embrace a cross and be filled with the Spirit. Everyone must be involved in this flow. It is the life of God, flowing through us, touching our world. We have had our mountain. Now it is time for us to go to the streets.

Matthew 17:1-8

Let's Talk About You

"Dear Jesus, when the disciples lifted up their eyes after the Mount of Transfiguration, they saw You only. We would have it that way in our lives. We want You only, not our performance. We do not want great singing or magnificent sanctuaries, but You only. We do not want to live with our focus on our problems. We want You only. Take us to the Mount, as you did the disciples, that we might experience You anew! In Jesus' name, we ask this, Amen."

Something strange and wonderful has happened to you. You want to tell others of your experience. To those who have had a like experience, your telling is easy. But what of those who have never had anything close to that happened to them? It is a difficult explanation. How would you describe a glorious, gorgeous sunset to some one who is blind? How would you express the wonder of friendship, or the intimacy of companionship, to one who has been alone all of his or her life? How does one who is mature in knowledge speak adequately to one who is a beginner? The mature have learned powerful lessons through great experience, but the beginner has never had such experiences. How can you explain the heavenly realm, if you have never been there?

One great author has captured this difficulty. A small boy came to his father. With his face full of confusion, the boy asked, "Father, tell me what it is like to be married!" How could he possibly explain to one of such a young age, the marriage experience? How would he explain to one so young, the intimacy of one flesh? It would not be possible for him to understand how two can join until they experience one purpose and desire? What would be a proper explanation of sexual relationship? The father leaned back and said, "Son, it is something like chocolate!" You and I know that marriage is nothing like chocolate. The father was reaching into his son's knowledge and attempting to find the finest, highest, and the most pleasurable of his experiences. He paralleled marriage with chocolate.

Jesus was facing the same kind of dilemma with His disciples. For three years He has been preparing them for these very moments. It has been on-the-job training. He has displayed truth by a miracle here and a message there. It has been day after day revelation from the heart of Christ. He has told them the seven parables of the mysteries of the Kingdom (Matthew 13). It was the kind of thing you could not understand unless someone revealed it to you. Surely, somewhere in this training, they have caught the message and seen the heart of Christ. They must be ready for the new revelation Jesus wants to share with them now.

Jesus and His disciples have been together in intimacy for six months. He thinks they are ready for the truth of the cross. In Caesarea

Philippi, Peter jumped to his feet and gave a great confession. In answer to Jesus' question, He states, ***"You are the Christ, the Son of the living God,"*** (16:16). This is a good sign. Now Jesus begins to explain to them the details of the cross (16:21). He begins to share with them that He will suffer, bleed, and die. This will be the cross style. He will identify with the sin of man, take that sin within Himself, and bring the liberation of a world. They were NOT ready. Peter began to rebuke Him (16:22). The other disciples, no doubt, joined Peter. Before it was over the debate lasted for almost one full week. Argument and rebuke filled the atmosphere. As Jesus attempted to teach them the truth of the cross style, the disciples rebelled. The arguments built walls between them. Outside these twelve men, Jesus was without any reliable following. They are all He has! The entire movement of the Kingdom of God, hangs in the hands of these twelve men. They must understand this cross and its style. Jesus is facing the closing months of His ministry. Time is pressing!

There must be a dramatic revelation, if the disciples are to understand it. Jesus takes three of the most influential disciples to the mountain. On the mountain He will open their eyes. Here on the mountain, the skies will split wide open, and the fog will clear from their minds. On the mountain, Jesus will be transfigured before them.

This is something of what revival is all about. In the middle of our arguments, confusion, and rebellion, we need to go to the mountain. With concentration, we can come to a radical break through. It will be a time when God can take His very presence and dump it all over us. If we can see Him, our minds will clear. Let us go to the mountain. If we go to the mountain, the same elements in the revelation to the disciples will become ours. Let us explore three such powerful elements.

DIRECT COMMUNICATION
Jesus is the Focal Point of All History
Matthew 17:3

"And behold, Moses and Elijah appeared to them, talking with Him," (17:3). This should not have surprised them. These are three disciples who have been steeped in the Old Testament tradition. From small childhood, until today, they have heard the ancient stories. They have memorized the Scriptures. This entire revelation of Jesus, the cross, and now this visitation, should not have been a surprise. They should have expected it. These disciples have been in Sunday School class and Sunday morning worship services, repeatedly. They have endured revival after revival. This should not have surprised them, but it did! It is amazing how easily we miss it. We can sit in the middle of all that God wants to give to us and let it slip right through our fingers. Is it not significant how the life changing power of God can permeate our atmosphere, and we are unaware of it? How easily we miss it! Yet, for these disciples, Jesus was giving **DIRECT COMMUNICATION.**

First, there is the presence of the law, **LET THE LAW SPEAK**. Look again at verse three, *"And behold, Moses . . . appeared to them, talking with Him,"* (17:4). Moses was the symbol of all contained within the law. It was Moses who led the Israelites into the wilderness wanderings. Finally, they came to Mt. Sinai where God would unfold the Divine law. This law of God was so forceful that it permeated every area of man's experience. The law spoke of family relationships, financial planning, daily activities, eating habits, etc. God, according to the law, literally reserved the right to dictate His will for man in every area of his life. The law was the fullness of man's duty to God. The law was the fullness of God's requirement of man's performance. The law was the standard of God's holiness brought into the practical ethics of man's daily living.

There is an obvious question in all of this. How successful was it? It was a total and absolute disaster. If you look to the law to bring righteousness to the life of man, it fails. The law never touches the inward heart of people. From the origination of the law, it has never accomplished righteousness in the life. Moses had gone into the very presence of God for forty days and nights. He experienced the fire of God's presence, burning Ten Commandments into tablets of stone. The people of Israel were supposed to anticipate this great occasion, but they got restless. They took their gold jewelry to Aaron, and he melted it into an idol. These Israelites, who had experienced one miracle after another from the hand of Jehovah, danced around a makeshift god. They had a wild party of sin and wickedness. At the very moment they should be anticipating the arrival of the law, they are breaking it. The law failed to bring righteousness from the very beginning.

Moses descends from the mountain. Upon seeing the wickedness of Israel, he breaks the freshly written tablets of the law. It was a symbol of what Israel was doing. If you are going to look to the law to produce any righteousness at all, you are going to be extremely disappointed. It did not accomplish personal righteousness. The real purpose of the law, according to Paul, was to be a school master. It would instruct us that we could not produce righteousness on our own. We have no goodness in ourselves. In our own self-righteousness, we produce nothing but filthy rags.

Life has discouraged and worn many of us. We have struggled in performance for so long, trying to do our duty. We have supposed God, with His law, is checking on us constantly. Doing our best is exhausting us. Our living is haunted with the sense that nothing we have, or ever will do, can bring us into intimate relationship with God. The law failed to accomplish righteousness in the life of man.

Can you see Moses? He has drawn close to the transfigured Christ. There is an intimate conversation taking place. What are they discussing? Luke tells us that they spoke of His decease, which He should accomplish in Jerusalem (9:31). It was the cross! Surely Moses is telling Jesus that what had taken place, through the presentation of the law, had been a failure. God gave the law to the people, but they had broken it. If their righteousness was to rule in the human heart, Jesus must go to the cross. The cross was the only hope for humanity. If man was to come into the presence of God, it could only happen through the cross. Jesus and His cross were the hope of the world. Their conversation must have been how Jesus would accomplish redemption on the cross.

When the law speaks, what does it say? It says, "Look to Jesus!" We must not look to our own strength, but to the bleeding Christ. Our own manipulations are not adequate. We need Jesus. We must look to Jesus, not our own attempts. Our morality will get us nowhere, but we must look to Jesus. Look to Jesus! Look to Jesus!

Secondly, we see the presence of the prophets - **LET THE PROPHETS SPEAK.** *"And behold, . . . Elijah appeared to them, talking with Him,"* (17:3). Elijah is the representative of all the Old

Testament prophets. In many ways he was the most dramatic. The stories of God working through him are dynamic. Elijah did miracle after miracle, through the power of God. He warned the people of Israel consistently. It was Elijah who preached with great passion. He was the one who built sacrifice altars and called down fire from heaven to consume them. He cut off the heads of the prophets of Baal. After all of this great demonstration, Israel went right on in her sin. When the final story of the prophets is told, what is the verdict? They did not bring righteousness to Israel. They failed.

Elijah has drawn close to the transfigured Christ. They are having a heavy conversation. What is the topic of discussion? They speak of His decease, which He should accomplish at Jerusalem (Luke 9:31). It is the cross to come. Elijah is urging Jesus to go to a cross. All of the preaching, miracles, and the foretelling of the prophets did not change the heart of Israel. If righteousness is going to come to the heart, it will take more than the prophets. It will take Jesus on a cross. All the prophets speak and say, "Look to Jesus!" We have only one chance. Look to Jesus! Look to Jesus!

Third, and last, is the presence of Christ - **LET LOVE SPEAK.** *"And behold, Moses and Elijah appeared to them, talking with Him,"* (17:3). God completed His love in one human being, and His name is Jesus. It is hard to comprehend the depth of this truth. The entire love action of God is literally moving through one man's flesh. Jesus is the epitome of the loving heart of God.

Listen to what this Love has to say. *"Behold, the days are coming, says the Lord, when I will make a new covenant with the house of Israel and with the house of Judah - not according to the* covenant that I made with the fathers in the day that I took them by the hand to bring them out of the land of Egypt, My covenant which they broke, though I was a husband to them, says the Lord. But this is the covenant that I will make with the house of Israel after those days, says the Lord; I will put My law in their minds, and write it on their hearts; and I will be their God, and they shall be My people. No more shall every man teach his neighbor, and every man his brother, saying, 'Know the Lord,' for they all shall know Me, from the least of them to the greatest of them, says the Lord. For I will forgive their iniquity and their sin I will remember no more,"* (Jeremiah 31:31-34).

Listen to what Love has to say. *"For by grace you have been saved through faith, and that not of yourselves; it is a gift of God, not of works, lest anyone should boast,"* (Ephesians 2:8-9).

Listen to what Love has to say. *"If we confess our sins, He is faithful and just to forgive us our sins and to cleanse us from all unrighteousness,"* (I John 1:9).

Listen to what Love has to say. *"In this the love of God was manifested toward us, that God has sent His only begotten Son into the world, that we might live through Him,"* (1 John 4:9). It is time to focus on Jesus. The law screams at us, "Look to Jesus!" The Old Testament prophets cry out, "Look to Jesus!" Love tells us that the only chance we have is to "Look to Jesus!" Should the passion of your life not be singular? Should not your internal love affair be with only One? Should not the complete movement of your life be in only one direction? Set everything aside and "Look to Jesus!" If we would experience radical revelation, as the disciples did on the Mount of Transfiguration, what would take place? It would be **Direct Communication.** This communication would tell us that Jesus is the focal point of all history. We are left with no one to look to except Jesus. Now let us move on to a second element.

DIVINE CONFIRMATION
Jesus is the Focal Point of All God's Dreams
Matthew 17:5

"While he was still speaking, behold, a bright cloud overshadowed them; and suddenly a voice came out of the cloud, saying, 'This is My beloved Son, in whom I am well pleased. Hear Him!" (17:5). It appeared in chapter sixteen, that Peter had come to a level of great comprehension. Peter, in a moment of great confession, was on his feet. He has responded to the question of Jesus, *"But who do you say that I am?"* (16:15). Peter responded, *"You are the Christ, the Son of the living God,"* (16:16). This great confession deeply moved Jesus. This was a bright moment. Peter had responded to the wisdom of the Father in heaven, (16:17). Peter's great moment appeared in a flash, and it disappeared just as quickly. As Jesus explained the cross style, Peter violently rebuked Him. He ceased to listen to the mind of God. Peter was again living out of himself. He actually came under Satanic influence, (16:23). After six days of Peter's rebuke and endless talking, Jesus takes him and two other disciples to the mountain. Something just has to happen on the mountain to change their minds, or Peter will never get it. What was it that would happen on this mountain? In Peter's life it was **DIVINE INTERRUPTION.** *"While he* (Peter) *was still speaking. . . ."* (17:5). This was so typical of Peter. We must

see the transfiguration of Jesus and the appearance of Moses and Elijah, in its context. Verse three is specific in its details. ***"And behold, Moses and Elijah appeared to them, talking with Him."*** Moses and Elijah did not even speak to Peter and the other two disciples. Their focus was on Jesus. All their conversation was with Jesus. But immediately after this Matthew writes, ***"Then Peter answered and said to Jesus. . . ."*** (17:4). Who is Peter answering? No one has asked, but he has decided to answer. Peter enters the middle of a heavenly conversation without an invitation. He has nothing intelligent to say. He is not contributing to what Moses, Elijah, and Jesus are discussing. Peter babbles out, ***"Lord, it is good for us to be here; if You wish, let us make here three tabernacles; one for You, one for Moses, and one for Elijah,"*** (17:4).

The grammar structure of the next verse tells us that while Peter is speaking and making his great suggestions, something amazing takes place. ***"Behold, a bright cloud overshadowed them; and suddenly a voice came out of the cloud. . . ."*** (17:5). It was the very presence of God, the Father, and He began to speak. He said, ***"This is My beloved Son, in whom I am well pleased. Hear Him!"*** (17:5). In other words, "Peter, keep still, and listen to Jesus!" Truth is here for his understanding, and he is missing it.

The only way God can ever talk to some of us is to simply interrupt. No doubt, we have made God feel like a sixth finger. We are so filled with our own plans, hobbies, family, materialism, and dreams, how could God ever get through to us with new truth? We must make Him feel like He is always crashing our party. He would have to interrupt us to get our attention. Maybe we need to go to the mountain. Oh, if only God would interrupt our lives. His love is so great for you and me, that He cannot give up on us. He continually crashes in upon us. He is constantly interrupting. Before any kind of confirmation of truth can come, there has to be a **Divine Interruption.**

Something great happened on this mountain. In Peter's life there was a **DIVINE EXPLANATION**. Can you hear the power of these words? *"**This is My beloved Son, in whom I am well pleased. Hear Him!**"* (17:5). You need to notice the key words in the statement. The Father uses the word *"My!"* This shows ownership. God, the Father, is speaking about Jesus. The eternal Father is confirming what the Son is all about. Jesus is not a rebellious child, Who has gone off to do His own thing. Jesus is fulfilling the dreams of the Father. The redemptive cross is a product of the entire Trinity. The word *beloved* means "the object of my entire love." Jesus has the total focus of the Father's loving heart. The word *Son* has to do with intimate relationship. It is the very flow of life from the Father to the Son. The Son lives by the Father. The words *well pleased* show the total approval of the Father. Jesus did everything just like the Father wanted it done. There was nothing missing from the will of God.

What is the Father saying to Peter? He is saying that all the focal point of His dreams for humanity center in Jesus. Everything the Father wants for us comes together in the person of Jesus. We must not get sidetracked. We must come back to Jesus. If we are going to be thrilled about something, it must be Jesus. Your life must be focused on Him. He is the focal point of all of God's dreams for you. What a powerful Jesus He is!

To make it even stronger, let me suggest that contained within this **Divine Explanation** is a **DIVINE ELIMINATION.** Let us look at it again. ***"This is My beloved Son, in whom I am well pleased. Hear Him!"*** (17:5). The disciples must listen to Jesus, not Moses. ***Hear Him!*** Listen to Jesus, not Elijah. ***Hear Him!*** It is not the law and the prophets I am calling you to follow. ***Hear Him!*** Please quit listening to your own wisdom and knowledge. ***Hear Him!*** Don't listen to your traditions, given to you by your forefathers. ***Hear Him!*** It is time to eliminate your own humanism. ***Hear Him!*** It is time to surrender your personal manipulation of circumstances. ***Hear Him!*** You must give up your self-centeredness. ***Hear Him!*** You cannot major on the minors. ***Hear Him! Hear Him!***

We are not bad people. We are people who have gotten sidetracked from what matters. Problems have become our focus, when our focus must be Christ. We are peace centered instead of Christ centered. It is so easy to go for the compromise and smooth things over. Our duty and our church activities are central in our thinking, but nothing matters except Him. ***Hear Him! Hear Him!*** If we would go to the mountain and see the vision, it would be a vision of Him. We would never get over it.

There is one more element to be drawn from this encounter.

DISTINCT CONTINUATION
Jesus is the Focal Point of Man's Destiny
Matthew 17:2

"And (Jesus) ***was transfigured before them. His face shone like the sun, and His clothes became as white as the light,"*** (17:2). God had an amazing dream for people. An invisible God decided to be visible to His universe, so He made a man and named him, Adam. The single purpose for man was to make God visible to the world. The spiritual realm was going to invade the physical realm. Upon the platform of the physical, God would reveal the spiritual. It is as if the spiritual needed the physical to be properly manifested. Man became the house in which God dwells. God made man in His image, so that He Himself could live in the flesh of man. The dream of God for your life is that He might fully indwell you. Then He would be visible through you. The community, in which you live, can then see Jesus.

There was a complication in the plan of God. Man sinned and marred the image of God. Instead of Adam being the demonstration of the Person of God, he became independent. He began to display himself. Man began to live out of his own resource, instead of God's resources. This went on throughout the Old Testament for thousands of years. Man was simply living out of himself. He got so accustomed to it that he thought it was normal. Everyone man saw was just like himself, each living out of his own resource. Surely if everyone was doing it, it must be normal. But it was not. Man was abnormal for so long, he now thought he was normal.

God decided to repeat something. He made a second man, just like the first. But instead of making a man as He made Adam, He Himself became that man. God became man and dwelt among us. He is called "the second Adam." His name is Jesus. What was His purpose? Oh, it centered in redemption of the abnormal, but there was another reason. God wanted us to see how He intended us to be. Jesus is what a normal man is all about. In Jesus is a picture of the full destiny that God has for your life. He wants you to be exactly what Jesus is.

What is Jesus like? That is the key message of the Mount of Transfiguration. The disciples were going to see what Jesus was really all about. The first aspect of the demonstration is **RADIATION or LIGHT SOURCE.** *"His face shone like the sun, . . ."* (17:2). A physical revelation of the internal spiritual light was indwelling Jesus. The grammar structure is very specific here. It tells us this was not an outside light shining on Jesus, causing Him to reflect the light. That is what happens when the moon reflects the light of the sun. Matthew is telling us that this is an inside light. From the deep inward heart of Christ, the indwelt light shines in its brilliancy. The disciples were seeing a physical expression of this internal light. It was shining through the face of Jesus.

Jesus was filled with the power of the Person of God. He was filled with the Holy Spirit. Paul tells us that it pleased the Father that in Him all the fullness should dwell (Colossians 1:19). He goes on to explain to us the content of the fullness. *"For in Him dwells all the fullness of the Godhead bodily,"* (Colossians 2:9). Jesus was totally possessed with the essence of God, having fullness of the Holy Spirit. You understand there is only one Holy Spirit, not two. The same Holy Spirit, Who indwelt Jesus, is the One Who has come to live in you. The same exact light that indwelt Christ on the Mount of Transfiguration is the same light that must indwell you and shine through you.

The Mount of Transfiguration was not just a revelation of the Divinity of Jesus. It was not to prove His Messiahship. The disciples knew that Jesus was the Messiah. They do not need proof. The problem lies in what it meant to be the Messiah. This mountain experience is a physical revelation of the spiritual dynamic inside Jesus. It is what each disciple is to have. But for each man to be indwelt with this light, there must be a cross. What else could bring it to pass?

The second element is **REFLECTION or LIGHT SPREAD.** *"And was transfigured before them. His face shone like the sun, and His clothes became as white as the light,"* (17:2). Again the grammar structure is very specific. The light source is from within Jesus. It is shining through Him, until His flesh shines. Even His clothes began to glisten as the light comes from within. His total being began to reflect this indwelt light.

This is the truth of the cross style. Jesus wants to indwell us making our total life reflect all that He is. He is shining through our face, hands, attitudes, actions, and reactions. Everything taking place in our lives is glistening with the brilliant light from within. We become one gigantic demonstration of Who He is. Isn't it interesting how we isolate Christianity into segments of our life? It is to touch only the religious activities. He wants to be in the total flow of our lives, but we choose to segregate Him.

The third element in this mountain experience is **REVELATION or THE LIGHT SEEN.** You remember what Peter's suggestion was to Jesus as he interrupted the heavenly conversation. He suggested that they might build three tabernacles and simply camp on the mountain. But that was not the purpose of the mountaintop. There is a valley that desperately needs this revelation. God has indwelt us that we might hit the streets. It is not here. It is there. Maybe the test of your personal fullness of the Holy Spirit is how much of Jesus is seen on your streets.

"Jesus, take us to the mountain. Please crash in upon us and disturb our world. If we could see You, we could see what we are to be. Give us the fullness of Yourself. We surrender to You. In Jesus' name, we pray, Amen."

Matthew 17:9-13

The Insignificant People

There is an interesting phenomena within the dynamics of relationship. It is the comparison between the way people perceive you and the way you perceive yourself. Someone looks at you in one of your finest moments, and they think you are that way all the time. However, you know your many moments of failure, and you know their perspective has you over rated. Another person may have seen you in your biggest failure. They think you are that way all the time, but you know that God is doing bigger things in your life through His power. They have underrated you and the power of God in your life.

How we rate ourselves, and how others view us, is important. In our moments of real honesty most of us view ourselves as just ordinary people, doing ordinary things, in an ordinary life. There really is not anything outstanding about us. Placed in the great sea of people, we somehow disappear. We are just one among them all, and we do not stand out. Our face blends in with all the rest of the ordinary people of the world. Our accomplishments are not superior. We just go through life wondering how we are going to pay our bills, which is what ordinary people seem to do. Most do not have visions of affecting the histories or hopes of inventing something which will revolutionize civilization. We have not thought much about finding the answer to hunger in the world. We are just ordinary people. What can we do?

There is a group of us, however, among these ordinary people just described, who do have a vision. Our perspective is on eternity. We have seen beyond the junk of this world, and we do not care about getting our names in the history books. Our gaze is beyond what we can handle. The eternal moving of the right hand of God has startled us. The fullness of the Kingdom of God is in our view. We long to make a dent in this world for eternity. We want to make a difference in someone's life forever. But we are just ordinary people, doing ordinary things. How can we accomplish this?

There were twelve disciples. They were ordinary guys, small time. They have been arguing with Jesus for one week. From the time of Peter's great confession (16:16) to the Mount of Transfiguration (17:1-8), the debate with Jesus carries on. The disciples have the traditional view of a powerful military Messiah. Jesus is a suffering servant and He is going to a cross. It is His style. The disciples resisted the cross style. Jesus takes three of them to the slopes of the mountain. He is transfigured before their very eyes. Moses and Elijah appear and carry on a conversation with Jesus. What are they talking about? They speak of His decease, which He would accomplish at Jerusalem. It was all about His cross. Suddenly a great cloud over shadows them. The voice of the Father speaks, ***"This is My beloved Son, in whom I am well pleased. Hear Him!"*** (17:5). The law, the prophets, and now the Father have all spoken about His cross. It is the truth. The disciples had better get wise. This is convincing verification of the truth.

Now they come down from the mountain. Jesus, commanding the three disciples, says, ***"Tell the vision to no one until the Son of Man is risen from the dead,"*** (17:9). Jesus returns to the same subject - the cross and its style. Are the disciples finally going to get it? Will they commit themselves to this style? This whole truth of the cross is so contrary to what their Sunday School teachers taught them. They are having a difficult time.

They turn to Jesus and say, ***"Why then do the scribes say that Elijah must come first?"*** (17:10). It is no wonder we are confused. They have heard too many conflicting stories. The scribes based their teaching on Malachi 4:5-6. It is a prophecy concerning Elijah. He was to come and bring some kind of restoration to the people of Israel before the Messiah would appear. He was to be the forerunner of the Messiah. Elijah appeared on the Mount of Transfiguration, but only for a brief moment. Could they classify this appearance as the restoration prophesied?

The prophecy, as interpreted by the scribes, told of a resurrection of Elijah. This important person was to come roaring out of the histories. He would drip with the dew of the resurrection. As a military genius, he would ride into Jerusalem on a great white steed. This genius would take over, bringing tax, economic, and social reforms, and he would establish a new kingdom. Rome would be overthrown, and Israel would come into world power. Elijah would bring all of this to pass, standing as a giant among men. Elijah would prepare the throne for the coming Messiah. The disciples are saying, "We have not seen any important persons who even come close to this description." Where is this important person who is to bring these great things to pass? How does this fit into the person of Jesus, Who is the Messiah? What does all of this talk about a cross - bleeding and dying - have to do with Elijah? When are the important people going to show? Jesus, bring on the important people!

Does this sound like us? We are always waiting for the important people to appear. Good things could happen in the church if we could just get some important people involved. We need some people with real talent. We need people with some real influence in the community. If we could just win some key business men, our church would grow.

Jesus cries to the disciples, "No! No! No!" They have missed it again. They have been in a dream world. The people who affect the eternities are just ordinary people. The people who are going to influence society for the Kingdom of God, are just ordinary people. It bears repeating!

It is the ordinary people who make the difference.

What are the characteristics of these ordinary people?

The Small Person
Matthew 17:13

"Then the disciples understood that He spoke to them of John the Baptist," (17:13). The disciples were looking for Elijah. Raised from the dead, he would probably stand seven feet tall and be impressive in his appearance. He would be an important person, a hero for all of Israel.

Who would have recognized John the Baptist as this kind of person? He was so strange. While Jesus said that John was the forerunner (11:7-19), it was just a passing truth. It obviously made no impact on the disciples. Who would have put John the Baptist together with this important person, Elijah? Why was it so difficult?

John the Baptist was an **OBSCURE FUNCTION**. It is easy for us to be on this side of the story and see the truth. We have a view of the entire picture, but they did not. Understanding the mind set of the disciples, how could they have recognized John the Baptist as the forerunner? John the Baptist was over in the corner. He was not in the main stream of things. He was not a military genius, and he made absolutely no impact on the Roman Empire. John the Baptist did not even have his own identity. If I were going to be the forerunner of the Messiah, I would want my name to be correct in the prophecies. I do not want everyone to be looking for Elijah when I am John the Baptist.

I certainly identify with this picture. I look at my life, and it is an obscure function. I work all week long on a Sunday School lesson and half of the people do not even have the decency to attend. Those who do come keep looking at their watches. I think to myself, "What did I go to all of this trouble for?" I spend a week at a local church for revival. Six months later the people are snapping their fingers trying to remember the name of the evangelist who preached their last revival. What kind of impact did I make? Did anything really important happen? Revival announcements were placed all over town. The name, Stephen Manley, appeared in every store window. We were there for an entire week, but Sunday morning I opened the bulletin to find my name is printed as Stanley Manley. Was I the right guy? Do I know who I am myself? I am here, and then I am there. What does all of this matter anyway? How does any of this impact the eternities or make a dent in society for the Kingdom's sake? I am just an obscure function.

John the Baptist was an **OBSOLETE FLICKER.** You tell me if a six-month's pastorate is a real success? If a person cannot stay longer than six months in the first pastorate then seminary did not teach him enough. John hit the scene, preached for six months, and was gone. Would you picture him as the great Elijah who comes marching in with power and might for reformation? If John had a successful pastorate, preached there for thirty years, appeared on television, wrote important books, they might have recognized him. But he was just there for a moment, and then he is gone. Besides that, his entire ministry (six months) was overshadowed by the ministry of Jesus. Jesus came right at the end of John's ministry and did these great miracles. Before it was over no one was talking about John the Baptist. Even his disciples could not be found. There was not even an old tabernacle left standing as a reminder. He was an obsolete flicker.

John the Baptist was an **OBVIOUS FAILURE.** It probably wasn't all his fault. He was trapped by the political atmosphere of his time. There was all of this unrest in the kingdom. The king was in turmoil. He had gone to Rome and had an affair with his brother's wife. He brought her back and kicked out his own wife. Her father, who was king over another country, was angry. War broke out between the two countries. It was a great scandal. John the Baptist just could not keep his mouth shut. He included this situation in his sermons. John said the wrong thing, at the wrong time, in the wrong place, when the wrong people were attending. He landed in jail and got his head cut off. It is too bad, but he was just an obvious failure.

Who would look at this obscure function, obsolete flicker, and obvious failure and see a man who affected the eternities? Who would recognize him? But Jesus said, ***"But I say to you that Elijah has come already,"*** (17:12). He was talking about John the Baptist. Behind all of the apparent lack in the ministry of John, there was the mighty moving hand of God. It is in this kind of unimportant person, the ordinary person, that God seems to have a way of moving in the histories. He pulls the rug out from under the Devil, brings a blow to the Satanic forces, and sets up the Kingdom. He invades new territory. It is the ordinary people who play the major roles in the redemptive process. It is the ordinary people who have the capacity of doing the job. Come on, ordinary people, you have the potential of dealing the blow that will make the difference in eternity. You, ordinary people, have roaring in your system all that you need to accomplish the task. Think big, ordinary person!

The Suffering Person
Matthew 17:12

"But I say to you that Elijah has come already, and they did not know him but did to him whatever they wished. Likewise the Son of Man is also about to suffer at their hands," (17:12). You can discover a great deal about a person by their heroes. It is not only true of the individual, but also the entire generation. Who are the heroes of our present age? Are they the big stars who can perform the best?

I grew up in some small towns. I spent much of my time at the local library. One particular library had only a main room with a storage room attached to it. One day I found my way into that storage room. I discovered a shelf that had some old dusty books on it. These books were outdated, so the librarian had removed them from the main room. They were the stories written by Horatio Alger. I fell in love with these stories. Every one of them was the same. You knew exactly how it was going to turn out from the first page. Each story was about a kid who was raised on the wrong side of the tracks. His dad was an alcoholic, and the boy was forced to help earn his living. He began by selling newspapers. The boy would save some money and then expand into selling flowers. With diligence, he went from selling flowers and newspapers to owning a newsstand on the street. By the time he was thirty years old he had bought the apartment store next to his stand, and in the end he was a millionaire.

It is the pattern of the Abe Lincoln story. As a boy, he was out in the woods cutting logs while other children his age were in school. To get his education he studied by the fireside at night. He somehow gets it together and ends up being president of the United States. It was the American dream. But our dream has shifted. Now our dream has become winning the lottery. We have lost the challenge to jump in the middle of the situation and bleed our way through it. The people who are going to impact this world with the Kingdom of God are going to be ordinary, insignificant people, who are willing to lose their lives for the cause of Christ. Those people will be willing to bleed.

John the Baptist was such a person. He was an **IMPRESSIVE SUFFERER.** Maybe strange is a better word to describe him. He was not one of the ten best dressed men of Israel. He wore a camel skin around his loins. Just thinking about his attire makes you want to scratch yourself to death. He must have been a man of great self control. If you got too close to him you would notice he had terrible breath, which smelled of locust. He must have been a health food nut, for he had a bit of left over honey lodged in the dimple on his chin. His was a strange life style. He lived out in the wild with no roof over his head, hidden from society. He would pop out from the wilderness on various occasions, ranting and raving, spitting and fuming. He would carry on so, you would think he was going to have a heart attack. But he was gripped with a great purpose given to him by God. This purpose dictated how he lived his entire life. A single, mastering dream consumed him. One passion obsessed him. He had one thing he wanted to do. Was his secret his focus on one thing?

God, give us ordinary people who will give all of their resources to lose their lives for one passion. God, give us ordinary young people who will give all of their youth, energies, and power for one cause, with one vision. It is ordinary people, who have one thing on their minds, who move a world. We are not calling you to stardom. This is not about an abundance of talent. There is a call from the cross for you to bring your entire system and lay it at His feet. Allow yourself to be consumed with one passion, one drive, and one dream. Be just an ordinary person who has one purpose.

John the Baptist was also an **INQUIRING SUFFERER.** I would not want you to get the wrong impression. You might think this is glorious. We are not talking about suffering before television cameras. This is not the afternoon soap opera. John is a free spirit of the desert, roaming with the wild animals. He has never known four walls and a ceiling in his adult life. Suddenly he is yanked from his environment, and he is jammed into a dudgeon cell. It has four walls and a ceiling. He can stand in the middle and touch all of them at the same time. The ceiling is pressing down upon him. The walls begin to move in on him. Despair grips him. His emotions begin to play tricks on him. His diet is upset. He begins to doubt and question. If Jesus is the Messiah and I am His forerunner, what am I doing in here? This is not the picture of a glorious conqueror. It is the depressed, discouraged, ordinary person, who is suffering.

You must understand that the suffering that affects the eternities is not glorious? Sometimes we must enter a Garden of Gethsemane where we sweat drops of blood. We find ourselves all alone praying, "Not my will but thine be done!" Sometimes it is expressed in great cries as in Hebrews 4, or it is under a Juniper tree, thinking, "Woe is me. Everyone is against me and I am all alone." We are not talking about Hollywood suffering. We are dealing with ordinary people who are going to be possessed with one cause, despite the price. If it takes a Garden of Gethsemane or a Juniper tree, or a dungeon cell and aloneness, it must be. Those are the people who affect the eternities.

John the Baptist was an **IMPORTANT SUFFERER.** *"Then Jesus answered and said to them, 'Elijah truly is coming first and will restore all things,"* (17:11). John the Baptist had to come first in order for the Messiah to do what He needed to do. The forerunner was essential to the plan. John was going to lay down a blood pavement over which Christ was going to walk to a cross. Eternity is not affected by accident. We will not just accidentally have revival. People do not just appear. Someone has to get involved. Someone has to pour their life out. Someone refuses to give up and bleeds until it happens. Someone cries. There has to be a core group that cannot live unless God brings revival. Who will suffer until it happens? It is the ordinary people who are willing to suffer who influence the eternities for God.

The Starting Person
Matthew 17:11

"Then Jesus answered and said to them, 'Elijah truly is coming first and will restore all things," (17:11). Did you notice the word *first?* Do you know how hard it is to get someone to go first? The most difficult thing in revival is to get the first person to come to the altar. It is hard to be the first one to say that you are sorry. When you go first, you are standing all alone. It is a great risk because there is always the possibility that no one else will join you. John the Baptist was an ordinary person who was willing to be first.

John the Baptist was a **STARTER IN SELECTION.** Again we see it in verse eleven. This is prophecy. God had selected him. The Old Testament stated this. John did not just happen to appear in the days of Jesus. You can read about the miracle of his birth and all that God did to cause His plan. Can you imagine knowing that before the Messiah could come and bring about world redemption, you had to do your work? God was counting on you. The entire redemptive plan of God hung on whether you completed your assignment? Jesus' cross could not be until John's cross was? Everything God did in the Old Testament was awaiting John? What about you? All God wants to do in the future in your community is waiting on you? All that God has been doing and all He wants to do comes together at your door step. You are the pivot point of the entire activity of God. I know you are thinking that you are just an ordinary person, but those are the kind that God has selected to affect eternity.

John the Baptist was a **STARTER IN SURRENDER.** *"But I say to you that Elijah has come already, and they did not know him but did to him whatever they wished,"* (17:12). The scribes have been teaching Malachi 4:5-6. They painted the picture of a great military giant who would be raised from the dead. He would march into Jerusalem; he would cause all the reforms necessary to grant Israel their rulership position in the world. He would prepare the way for the Messiah to come as the world ruler. All of Israel was looking for the Messiah, but the sign of His coming was Elijah, the forerunner. John the Baptist was a strange fulfillment of this dream. He was not a military leader. Some reform came about under his revival effort, but he was not a great leader in any area. He simply resigned himself for them to do to him what they wanted to do. He surrendered; there were no miracles, no gigantic feats. He experienced a dungeon cell, depression, failure in ministry, and had his head cut off. It was nothing but resignation and surrender.

Did you ever notice that the great manifestation of the power of God often appears to the world as weakness and failure? When I really surrender to God, I end up surrendering to you and submitting to your mistreatment? When I really give my life to Christ, I give my life to minister to you. I end up receiving your insults and condemnation without striking back. The world calls that weakness, but the Kingdom applauds that as greatness. All that the disciples were looking for in Elijah was present in John the Baptist, but not from the view of the world. He had this greatness about Him, which resigned him to all that they wanted to do.

I have discovered that the people out there do not move in here, until we who are in here, move up. We have to be first in surrender, if they are going to experience Christ. Get out of the way! We think that if we pray in the church house on special occasions, the lost will get saved. But it is not going to happen until you and I surrender to the cross. This process lays down a pavement of blood over which they can walk into the Kingdom.

John the Baptist was a **STARTER IN STYLE.** *"But I say to you that Elijah has come already, and they did not know him but did to him whatever they wished. Likewise the Son of Man is also about to suffer at their hands,"* (17:12). There has been nearly one week of argument between the disciples and Jesus over the subject of the cross style. He takes three disciples to the Mount of Transfiguration. Heaven descends and verifies the cross style. On the way down from the mountain Jesus is telling His disciples about the cross style again. They have had the wrong idea. Did they get their thinking corrected? Have their eyes been opened to the truth?

In Matthew chapter ten Jesus took the power He contained within and transferred it to His disciples. He sent them out to duplicate His ministry. All the miracles that Jesus had displayed for them, they could now do. They cast out demons and raised the dead. They were absolutely thrilled with this miracle ministry. The crowds flocked around them, and their stardom was building. They were getting their names in the newspaper, and they loved this kind of ministry. They were stars in evangelism. Where is John the Baptist during this time? He is in jail. He is depressed with the threat of getting his head cut off. The disciples must have gathered at sometime and talked about poor John the Baptist. He was such a failure and could not make it in the ministry. What was wrong with his technique? He did not do miracles; he could not draw the crowds. His personal appearance left a lot to be desired, and he certainly did not have much tact. Maybe that was the cause of His failure.

This is our view. You can gage your success by the crowds, money, or size of your home. But Jesus states, "Disciples, you have it backwards." While they were out holding their big campaigns, John the Baptist was starting a new style. It is the style of the Kingdom. It is the style of bleeding, suffering, and dying. It is time now for the disciples to become a part of that style. John the Baptist started the style; Jesus was walking over his blood to continue the cross style; the disciples must follow in a like manner. The style of the cross is the style of the Kingdom. It is not big success stories, not massive crowds, not demanding your rights. It is the style of bleeding, suffering, and giving your life away. It is a style of resigning, and being used. It is the cross.

Do you qualify to be in the Kingdom? What is your style?

Jesus, I am so ordinary. But You have called on ordinary people who will surrender themselves totally to You. Will You give me one passion and one drive? I will be totally expendable by You. Use me to make a dent in eternity for the Kingdom's sake. Use me to be a person who makes a difference. In Jesus' name we pray, Amen.

Matthew 17:14-20

Transferring The Power

It is impossible to read this great chapter without being reminded of the ancient Renaissance painting by Raphael. It is a classical master-piece entitled "The Transfiguration." Raphael worked himself to death to paint it. The genius of the painting is that Raphael captured Matthew chapter seventeen on canvas. He grasped the theological truth that Matthew is attempting to portray to us. The great painter took the two pictures of this chapter and fused them together.

The top of the canvas is the brilliancy of the Mount of Transfiguration. He used bright colors to show the radiation of light coming from the inward heart of Christ. Jesus is floating in midair, just off the mountain. Elijah is on one side; Moses is on the other. They are talking about the cross that Jesus should accomplish in Jerusalem. The disciples are prostrate on the ground. The magnificence of the transformation of Jesus has struck them with awe. They are in great fear.

On the bottom of the canvas Raphael painted the valley scene. There are dark lines to depict the overwhelming despair that has gripped the crowd. The Pharisees are making fun of the disciples. The disciples are defending themselves. There is a father who is very anxious about his son who is possessed by a demon. He is pleading with the disciples to please do something. A disciple is seen pointing his finger toward the top of the mountain where Jesus is being transfigured. The boy in the midst of his possession is reaching out toward the mountain as if to say, "Help me!" All the paint strokes on the canvas are in the direction of the transfigured Christ. Your eyes are just naturally drawn to this central figure of the painting. No matter where you look, your eyes draw you back to Jesus.

Raphael has put on canvas what Matthew is writing about on paper. It is a lesson with which we have all struggled, and it has to do with the plight of each of us. It asks the fundamental theological question, "How do you get the power of the mountain to the need in the valley?" If we could discover this answer and apply it, we could rescue a world. If we could find this solution and apply it, we could grow a church. We do not need to discuss the power that the disciples witnessed on top of the mountain. That is a fact we all accept. We know God is there, but we are here. If some how we could get Him from there to here, or if we could go from here to there, we could find the answer to our need. How do you get the power of the mountain to the valley?

We have seen Him on Mount Sinai. He was thundering out the law in power and majesty. But we do not live on the mountain; we live in the valley. How do you keep this law, day after day, in the struggle of the valley? We have seen Him in the burning bush. But we need a God who can indwell us in the midst of our burning hate, when we need love and cannot find it. We have seen Him in the pillar of fire by night, and knew

He was there. But we need Him down at our home when argument is blazing. How do you get the power of the mountain to the valley?

We do, however, have the answer to this question! God, Himself, has come from the mountain to the valley. He has answered the question Himself. God has solved the problem. He is Immanuel, God with us. God is no longer on the mountain, isolated from the need of the valley. He has moved to be where we are. It is our message. It is the fullness of the Holy Spirit that will literally indwell every individual. He is not just here in the valley; He has come to live within us. It is the message of Christmas. Christ has come to dwell among us. He sends His Spirit to be in us.

Are you like I am? God has solved the problem; it is a marvelous truth. I applaud it and believe it with all of my heart. Meanwhile I scratch my head and say, "It still does not seem to work." We live such powerless lives. God has taken the initiative and moved out in our behalf, but still there is something missing. It is not that I am blaming Him; the blame is mine. I have a problem. Even when He has come from the mountain to the valley where I am, there is a blockade to the flow of the power to my life. How do I experience Him in His fullness? He has come near, but there is a gap between me and Him. But Jesus has given detailed instructions concerning this need. Jesus focuses us on the problem of faith.

Here is the proposition of the valley scene. It is the summary statement of all that Jesus is teaching us. The attitude of the heart, which takes the power of the mountain and flows it through life, is faith. The key is faith. The channel through which Jesus can flow is faith. The means by which He is appropriated is faith. The attitude of the heart, which brings this all to pass, is faith. Let us look at some details.

Faith Is The Point
Matthew 17:19-20

"Then the disciples came to Jesus privately and said, 'Why could we not cast him out?' So Jesus said to them, 'Because of your unbelief, . . ." (17:19-20). You understand the real emphasis of this scripture is not another miracle. Matthew has given us tremendous miracles involving the deliverance of demons. This story is not just another miracle. The central theme of this story is the teaching of Jesus to His disciples, when they could not cast out one demon. This story tells us what Jesus thinks about faith. Faith is the point.

Faith is a **DEFINED OBLIGATION**. Jesus teaches that our need is not for "more" faith. I have said, "If I just had more faith, I could have victory in my life." We speak, having small faith, when we need a large faith. Our focus is on the amount of faith. Jesus says this is not the problem. His emphasis is not on the amount of faith, but on the definition of faith.

I have had difficulty with the subject of faith. I cannot seem to define it or talk about it. It is an allusive subject. We hear a ninety minute sermon on faith, and think it was wonderful, but still do not understand it. We talk about it, but it is difficult to make it reality. There are concretes and there are abstracts. Abstracts are those things you cannot buy at the store. They do not seem to have substance, and yet they are real in our lives. Concretes are those things you can feel with your hands; they are pulpits you can pound. Abstracts are allusive; they slip through your fingers when you try to hold them. Faith is an abstract.

I was a junior boy kneeling at an altar of prayer. I was sincere in wanting God in my life. Some dear saint would come, hit me on the back, and yell, "Just trust Jesus, son. Just trust Jesus!" I would turn around with a look that said "I would if I could! Could you tell me how to do it? Could you give me steps one, two, and three? Could you tell me where to buy it? Do you have some with you? Do you have some you could lend me?" Someone else, seeing my problem, would quickly jump in and say, "Now do not get confused. Just believe in Christ." I would look at them with the obvious questions, "He told me to trust Jesus. Now you say that I should believe in Christ. Where do I find this belief? Do you have some of it available? What will it feel like when I have it? How will I know when I do it?" A third saint would quickly move in to rescue the situation, "Well, what we are talking about is having faith in God." I would stare at the wall thinking, "Am I to trust in Jesus, believe in Christ, or have faith in God? I do not know how to do any of these things." I would go in this vicious circle, round and round again. I would gladly have done anything to have clear experience with God. It all seemed to hang on something I could never understand, and no one could explain to me.

If faith is that important to our experience with God, should it not be clear? Perhaps we can be vague on some minor points, but faith is major. This major item of our relationship with Him should be unmistakable? Jesus gives us the answer in this passage. He puts cement in the matter of faith. It is now clear so all can understand it. A definition is - faith is invoking the activity of the Second Party. Let us investigate this definition.

Faith is the act of invoking. Invoking is what happens when you call your children to supper. You lean out the back door and yell, "Supper is ready." You are invoking the children. You are wanting, calling, and earnestly demanding their presence. We all understand at the heart of faith is a sincere desire. Any double mindedness will destroy faith. The invoking must be absolutely sincere. It must possess the entire being of beings.

Faith is invoking the activity. The children hear your invoking and begin to run toward the back door. They are in action, moving their muscles, flowing with energy. Faith is a clear call from deep within the heart for the flow and movement of the energy and power that is beyond us. Any attempt to think we are the source of this flow is destructive to faith. Any self-centeredness is like cancer to faith. Self-centeredness will destroy faith.

Faith is invoking the activity of the Second Party. Who is the Second Party? It is Jesus! He alone is the resource needed. He alone has the power to accomplish all that needs to be done in me. Faith is saying, "I can't, but You can. I will let You." Faith states, "I cannot handle this, but You can. Take over!" Faith says, "I am resting. I am leaning. I am pushing my puny resource aside. I am going to cling to Yours and Yours alone!"

Let us imagine you are a major league baseball player. Your team has done very well this year. You are participating in the World Series. Your team has won three games and lost three games. You are now in the play offs. The pressure to win is on. The rival team is one run ahead, and the game is just about over. Your team is up to bat, and that will decide the game. Two of your team mates have already made outs, and there is one man on base. This could be a positive situation except you are up to bat. You have never hit a home run in your life, and one is desperately needed now. You are very nervous. On your way to home plate, you trip over a bat and break your arm. Your team mates all cheer. They know what a lousy batter you are. They call in a substitute hitter for you. He walks in confidence to the home plate. The pitcher throws his first pitch, and the substitute hits it out of the ball park, making a home run. Your team wins the game! You were not adequate, but your hitter was. He did for you what you could not do for yourself. That is faith!

No illustration is complete in all areas. It always misses it some point. In the baseball illustration there is an obvious flaw. You are sitting in the dug out nursing a broken arm. Your substitute is at home plate hitting a home run. But in the reality of life, you are at home plate. Everyone is seeing your flesh. Your arm is hanging by your side. Everyone knows you are incapable of hitting home runs. But you keep doing it anyway. Everyone is yelling, "How are you doing that?" You keep trying to tell them that it is by faith. You are invoking the activity of the Second Party. The Substitute Hitter lives within you. He is doing through you what you cannot possibly do. You are simply invoking His activity in your behalf. He does, through your flesh, what you cannot do. You have to constantly remind people that it is not you. You are living by faith. They think it is because you are extra clever, but you keep telling them it is Jesus. They think it is because you are a disciplined person, but you keep telling them, "No! No! It is Jesus!" You are constantly invoking the activity of the Second Party. You are always saying, "I can't, but You can. I am going to let You."

How does that come out of this Scripture? In Matthew, chapter ten, Jesus has reached into Himself and transferred something of His power to His disciples. They have become apostles. He gives them an entire chapter full of instructions on how to use this power. He then sends them forth to duplicate His ministry. They go forth to do miracles. They heal the sick, raise the dead, and cast out demons. How are they able to do these miracles? Any one of the disciples could tell you. Before chapter ten they could not do miracles, but after chapter ten Jesus enables them with His power. They operate in a power that is not their own. The Spirit of Jesus is doing through them what they cannot do themselves. They are doing miracles by faith - invoking the activity of the Second Party. They are leaning and trusting the power that is bigger than they are!

Jesus shares with the disciples the content of His Messiahship. He tells them the style of the cross. He is a bleeding, suffering, dying Messiah. New light comes to them. Jesus calls them to lose their lives. Instead of living by faith, as they have been, something new happens. They have invoked the activity of the Second Party. They have trusted the power of Jesus flowing through them. Now in chapter sixteen they decide to trust their own prejudices and traditions. They invoke the activity of the first party. They revert to trusting themselves. They begin to argue with Jesus and the resource that has made everything they have been doing possible. For nearly one week they debate with Jesus. They come to the base of the mountain, and they are confronted with demon possession. They find themselves totally unable to handle one boy with one demon. They are amazed! What has happened to them? They ceased to live by faith. They ceased to invoke the activity of the Second Party.

Matthew is giving us a clear definition of faith. It is your obligation, twenty-four hours a day, to always, consistently, and constantly, invoke the activity of the Second Party. Get out of His way! He has some powerful living He wants to do through your life. Live by faith!

In the "Defined Obligation" there is a **DIRECT OBJECT**. The key in the definition that Jesus is giving is found in the Second Party. He is the direct object. The problem is not in the size or the amount of faith, but in the object of faith. Everyone has all the faith they could ever need. The problem is we do not have the correct object for our faith.

Let us go back to chapter ten in Matthew. Christ has released His power into the disciples. They are invoking the activity of the resource that is bigger than they are. The object of their faith is the resource of the person of Jesus. He has released His power within them. In chapter sixteen they shift objects. Where their object of faith was the indwelt power of Christ, they have shifted to themselves, being prideful and self-centered. The moment they revert to the object of themselves, they are powerless in the face of one demon. The problem is not in the amount of faith, but in the object of their faith.

Let me illustrate. Every Sunday morning you come to church. You have your favorite church pew. We have copied the habit of milk cows who have been trained to go to the proper milk stall. Every Sunday morning you go to the same pew. Sunday after Sunday, fifty-two Sundays a year, you go to the same pew. Year after year, you go to the same pew.

It is a great act of faith. The object of your faith is the church pew. Each Sunday you invoke the activity of the church pew and believe that it will hold you. Of course, it always does. You do not come to the church pew and kick it. You do not make your wife sit first to test it. You have full confidence in the object of your faith - the church pew. Then one Sunday you come to the church pew, and with total faith you plop yourself down on the object of your faith. Crash! You find yourself on the floor with broken pieces of pew all around you. The pastor rushes down to help you. He says, as he picks you up off the floor, "Your problem is your faith. If you had more faith, you would have been fine." You look startled. The truth is you had total faith. You had so much faith you never even thought that the church pew might fail to hold you. The problem was your faith, but it was not the amount of faith. It was the object of your faith. That pew was an inferior object.

Our problem is not in the amount of our faith. You and I have all the faith we need. The problem is in the object of our faith. I have a little faith in my wife, a little faith in the church, some faith in Jesus, and a whole lot of faith in me. Someone tells me I need to believe. But I have believed. The problem is I have believed in an unworthy object. I have been invoking the activity of the wrong party. I need to get all of my faith on one focus. My faith must be on Jesus alone. The power has come from the mountain to the valley. How will I use it in my life? The key is faith. Faith is invoking the activity of the Second Party. We are going to live in the state of invoking His activity through us. Our entire focus is going to be on Him instead of on us.

Faithless Is The Plight
Matthew 17:17

"Then Jesus answered and said, 'O faithless and perverse generation," (17:17). Those are strong words. From the context of this passage, we have a proper understanding of the word "faithless." It is the generation who has not been invoking the activity of the Second Party. It is not the generation who has small faith compared to large faith. It is the generation who has placed their faith in an unworthy object. They have placed their confidence in themselves. This generation is steeped in their traditions. They have trusted their own way of doing things. Their style has been to invoke the activity of their traditions instead of the Second Party.

"Faithless is the Plight" that is **EVIDENCED BY THEIR LACK.** Did you see their lack? Outsiders saw their lack. *"So I brought him to Your disciples, but they could not cure him,"* (17:16). This was the statement made by the father of the boy who was demon-possessed. He knew that the disciples were lacking. There is no doubt that the crowds also knew that the disciples were not adequate. The disciples were embarrassed. How can they win a world to the Kingdom when the world sees them lacking. How do you convince the world that we have a Kingdom of love when we of the Kingdom cannot get along with each other?

The disciples knew that they lacked. *"Then the disciples came to Jesus privately and said, 'Why could we not cast him out?"* (17:19). We need to qualify the reason for the lack of power. The test of whether you have proper faith is not physical results. Jesus came to His hometown of Nazareth, but He could not do mighty works there. He invoked the activity of the resource of God, but there were no results. The problem was not Jesus; the problem was those who would not receive Him. Results are not the test of faith. It is a trick of the Devil to get us focused on the results instead of on the resource. It is very easy to be tricked.

The qualifying factor of faith is not results. It is the flow of life. The disciples have lost the flow of His life through them. They did not invoke the activity of the Resource that was bigger than they are. The outsiders recognized there was no flow, and the disciples knew that the flow had stopped. Here is the supreme question for you and me! Do we know the flow of His life? The results are none of your business. Your sole attention should be on flowing His life. Do you know what it is to live in the Spirit until through you, the power that is bigger than you are, is touching your world? Do you know what it is to moment by moment invoke the activity of the One who is beyond you? You become the flesh through which the Divine God is flowing! You are flowing His life. If you lack the flow, you are faithless.

"Faithless is the Plight" that is **CAUSED BY THEIR PAST.** *"Then Jesus answered and said, 'O faithless and perverse generation"* (17:17). A literal translation of that phrase would be - "O two faced and twisted generation." The grammar structure of those words suggests to us that there was a perversion in their past. This perversion has been maintained to the present moment. It has left them victims in a distorted position. In the past, the training of the disciples had taught them the untruth, as if it were true. They believed it as truth and committed themselves to this untruth. Jesus now comes into their lives and exposes the untruth. This exposure would correct their perversion, if they will give up the untruth, but they refuse to believe it is not the truth.

The untruth was their past tradition and what they had been taught about the Messiah. He was pictured as a military commander, when He was a suffering servant. They saw Him riding into Jerusalem on a great white steed, when He would come into Jerusalem riding on a donkey. Their teaching said He would have hundreds bowing at His feet to serve Him, when He would come to serve with a bowel and towel. Jesus tells His disciples the truth, but they refuse to give up their untruth. They are trapped. What a tragedy! Jesus came with the new revelation of the cross and its style. It was a revelation of new light, but they were so trapped in their past tradition that they missed it. Faith is invoking the activity of the Second Party. Faith means I am invoking His flow instead of my own traditions, prejudices, and thought patterns. This means that I will be teachable by the truth of His Spirit. I will expand in the Kingdom truth. It is the adventure of investigating the mind of God.

"Faithless is the Plight" is **REBUKED BY THEIR CHRIST.** Jesus has looked at the disciples and said, *"O faithless and perverse generation, how long shall I be with you? How long shall I bear with you?"* (17:17). Jesus expresses Divine impatience here. How long will He need to put up with this? How long will He allow them to invoke the activity of their own thought process instead of His?

The Bible says, *"for whatever is not from faith is sin,"* (Romans 14:23). What is faith? It is invoking the activity of the Second Party. Every time you are not invoking His activity and flowing with His life, you must be flowing with self. This is sin. The Bible says, *"But without faith it is impossible to please Him,"* (Hebrews 11:6). What is faith? It is invoking the activity of the Second Party. What pleases God? His pleasure comes when you allow Him to act for you. You please Him when you say, "Not me, but You! I can't; You can! I am depending upon You. Do in and through me what I cannot do for myself." God is never pleased with what you do for Him; He is only pleased with what He gets to do through you.

Faithful Is The Possibility
Matthew 17:20

"So Jesus said to them, 'Because of your unbelief; for assuredly, I say to you, if you have faith as a mustard seed, you will say to this mountain, Move from here to there, and it will move; and nothing will be impossible for you." (17:20). We love this Scripture. We claim it as a great promise. It becomes a license for our selfishness. All I have to do is believe and nothing is impossible for me. Suddenly we believe and expect to win the lottery. We believe and expect to win all of the ball games this year. But Jesus is not referring to those things at all. This is not a statement regarding your self-centered agenda. It is not a blank check written on the bank of God and you fill in the amount. I fear we have taken this Scripture out of context and have read into it what we want.

This passage deals with a single issue. It is ministry. There is a demon-possessed boy who desperately needs help. There are disciples who are lacking in the flow of ministry to that boy and his father. Then Jesus comes to the rescue and ministry is accomplished. The whole context of the conversation between Jesus and His disciples is ministry.

Ministry is what Jesus is discussing. When Jesus flows through His disciple nothing will be impossible.

Therefore, **MINISTRY IS FUNDAMENTAL**. Jesus and the three disciples are experiencing the Mount of Transfiguration. Let us be reminded about the larger context of this passage. Peter's response to this whole scene was a desire to build three tabernacles and camp right there on the mountain. We can forget the cross and all of those rotten people who are at the base of this mountain. We can have perpetual camp meeting right here on this mountain side. Let us just come to church every Sunday morning, and pat ourselves on the head for being so good, fellowship and have a good time. Jesus would not tolerate Peter's idea for one moment. The Mount of Transfiguration was not designed for the disciples to have a good time. The indwelt presence of God is not for the purpose of making you feel good. The focus is ministry. Ministry is fundamental.

MINISTRY IS FOCUSED. If you come to the valley with an open heart, what is the focus of the story? You might think that the focus is on the family. A father is concerned about his son. He has a major problem in his family, and they need someone to minister to them. We find an element of truth here, but it is not the focus of the passage. Physical healing is not the focus, though the son does have a physical condition that is ruining his life. He needs to be restored, but that is not the focus of this passage.

The great need in this story has to do with demonic activity. It shows up in the contrast between the Mount of Transfiguration and the scene in the valley. On the mountain there is Divine power; in the valley there is demonic power. The power of the mountain comes to the valley.

It invades the territory of demonic dominion. It seems so difficult for us to keep focused on what we are really trying to accomplish in ministry. Someone says, "Our goal is to have ten more in Sunday School this year than we did last year." That is sick. Someone else says, "We are trying to raise some money to pay off our mortgage." That is sick. We become consumed by these projects, as if that were to be the focus of our ministry. We forget what we are all about. Jesus does not call us to maintain a program. We are men and women who are to constantly invoke the activity of the Second Party and invade demonic territory. We are at war. We live in a society possessed with demonic activity. God asks us to take the power contained in His person and do something about it. That is our mission.

MINISTRY IS FELLOWSHIP. *"For assuredly, I say to you, if you have faith as a mustard seed, you will say to this mountain, 'Move from here to there,' and it will move;"* (17:20). Some have tried to take the moving of mountains literally. But you do not need faith to move mountains. You can rent a bulldozer.

To understand this phrase, you must go back into the cultural setting of Jesus' day. There were key scholars at the head of the Jewish schools in Jerusalem who were the final authority regarding the law and the prophets. Everyone listened when they spoke. These individuals were called "the movers of the mountains," or "the pulverizers of the mountains." When problems needed solutions, these men, who were educated and knew the answers, were consulted. They had the answers to the toughest questions.

Jesus now turns to uneducated fishermen. He declares to them, "You are going to be the movers of the mountains." The task of changing your world, invading demonic territory, and answering the needs of your society, is not going to be delegated to a few educated individuals.

Jesus delegates the task to you, the uneducated and ordinary people. You are going to invoke the activity of the Second Party. Through you, the flow of God is going to pour into your world. You are going to be in such fellowship with the Divine that you can be used by Him to move the obstacles of your age. It will not be done by your traditions, nor by those who are highly educated. It will be accomplished by those who will open themselves to total dependency upon God and invoke His activity rather than their own. You can shake your world. It is all by faith. It is all ministry. Are you available?

Matthew 17:22-23

Cross Style Evangelism

I realize it is a bold statement to make, but I believe that verses twenty-two and twenty-three could possibly be the most important verses in the New Testament. The reason is not because they give us valuable new information; they do not. It is not because Jesus has given deep, deep insight into what He has spoken. It is not new light to startle you. These verses contain old truth. It is the truth Jesus has been exposing to His disciples as they argue with Him. It is the revelation on the Mount of Transfiguration.

These verses are important because they give us a great summary or climax. Their immensity of truth is startling. We see in them the sequence of events taking place and the truth Jesus has been teaching His disciples.

To grasp it fully, you must return to chapter ten. It was there Jesus reached down deep inside Himself, took the power He contained within, and transferred it to His disciples. They went forth with that power and the results amazed them. They could do the same miracles as

Jesus. After sometime of ministry they returned with glowing reports. Even the demons came under their control. Nature listened to their voices. The crowds were thronging around them, and everyone was applauding them. People lined the altars; they received great offerings. The television cameras were on; the press was present. The disciples were loving every moment of this great ministry. They believed they were building the Kingdom, and they based it on miracles, performance, great crowds, and popularity.

Then you see the disciples in chapter sixteen. In Caesarea Philippi, Peter makes his great confession. He shouts, ***"You are the Christ, the Son of the living God,"*** (16:16). He was saying that he really believed Jesus was the Messiah. He thought he saw the whole picture. The miracles of Jesus and His disciples would win the world. It would be no problem! As the thirteen of them called the multitudes together, and worked their miracles, they could overthrow Rome. They could usher the Kingdom of God onto this planet. The disciples could establish a new order, and they could be in charge.

This was not the direction of Jesus. He began to talk with the disciples about an opposite procedure (16:21). They had focused on the wrong thing. Fame and power possessed the disciples. Miracles were a big thing to them, but though Jesus did miracles, they were not His focus. He was going to a cross. It would be cross style that would shake the world to the core. He began to reveal to them the reality of His trip to Jerusalem. He was going to suffer, bleed and die. Redemption would not come through Hollywood stunts, television, or miracles. Only a cross and the shedding of blood could accomplish redemption.

The disciples reacted to this by argument. But you cannot blame them, can you? Miracles are the logical way to proceed with the building of this new Kingdom. It is stardom! The Sunday night crowd will double in attendance with this kind of performance. On the other hand, the cross style is definitely not attractive. The very idea of bleeding and suffering is not a crowd pleasure. If you want to sway the multitudes, you must have the right kind of production. Miracles are the way to go. Is it any wonder that the disciples argued with Jesus?

They argued for six days. Jesus took three of the most influential disciples with Him to the mountain. On the Mount of Transfiguration, Jesus was transformed and carried on a conversation with Moses and Elijah (17:1-3). The topic of the conversation was the cross. Heavenly beings are stating the foundation of the Kingdom. This is the issue. Here is what is important and what matters. This is the method through which God was going to build the Kingdom. It is the style of the Cross. Suddenly the Heavenly Father descends and places His stamp of approval on Jesus (17:5). He closes His great statement by saying, **"Hear Him!"** (17:5). Jesus has the key to winning the world; listen to Him. He is the One who knows where He is going. It is time to get in on His style.

On the way down the mountain, Jesus turns to His disciples. The very first words out of His mouth are a reference to the cross and its style (17:9). This is the way God is going to be build His Kingdom. The procedure is not performance, miracles, and popularity. The style is that of the cross. Come and die!

At the base of the mountain a miracle is needed. Jesus delivers a young boy from the clutches of a demon (17:18). The deliverance power amazes the crowds. The performance is sucking the disciples in again. They are, no doubt, giving out autographs, having interviews with the local press, and enjoying the great fame. Jesus reaches out and gets hold of His disciples. He pulls them behind a great rock where they can be alone. He leans into their faces and gives them strong instruction. He calls them not to be like the crowds. Do not get caught up in the spectacular and the miracles. The fundamental of the Kingdom of God is the cross style. That is how God will build the Kingdom. This is what I am calling you to embrace. I want you to be like I am. I am going to bleed, suffer, and die. He calls the disciples to join him in the style of the cross. It is a process of blood and death that is going to build the Kingdom.

Jesus sharply clarifies the truth by strong teaching and a variety of events. How could they miss it? Glamour and hot shot programs will not build the Kingdom of God. Bigger churches and television stars will not build it either. Only redemptive blood process will build the Kingdom of God. It is the cross and its style. As you allow Jesus to indwell you, and you get involved in the hurt and pain of your world, at the point of your involvement a cross is produced. This cross produces blood, and this bleeding process will shake a world. When you leave the four walls of the church building and embrace the pain of your next door neighbor, you become an extension of Jesus. He then flows His style through you - the cross style.

Jesus is calling us to allow Him to do what He does best. He takes the sin, pain, and hurt of another into Himself. Then that person is free, and God can do a new thing within him. Will you allow Him to do that through you? The minute you allow Him to do it, He produces the cross through you. The moment He produces the cross in you, your blood is spilt, and redemption takes place. This is the style of Jesus. No wonder Jesus is stating to His disciples that the plan of redemption is a cross - a cross - a cross.

THE MOVEMENT OF THE CHRIST
Embracing the Cross
Matthew 17:22

Christianity is not a mutual admiration society where we talk about love and more love, but never get anything done. On the other hand, it is not a performance scale where we measure our actions. That leads to a legalism that is destructive at its heart. The New Testament keeps a strong balance or tension between internal attitude and external action. We see this balance in the life of Jesus.

There is **DIRECTION** in "The Movement of the Christ." *"Now while they were staying in Galilee, Jesus said to them, . . ."* (17:22). Jesus had finished His ministry in Galilee as recorded in Matthew, chapter fourteen. He celebrated the end with a great banquet where He fed five thousand men, besides women and children. Then He took His disciples into Gentile territory to focus them. He desperately needed to convey to them the cross and its style. He needed time alone with His disciples to prepare them for the cross. They must learn the principle of its style. Jesus took the disciples to the eastern side of the Sea of Galilee. Though we do not know the length of time spent in this area, we do know that three important things took place there. In Caesarea Philippi Peter gives his great confession (16:16), the Mount of

Transfiguration happens (17:1-7), and in the valley Jesus teaches the disciples a great lesson on faith (17:20).

Now, for the sake of the cross, Jesus brings His disciples back into Galilee. They seem to slip in unnoticed. ***"Now while they were staying in Galilee, Jesus said to them, 'The Son of Man is about to be betrayed into the hands of men,"*** (17:22). The first phrase of verse twenty-two is very important. A better translation of this phrase would be, "Now while they were gathering together in Galilee, . . ." In other words, the grammar structure of this phrase tells you that Jesus and His disciples were on the move. You can expand that to include other groups also. It is as if there were several groups meeting together at a selected place in Galilee. Their purpose was to form a larger group to begin the journey to Jerusalem for the Feast of the Passover.

Jesus knew He was headed for the cross. It is significant to understand that as Jesus was speaking to His disciples about the cross, He was marching toward it. He was gathering His forces around Him and moving out. This was not a class room lecture. This was rolling up your sleeves and moving on it. This was not theory He was offering. This would put shoes on your feet and march you toward a cross.

I am deeply concerned about us. The theology of the cross is a part of our discussion. We sing the hymns about the cross, and we have memorized the details concerning the cross. The class room has answered our questions involving the cross. The benediction has been given; the class has been dismissed; the theology is now made clear. It is time to hit the road. It is time to stop analyzing the cross; it is time to embrace the cross. When the cross style becomes reality, you will experience the pain of your neighbor. Upon embracing their pain, a cross is erected, and you are on it. The cross becomes the reality of your living in the style of blood redemption process.

The movement of the Christ has a direction. He is headed for the cross. There is **SELECTION** in the "Movement of the Christ." We see the strength of this truth strongly in verse twenty-two. The framework of the context is the balance between action, motive and attitude. Jesus not only had action toward the cross, but He had internal attitude about the cross. His attitude was singleness of mind.

It is impossible to read chapters sixteen and seventeen without seeing that Jesus was stuck on the idea of the cross. He was like a piano with only one note. He had only one subject on His mind. A single thing was taking place. Only one thing concerned Him. He was stubborn about the cross and its style. When you come to the first prediction of His cross (16:21), a great avalanche of this teaching begins. You are flooded with the truth of the cross from that point on. There is no compromise on the subject. You cannot argue Him out it. It was not a matter to vote on. It was settled in the heart and mind of Christ.

What does the cross mean to us? We wear it as a gold plated symbol on a chain around our neck, or we display it as a beautiful piece of wood in the sanctuary of our church. We sing songs about the cross while we maintain our comfortable programs. The cross means very little to us unless we have a stubborn commitment to involvement with the hurt and pain of our world. It is in our involvement that a cross is produced and our blood is shed. He is calling us to be single minded about the cross style, although there are people who will tell us it is not reasonable. We cannot become casual about it. Only God can help us with the process of spilling blood - our own blood. He is calling us to the cross style.

The movement of Christ has a direction; He is headed for the cross. The movement of Christ has a selection; He is single minded about the cross. But there is another aspect of this truth to consider. There is **CONNECTION** in the "Movement of the Christ." Now if Jesus wants to go to a cross, why should we stop Him? If He wants to do something wonderful for us, why will we not let Him do it? If He decides to be single minded about the cross, why should we attempt to persuade Him otherwise? But when He shifts from speaking about His cross to our cross, that is a different message. He is talking about the requirements of being a disciple, bringing us to cross style. This makes me nervous. I do not mind if Jesus dies for me! I can glory in that and praise Him forever. But when you put me into the same style of the cross, it is a different situation altogether. Jesus, in speaking to His disciples about the cross, literally connects them to His cross, as if they will have a cross also.

When Jesus started talking about the cross and its style, He definitely messed up the plans of the disciples. They had great dreams of bigger miracles. Great crowds would continue to follow them and Him. It could easily become a world wide movement. But the very idea of a cross puts a damper on all of those dreams. They were devastated when Jesus connected them to this cross. They were being called to lose their lives as well. This factor causes us to ask whether we even want to be His disciples.

Jesus stated it plainly to His disciples, ***"If anyone desires to come after Me, let him deny himself, and take up his cross, and*** *follow Me,"* (16:24). Jesus illustrated it clearly in the person of John the Baptist, *"But I say to you that Elijah has come already, and they did not know him but did to him whatever they wished. Likewise the Son of Man is also about to suffer at their hands,"* (17:12). Jesus displayed it effectively, *"And was transfigured before them. His face shone like the sun, and His clothes became as white as the light,"* (17:2). The heavenly beings spoke of the cross and the Father verified it (17:5). Jesus said it forcibly, *"Because of your unbelief; for assuredly, I say to you, if you have faith as a mustard seed, you will say to this mountain, 'Move from here to there,' and it will move; and nothing will be impossible for you,"* (17:20). The disciples had no faith in His message of the cross; power for deliverance ceased to flow. Jesus was determined the disciples were going to have intimate connection with the cross. His plea to them was, "Oh disciples, come with Me and embrace the cross style!"

How can we in this modern generation be expected to experience the cross and its style? The cross is produced in touching the need of your world. The moment the Jesus within you intersects the hurt of your world, a cross is erected and fresh blood will flow. Will you join Jesus in His journey to the cross?

MANIPULATION OF THE FATHER
Evolving the Cross
Matthew 17:22-23

An outstanding truth of this passage is the tremendous interaction between man, the Devil, and a Sovereign God. What is so startling is that these three parties are all involved in bringing about the event of the cross! The meeting point of all the interaction is at the place of the hurt and need of a world. How could these three parties be brought into such strong cooperation?

There is **DIRECTION** in the "Manipulation of the Father." *"Now while they were staying in Galilee, Jesus said to them, 'The Son of Man is about to be betrayed into the hands of men,"* (17:22). The factor of betrayal is a powerful statement. A literal translation would be something like this, "The Son of Man is about to be given over into the hands of men."

Now we come to Judas and his action of laying the betrayal kiss upon the cheek of Christ. Judas gave Jesus over to the leaders of Israel. It happened in the staggering loneliness of Jesus when the disciples did not have the decency to watch with Him in loyalty. Jesus was agonizing over a world redemption to the point of sweating drops of blood. Can you believe the scene? Six hundred to a thousand men came stomping through the midnight hours to get one lonely man. Judas was leading the parade. It is a horrible story.

There is something bigger being spoken here. When we approach this truth through chapter sixteen and the first part of chapter seventeen, we begin to understand the Divine Sovereign God has planned this. This is not the plot of a betrayer, but the plan of the Divine. The impact of this phrase is that the Father Himself gave Jesus over. There is a verse in Isaiah, chapter fifty-three, which gives us this same truth? *"Surely He has borne our griefs and carried our sorrows; yet we esteemed Him stricken, smitten by God and afflicted,"* (Isaiah 53:4). We read it again in Romans. *"He who did not spare His own Son, but delivered Him up for us all, how shall He not with Him also freely give us all things?"* (Romans 8:32). God the Father has stuck His fingers in the middle of this entire scene. He has manipulated all the actions of man to cause His plan. He is the One who has given Jesus up to a cross.

In the manipulation of the Father there is a direction; it is the Divine plan of the cross. But there is **SELECTION** in the manipulation of the Father. He states, *"The Son of Man is about to be betrayed into the hands of men,"* (17:22). It is the direction of a sovereign God to give up His Son. However, He has selected to do this through the hands of sinful men. Does that not have tremendous significance?

There are sinful men who are parading their abilities, as if they are in charge. Men, in their self-centeredness, think they are accomplishing a great feat. The chief priests, scribes, and elders think they have executed an excellent plan, while Judas thinks he has fooled everyone. All the while they are simply tools in the hands of a sovereign God with a plan. There is a word play taking place between the phrases "Son of Man" and "hands of men," (17:22). Men, acting in the fog of their own deception, are becoming instruments of the Father's redemption for a world. The Holy Father is using the guilt of men to accomplish His Divine bidding.

Let us note that we could criticize those individuals who were physically on the scene and played the role. But the truth is, we are speaking about ourselves. I can hear my screaming voice in the crowd surrounding the cross crying, "Crucify Him!" God, forgive us, for we have participated in that scene.

There is direction in the manipulation of the Father; it is the Divine Plan of a cross. In the manipulation of the Father there is the selection; He has chosen to do this through the hands of sinful men. But notice there is **CONNECTION.** How could you not see the strong connection between the plan of the sovereign God and the activities of sinful men? When a sovereign God with a plan touches the wickedness of men, the inevitable result is a cross. Blood is going to flow. Redemptive process is going to take place.

"And they will kill Him, and the third day He will be raised up.' And they were exceedingly sorrowful," (17:23). Did you notice that the three phrases used in this verse start with "and?" I would suggest the first and third "and" are proper, but the one in the middle should be translated "but." *"And they will kill Him."* It begins with murder from the hands of sinful men. *"And they were exceedingly sorrowful."* It ends in defeat, sorrow, and dismay. But sandwiched in the heart of all of this is the phrase "but *the third day He will be raised up."* This is good news! In the middle of murder, sorrow, and defeat comes the resurrection. It is the style of the cross. Life is at the heart of death. For those who lose their lives and embrace a cross, they find they are embracing life. While circumstances pressure you on one side, the other side is filled with weeping and sorrow. Coming out of it all is resurrection - the style of the cross. Every time the sinful lives of men are intersected by a sovereign God, a cross is produced and life begins to flow.

MISINFORMATION OF THE DISCIPLES
Extension of the Cross
Matthew 17:23

You and I have no problem identifying with the disciples, especially in this scene. It may be here we will find our true calling. May God speak to us clearly.

In the misinformation of the disciples there is a definite **DIRECTION**. As you view verse twenty-three you can see how hard it was for them. They had a strong heritage, the past, their tradition, and all of their training. They were steeped with prejudices. Their perception had always had a certain focus. They believed the Messiah would be a military commander who would bring victory. Their conception of the Messiah was from the physical view alone. Jesus has turned to them and said, ***"And they will kill Him, and the third day He will be raised up,"*** (17:23). You would think they would be shouting for joy over the news of the resurrection. How greatly this will affect their lives. But their reaction is quickly recorded by Matthew. ***"And they were exceedingly sorrowful,"*** (17:23). The subject of the cross hit them with such force that they seemed to miss the great truth of the resurrection. It was tragic! They were going in a terrible direction. It was the direction of great darkness. It might be good to ask you about your direction. Have you missed the truth of life out of death? It is the heart of the cross style.

In the misinformation of the disciples there is also the **SELECTION.** The great tragedy of this was that the disciples did not grasp God's plan. He has selected the cross and its style to bring redemption to the world. They were so filled with themselves. But we know how the story unfolded. We know that there came a time when the disciples did get it. They did experience the cross in their lives and it did become their style. They no longer cared about television cameras and stardom. They embraced the process of bleeding and risked their lives. They shook their world as they became an extension of the cross. After they had been beaten by order of the Sanhedrin, they looked at one another in great joy. They reported to each other, "Isn't it great! We got to suffer for Jesus." They have a new outlook.

In the Philippi jail we see the selection. It was a privilege to have your back beaten. In the midnight hour, as you embrace the pain, you can sing praises unto God. Through that embracing of the cross style, a Philippian jailor is shaken. His whole family is won to the Kingdom of God. God has selected the cross style to bring it to pass. Men and women will not be won by Hollywood stunts and big programs. They will be won by people just like you. It happens when we embrace the cross and become a part of the pain of our next door neighbors. When you embrace that pain, blood is shed and a cross is erected. This is the style.

But you must not miss the truth of the **CONNECTION**. It is not a simple matter of disciplining our lives and caring for people. This is not simply doing charity work for the rest of our lives. In fact, this is not about us at all. This is about being connected with Him, until He can do through us what He did two thousand years ago. Two thousand years ago He had His own body; now He wants yours. He had His own face; now He wants yours. He had His own hands; now He wants yours. If He possesses your body, what will He do with it? He will do the same thing He did with His own! The cross is you dying to yourself, so Christ can do through you what He does best. He wants to flow His life through your death as you join Him in His suffering. Are you available?

Matthew 17:24-27

Free Like Christ

"Jesus, we want to be exactly what you want us to be. We want to get the chip off our shoulder. Enable us to set aside the internal insecurity. Cause us to get our fist down so we no longer defend ourselves. Make us free from self, hang-ups, bondage, and prejudices. Oh, how we wish to be free! In the name of Jesus, we pray. Amen."

Several years ago I met a teenager who was within a few months of being eighteen years of age. He was in total rebellion against everything decent. Pushing drugs and stealing from his parents supported his personal drug habit. He was flunking out of school, wanted nothing to do with the church, and was in trouble with the law. His mother called me one night requesting that I come and visit him. I did not want to go. There was so little chance of communication with him. When I appeared at their door, this teenager was sitting in a lounge chair. The expression on his face told me he was displeased that I had come. I tried to carry on a conversation with the boy and his mother, but he did not want to talk. It appeared that he was about to get up and leave. I said to him, "Would you take a walk with me?" Reluctantly he followed me out the door. It was dark outside except for the lights on the street. I asked, "What is going on in your life? Tell me what you feel inside."

The expression on his face matched his words. He said, "I don't want anyone telling me what to do! I don't want the church, my parents, the principal, or the police telling me what to do!" I replied, "Hey relax, I am not here to tell you what to do." We continued to walk in dead silence for a short while.

As we returned to his house I turned and asked, "What are your plans for the future?" In dead seriousness he turned to me and said, "In a few months I will turn eighteen and I am going to join the Marines." I had to bite my lip to keep from laughing in his face. He had no idea what he had said. He did not want anyone telling him what to do, yet he was going to volunteer for the Marines.

This is a classic illustration. The reason is that it shows us the internal tension in each of us. We all have this driving passion to be free. We all have this great need to belong to something bigger than we are. We want something that will command us and have authority over us. Yet, we scream inside to break over the traces, to do what we want to do, or to be what we want to be. There is this strong desire to find someone bigger than we are, who can solve our problems. We want some one who can take charge and tell us what to do. We need one who can be Lord. This is why we are so attracted to Jesus. He can take these two great drives and bring them into perfect balance within the heart. In Jesus we find the kind of freedom for which people were built. It is in relationship with Him that we begin to experience freedom in our lives.

If the drive for freedom is allowed to dominate, we end in self-destruction. This is not freedom. It is bondage. On the other hand, if all you have is control and authority, you have legalism which brings death at the heart.

Jesus can take these two aspects and bring them together. He maintains perfect balance. I have found freedom in Jesus that I could not have imagined. It is the freedom a train has as long as it runs on the track. In the balance of Christ, I begin to experience life. I find fulfillment of personality. It is under His Lordship that I become free. It sounds like a contradiction, but it is not. It is freedom.

Jesus discusses this truth in Matthew 17:24-27. The miracle of taking a coin from the mouth of the first fish caught is not the main truth of this passage. There are some scholars who are very skeptical about this miracle. They find difficulty in the fact that this miracle was not recorded as actually being done. Others are troubled by the apparent violation of a basic principle Jesus maintained. Jesus never used the power of God for Himself. It would be easy to miss the main path of truth Matthew is attempting to share with us. Other scholars have felt this passage is to teach our responsibility to government. They think Matthew is telling us to meet our obligation of paying our taxes.

In verse twenty-five, Jesus asks Peter a leading question. Peter answers and Jesus says, ***"Then the sons are free,"*** (17:26). This is the heart of the passage! It is a bold statement. Freedom is the basic element of the Kingdom of God. What kind of freedom does the Kingdom offer to us?

Freedom As Sons Not Strangers
Matthew 17:25- 26

You need to review the context of the statements made in these verses. The disciples have argued with Jesus for six days. They do not agree on the style of the Messiah, (16:21-28). Jesus proclaims the cross style, but the disciples will not accept it. Jesus takes three of the leaders to the Mount of Transfiguration. They experience the conversation of heavenly beings speaking with Jesus about His cross. They hear the Father instructing them to listen to Jesus. The nine disciples who remained in the valley are defeated because they have not accepted the truth Jesus has given. Now all are on the move back into the territory of Galilee. Followers of Jesus are gathering to go on a journey to Jerusalem. Jesus is moving toward the cross with great determination.

They have come to their adopted home town of Capernaum (chapter 4). Peter evidently had a home there (8:14). So a Pharisee confronted Peter concerning their payment of the temple tax. After all, this was the place in which they were responsible for paying it. The question is a little blunt, *"Does your Teacher not pay the temple tax?"* (17:24). The indication is that the Pharisee thought Jesus and the group were trying to escape meeting their obligation. Peter immediately bristles in his spirit. "What do you think we are? Cheap?" he must have yelled! "We have been traveling. Sure we are going to pay the temple tax," he continues.

Peter thought Jesus would really be pleased with the way he handled the Pharisee. He comes to the home where they are staying. He expects to brag about his superior ability. Jesus anticipates what has taken place and meets Peter at the front door. Jesus asks him to step out back. He wants to meet him in the woodshed. Jesus begins to ask Peter some questions. It is almost a parable in question form. Jesus asks him, ***"What do you think, Simon? From whom do the kings of the earth take customs or taxes, from their own sons or from strangers?"***(17:25). This is a clear and logical question that any child could answer. Peter responds, ***"From strangers,"*** (17:26). No king collects taxes from his own sons; he would collect taxes from the citizens of the country or strangers. Since this is true there is a logical conclusion to the answer. Jesus says to him, ***"Then the sons are free,"*** (17:26). What a bold statement!

Did you notice the **BASIS OF THE FREEDOM** about which Jesus is speaking? It is "Relationship!" The context of the discussion on the subject of freedom is not about circumstances. It is not about politics. Jesus is not giving new techniques on overthrowing Rome. He is not giving new ways to stay out of jail. This is not about our surroundings. In the mind of Christ, these things have nothing to do with freedom. However, Peter's thoughts about freedom are altogether different. If you ask Peter about freedom, he would start talking about the domination of the Roman Empire. He would talk about taxation and suppression. This was the same problem Peter has about Jesus as the Messiah. His picture was that of a military commander, not a cross bearing Savior. He wants Jesus to lead the way to military and political freedom, but this is not in the framework of Jesus' discussion of freedom.

Jesus is highlighting a freedom that is bigger than circumstances or the political atmosphere in which you live. I wonder about us. We also think of freedom in terms of the removal of pressure. Teens think when they get away from the control of their parents they will be free. Parents feel they will be free when they get their bills paid. Business men think freedom will come when they get a signature on the new contract. The working person thinks he will be free when he finally reaches retirement. None of these ideas are true. Freedom has absolutely nothing to do with circumstances, exterior activities, or pressures from without. The heart of freedom is relationship.

You must also see the **BENEFIT OF THE FREEDOM** Jesus is discussing. It is "Release!" Jesus presents great contrast in His statements (17:25-26). It is seen in the words "sons" and "strangers." There are two basic ideas Jesus might have had in mind as He spoke of this. One is the common understanding of the royal family. The king of a country does not tax his own children. The son of the king, the prince, does not pay taxes. In fact, he lives off the taxes. The ones who pay the taxes are the citizens of the kingdom. Where do we fit into this contrast? Jesus is declaring that we are sons. We have royal blood running through our veins. We are free! What about the domination of the Roman Empire? Political freedom is not the discussion in this passage. Jesus is speaking about royal blood, sonship, and relationship. We are free.

There is a second idea Jesus may have had in mind. Sometimes it was not just the royal family that was exempt from taxes, but all of the citizens of the kingdom. A King and his people might have conquered a neighboring kingdom. They would tax the conquered strangers and this would release their own people from paying taxes. Taxation was a result of being conquered. Jesus is saying that we have not been conquered. We are not trapped. We are people of the Kingdom of God; we are free.

I fear some of us have a Christianity that is like a bad pill. We have been socially and culturally trapped by our Christian training. We know too much good to feel comfortable about being bad. Yet, we really do not want to commit ourselves to righteousness. What are we to do? Christianity is some kind of bad unnatural element that has been thrust upon us. We are now obligated to pay these Kingdom taxes - go to church and tithe. Jesus says, "You do not understand!" There has been no external force. There is no king who has trapped us and is pushing us into the unnatural. Sin is bondage! The unnatural is that which is wrong. Christ is saying that the natural, normal, royal sonship, and being in the Kingdom, is the flow of life. It is here that we are turned loose and released to be free.

The basis of freedom is relationship. The benefit of freedom is release. Then there is a **BURDEN TO THE FREEDOM**. It is "Responsibility." After telling Peter that the sons are free, Jesus continues, ***"Nevertheless, lest we offend them, go to the sea, cast in a hook, and take the fish that comes up first. And when you have opened its mouth, you will find a piece of money; take that and give it to them for Me and you,"*** (17:27). We do not have to pay the temple tax because we are sons of the Kingdom. We are free, but we are going to pay anyway.

To grasp the full impact of this statement, you need to understand the Old Testament framework. The Israelites were obligated to take care of the poor, the widows and the orphans. They also had to pay the temple tax. It was an obligation to keep the temple functioning. They did not view it as an obligation. The children of Israel were in Egypt. What did they have? They were slaves who had been stripped of all their dignity and possessions. They did not have land, freedom, or family life. All they knew was the crack of the whip over their backs. But God, Jehovah, intervened in their lives. They were delivered into a land flowing with milk and honey. Now they had an abundance of possessions - lands, homes, family life, freedom. They went from nothing to everything. They could afford to be generous. For them to take care of the poor was no problem; they remembered how they had been poor. They gave out of their abundance. In Egypt they had no place to worship and no right to do so. Now they had religious freedom and a beautiful temple. It was nothing for them to be generous in the support of the temple. What a joy! This is the context from which Jesus is speaking. You can afford to meet your responsibilities!

You can afford to forgive seventy times seven. Do you understand why? Once you were overcome with guilt and defeat. The Divine God came in great deliverance through the blood process and has forgiven you more than you will ever be called upon to forgive. You should have no problem forgiving in abundance. You can afford to forgive extravagantly. You once had nothing in forgiveness, now you have everything. You can afford to lavish forgiveness upon everyone. You are free to do it.

You can afford to be generous with love. Once you had no love at all. You experienced nothing but loneliness. There was no one who cared for you. Then you met Christ face to face and experienced the entire power of the redemptive love. He has abundantly poured out His love over you day and night. You have gone from nothing to everything. You can afford to pour love out to everyone. You are free to do it. You are released to generosity.

Freedom As Secure Not Self-Centered
Matthew 17:24

"And when they had come to Capernaum, those who received the temple tax came to Peter and said, 'Does your Teacher not pay the temple tax?" (17:24). In our present day situation we link freedom and security together. From a political view, freedom is linked with having a secure military power. We continue to play war games. As long as our military is strong, we feel secure, and thus free. We stockpile enough bombs and missiles to destroy the world several times. How many times do you need to be able to destroy the world to remain secure? We are the same in our personal lives. How many locks or alarms do you need on your home to feel secure, and thus free? How much money is enough to make you feel secure?

Did you notice that the context of this discussion has all been external rather than internal? Can freedom come from an internal security? What would be the **BASIS OF THE SECURITY**? It is "Relationship." Now the question becomes, "Of whom are you a son?" The security of the relationship is in the one to whom we are related. We are sons of the almighty sovereign God. If that factor ever really grips us, we will be shouting for the rest of our lives. Matthew has written seventeen chapters, so far, in an attempt to convince the Jews that Jesus is the Kingly Messiah. He is King of the Kingdom. He is the One to whom we are related. It appeared in Peter's great confession, *"You are the Christ, the Son of the living God!"* (16:16). The Mount of Transfiguration experience visualized it for us. We saw the Divine power that indwelt Him. The Father came down and verified it.

The temple tax has an interesting background. It began back in Exodus chapter thirty. The temple was very expensive. The draperies, ornaments, and fixtures of the temple were elaborate. Two perfect lambs were needed each day for the offering. The clothes of the priest were the finest that could be bought. The incense that burned was a high-priced variety. These were on going expenses. Therefore, a temple tax was established to offset these expenses. Every Jewish male who was twenty-years and older had to pay this annual tax, and the amount equaled two days' wages.

The motivation for this tax was greater than just the expenses of the temple. Here are the instructions, ***"The rich shall not give more and the poor shall not give less than a half a shekel, when you give an offering to the Lord, to make atonement for yourselves,"*** (Exodus 30:15). In other words, you pay the temple tax because you are a sinner and you desperately need the temple. Now the Pharisee has come to Peter and asked, ***"Does your Teacher not pay the temple tax?"*** (17:24). The question is about the spiritual condition of Jesus. Is not Jesus a sinner in need of forgiveness, just like the rest of us? Is He not under the same obligation as the rest of us? Does He not need to pay the temple tax to make atonement for His sins? Peter answered, ***"Yes,"*** (17:25). He falls into the trap every time.

Jesus corrects Peter when he arrives at the house. He attempts to get Peter to think through what is taking place. Peter made the great confession (16:16), when he declared Jesus to be the Christ, the Son of the living God. Now he tells the Pharisee that Jesus is an ordinary sinner just like everyone else. What do you believe, Peter? In believing Jesus was the Messiah, Peter was accepting Jesus as the spotless Lamb of God.

As a son you are in relationship with the Righteousness of Israel, who is free. You also are free in the security of who He is!

The **BENEFIT OF THE SECURITY** is "Release." You find freedom in release when you have security within! This passage holds a three-way contrast. The contrast involves the Pharisees, disciples, and Jesus. The Pharisees are laying another trap. Peter responds with his impulsive spirit. He lives with his fists up and ready to fight. The Pharisees ask the question, *"Does your Teacher not pay the temple tax?"* (17:24). Peter responds in defense, *"Yes,"* (17:25). He is defending Jesus. We are not a cheap group. We pay our own way. You are not going to trap us. This describes most of us, does it not? Oh, what bondage we are in. Our pride or self-centered carnality has mastered us. We spend our energy defending ourselves. Every church fight reveals insecurity. Every upset in our homes declares to the neighborhood our deep internal insecurities. In the cities of Israel, there was a court that convened at the city gates each morning. Any Jewish male could appear in the court. All injustice to him or his family could be presented. He had a right to be defended in the court. There were two kinds of people who had no right to ever appear in the court. There was no defense for them in this judicial system. They were the widows and the orphans. Do you realize what God said about this in the Old Testament? He declared that He would be the defender of the widow and the orphan. Anyone who touches one of those would have to deal with God Himself! How is that for great security? Is this not the position into which He is calling us? We do not have to defend ourselves. We have an almighty God who is going to speak for us! I am released into freedom.

There is a great **BURDEN OF SECURITY**. It is "Responsibility." Now that you are free inwardly, you can focus your entire attention on ministry to others. You are released from spending your energies defending yourself. You are trusting God for that. Your energy can now be used for the sake of others. You are now free and God can use you for others. The walls of defense that kept you from ministering to certain people are now gone. You are free.

Freedom As Servants Not Slaves
Matthew 17:27

"Nevertheless, lest we offend them, go to the sea, cast in a hook, and take the fish that comes up first. And when you have opened its mouth, you will find a piece of money; take that and give it to them for Me and you," (17:27). Jesus does not need to pay the temple tax. There is no "have to" in this passage, but He is going to pay the temple tax any way. When you "have to" you are a slave; You are a servant when you "want to." You are free. There is freedom in your motive.

What is the **BASIS OF THE SERVANTHOOD**? It is "Relationship." The Pharisees are to be pitied. Jesus is calling them strangers. They are insiders who had been chosen by God to play a role in the style of the cross. They have now become outsiders. They have become slaves to their own self-centered carnality, and it expresses itself in terms of their relationship with the law. They have taken the law, that was good and proper, and twisted it. It has become a tyrant that is cracking the whip over their backs. They are slaves to the law. They spend most of their creative time attempting to find loop holes to get around the law that makes them slaves. They are not free; they are slaves.

Paul gives us great insight into this. He parallels the bond slave and the love slave. Once we were forced, "had to" bond slaves, now we are joyful, "get to" love slaves. This turns us loose (free) to be servants. We are free to serve. There is no whip beating on our back, but a great release of love has brought us to freedom.

All of this brings us to the very heart of servanthood. It is the **BENEFIT OF SERVANTHOOD** that is "Release." The Pharisees have been trapped within their own spirits. They always have a hidden agenda. When you talk with them, you depart feeling like they are after something. There is something going on which is not fully expressed. There is a hidden motive. There is a battle going on between the Pharisees and Jesus. The basis of it is this hidden agenda. The Pharisees were always trying to get the upper hand. They were threatened by Jesus' popularity.

I have been in homes where I felt like that. The conversations were always one person trying to get one on the other. I felt like a recorder was taping everything being said. It will, no doubt, be held against you forever. I have been in church board meetings that had this kind of atmosphere. You have to carefully select every word you speak, because you are going to be quoted. It is a trick. There is no freedom to express your heart. I also have friendships like that. There is no way to be open and free. It is an awful way to live, but the cross has brought us to freedom. We do not have to live like that. Jesus is presenting a life where the internal motive has been purified until there is no hidden agenda. You are free in the heart. It is the style of the cross.

If the basis of servanthood is relationship, the benefit of servanthood is release from hidden agendas, then the **BURDEN OF SERVANTHOOD** is "Responsibility." We have been released to be like Him! I am free not to claim my rights. I am free not to defend myself. I am free now to become the life and death of Jesus to my world. I am now free to deny myself. I am free to make a difference in the life of someone else. I am free now to give myself away. I am free!

"Jesus, some of us are in great traps of our own making. Not outward circumstances, but internal traps have been created which defeat us. We are in such bondage. Our self-centeredness has become an amazing tyrant that is destroying our lives. Jesus, save us from ourselves. Redeem us out of ourselves and bring us into the flow of Your Life. Make us free to serve. In Your name, I pray. Amen."

PART FOUR

Matthew 18

Self or the Cross

Confessions of the Cross Style

Matthew 18

Introduction

Personal Relationships Through the Cross

We are a talking generation. Television reveals the popularity of talk shows. Conversation is taking place everywhere. Experts proclaim information on every subject for all to hear. I fear there is much talk about everything except the real issue. In our homes we yell about minor issues, and never have the courage to discuss what really matters. In our church board meetings, we spend hours discussing issues that will not matter one hundred years from now. One great marvel about Jesus is that He never discusses the side issues. He cuts through the surface and goes to the very heart. If you do not want to face the central issue of your life, do not come to Jesus.

In Matthew chapter thirteen, Jesus exposes the major subject. It is the Kingdom of God. Matthew presents Jesus as the King of the Kingdom. He is spending His energies and resources on building the

Kingdom. Seven parables describe the hidden secrets of the Kingdom. This information reveals what no one could possibly know.

A theme is flowing through these revealed secrets. The throbbing heart of the Kingdom is relationship. If you are going to fight for something, let it be relationship. In your daily interactions the eternal issue is relationship. You can sacrifice anything except relationship. If you are going to take a stand in the board meeting, let your stand be for relationship. The color of the carpet is not worth division. You must always build bridges and protect relationships. Relationship is the one thing that will last forever.

The Pauline term for this concept is *reconciliation.* **"For if when we were enemies we were reconciled to God through the death of His Son, much more, having been reconciled, we shall be saved by His life,"** (Romans 5:10). Sin estranged us from Him. There was a gulf between us. God reconciled us through Christ and brought us into relationship. Relationship, relationship, relationship is the theme of the Kingdom of God.

Beginning with chapter thirteen, you can follow the progression. For six months Jesus has special training for His disciples. His theme is relationship. It is the strong thrust of the cross style. He calls them to lose their lives in the cross experience. The subject gains strength in chapter sixteen. Jesus calls each disciple to **"deny himself, and take up his cross, and follow Me,"** (16:24). The disciples revert to much talking. They discuss the subject until it becomes meaningless. In chapter seventeen, the heavenly beings come forth and announce that the cross is not going away. Moses and Elijah verify the cross teaching on the Mount of Transfiguration. God, the Father, pronounces His approval of this style. Chapter seventeen verifies chapter sixteen. The cross is the basis of the relationship as discussed in chapter thirteen.

Now we come to chapter eighteen. The study of relationship continues. The means of relationship is ***forgiveness.*** Man cannot have relationship expect in forgiveness. Picture in your mind a series of concentric circles. The largest circle represents the Kingdom of God. Jesus is establishing the structure, and it is all possessive. The circle within the Kingdom circle represents relationship. It is the fiber that lines the very structure of the Kingdom. Within the relationship circle is a third circle. It represents forgiveness. It is impossible to have relationship without forgiveness. Because of the guilt and sin in your life, there is no way you can have relationship with God without His forgiveness. You have offended many people. Relationship with them is not possible without their forgiveness. Every relationship has strong forgiveness flowing within it. The inner circle represents the cross. There is no possibility of God's forgiveness without the cross. In the cross, God did what was necessary to bring you to Himself. Jesus died on the cross so that you might have forgiveness and be in relationship with God. But the cross is just as important if you are to have relationship with others. Unless you come to the cross in death to self you will never experience the ability to forgive others. Forgiveness comes from the cross and produces relationship. That is the heart of the Kingdom of God.

This brings us to the introductory proposition of this great chapter. Personal relationship through the cross is forgiveness. Matthew shapes this chapter like a pyramid. The peak of the pyramid is the end of the chapter. The foundation upon which it all sets is the beginning of the chapter. Let us look at the chapter in reverse, beginning with the peak.

FORGIVENESS IS FUNDAMENTAL
Emphasizing Forgiveness
Matthew18:21-35

In verses twenty-three through twenty-five, Jesus is telling a parable. Like many of Jesus' parables, the details are very simple. A wealthy master has summoned his servants to give an account. He discovers one servant owes him ten thousand talents. The master demands immediate payment of the total amount. The servant is in an impossible situation. He cannot possibly pay this huge debt. The master orders those in charge to sell the servant, his family, and all of their earthly goods. All of that does not even begin to pay back the debt. The servant bows before the master and pleads for mercy. Compassion moves the master, he releases the servant, and cancels the entire debt. In the next scene, Jesus tells how the forgiven servant meets a fellow servant who owes him one hundred denarii. He demands payment immediately from this fellow servant. In a spirit of hatred he threatens to throw the fellow servant in prison until he pays the debt. News of this returns to the master, and the master is irate. He cancels the forgiveness of the ten thousand talents and gives the servant to the torturers until he pays it all. What a powerful story!

The emphasis of this story is forgiveness. The great truth of this parable and its context is **PLENTY OF FORGIVENESS.** This calls for an investigation of the question that prompted Jesus to tell this parable. Peter interrupts Jesus' discourse. He asks, ***"Lord, how often shall my brother sin against me, and I forgive him? Up to seven times?"*** (18:21). Peter is bold. He desperately wants to be number one. He thinks forgiving seven times will impress Jesus. The Roman pagans never forgave. The Jews only granted forgiveness after they had done to the individual what had been done to them. So Peter is being extravagant in suggesting forgiveness up to seven times. He expects Jesus to brag on him.

Jesus disappoints Peter. What is extravagant in the Kingdom of earth is puny in the Kingdom of God. Jesus says, **"*I do not say to you, up to seven times, but up to seventy times seven,*"** (18:22). This statement says that you should always forgive. Live in forgiveness all the time and in all circumstances. We must forgive every hurt and abuse, in the past and the present. There is never a time you should not forgive. Forgiveness should be total, absolute, consistent, and inclusive. This is beyond shocking. It is life shattering. This must have shaken Peter to his very core. How could this be possible?

Forgiveness is not optional in the Kingdom of God. It is the very heart beat of what is taking place. If you and I are going to live in the Kingdom's style of the cross, we must have an inward attitude of continual forgiveness. It is a forgiveness that is beyond conditions. It is forgiveness that takes place in the heart before repentance is received from others. Forgiveness is an automatic response of the inward spirit. You are to always forgive.

It is easy to write bold statements in a book when you do not know the details or circumstances of the reader. A person should be generous with forgiveness on small, petty hurts or wrongs. But there are some things that are too painful for us to forgive. There are severe abuse, murderous acts, and hideous crimes that we cannot forgive. How can you lump all wrongs into the same category and declare total forgiveness?

I confess I would agree with you except for the **PATTERN OF FORGIVENESS.** We see this pattern in the master of the parable. *"Then the master of that servant was moved with compassion,"* (18:27). This is a picture of the heart of God. The parable relates that the servant owed the master ten thousand talents (18:24). There may be some disagreement concerning what this amount would be in our currency. However, a LOW estimate would be two million three hundred and seventy thousand dollars. Jesus is describing a situation where the debt is far too great to ever repay. The servant could not repay this if he had ten life times.

That is why verse twenty-seven is so significant. Compassion moves the master. The debt of my life was so overwhelming there was no possibility of repaying it. The guilt and sin in the amount of two million three hundred and seventy thousand was on my account, but compassion moved Jesus. It was not faceless people He saw that moved Him. It was not an entire church that gripped Him. I was not one among several thousand people. It was not numbers on attendance boards that got through to the master. It was one lonely servant standing before Him. This servant was in debt for two million three hundred and seventy thousand, and there was no way out. I was that servant. Somehow my need got to the heart of God. I had no way to merit His attention except to receive wrath and judgment, but compassion moved Him.

There is another important aspect to this great verse. *"Then the master of that servant was moved with compassion, released him,"* (18:27). It is so abrupt. The master dismissed the guards who dragged the servant to him. There is no locked door or prison cell. The master simply released the servant. He was free to leave. There was no bondage. It is incomprehensible. Often in church we sing the song "Glorious Freedom." Why do preachers always speak of sin as bondage and Christianity as freedom? Sin is a trick. It looks fun. I am free to satisfy myself as I want. Yet, before long, sin traps me into what I cannot give up. Quickly it becomes apparent that I am serving sin because I have to. I am in bondage. There is no way out. Christianity, however, is not a ball and chain on my ankle. Jesus releases me to the freedom of choice. Every service to Christ is a voluntary act of my will.

"*Then the master of that servant was moved with compassion, released him, and forgave him the debt,*" (18:27). The content of the release is that He has forgiven the debt. Jesus cancels the debt of two million three hundred and seventy thousand dollars. There is no record of it. It is as if he never owed it. We call this GRACE. There are no strings attached. Can you see the servant turning to the master and whimpering, "I suppose I am going to have to mop your floors for the rest of my life to pay you back?" The master replies, "No!" The servant whines, "Do I have to milk your cows at four o'clock every morning from now on to pay you back?" The master in compassion cries, "No! You are free. There is the door." It is just too good to be true. Now that I have received His forgiveness, do I have to come to church every Sunday? The answer is NO. Do I have to be good? Again, the answer is NO. Holiness is always the out spill of love, not obligation. The moment it becomes obligation or bondage, it is in the pattern of sin. This is the picture of what He has done for you. In the Kingdom of God, extravagant, gracious, generous forgiveness is the very heart beat of the cross style.

I wish we could just stop right here in the parable. However, the truth continues to present the **PROBLEM OF FORGIVENESS.** The problem is that I have a fellow servant, a brother, who owes me one hundred denarii (18:28). This amounts to sixteen dollars and sixty-seven cents. I grab him by the throat and demand he pay his debt. After all I worked hard for that money and lent it to him in good faith. It is only right that he pays me back. But the master has just forgiven me two million three hundred and seventy thousand dollars. Should not the joy of my forgiveness so capture me that it would spill over to my brother?

The master hears of my actions. He demands I appear before him again. He cancels my forgiveness and demands full payment immediately. ***"And his master was angry, and delivered him to the torturers until he should pay all that was due to him. So My heavenly Father also will do to you if each of you, from his heart, does not forgive his brother his trespasses," (18:34-35).*** My lack of forgiveness sets up barriers which blockades my heavenly Father's forgiveness to me. My lack of forgiveness, hatred, and bitterness literally nullifies any forgiveness I might receive from God. Forgiveness is fundamental in the Kingdom of God. You and I must consistently live in the state of forgiveness.

Jesus uses the phrase ***"from his heart,"*** (18:35). Forgiveness is not spoken words. Forgiveness is not meeting your obligation because you know it is the right thing to do. Forgiveness is not learning to control your hatred so you can push it aside. Forgiveness is from the heart and forms the atmosphere around you. It is the awesomeness of how much Jesus has forgiven you. The amount you are to forgive will never equal the amount He has forgiven you. You will never be wronged as much as you have wronged. The peak of the great pyramid in chapter eighteen is Forgiveness is Fundamental.

FORGIVENESS IS FUNCTIONAL
Embracing in Forgiveness
Matthew 18:6-21

This is the middle of the pyramid, and it is powerful. On the peak of the pyramid the high altitude may cloud your thought. Maybe you are having illusions about living a life of forgiveness. But in this section your feet are on the ground at sea level. You have come to the practical living out of forgiveness.

In verses six through twenty-one, the summary is **PLENTY OF FORGIVENESS.** A key thrust resounds throughout these verses, and it is *whatever it takes.* Whatever it takes to live in forgiveness, do it! No cost is too high to maintain constant forgiveness. No wall or barrier is worth missing relationship. Live in Plenty of Forgiveness.

"And if your hand or foot causes you to sin, cut it off," (18:8). This is severe! *"If your eye causes you to sin, pluck it out,"* (18:9). We have failed to see these verses in their context. We have concluded that He is talking about resisting sin. We are to resist sin with all our being, but that is not the context of these verses. This chapter highlights the subject of forgiveness. Offenses come your way (18:6-7). People hurt you, do things to offend you, or talk behind your back. The instruction given is to live in forgiveness whatever the cost. Whatever it takes to stay in a state of forgiveness, do it!

You and your next door neighbor are arguing over the line between your property. Division has arisen between the two of you. Is one foot of property worth the terrible knot you feel inside every time you look at him? Jesus tells us to live in forgiveness. Whatever it takes to live in forgiveness, do it! Give him the foot of property, and live in the atmosphere of forgiveness.

You and your brother have a business deal. There is a disagreement over one hundred dollars. What are you doing? One hundred dollars is not worth the internal upset and conflict you experience. It is not worth the broken relationship that spreads through your family and friends. Give him the one hundred dollars and live in forgiveness. In fact, give him two hundred dollars just to be sure. Break down every wall that would stop you from basking in the greatness of the forgiveness you have received. Whatever it takes to live in forgiveness, do it!

Well, what about the other person? Look at how Jesus covers that subject. ***"Moreover if your brother sins against you, go and tell him his fault,"*** (18/15). We have no problem with this part of the verse. I will be glad to go to my sinning brother and straighten him out. If he does not repent, I will take a couple of others who agree with me and talk to him strongly (18:16). If the confrontation does not cause him to change his ways, I will tell it to the church (18:17). Do you see what we have done to these verses? We think Jesus is giving a pattern for handling church squabbles. So we strongly rebuke our brother and are not a bit surprised when he does not respond positively. We follow through with the Biblical pattern until we can justify our dislike for him. Sadly, we have missed the impact of these verses. Jesus is not giving a pattern for dealing with church squabbles. Jesus tells us to do whatever it takes to live in forgiveness. Go to any extent to win your brother back.

Sacrifice your pride and go to your brother with a broken heart, dripping with love. In practical everyday living, we are to be saturated in forgiveness. It is the heart of the Kingdom.

It is vital that we have a **PATTERN OF FORGIVENESS.** *"What do you think? If a man has a hundred sheep, and one of them goes astray, does he not leave the ninety-nine and go to the mountains to seek the one that is straying?"* (18:12). This is the parable of the Shepherd Father's heart. It is the parable form of what Jesus did in reality! He is the pattern. Yes, there are those who are safe in the fold, but He is risking Himself to find the one who has gone astray. He cannot tolerate one being out there without proper relationship. Whatever it takes to win him back, He will do it. He will give His life to bring forgiveness and reestablish relationship. He will leave His throne and take on flesh. He will die a criminal's death. He will go to any extent to bring forgiveness to you. This is the pattern.

He ends the small parable with the following words. *"Even so it is not the will of your Father who is in heaven that one of these little ones should perish,"* (18:14). It is the total will of God that forgiveness and relationship extend to every individual. His will has driven Him to *whatever it takes.* But there is the **PROBLEM OF FORGIVENESS.** I have no problem living in an attitude of forgiveness until you offend me. Most people in close relationship with me always end up offending me. *"Woe to the world because of offenses! For offenses must come, but woe to that man by whom the offense comes!"* (18:7). Do not miss the statement, *"For offenses MUST come."* I wish He had said that offenses **MIGHT** come. With absolute certainty, offenses will come if you live in this world. In this society, even in church and Sunday School, someone will offend you.

The issue is not whether someone will or will not offend you. That is settled - someone will offend you. Your willingness to forgive is the issue! Will you decide to abide in the Kingdom of God? Will you receive the forgiveness of God that is worth two million three hundred and seventy thousand dollars? Will you live in the attitude of forgiveness because of the lavish forgiveness that has come to you? Will forgiveness constantly flow from you to every one who offends you? This is the life style of the Kingdom of God.

FORGIVENESS IS FACTUAL
Experiencing God's Forgiveness
Matthew 18:1-5

This is the source from which all forgiveness comes. It is the foundation of the whole matter. At the very outset of this chapter we established that there is **PLENTY OF FORGIVENESS.** In verses three, four and five, there is absolutely no condemnation in the voice of Christ. There is no sense of put down or scolding. To adequately understand this I must remind you of the experiences of the last few days. In chapter sixteen, verse twenty-one, Jesus explains the cross to His disciples. They rebel against this idea as expressed in their rebuke (16:22). The argument extends through six days (17:1). Jesus takes three disciples to the Mount of Transfiguration (17:1). It is here that Moses, Elijah, and the heavenly Father verify His teaching about the cross (17:3 - 5). On their way down from the mountain, Jesus speaks to the disciples again about the truth of the cross (17:12). In the valley, Jesus does a miracle the disciples are powerless to do (17:18). The disciples ask Him privately to explain their problem (17:19). Their defeat is traceable back to their rebuke of the new truth about the cross. After all of this intense training and teaching, the disciples have the nerve to ask Him, **"Who then is greatest in the Kingdom of Heaven?"** (18:1).

Did they sleep through all of the messages? They seem to have ignored the training of the last week. The very fact they would ask this question tells us they did not listen nor comprehend what Jesus has been teaching them. I would have yelled at those disciples. I would have scolded them until they would have considered leaving the group. But Jesus tenderly and lovingly tells the disciples to seat themselves, and He explains it all over. There is **plenty of forgiveness** in Jesus.

The message is true. No matter what you have done, there is **plenty of forgiveness** with Jesus. In the midst of all the stupid stunts you have pulled, there is **plenty of forgiveness** with Jesus. After all you have done, there is still **plenty of forgiveness** with Jesus. Although you have asked for forgiveness for that very same thing repeatedly, there is **plenty of forgiveness** with Jesus. This establishes the **PATTERN OF FORGIVENESS**. Over and over again Jesus has extended forgiveness to you. He has never altered this pattern a single time. He is the King of the Kingdom, and this is the foundation of it all.

Again, there is a **PROBLEM OF FORGIVENESS**. God does not have the problem; the problem is within us. **"Therefore whoever humbles himself as this little child is the greatest in the Kingdom of Heaven,"** (18:4). As we read this verse, there is one word that causes most of us trouble. It is not that it is hard to pronounce. It is a word that repulses us. The word *is humbles.* After you say it, you want to wash your mouth out with soap. We must see this word in the context of these verses if we are to know its true meaning. It is the opposite of the self-seeking of the disciples in verse one. Self-seeking is contrasted with the self-giving of a cross. Wanting position is contrasted with promoting others. Grabbing for ourselves is seen against the backdrop of giving to others. The only way to live in forgiveness is to come to the cross.

There is only one reason you cannot forgive others. Listen to your excuses. You say, "You don't know what they have done to me. You don't know how they have hurt me. My life will never be the same because of them!" Every statement is a self-centered statement. Your total focus is on yourself. It is because of self-centeredness that you cannot forgive. You must come to the cross.

There is only one reason you cannot receive God's forgiveness in your life. Again, listen to your excuses. "But you do not know the terrible things I have done. How could God forgive a terrible person like me? I know the depth of my heart and what I have done." The total focus of these comments is on yourself. You are self-centered. It is keeping you from receiving God's forgiveness.

What is the blockade that keeps you from forgiving yourself? It is self-centeredness. Here are the excuses, "Oh I believe God will forgive me, but I cannot forgive myself. I have to live with what I have done. The scars of sin in my life remind me of how terrible I have been." Do you see the number of times the word *I* is used? You are self-centered. It is keeping you from forgiving yourself. There is only one thing that keeps you from a total state of forgiveness. It is your self-centeredness. We, like the disciples, have failed to grasp the cross and its style. This is not a message about forgiveness, but it is a call to the cross. Will you lose your life?

"Dear Jesus! Tenderly call us back to the cross as you did your disciples. We must lose our lives. Bring us to death until forgiveness flows from us to our world. We give you the right to accomplish this in our lives. In Jesus' name we pray, Amen."

Matthew 18:1-5

Like a Child

"We have a desperate prayer request to make of You, dear Jesus. How much we want to receive You! We want You to be an intimate part of our lives. Please flow in and through us, making us like You are! We pray that you would convert us, change our direction, alter our minds, and uproot our heart structure. We make ourselves available for this purpose. In Jesus' name we pray, Amen."

It is very easy to get sidetracked in planning your life. There are many aspects of living in the Kingdom of God. One cannot concentrate on all of them. The minor issues often become major; we find we have been tricked. There is legalism on the far right and liberalism on the far left. Somewhere in the middle of all this, is the central thrust of Christianity, which demands our focus. That is why I keep coming back to the person of Jesus. It is in Christ that I find the major thrust of Christianity. With Jesus there are no tangents or dead ends. He brings me back to what really matters.

Jesus always did this with the disciples. ***"At that time. . . ."*** (18:1). The moment you see this phrase, you know that Matthew is going to make a connection between what has taken place and what will happen. ***"At that time"*** connects the events of chapter seventeen with those of chapter eighteen.

In the opening chapters of Matthew, Peter does not have a major role. He appears briefly in the closing chapters of Matthew. He denies Jesus three times before the rooster crows, and he appears at the resurrection scene with the other disciples. He is there, but he is not in the lime light. In the central section of the book, Peter is on the center stage. From chapters fourteen to nineteen, Matthew mentions his name constantly.

In chapter fourteen, Peter stepped out of the boat in the midst of a raging storm and walked on the water. It is true that he only walked a few steps, but it beats anything you have done lately. What a powerful act of faith! Jesus dramatically rescues him. In chapter fifteen, the big boys have come from Jerusalem to trap Jesus. They have chosen the big theological issue of unwashed hands. Jesus gives them a powerful answer in a parable. It is Peter who has the courage to approach Jesus and say, "I didn't get it!" Do you know how much material would be lacking in the New Testament if it had not been for Peter's admission? Jesus launches into an additional explanation concerning the inner heart as the source of life. I wonder what would happen in your church if you would admit to your pastor, "I didn't get it!" We shake hands and say causally, "It was a great sermon." If we would be bold enough to admit our lack of understanding as Peter did, maybe an additional explanation would turn our life around.

In chapter sixteen, Peter comes through in a great confession while the other disciples set silently. He states, **"You are the Christ, the Son of the Living God,"** (16:16). Peter's response amazed Jesus. It was Peter Jesus turned to and said, **"And I also say to you that you are Peter, and on this rock I will build My church, and the gates of Hades shall not prevail against it,"** (16:18). Jesus has given Peter a powerful position. He is a star in this chapter.

Jesus selects Peter as one of three disciples to experience the Mount of Transfiguration in chapter seventeen. He gets in on the heavenly conversation between Moses, Elijah, and Jesus. At the end of the chapter, Peter participates in the miracle that pays the temple tax. Peter is definitely in the limelight in this great chapter.

To tell you the truth, I am sick of hearing Peter's name. He thinks he is a big shot and is better than the rest of the disciples. Peter is always throwing his weight around. Everyone is supposed to follow him. He thinks he has a special position in the Kingdom of God. He feels he is number one, or greatest, in the Kingdom. But there are other disciples who operate powerfully. James and John experienced the Mount of Transfiguration. The other disciples have done as many miracles as Peter. Peter has nothing over the rest of us. He has had some very dark moments in his life. Shortly after his confession he rebuked Jesus, as if Jesus did not know what He was talking about. Jesus said what Peter was saying was coming from Satan (16:23). So Peter does not need to be so high and mighty. He missed the mark on the Mount of Transfiguration. When he interrupted the heavenly conversation, he placed Jesus on the same level with Elijah and Moses (17:4).

I wonder who will be greatest in the Kingdom of Heaven? When the shake down finally comes, who will be standing taller than all others? Who will get to be number one? Does this discussion sound familiar? You can hear it often in the local church. Rank, competition, and political power are so important to us. Who got the most votes? Who will get to be chairperson of the board? Perhaps this is not wrong, but it is the position we give to it. **"Who then is greatest in the kingdom of heaven?"** (18:1).

A remarkable thing about this whole setting is that at first glance it appears as if Jesus totally ignored their question. Does this question not have enough value to merit an answer? It appears that Jesus is addressing another question. "How do you get into the Kingdom of Heaven?" A deeper look into the material shows us that Jesus is answering their question in a most profound way. Does it not seem strange that He would speak to these twelve experienced disciples on how to enter the Kingdom? They have cast out demons and raised the dead. Surely Jesus does not need to tell them the beginning truths of the Kingdom. Could it be that the same power that brings you into the Kingdom is the power that keeps you there? There is no difference between entering and maintaining here.

THE CONVERSION OF CONCENTRATION
Matthew 18:3

Jesus said, **"Assuredly, I say to you, unless you are converted and become as little children you will by no means enter the kingdom of heaven,"** (18:3). After three years of teaching and ministry, Jesus brings the disciples back to the central issue of the Kingdom of

God. It is conversion. Jesus is not discussing a conversion from bad deeds to good deeds. He is deeply concerned about the conversion of their concentration. The wrong thing has their focus.

Did you notice what started this whole discussion? It was the **ASKING. "*At that time the disciples came to Jesus, saying, 'Who then is greatest in the kingdom of heaven?'*"** (18:1). A difficult thing to do is to get some one in a large group to ask a question. The reason this is so difficult is that you reveal yourself when you ask. Your question reveals your level of comprehension. You reveal your inward thinking. The question tells something of your priority structure. In a sense, it acts like a knife that literally opens you up. Your question exposes you! It is true with the disciples. They have revealed their concentration with the question concerning which one of them will be first in the Kingdom of Heaven. Their question exposes their motivation. It is very evident they have missed what Jesus has been telling them. They are going in the wrong direction and need a complete turn around. They need a conversion. They do not need this because they have been committing sinful, evil deeds. They have been serving the Kingdom for nearly three years through the means of miracles, preaching, and assisting Jesus. They have been ushers in Jesus' campaigns. They do not need a conversion from wrong deeds done, but oh how they desperately need a conversion in their concentration. Their focus is on the wrong thing.

Surely every one of us has faced this. Quickly our walk with Jesus shifts from right and wrong to concentration. To what are you going to give yourself? What is your burning passion? What tires you? What makes the hair stand up on the back of your neck? What causes your excitement or thrill? What is your love? Through their asking the disciples have revealed their focus. It is on themselves. Their driving passion is position and power for themselves. Selfish desire is the focus of each disciple. Repeatedly, Jesus has been talking to them about the cross and its style. But their focus is on themselves, and they have missed His message. They have not heeded the call to lose their lives. Their focus is on fulfilling their own agenda, building their own prestige, and remaining in their comfort zone. Conversion is their need. It is not a conversion from bad to good, but a conversion in their concentration. Their *asking* reveals their need.

There is an **ASSUMPTION** underlying their asking. *"At that time the disciples came to Jesus, saying, 'Who then is greatest in the kingdom of heaven?'"* (18:1). Can you sense that this question must have cut the heart of Jesus? Out of Peter's great confession Jesus leaped into the discussion of His cross. He would be a bleeding, suffering, dying Messiah. He was calling them to this style. They argued with Him for nearly an entire week as He tried to express the fundamental principle of the Kingdom of Heaven. In desperation He took three disciples to the Mount of Transfiguration for prayer. Surely a revelation from heaven would convince them of the cross and its style. Moses, Elijah and God, the Father, said that the heart of the Kingdom was a cross and its style. On their descent, the disciples asked about John the Baptist. Jesus instructed them that John had started a new style. It was the heart of the Kingdom. *"Likewise the Son of Man is also about to suffer at their hands,"* (17:12). When they arrived in the valley, Jesus did a miracle the disciples could not accomplish. Upon their inquiry He told them it was because they had not accepted the truth of His cross and its style. He again boldly stated the truth to them. *"The*

Son of Man is about to be betrayed into the hands of men, and they will kill Him, and the third day He will be raised up," (17:22-23).

Now after all of this focused training, how much did the disciples grasp? They have had a four-hour board meeting. They could not get beyond one issue on the agenda. They have come to Jesus demanding an answer. The Sunday School cannot continue until we settle this issue. Until we solve this problem, there will be no more tithing. Their question is, "Which one of us gets to be number one in the Kingdom of Heaven?" It is obvious they have not been listening. They have not lost their lives. The question violates the fundamental principle of the Kingdom, which is the cross.

Their question tells you that they assumed that one of them would get the position. And why not? After all, who does Jesus have except them? They are His called ones. They received His power to duplicate His miracles and ministry. Except for them, He has no one. Why should they not assume that one of them will fill the number one position?

Jesus was forceful in His answer. The issue is not which one of them will be number one in the Kingdom? The question is "will they even get into the Kingdom?" This must have shaken them to the core. They had assumed too much! How does this apply to us? A great saint of old stated, "We are not able to even reach the faults of the twelve disciples. We ask not who is greatest in the Kingdom of Heaven, but who is greatest in the Kingdom of Earth?" I have deep concerns about the assumptions we make as we come to church Sunday after Sunday. We keep a few acceptable standards of a church denomination and assume so much. This is not an attempt to cast doubt in your mind concerning your salvation. It is a call to realism.

Mary and Joseph traveled a day's journey, assuming that Jesus was in the company (Luke 2:43-44). Samson went out to do great feats of strength. He simply assumed the Lord was still with him (Judges 16:20). The disciples have walked with Jesus for nearly three years and assume that they are the leaders of the Kingdom. Yet Jesus said that the issue was not who would be number one, but would they even make it into the Kingdom.

Jesus brings the disciples back to the possible **ACCESS** of the Kingdom. *"Assuredly, I say to you, unless you are converted and become as little children, you will by no means enter the kingdom of heaven,"* (18:3). The message is that you do not have to miss it! Conversion can go beyond just good deeds and bad deeds. The cross will radically change the very heart focus. It is time to change deep within. You do not have to be like you are. It is a call to the **Conversion of Concentration.**

SINCERITY OF SORROW
Matthew 18:4

"Therefore whoever humbles himself as this little child is the greatest in the kingdom of heaven," (18:4). Jesus begins this statement with the word *therefore*. It means that what He tells us in verse four, He bases upon what He has already told us in verse three. He reveals to us in verse three the great need for a conversion of our concentration. But how will He accomplish the meeting of that need?

What steps are necessary to experience this transformation? In verse four He gives us the answer.

He begins with **REPENTANCE.** *"Therefore whoever humbles himself. . . ." (*18:4). Repentance means to change your mind. Divine actions must cause the conversion needed deep within. Repentance is a response to the call of God. Jesus called His disciples to the cross style, but they did not respond. They were not open to such a change.

The word *humbles* gives the thrust of this necessary repentance. We can only understand it when we see it in its context. He is not calling us to a wimpy, jellyfish life style. *Humbles* is the opposite of the attitude the disciples have been expressing. They have been fighting among themselves. *Humble themselves* would mean submitting to each other. They were seeking the position of power. They should have sought position of service. They were demanding their rights. They are to die to their rights and become usable. They were protecting themselves. They must come to the cross and live its style. Humbling themselves would mean the exact opposite of everything expressed in their question to Jesus, *"Who then is greatest in the kingdom of heaven?"* (18:1).

Would not this kind of change require a response or admission of wrong? It is difficult for people who are so right to admit they are wrong. There is a difference between being wrong and being bad. We can be so right we are wrong. People who have taught so many *right* Sunday School classes, testified so many *right* testimonies, and given so many *right* tithe checks, find it hard to get on their knees and say, "I have been wrong!" Perhaps our deed has not been wrong, but self-centeredness has filled the motive or attitude of the deed. Our focus is upon ourselves. We demand our rights as if we deserve them. We look out for our own interests. We play the political game of selfish positions. We must see it for what it is! "I have been wrong!" That is the proper response. It is repentance.

There is second part to the answer Jesus gives in verse four. He continues with **RELATING.** *"Therefore whoever humbles himself as this little child. . . ."* (18:4). It is in the act of repentance (*humbles himself*) that we become as a little child. We are to relate to Jesus (*the kingdom of heaven*) as a little child. I have heard many explanations of what this means when applied to our personal lives. Some explain that we must take on childlike qualities. Children are trusting; so I must be trusting. A child is naive; I must become less skeptical. I have to admit to you I have some difficulty with that interpretation. I have not seen very many children after whom I would like to pattern my life.

There is no question in my mind that Jesus is not referring here to the characteristics of a child, but to the status of a child. If you are to properly understand, you must place yourself into the setting of Jesus' day. A child in Jesus' culture was without status. He had absolutely no rights. He had no platform upon which to fight for himself. A Jewish father, needing some extra money, could sell his child into slavery. The child was an instrument, a thing he owned. He was in total control of his child. The child had no voice in the legal system except through his father. He was totally dependent upon the love and care of his father.

This is the style of Kingdom living. We are to repent of our self-seeking. We are to come with no demands or rights. We must place ourselves totally in the hands of Jesus, allowing Him to do to us as He pleases. We must relate to Him as a child and throw our lives away. We must give up all of our supposed rights. We must tear down our walls. We must come to the cross and die to ourselves. Have you ever come to Jesus like that? Have you ever literally lost yourself to Him? Have you allowed Him to strip you of everything except Himself?

Jesus has called self-seeking disciples to repentance. He has challenged them to relate to Him as a little child. The proper response is to **RELINQUISH.** *"Therefore whoever humbles himself as this little child is the greatest in the kingdom of heaven?"* (18:4). Jesus elevates to the position of greatness the person who has become like a child with no rights. But do you see the interesting paradox in that? If you die to your rights and receive the status of a child, you would not care about being greatest in the Kingdom. You would only crave relationship with your Father. Power and position are all a part of the self-seeking life of which you have repented. In other words, if you want to be great in the Kingdom of Heaven, you are not. If you do not care to be great, you have the heart of the Kingdom style and become the greatest.

Jesus has told us that the question is not *"Who then is greatest in the kingdom of heaven?"* (18:1) The real issue is "Will you even get into the Kingdom of Heaven?" The entrance into the Kingdom of God is the same as staying in the Kingdom of God. It requires a radical, deep conversion of your concentration (18:3). It is not a conversion from bad deeds to good deeds, but a conversion of self style to the cross style. You do not achieve this by your discipline or skill. It is the action of a Divine God within your life because you have lost yourself. You must respond to His moving upon your life by repentance, *humbles himself,*

(18:4). The concentration of the cross happens when you release your self focus. You respond by relating as a child who has no status. There is no bargaining or demanding. It is surrendering and yielding.

RECEPTION OF THE REDEEMER
Matthew 18:5

"And whoever receives one little child like this in My name receives Me," (18:5). This is not some kind of mind game we are playing. This is not just an adjustment in my philosophy of life or an addition to my theological understanding. We are not discussing a correction in your style of living. This whole change in your focus is not a step in the direction of positive thinking. We are speaking of **RECEIVING CHRIST.**

The grammar structure of verse five is very significant. In the original language of the Bible, Matthew delays the reference to the child until after the verb. Thus, the emphasis in the verse is upon receiving Christ or the last phrase that says, *receives me.* In our translation it appears the emphasis is upon our response to the child, but Matthew begins in his statement with receiving Christ. Thus, the dominate idea of the verse is placed upon receiving Christ.

What a powerful mystery! We are referring to the actual person of Jesus Christ coming to live in the depths of the inner soul. The reality of Christ is flooding the whole being of man, until the Spirit of Christ fills the man. Christ cleanses the man from the concentration upon himself, and the presence of Christ now consumes the man. It is impossible to get away from this message. This is not a call to receive the church - please receive Him! We are not pleading for you to do certain good deeds - please receive Him! We are not suggesting you turn over a new leaf or reform - please receive Him! The actual presence of the person of God makes entrance into the depths of your soul. It is the call of the cross. The question of this moment is "Do you have the throbbing, passionate, internal presence of God within your being?"

There is a strange twist in verse five. It has to do with **RECEIVING A CHILD.** *"And whoever receives one little child like this in My name receives Me,"* (18:5). Matthew ties the fact of receiving Christ to receiving a child, or others. It is presented to us so that you realize it is the test of whether you have received Christ. We are always asking, "How can I know for sure have totally surrendered to Christ?" What is the sign of the fullness of the Holy Spirit? Is it a special language I speak, or a feeling I have? How can I know when I am really His? That is answered in this verse! "Receiving a child" is the test contained in verse four.

We might respond, "Of course, I love children. This is no problem for me." You need to understand clearly to what Jesus is referring. As this discourse in chapter eighteen unfolds, you realize Jesus clarifies the concept of the word *child.* At the beginning of the discourse He has called a child to sit on His lap. The child becomes the focus of everyone's attention. Jesus then expands the concept to the phrase *little ones,* (18:6, 10, 14). He then begins to speak of *your brother,* (18:15). Clearly Jesus is not just referring to a child in relation to age. He is speaking about anyone who is less than you, one who is not on your level, an individual who does not match your abilities. It is the individual who does not have your educational level and knowledge. The test is found in how you treat the one who does not dress as well as you, does not drive your kind of car, does not live in your part of town, or does not smell like you smell.

Why is this the test? There is only one way you can treat these kinds of people as equals. We want a mutual admiration society. We establish our relationships with people who can help us. We fellowship and share with people like us. I fix your plumbing, and you do my electrical work. You help me with contacts, and I provide a certain amount of prestige for you. But there are people who have nothing to offer us? There is no way they can benefit us. Why would we want to be friends with them? The only way we can have relationship with them is to lose our lives. There can be no self-seeking here. This is the test.

Jesus is very specific in His presentation of this truth. *"And whoever receives one little child. . . ."* (18:5). Jesus is pointing only to one. The masses of people often move my heart and bring tears to my eyes. There are hundreds of starving people in the world. There are multitudes of homeless people of the streets. That moves me to compassion. But it is the poor, worthless, bum who lives next door to me that I cannot stand! His junk cars clutter our neighborhood. He is always begging food from me. I have no problem with the hypocrites in your church. It is the one who sets next to me at the board meeting that I cannot tolerate. The test is not the masses of people; it is the one who bugs you, bothers you, rubs you raw. You just cannot stand to be around him.

There is another factor in this verse to consider. We are to **RECEIVE IN HIS NAME.** *"And whoever receives one little child like this in My name receives me,"* (18:5). His name bespeaks His person, which is His style. You are to receive this *little one* who bothers you, like Jesus would receive him. It is a New Testament principle. Jesus has attached Himself to my fellow person. If I want to receive Jesus, I must receive my fellow person. If I want to do something for Christ, I must do it for my fellow person. What I do for my fellow person, I do for Jesus. It is a fundamental in the Kingdom of God. Indeed, the question is not **"Who then is greatest in the kingdom of heaven?"** (18:1). The question is, "Will you and I even get into the Kingdom of Heaven?"

"Jesus, we have no ground to walk on that makes us secure. We have no reason to be cocky. We find nothing we have done gives us an assurance that we might get to be greatest in the Kingdom of Heaven. We come back to the fundamental of conversion. Would you change us in our concentration? We have changed many outward activities, but would you change us inwardly. Save us from ourselves! In Your name, we pray. Amen."

Matthew 18:6-9

Being a Temptation

Personal struggles are common in life. None of us are exempt. In the early days of my Christian experience, I struggled with the linkage of desire, temptation and sin. The heart of the confusion seemed to settle in the idea that temptation was sin itself. If I were really a Christian, I would not have evil desires. I thought that the very presence of the temptation producing desire was the reality of sin. Where there is no desire, there is no temptation. Yet, the basis of my temptation came through my normal body drives. If I were truly what God wanted me to be, evil desires would be gone.

Then I read, **"For in that He Himself has suffered, being tempted, He is able to aid those who are tempted,"** (Hebrews 2:18). This passage refers to Jesus. Since Satan could tempt Jesus it obviously means that Jesus also had desires. Yet, He was without sin. The conclusion then is that desire and temptation are not sin. Sin happens in the yielding to desire and temptation. With this revelation, I experienced new victory in my life.

Later I came to Matthew chapter eighteen. Jesus is speaking to His disciples on the subject of temptation. I dismissed this passage (18:6-9), because I had already settled the issue of temptation in my life. However, the Lord kept probing me with this subject. There is another view of the subject, one I may have missed. In this passage He is not dealing with how the enemy is tempting me. He is dealing with how I am being a temptation. Could it be that Satan is using me as a temptation in the lives of others?

In verses six through nine of this chapter, Jesus is presenting a proposition. Being tempted, or being a temptation, is undesirable. These verses are severe. Jesus is very forceful in this passage. There is fire burning in His eyes. The verses are spoken in love and kindness, but with the sense that He means every word He is saying. I really thought I was a cut above this kind of discussion. I even managed to laugh when the thought was first presented. "You think I am being a temptation to someone? How absurd!" was my reply. I could point out many people who probably could benefit from this message, but this simply did not apply to me. But Jesus kept pressing. Could we be open to His message? Let us begin our investigation.

ENTRAPMENT FROM WHOMEVER
Matthew 18:6

"But whoever causes one of these little ones who believe in Me to sin, it would be better for him if a millstone were hung around his neck, and he were drowned in the depth of the sea," (18:6). I wish I could have been there when Jesus was preaching this great verse to the multitudes. But He did not preach this to the

multitudes. I could see Jesus gather the liquor industry together and put His bony finger in their faces. I do not doubt that He would yell at them about how they are entrapping little ones for the sake of their own materialistic gain. But He is not preaching this to that group. How about the drug pushers? Jesus could go after them with great fierceness. He would warn them about entrapping little ones and ruining their lives for personal, selfish gains. But Jesus was not speaking to that group in this verse.

Jesus addressed this verse to twelve disciples. They represent the local church membership. He is having a closed meeting with the official board. These are not outsiders, but insiders. They have received power from Jesus. They have duplicated the miracles of Jesus regularly. They have preached, witnessed, and followed. These are the best Jesus has! Jesus is speaking to us! It becomes clear when you see verse six in its context. Jesus is saying that you and I are the ones who have the highest potential for tempting *little ones*. This is a very severe statement.

Considering this overwhelming responsibility, it would be good for us to look at the **POSITION WE ARE IN**. Jesus focuses our position in the word *offend* or *offense*. In verse six, as quoted above, this word is translated *causes. . . . to sin.*

The word *offend* has great strength. This word has degrees of severity. It can mean a light, superficial, involuntary offense. It can also mean to plan, set a trap, on purpose offense. Matthew labels both extremes with this word. What is the tone in Jesus' voice as He speaks this word? As we come to this passage, we must carefully discover how Jesus uses the word. This is found in the context or flow of the passage. The author uses this word once in verse six, and three times in verse seven. He uses it once in verse eight and once in verse nine. This word is the key to understanding the entire passage. Anytime the Scriptures repeat a word, you need to pay special attention to it. There is a reason for the repetition. Matthew is giving the word great strength by the constant use of it.

Also, in the larger context of this passage, we find an illustration of this word. In chapter sixteen Peter gave his great confession. His statement was, **"*You are the Christ, the Son of the living God,*"** (16:16). This is a high moment for Peter and the other disciples. Jesus begins to explain the content of His Messiahship. He is going to a cross. It will be a culmination of the cross style that He has been involved in from the beginning. He will establish the path upon which everyone will walk in the Kingdom of Heaven. Peter rises in self-centered carnality and rebukes Jesus (16:22). This is not the kind of Messiah he wants. Jesus turns to Peter and says, **"*Get behind me, Satan! You are an OFFENSE to Me, for you are not mindful of the things of God, but the things of men,*"** (16:23). Peter slips into his self-centered, carnal focus and reacts out of the things of men. His self-centered carnality becomes a platform for Satan to stand upon and accomplish his desires. Satan sets a trap for Jesus that could hinder the accomplishment of the cross. The enemy uses Peter to set that trap.

There is a second illustration given to us of this word. It is found at the end of chapter seventeen. The disciples have come with Jesus to Capernaum. The one who collects the temple tax comes to Peter and asks him, **"*Does your Teacher not pay the temple tax?*"** (17:24). Again Peter's self-centered carnality comes to the surface. He rises and rebukes this individual. He returns to the house where Jesus is staying.

Peter thinks He has done a great thing. Jesus anticipates him and meets him at the front door. He takes Peter outback to the woodshed. Jesus asks him some key questions which bring revelation to Peter. Then Jesus states, **"Nevertheless, lest we OFFEND them, go to the sea, cast in a hook, and take the fish that comes up first. And when you have opened its mouth you will find a piece of money; take that and give it to them for Me and you,"** (17:27). Jesus was saying that He did not have to pay the temple tax, but He would pay it now, rather than offend them. Jesus often spoke strongly to Pharisees and scribes. How is what Peter did any worse than what Jesus did? The difference lies in the source. Jesus never spoke out of self-centered carnality. Peter was consistently speaking from that base. This is the base that gives Satan a foot hold in the life to manipulate the individual, creating the trap he wants. This is a repeat of Peter's actions in chapter sixteen.

Now we come to Matthew chapter eighteen. The disciples have come demanding from Jesus an answer to the question, **"Who then is greatest in the kingdom of heaven?"** (18:1). Jesus gives the answer in the action of a child coming to sit upon His lap (18: 2). He calls the disciples to humble themselves and become as this little child (18: 4). They need a conversion in the concentration or focus of their lives (18:3). The conversion of their focus will result in them receiving Jesus, and thus, receiving a little child (18: 5).

The words of verses six through nine are a contrast to what Jesus has just said. Jesus has spoken of receiving a little child. Now he speaks of the opposite, which is offending a little child. A little child is not just referring to age, but to anyone less than you are. How are you to receive a little child? You should receive one less than you are just as you would receive Jesus. Can you imagine the sudden physical appearance of Jesus? How would you receive Him? I would get on my knees and bow before Him. He is the sovereign Lord of life! I would not manipulate Him or be thinking of how I could use Him. He, Who knows all, has just arrived. I would humble myself. This is exactly how Jesus is instructing us to treat the little ones. If I rise in self-centeredness to dominate and control the little ones, or talk down to them, or have a motive that wants to use them, then I have caused an offense to entrap them.

The literal word *offend* in the New Testament has a clear meaning. It is "a stick in a death trap." Picture a small cage with wire all around it. We are not discussing the wire or the post in the corner that gives shape to the cage. The trap is not the piece of meat or bait placed in the cage. Our subject of discussion is not the entrance into the cage or the door swinging down from above. There is a stick that holds the door in place. That is the death trap! When the animal comes into the cage to get the bait , he hits the stick. The door slams shut and traps him. The word *offend* refers to that stick. It is the trigger. It is the spring or the lever that holds everything in place. That is what makes the cage a trap.

Jesus is saying that by lording it over little ones we become this stick in the death trap. Perhaps we would not intentionally hurt anyone, but our self-centeredness has become Satan's foothold. Our self-centeredness is a handle for him to grab. You may not even be aware of it. In the board meeting you find yourself disagreeing. It is quite acceptable to disagree. The problem comes when we disagree from a self-centered motive. It is then that the death trap is set into motion. One way to know if you are disagreeing out of a self-centered motive is to notice the kind of things you disagree about. Is it a major or a minor issue? A minor issue is that which will not matter one hundred years from this moment. This includes all material things like the color of the carpet or the location of the communion table. The only things worth yelling about are eternal issues that will matter forever. When out of self-centered carnality we find ourselves yelling about the wrong things, we create a death trap to allure little ones. They simply do not know better. It is a foothold of Satan to destroy them.

Jesus is warning self-centered disciples. They are the ones whom Satan can use in such a manner. We must heed His warning for this is the position we are in.

Verse six give us the **PUNISHMENT WE WILL RECEIVE.** *"But whoever causes one of these little ones who believe in Me to sin, it would be better for him if a millstone were hung around his neck, and he were drowned in the depth of the sea,"* (18:6). The language of this verse is very specific. This is not a small hand held grind stone that a lady would have in her kitchen. The word is *millstone*. This refers to the huge millstone in the center of town. The bottom stone is stationary and the top stone can rotate. Jesus is referring to the top stone. It weighs several tons. It takes two oxen just to move it. Jesus' instructions include the use of this millstone. It is so big and heavy we will need a hundred men to help us. Tie one end of a rope around your neck and tie other end of the rope to the millstone. Do not go down to the edge of the sea where the water is shallow, but you are to go into the deepest part of the sea. Now jump out of the boat with this huge millstone around your neck. The results of this are obvious.

Jesus' words are specific, but notice carefully, this is not the punishment you will receive. If you offend a little one, your punishment will be much worse. Jesus says that you should avoid offending a little one by using the millstone to drown yourself in the depths of the sea. If you recognize self-centeredness within you, think carefully about this solution. It will be better in the coming judgment if you jump into the sea now with the millstone around your neck, rather than offend a little one. This is very severe. This issue has Jesus' determination! Offending a little one will bring drastic results.

This helps us to understand the **PERSUASION WE MUST GRASP.** The conclusion of verse six is obvious. We must not offend a little one. We must protect the little ones at all costs. We must continually guard against becoming a stick in the death trap. The greatest cause of offending is self-centered carnality. This is why Jesus is so specific with the disciples. The disciples plainly display their self-centeredness as they argue over who will be number one (18:1). It is our carnality that helps to damn the world. It is our self-centeredness that establishes the trap that allures little ones. We cannot tolerate one small speck of self-centered carnality, or even the slightest hint of it. We must come to grips with any expressions of self-centeredness. Looking through the eyes of Jesus, we must sweep the house carefully to discover any hint of its presence. It is a death trap.

Peter's leadership is interesting in the expression of self-centeredness. If he were an offense to Jesus through this carnality (16:23), what do you suppose he was to the other disciples. Judas betrayed Christ. Does Peter's self-centered leadership have any responsibility in the act of Judas' betrayal? If Peter would have surrendered to the cross style and become the flow of the movement of God to his fellow disciples, what would have been the end result? Jesus and Peter, linking arms to display and teach the cross style, could have made the difference. It might have made a difference in the life of the betrayer.

A man kneels at the altar of prayer and confesses change in his life through Jesus Christ. We all hang back and look at him. We wonder how long it will last. In three weeks we hear the news that he has fallen by the wayside. It does not surprise us. What would have happened if we had not stood back in our self-centeredness? Could we have made the difference if we had wrapped the loving arms of Jesus around him? If we had saturated him with prayer instead of criticism and skepticism, could Jesus have used us to conserve his birth in the Kingdom?

INDUCEMENT FROM THE WORLD
Matthew 18:7

"Woe to the world because of offenses! For offenses must come, but woe to that man by whom the offense comes!" (18:7). I am afraid we are too casual about these verses. I am not sure we have comprehended the absolute severity of the situation! Because of that, let us analyze **THE POSITION WE ARE IN.** Jesus says that when you offend a little one you have become a part of the world. When you become a stick in the death trap and allure a little one, you cease to be a part of the church and become the world.

We all understand that temptation is inevitable in everyone's life, including the little ones. There is no way to protect them from all the temptations of Satan. However, the issue of this verse is that you and I do not have to participate in it. The significance of this concept roots itself in the theology of the Jews. If a Jew sinned, he could go to the temple and make adequate sacrifice for that sin. Then he could experience forgiveness. However, if a Jew caused his brother to sin, he crossed into the severe danger zone. What could he do about his brother's sin? He does not have the power to stop him from sinning, nor can he ask forgiveness for his brother's sin. His brother may teach another to sin, and that one teaches another, and that one teaches another. Who knows where it will end? The responsibility falls back upon the original person who caused his brother to sin. This is the picture Jesus is describing. According to Jesus, you and I can participate in this.

How severe is this participation? The Scriptures explain this to us as we examine the **PUNISHMENT WE SHALL RECEIVE.** Look carefully at the beginning of verse seven. The first word is *Woe*! As He continues in the verse, He uses this word *Woe* again. This is a double *Woe* verse! In chapter eleven Jesus gives three woes to the three major cities of Chorazin, Bethsaida, and Capernaum (11:21-24). Jesus did most of His mighty works in these three cities. His purpose was to form an evangelistic base from these three cities. From there He would launch the winning of the entire world. However, these three cities had no time for the miracles of another budding Messiah. God walked on their streets, and they treated Him as nothing. Jesus' answer to that was *Woe*! He states, *"But I say to you that it shall be more tolerable for the land of Sodom in the day of judgment than for you"* (11:24).

The literal definition for the word *Woe* is "you are damned." Jesus starts verse seven with, *"Woe to the world. . . ."* This is a general statement to all who are participating in the worldly activity of damning little ones. However, as He continues on in the verse, He states, *". . ., but woe to that man. . . ."* This statement points to the individual. We cannot hide in the group of those who are guilty. We are selected to stand responsible for what has happened through us. This brings us to the conclusion of the **PERSUASION WE MUST GRASP.** It is an overwhelming warning. We cannot afford one ounce of self-centered carnality. We cannot risk having our own way. In honesty, we must face not just the deed done with our hands, but the very attitudes of our hearts. Jesus must expose the depravity of the inward mind in us. We must open the door for the search light of Jesus to engulf us. He must expose what we are inside. There can be no more cover up. It is the call of Christ.

Did you notice at the end of verse seven that the **woe** addresses one individual who only did one offense? **" . . . *but woe to that man by whom the offense comes!"*** (18:7). This relates us back to the beginning of verse six where He is speaking about one little one. ***"But whoever causes one of these little ones who believe in Me to sin. . . ."*** (18:6). Jesus is discussing one offense against one little one. In casualness we say, "Well, he wasn't that important anyway." Jesus tone says this is a lie right out of the pit of hell itself. There is no little one who is not important. "Sometimes you have to sacrifice the one person for the sake of the many people," we say. This was never the concept of a sovereign God who knows the very number of hairs on the head of that little one. You need to discuss this issue with Jesus who came specifically to die for that little one. We cannot risk offending even one little one.

It is a call to total honesty in total surrender. We must seek His cleansing as we never have before. We must not rest until every area of our life is under His sovereign control. We cannot tolerate pride in any form. We must die to ourselves. The cross and its style must dominate us completely. We cannot tolerate division, quarreling, bitterness, or hatred. We must deal with it directly. This brings us to the last emphasis in this section.

ENTICEMENT FROM WITHIN
Matthew 18:8-9

"And if your hand or foot causes you to sin, cut it off and cast it from you. It is better for you to enter into life lame or maimed, rather than having two hands or two feet, to be cast into the everlasting fire. And if your eye causes you to sin, pluck it out and cast it from you. It is better for you to enter into life with one eye, rather than having two eyes, to be cast into hell fire" (18:8-9). These powerful verses are a summary of verses six and seven. There is a climax to what He is saying. Matthew has quoted these verses one other time in his book. Jesus spoke these words in The Sermon on the Mount (5:29-30). Anytime the Bible states something twice, you know it is very important.

The tone or context of this statement in The Sermon on the Mount is extremely different from the tone in this private discussion between Jesus and His disciples. In His sermon the context is sexual lust. The focus is on the person and his victory over his personal body. But in this private discourse, Jesus is using language that He only uses concerning the Church. It is a group of disciples who are fighting among themselves for position and power. He points to the Body of Christ, the Church. He is calling us to eliminate self-centered carnality within the Body of Christ, the Church.

This is definitely not a call for a "witch hunt." It is a call to not tolerate self-centered carnality within the heart of the church. Far too often we have allowed individuals that we know are carnal to have leadership roles in the church. The carnal pride and desire to control motivate these people to serve. Since they are so willing, we do not have to bother with the responsibility. We can sit back and criticize, and we become as self-centered as they are. We should develop our spiritual senses enough that we can spot the expression of self-centered carnality. We must not vote this kind of person into leadership. In the leadership of the church, we cannot tolerate self-centered carnality. Let us pray and weep before God until there is a revival and cleansing at the heart of the church.

It is necessary to see these verses because of the **POSITION WE ARE IN.** It is one thing for temptation to come from whomever (18:6); it is another thing for temptation to come from the world (18:7). However, it is very different for temptation to come from within the Body. I expect self-centeredness to fill the world, but not the Body of Christ. I expect there to be hypocrites at the local bar, but not at the board meeting. Political manipulation, behind the scene adjusting, and deception in the world political system does not surprise me. I am shocked when it happens in the Church. I am not hurt when the world commits adultery; it is the way of sin. But to find self-centeredness in the Church causes me great pain. Jesus is telling us that we must not tolerate it. An unredeemed world may go on lying, but we cannot do it. A brother within the Church gives expression to self-centered carnality and we cover it by saying, "That is just the way he is." The heat of the Spirit of God should be so hot within the Body that he would find himself daily pressured in his carnal condition. We must weep and pray until the cleansing comes. We cannot tolerate lukewarmness. That lukewarmness must tear up our spirits until it drives us to the cross. The position we are in according to these verses is one of great responsibility.

The severity increases when we see the **PUNISHMENT WE SHALL RECEIVE**. Jesus climaxes verse eight with the words *everlasting fire.* He continues in verse nine with the words *"hell fire."* Matthew has used the Greek word so often that you are familiar with it. It is "Gehenna." This was an actual valley located outside Jerusalem. It was a cursed valley because of the activities that had taken place within it. Evil Jews had offered their children as blood sacrifices to pagan gods. It was a defiled valley; it was off limits to the Jews. The city of Jerusalem decided to use it as a garbage dump. The people of Jerusalem dumped all of their refuge into this valley and burned it. At one point Rome had crucified so many people in Jerusalem they could not bury them all, so they threw them into this valley. They burned these bodies. For days there was the stench of burning flesh. When Jesus wanted to talk about hell, He used this valley as an illustration. This elevates the idea from just a philosophy or theology to a reality. This is not just a scare tactic, but a reality of life.

The thrust of what Jesus is saying to us comes in the **PERSUASION WE MUST GRASP.** Can you see Jesus pointing a finger to this valley as He refers to the punishment we shall receive? Terrible sinners deserve this kind of treatment. After all *"the wages of sin is death"* (Romans 6:23). The prostitutes, drug pushers, and the liquor traffic deserve death in the valley of fire. BUT, remember that Jesus is not addressing these kinds of people. He is speaking to twelve disciples who are self-centered. They have duplicated the miracles of Jesus and helped Him in His ministry. They are the ushers. They are the ones He is counting on to carry on the Kingdom of God. They never miss Sunday morning or Sunday evening services at the synagogue.

Often after an evening service someone will approach me with the idea that they never hear preachers talk about hell. They are concerned for the young people whom we need to warn about the terribleness of hell. They urge me to confront the sinner with the fact of hell. I am deeply concerned about preaching the truth. If God wants me to preach upon the subject of hell, I am willing to do just that.

It was out of this concern I decided to commit myself to preach on hell as Jesus did. This meant that I would have to study the Gospel accounts where Jesus mentions the word *hell.* My first stop was at a sycamore tree (Luke 19:4). If there was ever an occasion when a red-hot sermon on the subject of hell was needed, it was at this tree. A short man by the name of Zacchaeus was sitting in this tree. He had climbed up the tree to get a look at Jesus who was passing by that way with a crowd. He was the worst cheater society could produce. I could just imagine Jesus stopping under that tree and looking Zacchaeus in the face. He would no doubt shake a bony finger at him and warn him about the fires of hell. Yet, to my amazement, Jesus instructed Zacchaeus to come down, for He was going to stay at his house. Jesus never mentioned the subject of hell. It surprised me.

There was a confrontation between Jesus, the Scribes and Pharisees, and a woman caught in the act of adultery (John 8:3). I saw an ideal place for a blistering sermon on hell. This woman was so bad even the law of Moses commanded that they could stone her to death. But

Jesus said things like, **"*He who is without sin among you, let him throw a stone at her first*"** (John 8:7). When the men had all departed He turned to this wicked woman and said, **"*Neither do I condemn you; go and sin no more*"** (John 8:11). There was no mention of the subject of hell. It was such a good opportunity to warn her.

I continued to a tax collector's table set up in the middle of the block (Matthew 9:9). There were weeds growing up everywhere because no one would go down that side of the street. Jesus is going right over to that wicked cheater. Surely we will see Him give this man a strong sermon on hell. But to my amazement He simply said, **"*Follow Me*"** (9:9). There was no warning or condemnation.

It seemed like every place I went where I thought there would be a good opportunity for Jesus to preach on hell, He never mentioned the subject. I saw this was not going to be as easy as I had thought. I got out my concordance. It became clear when Jesus preached about hell. It was always to self-centered, carnal, religious people. Jesus never mentioned hell to the street people, the multitudes, or the wicked sinners of the world. He was constantly talking about hell to the religious leaders and the self-centered disciples, who wanted to be number one in the Kingdom. What is the conclusion of this fact? The issue of self-centered carnality is serious. Carnality is death; it is enmity against God. We cannot afford one drop of it in our lives. We must go on a search. We must look in every closet, under every carpet, and in every cupboard. We can neither tolerate nor excuse it in our lives. The slightest hint of it in our lives or in the church must send us to our knees, weeping our way through to God in victory. It is our carnality, our pride, our self-centeredness, our self-manipulation, our lukewarmness that causes us to put the stick in the death trap that destroys the little ones.

"Jesus, I am not sure how You delivered this message to Your disciples. Perhaps You were yelling in intensity before You were through. You have confronted us with the same message. Please strike deep into our hearts with the truth of Your Word. We will be obedient. In Jesus' name I pray, Amen."

Matthew 18:10-14

As God Sees

"Our great desire, Jesus, is to align our heart with Yours. We want to concentrate on what You concentrate on, be interested in what You are interested in, give ourselves to what You give Yourself. Would You show us Your heart? We will respond! In Your name we pray, Amen."

I grew up with a statement made of a saint of old. I am not sure of the exactness of the quotation or where the source can be found. It goes like this, "If a man does his merchandise and his recreation, cheerfully, promptly, readily, speedily, and the works of religion slowly, flatly, without appetite and his spirit moves like Pharaoh's chariots when the wheels are off, it is a sign his heart is not right with God, but he cleaves too much to this world."

This statement sends me to the floor. I must ask myself if I serve Jesus like I play ball. Am I as excited about Jesus as I am the fishing trip? In less than thirty minutes, I am to meet a client in my office. We will sign papers that will net me several thousand dollars in profit. As I leave the front door of my house, I notice a flat tire on my car. Do I cancel the appointment? Hardly! I call a taxi, get my jogging shoes, or hitchhike, but I am going to the office. Is that the way I go to church Sunday morning? As I am on the way to my car, company pulls into the driveway. How can I keep the appointment and make the large profit when company has arrived? That is not going to stop me. I simply turn the house over to them and race to the office. Is that the way I come to church Sunday evening?

The great thrust of the above statements is it not centered on deeds, duty, obligation, or standards. Their center is the internal concentration of the heart. It deals with what turns you on! What races your engine? What brings you to the peak of excitement? This is the subject Jesus emphasizes in almost all of chapter eighteen. There is a great contrast between the disciples' concentration and the Father's concentration.

Jesus begins His lesson with a call to a radical conversion experience (18:1-5). It is not a conversion from evil or bad. This call is to disciples who have been faithful to minister under the direction of Jesus. They left all to follow Him. However, the conversion needed is in the area of their concentration. They need to make an about face in the area of focus. It is our personal need, also. When the major issue does not possess us, we will dabble in the minor issue. The minor issues soon become major with us. We find our entire lives consumed with things that do not matter, thus, we have missed it! When we are not possessed with the supreme task, the unimportant tasks soon dominate our lives.

The unimportant become the important for us. It is a waste of life to focus on what does not matter.

An inevitable truth is that we will concentrate on something. No longer can we say, "I do not have time to do what the Lord wants." It is not that you and I do not have time, but we have squandered our time on unimportant matters. Confronted by the supreme, we find ourselves wasted and wanting. We seem to have time and resources for what we really want to do. It is a matter of internal priority and concentration.

Jesus is definitely confronting the disciples (and us) with a major contrast. The foremost question on the minds of the disciples is, ***"Who then is greatest in the Kingdom of heaven?"*** (18:1). Their concentration is on themselves. Jesus gives a vivid picture of the Father's concentration. He says, ***"Even so it is not the will of your Father who is in heaven that one of these little ones should perish,"*** (18:14). The supreme concentration of the Father is on rescuing the little ones - others. The great concentration of the disciples is on positions for themselves - self-centered.

It was a major conference of The Salvation Army. The leaders and delegates numbered into the thousands. There was high expectation on hearing their beloved leader, General Booth, speak to them during this conference. Many believed that due to his health this might be the last time they would hear from him. They assembled in the great hall, only to be disappointed. The General's ill health prevented him from making the trip. Those in charge requested that General Booth send a message to the followers who were anxious for leadership. It came by way of telegram. A man made his way to the platform. His hands were shaking. Through trembling lips he read this final message from General Booth. It said, "Others, others, others!"

This may be the supreme test of Christianity. It is not how often we come to church, but how much do we spill our lives out for others. What if we were to take all of the rules that the evangelical church imposes on its people and bring them together in one summary? Should it not be - others, others, others? The driving passion of Christianity is the opposite of self-centeredness. It is - others, others, others!

E. Stanley Jones, in one of his writings, tells of an opportunity he had to speak in the chapel of a mental institution. This facility was for ladies only. He took a tour of the facility. The sewing equipment available to them amazed him. Most of the women had great skill in making lovely garments. At the close of his message, he turned to that great crowd saying "I have brought many boxes of garments that need repair. Each garment has instructions attached to it. I want to ask each of you to come and get one garment, repair it, and place it back in the box. I will take them to the mission field for the poor and needy." When he finished his appeal, he stood back anticipating that most of them would begin to come. To his surprise, not one lady moved forward. No one sewed a stitch. He turned to the head of the institution with the obvious question, "Why?" The reply was, "Oh, you do not understand, Dr. Jones! You do not understand why they are here. If they could do something for someone else, they would not be in this place."

Could it be to the degree we are self-centered, to that degree we are insane? Could the great insanity of this century be our preoccupation with ourselves? Self-centeredness is absolute destruction. This is why we center our attention on the holiness message. It is a call for radical change in the focus area of our lives. Here is the deep need of this hour. We have focused on ourselves and only God can change this!

Jesus points out what a proper focus should be. The Father's heart shows it. Jesus calls us to concentrate as the Father concentrates. What are the elements of the Father's concentration?

THE FATHER'S ATTENTION
Matthew 18:10

"Take heed that you do not despise one of these little ones, for I say to you that in heaven their angels always see the face of My Father who is in heaven," (18:10).

As a child I would listen closely when my mother called my name. I gave close attention to the tone of her voice, and to what parts of my name she used. When she used my whole name, I knew I needed to act immediately. Jesus is doing the equivalent to using your whole name in this passage. It is found in the statement *"for I say to you."* A literal translation of that phrase would be "for I declare to you with all of the authority at My command." He reaches back into His oneness with the Trinity. He gathers all of His creative power, which brought the worlds into existence, and grabs the future moment of the redemptive power of the cross. Pulling all of this together, He uses it as a basis to speak to the disciples. This is severe; He means every word He is speaking.

What does He have to say to us? First, we must see **THE SOVEREIGN PERSON.** Jesus states, *". . . for I say to you that in heaven their angels always see the face of My Father who is in heaven."* (18:10). The one we face is *My Father.* He is the Sovereign

Person. Jesus is claiming intimate connection to the sovereign God, Who is *My Father.* He is in full agreement with all that is taking place in the heart of God. All that God thinks is what Jesus thinks. What spills forth from the heart of God, spills forth from the heart of Jesus. What He focuses on is what Jesus focuses on. They are in total agreement. Jesus' heart aligns with the heart of the Father, and they are beating the same.

The significance of this is found in chapter seventeen when the Father descends on the Mount of Transfiguration (17:5). It is a powerful moment as the Father begins to speak. *"This is My beloved Son, in whom I am well pleased. Hear Him!"* (17:5). The Father is claiming attachment to the Son. What is taking place in the heart of the Son is taking place in the Father. What the Son is thinking is what the Father is thinking. The Son's concentration is also the Father's concentration. They are one. They have linked themselves together. When you have seen one, you have seen the other.

Jesus added the phrase *"who is in heaven,"* (verse 10). This underscores the sovereignty of the Father. The Father, Who is in heaven, and the Son, Who is on the earth, are in complete harmony. They flow one to the other in great spiritual linkage. They are together in their concentration.

What is this Sovereign Person like? He has a **SERVANT PATTERN.** Look closely again at the statement of Jesus. *". . . in heaven their angels always see the face of My Father. . . ."* (18:10). This statement means that the sovereign, Person of God, has placed Himself at the disposal of all the needs, concerns, and hurts of the little ones. The sovereign, Person of God, has given His entire attention to the cries of the little ones.

Do not come to verse ten in an attempt to prove an angelic hierarchy. If you do that, you have missed the entire point of the passage. You have detoured to the minor aspect of what He is telling us, or even into what He is not telling us at all. The impact of the verse is not to tell us that everyone who is born has an assigned angel who hovers around them. The impact of this verse is to show us the extreme concentration of God upon the little ones. They have His full attention; His heart beats for others.

No doubt, when Jesus spoke these words, He was thinking of the Eastern court system that was a part of the culture of His day. There was the large public court room. Here the King ruled over the many cases that needed his judgments. However, off the inner halls of the King's palace there was a private, smaller court room. This was the meeting room of the King and his most trusted counselors. Here is where the King accomplished the real work of the Kingdom. They opened the books, planned the strategy for war, and settled economic issues. It happened in this room as these trusted men stared into the face of their King. Now translate that into the Kingdom of Heaven. There is the public court room where God rules and judges, but in the inner palace of the King there is an inner court room. The most trusted angels get to be in this room. They stare at the face of God, the Father, as they discuss the plans for the Kingdom.

Suddenly something takes place outside the room that distracts the attention of God. He is now staring out the window. The angels have joined Him. The agenda has been pushed aside as if it does not matter. What could be so important to God that it could shut down the entire business of heaven? What could be so significant that it could demand the attention of God and all the angelic hosts? The answer is the cry of a little one. God gives His complete attention to the needs of the little ones! There is no question to the why of God's heart. His entire concentration is on others.

What makes this so dramatic is the contrast between the Father's concentration on others and the disciples' concentration on themselves! The Father gives His total attention to the needs of the little ones. The disciples give their total attention to **SELF-PROMOTION.** *"At that time the disciples came to Jesus, saying, 'Who then is greatest in the kingdom of heaven?'"* (18:1). What a contrast we see here! The disciples' focus is self-centered; the Father's focus is self-giving. The disciples are concentrating on their own needs; the Father is concentrating on the needs of others. The disciples are seeking their own fulfillment; the Father is seeking the fulfillment of others. The disciples are building the kingdom of self; the Father is building the Kingdom of life for others.

"Take heed that you do not despise one of these little ones . . ." (18:10). *Take heed* is in the imperative. It is a command meaning "see to it!" *Despise* means to look down on in self-centeredness. It means to view someone else as lower than you. The call of Jesus is that you must not tolerate one bit of self-centeredness in your life. You must watch for it carefully. The moment a hint of selfishness appears, you must drop to your knees in repentance. You must die to yourself. It is a call to the style of the cross. We must align our hearts with the heart of the Father. His concentration must become ours.

THE FATHER'S ACTION
Matthew 18:12-13

There are multitudes of people in our world who know what they need to do, but never get around doing to it. There are hordes of people in the church who can tell you in clear terms what ought to be done, but they never do it themselves. That is not the picture of the Father. The Father has given His attention to others, and He has backed it up with an overwhelming dynamic action.

"What do you think? If a man has a hundred sheep, and one of them goes astray, does he not leave the ninety-nine and go to the mountains to seek the one that is straying? And if he should find it, assuredly, I say to you, he rejoices more over that sheep than over the ninety-nine that did not go astray," (18:12-13).

Jesus gives us a picture of **THE SOVEREIGN PERSON** in parable form. The picture is of a man who owns and controls one hundred sheep. They are all under his command. He is free to do with his sheep as he sees fit. If he wants to let one remain lost on the mountainside, it is his right as the owner to do so. No one can bring judgment against him. The Sovereign Person can do exactly what His heart tells Him to do.

What does His heart tell Him to do? The Sovereign Person has **A SERVANT PATTERN.** His heart demands that He respond in love action. It is amazing that all Biblical scholars agree on the central teaching of this parable. From every different theological persuasion, they all seem to come together here. The agreement is that the central thrust of this parable is the anxiety of the Father's shepherd's heart, over one lost sheep! The anxiety over one lost sheep is so strong that it overrides any joy He feels over ninety-nine safe sheep. This creates a situation in which the ninety-nine cannot satisfy Him. His anxiety drives Him to action for the one lost sheep. What a picture! It is the Father's shepherd's heart. He cares more for one lost sheep than He cares for Himself. He must risk Himself for even one.

If we are to really grasp the meaning, we must go back to the cultural setting in which the parable was spoken. The disciples clearly understood the concept of the shepherd's heart. The sheep became the shepherd's children. He knew them by name and built close relationship with them. He would easily move to protect them with his life. The shepherd loves his sheep more than he loves himself.

I am afraid we have no way to identify with these feelings in our culture. What if Jesus had spoken this parable in our day? Can you imagine Jesus speaking of a computer technician, who has lost his computer program? He is setting in an air-conditioned room, in an overstuffed office chair, looking for the program he has lost. He is running his fingers carefully over his key board. He cannot find it. He goes to his storage room, secures the original software, and reinstalls the program. Can you imagine Jesus speaking of a homemaker who has baked a cake only to find it did not rise? She simply throws it away and goes to the bakery to buy another one. In our throw away society, how can we identify with the cry of one little one?

Did you notice the action words given to us in verse twelve - *'leave, go, seek?'* The emphasis is upon the urgency, the anxiety of the Father's shepherd's heart. He cannot tolerate one sheep in trouble. The Father is on the move. This is the Sovereign Person who has a Servant Pattern.

SELF-PROMOTION characterizes the disciples. Their priority question is, *"Who then is greatest in the kingdom of heaven?"* (18:1). Jesus is calling the disciples to get in line with the Father's shepherd's heart. In our church attendance, our tithing, and our goodness, does our chest beat with the Father's shepherd's heart? His heart beats for others, others, others! It is a call out of ourselves, out of self-centeredness into others, others, others! We must lose our lives. It is a call to the cross and its style.

FATHER'S AGGRESSION
Matthew 18:14

Jesus says, *"Even so it is not the will of your Father who is in heaven that one of these little ones should perish,"* (18:14). There is a progression going on in these verses. This progression teaches us that His passion for others is deeply ingrained into the heart of the Father. Jesus begins in verse ten by telling us this passion is not a light or casual attention for others. It is not one item on the Father's agenda. He has literally interrupted the entire business of heaven to concentrate on others. Others have become the business of heaven. In verses twelve and thirteen, Jesus continues by sharing with us the moving action of the Father for others. The picture is the shepherd's heart, who risks his life for his sheep - others. He could not be content to sit on the sidelines and watch. His heart drove Him to a cross. We must examine the aggression of this Father's shepherd's heart.

How does Jesus describe Him in verse fourteen? He is **THE SOVEREIGN PERSON**. *"Even so it is not the will of your Father . . . ."* (18:4). There is a definite contrast between His statement in verse ten and now in verse fourteen. Jesus describes the Sovereign Person as *My Father* in verse ten, but now He calls Him *your Father.* There is a great difference between the two. Since He is your Father, the consequences do not worry me. You are the one He holds accountable, and you are the one who has to face Him. I can always go out the back door, down the alley, and enter my home. But when He is my Father, I must go into the living room and stand before the big chair. He calls me in on the carpet. I must face the consequences.

If He is simply the Father of Jesus, I do not have to worry too much about it. After all I am simply a disciple. But Jesus reminds us that we cannot reside in that false security. For the Sovereign Person is your Father. We are going to have to face Him in all of His sovereignty. He is going to confront us with His concentration and whether we have aligned our will with His. This is not a church program you can take or leave. This is the Father, the Sovereign Person! This is not the vote of some board; it is the Father.

He is concerned about **THE SERVANT PATTERN**. Jesus states, *"Even so it is not the will of your Father . . . ."* (18:14). The word *will* is the key word in the verse. We understand the will as the decision making part of our being. God, the Father, has made a decision. He has chosen that not one little one will perish. But the meaning of the word in this verse is much deeper than that. In other places in the New Testament, the writers translate this word "good pleasure." This means that there is a key atmosphere surrounding this decision or act of His will. There is an attitude that is the heart of the motive behind this decision to rescue little ones. It is His delight, thrill, pleasure, excitement, enjoyment, fun, and turn on. Do you have any idea what it is that turns

God on? Do you know what excites Him until He literally jumps off His throne in great joy? Can you imagine Him standing in heaven, waving His arms, and jumping up and down? What could bring God to that kind of hilarity? It is the rescuing of a little one. It may be we have missed something in all of this. Perhaps we have fooled ourselves into thinking that large sanctuaries, full of people raising their hands in worship, are what pleases God. Perhaps we thought it was the harmony of our quartets or the volume of our choirs. Most of our references for praise and worship, we gathered from the Old Testament. It is Israel who had an exclusive on God gathering around sacrifices and doing ceremonies as they chanted psalms. The New Testament thrust is the cross and its style. Come and pour out your life for others! It is time to rescue the little ones, others - others - others! This is the passion of the heart of God. This is His excitement.

Look at this in contrast to the disciples. What excites the heart of the disciples? What is their great delight? It is **SELF-PROMOTION.** Their great concern is ***"Who then is greatest in the kingdom of heaven?"*** (18:1). There is great embarrassment in this contrast. The disciples are persistently and aggressively promoting themselves. They argued with Jesus for nearly one week about the cross and its style (chapter 16). They were not interested in bleeding and dying for a world; their concern was their own protection, with miracles and power positions. Jesus took them to the Mount of Transfiguration in a desperate attempt to express the Father's heart to them (Matthew 17). But the disciples were persistent and stubborn in their concentration on themselves.

Jesus wanted a shift, a radical change. It was not that the disciples should give up their persistency or stubbornness. They needed to focus their persistency and stubbornness on others, instead of themselves. If they would be as aggressive for others as they have been for themselves, they would win the world. Is it not a message to us? We must now match the energy we have spent on ourselves with the energy we spend on others. All the time we have focused on ourselves, we must now match with time for others. We must aggressively fight for others as we have aggressively fought for ourselves.

This is not another appeal to help us in church growth. This is not a motivational message to help stimulate more activity for the fall Sunday School contest. We are talking about the heart of God. If we do not align our lives with His heart, we cannot call ourselves by His name. This is the central heart beat of Christianity!

"Dear Jesus, the greatest deterrent to burnout, boredom, and dead churches, is pouring our lives out for others - others - others. The greatest blockade to evangelism is our own self-centeredness. The biggest hindrance to the growth of the Kingdom are the walls we have built around ourselves for isolation. We have fought for position in the church, demanded our own way on the board, and we have missed Your heart for others - others - others. Forgive us, and please give us another chance. Bring us to death! We have met together to discover who is going to be the greatest, when we should have sought your heart and cried out for others - others - others. Change us within. Give us your heart! This is our prayer. In Jesus' name we pray, Amen."

Matthew 18:15-20

Who Cares About My Brother?

"Jesus, You constantly astound us by the amazing promises You give us. If we, the church, could just get together and agree. If we could come to intimate unity through dynamic love, we would link with the heavenly realms. You could then flow through us and move our world. You amaze us with all of the resource you have placed at our disposal. We have all we need to accomplish what needs to be done in our generation. We yield ourselves to Your Word. In Your name we pray, Amen."

The interaction of personal relationships is a most intriguing study. The conclusions of such a study would be humorous if they were not over shadowed by such seriousness. For example, we criticize in our brother what is our own biggest fault. We seldom recognize the fault in ourselves. The Parable of the Prodigal Son is a good illustration. The youngest son went to the land of riotous living, and squandered his money. Those are about the only details we have of his sinful activity. When his money ran out and his friends abandoned him, he found himself in the pig pen, attempting to stay alive. It was a good place to come to himself. He went home in repentance. The Father killed the fatted calf and threw a great party of celebration. The elder brother was standing outside the party, refusing to attend. When confronted by his Father, he criticized the prodigal son saying, **" . . . who devoured your livelihood with harlots,"** (Luke 15:30). It never says the prodigal son was with harlots, but the elder brother was saying that is what he would have done. It was his own biggest problem. We often treat people who have wronged us by returning to them exactly what they have done to us. We stoop to become what we have said is so terrible.

"Why did you hit him?"

"Well, he hit me!"

"Do you like people who hit you?"

"I cannot stand people who hit other people, so I hit them."

Thus we become what we cannot stand.

"Well, you are right! We should not criticize other people. We should not stoop to their level, to correct them when they are wrong. There is only one way to handle this situation. I will walk away from them and ignore them. I will act like it is none of my business."

The Word of God does not allow us that option either. The Scriptures do not allow us to walk away from relationships. Do you think that the actions of others are none of your business? We are personally responsible for the activities of our brother. This issue was settled back in the Old Testament. Cain killed Abel (Genesis 4). Abel's blood soaked into the ground and screamed to God Who was listening. God confronted Cain with the question, ***"Where is Abel your brother?"*** (Genesis 4:9). Cain replied, ***"I do not know. Am I my brother's keeper?"*** (Genesis 4:9). The obvious answer to that question is "YES." This answer echoes down through the pages of the Old Testament, and the New Testament shouts it repeatedly. There is no way to wipe our hands of our brother. We are responsible for the spiritual welfare of our brother. Our brother is our responsibility.

The disciples have come to Jesus with a question. It reveals exactly what is taking place in their hearts. They want to know, ***"Who then is greatest in the kingdom of heaven?"*** (18:1). Their focus is upon themselves. They are reporting that they are only responsible for, and interested in themselves, their own position, or their own spiritual condition. After all, they have to look out for number one. Jesus quickly moves to correct their thinking, (18:2). He lets them know they are backwards in their thinking. They need to be converted. They need a radical about face. They have wiped their hands of responsibility. A change needs to take place that will cause them to realize they are responsible for others, to the least of them. Jesus has a child on his lap, and He is calling the disciples to lose their lives for the little ones.

Jesus then gives His disciples a strong warning (18:6-9). If they do not allow Him to convert their focus, and they do not begin to take responsibility for their brother, there will be a heavy punishment. He introduces the subject of everlasting fire and hell fire (18:8-9).

It is easy for the disciples to say that what happens to the little ones is really none of their business. After all, they are busy about the work of the church, and they cannot allow the needs of such unimportant people bother them. Jesus gives them the example of His

Father in heaven (18:10-14). The Father has set aside the entire business of heaven to concentrate on the needs of the little ones (18:10). This has become the business of heaven. God has focused His attention, resources, and the angelic host upon the cry of one little one. The Father has set the pattern of a shepherd who risks all to rescue one lost sheep. Jesus calls the disciples to this pattern. They are responsible for their brothers.

The proposition for our study of chapter eighteen, verses fifteen through twenty is, "We are responsible for our brother." This is not limited to the innocent little one, who reaches out to us. It includes the supposed hypocrite, who has sinned against us. Jesus includes our sinning brother in the little ones.

THE STRAYING SHEEP
Matthew 18:15-16

We must see these verses, fifteen and sixteen, in their context. It is essential to proper interpretation. The context is found in the parable Jesus has just told (18:10-14). He highlights the heart of the heavenly Father. The whole attention and action of heaven is focused on the need of a little one. The parable is descriptive of the Father's action for the little ones. The Father has a shepherd's heart. Ninety-nine sheep are safe in the fold, but one is going astray. The Father cannot tolerate that because of the anxiety that possesses Him. The joy over ninety-nine safe sheep is over shadowed by the anxiety for one straying sheep. He has to do something about it!

Who is the straying sheep in the parable? The sheep is not an unbeliever. He is one who has been in the fold. One of us is straying, and he will ultimately be lost unless a shepherd intervenes. How did this straying come about? The context of this chapter blames the offenses of the disciples (18:6-7). They have become the stick in the death trap that allures and traps little ones. The selfish agenda of the disciples is causing the little ones to stray. We must rescue them.

Jesus is speaking. ***"Moreover, if your brother sins against you, go and tell him his fault between you and him alone. If he hears you, you have gained your brother. But if he will not hear, take with you one or two more, that 'by the mouth of two or three witnesses every word may be established,'"*** (18:15-16).

Who is the brother in ***". . . your brother sins against you. . . ."*** (18:15). He is not an unbeliever, but he is the lost sheep of the parable. Another has offended a little one. While straying, this little one has sinned against you. He will be lost unless someone rescues him. He is your responsibility.

In verse fifteen, Jesus gives us an **IMPERATIVE**. ***"Moreover if your brother sins against you, go. . . ."***(18:15). The imperative is to go. Do not just sit there! Go! If your brother has sinned against you, immediately go to him. Do not talk behind his back about how much you have been hurt and how bad he is. Get yourself together and go. Do not allow internal hatred and bitterness to build up within you. Get with the program and go! Do not allow backbiting and gossip to take place in your life. Pull your skirts about you and go! Do not sit back passively, as if it does not matter, and withdraw from your sinning brother. Extend your arms of love and go. If he has sinned against you, do not build calluses over the hurt and become numb. You must go! Go! Go! Go!

There is a second imperative. *"Moreover if your brother sins against you, go and tell him his fault. . . ."* (18:15). The word *tell* means "convince." The weight of responsibility is upon you, not him. You are to take the initiative. Though he has wronged you, do not set back and wait for him to apologize. You are to begin the process. You are to go!

Do you understand the **IMPACT** of that kind of action? A part of the impact is in your attitude. You are not going in your righteousness to put him in his place. You are not one who is more holy. You are not lording it over him as if you are better than he is. You are going with your hat in your hand, because you too have sinned. You know what it is to be lost. You know how it feels to be away from the fold and to have the danger of damnation pressing in upon you. After prayer and fasting, broken in spirit, with tears streaming down your face, bleeding from your heart, you go to your brother.

The impact is not only who you are, but how you care. You cannot leave your brother alone, because you care so much. Love demands your going. You have been possessed with the Father's shepherd's heart. The anxiety of the Father's heart has been placed within you. The fact that someone will be lost is too much to bear. It drives you to go on your knees, dripping with love, and a broken heart. You cannot tolerate the thought of your brother being lost. You have to go and convince.

The impact is not only who you are, and how you care, but why you go. You are to go and convince. This word means "to rebuke, to bring under conviction." This is the Holy Spirit's job in our lives. You are linking arms with the Holy Spirit so He can use you in Divine work.

You are going to be an instrument of Divine convincing. You are not doing your duty. You are to go with a broken heart and dripping with love. Linked with the Holy Spirit, you are to touch the life of your brother.

The **IMPLICATIONS** of this are overwhelming. Jesus is so wise. He understands the depth of His instructions. He knows the human personality. He is saying that you and I are to do everything we can to protect and rescue our straying brother. We are to make it easy for him to repent. The path that leads back to the fold must be cleared, and we must erect signs so there will be no confusion. You are to remove every obstacle, and you should cover the path with flowers of welcome. We are to go to him with our hat in our hand. Do not put him on the spot in foreign territory, but go to his home. We are not to drag him in on our carpet, where we put him on the spot, but we are to go to his territory. We are to make it as easy for him as possible. *"Moreover if your brother sins against you, go and tell him his fault between you and him ALONE,"* (18:15). No one needs to know. Do not spread the problem around the church or community. A big parade will pressure him, so go alone. After prayer and fasting, broken in spirit, with tears in your eyes, and dripping with love, you are to go. Go to his territory alone, to gain your brother. You and your brother can settle the issue, and no one will ever need to know. God can use you to rescue a straying sheep.

THE CARING CHURCH
Matthew 18:17

Let me remind you of the context of the verses we are studying. It is the parable that illustrates the Father's concentration (18:10-14). It is the shepherd's heart. Jesus is stating the mission of the Father. The mission is redemption. The Father has only one thing on His mind. Every other activity stops in the heavenly realms to focus on the redemptive mission. He did not come to cut us out; He came to cut us in.

It is amazing! God has called us to join Him in this. This redemptive mission has consumed God, and He wants to involve me. You get the feeling from these verses that the Father has placed Himself in a strange position. Redemption has become bigger than what He can do on His own. He needs to link the church with His shepherd's heart. It is out of this that He gives the church an **IMPERATIVE.**

Jesus has already given me an imperative to go (18:15). The manner of my going paves the way. I must go weeping, in a broken spirit, crawling on my hand and knees, with my hat in my hand. I must go to his territory, dripping with love and the moving of the Holy Spirit. His straying brings my intervention. It is an expression of the Divine heart through me.

Now let us play the "what if" game. What if this does not work, and my brother does not respond in repentance? What if I go with all of my love, but he refuses to hear me? What should I do then? Jesus' response to this question is obvious. I should increase my love! If I have gone with all of the love I have, how can I increase my love? I get one or two, who love like I do, and go, (18:16). Then my love is doubled or tripled. We go to our brother with a broken spirit, with tears in our eyes, and dripping with the love of God. This will win our brother for sure.

Well, that sounds good, but what if he still does not respond to our love? What should we do then? Jesus' response is to increase our love. How can we increase our love? ***"And if he refuses to hear them, tell it to the church,"*** (18:17). Let the entire church link together in agape love. Let the entire church, with broken spirits, with tears in their eyes, praying and fasting, come to the straying brother and pour the love of God all over him. This will break his heart for sure. How can he resist such passion expressed? Do you see the **IMPACT** and power of this? It is the entire, local, Body of Christ, mobilized in love to win one straying sheep back to the fold. Is this not the acted out parable Jesus told? This is the Father's shepherd's heart acting today.

There is not one individual in our community we could not win to the Kingdom of God in this manner. If we would mobilize and concentrate the entire love of the church on an individual, we could keep them in the fellowship. How does a visitor come to your church? Does he look in the yellow pages of the telephone directory? After discovering the name of your church, does he write and request a doctrinal statement of belief? After reading it, does he decide to attend your services because he agrees with your beliefs? The answer to these questions is no. A person who visits your church has no idea what the doctrinal belief of your denomination is. Why did he come? Someone knocked on his door and became his friend. A concerned individual helped her with her flat tire or visited the family in sickness. Someone at work got next to him or her in the middle of a need, and offered love and friendship.

Have you wondered why so many people who kneel at our altars as converts do not stay in the church? We have a trail of people going out the back door of our fellowship. Half the people joining our church do not remain members. A strong Christian told me of moving to a new town where he spent two years fighting his way into the fellowship of a church. This is a church with barred doors and strong walls. How could they ever win a sinning brother?

Holiness evangelism is a broad view of evangelism. It includes the movement of God in prevenient grace, the new birth, discipleship, reproducing yourself in the lives of others, and finally making it to heaven. To accomplish this in someone's life, it will take the combined, mobilized love of the church toward the new convert.

The **IMPLICATIONS** are startling. Jesus is telling us that, if we, as the church, do not do this, we have ceased to be the church. The opposite of being the church is to be the world. Let us play the "what if" game again. What if the entire church mobilizes their love passion, and concentrates it on a sinning brother, but he still does not respond? Jesus' answer is clear. ***"But if he refuses even to hear the church, let him be to you like a heathen and a tax collector,"*** (18:17). Does this mean we can finally wipe our hands of this individual? Have we fulfilled our responsibility to him? Do we need to care for him anymore? How did Jesus treat the heathen and tax collectors? He ate with them, and He said He came to redeem them (9:12). Those who are whole do not need a physician. We are to treat those who refuse to hear the church just like Jesus did. We must put our blood into our evangelism. This is not a reduction of love, but it is another increase. We must be a caring church.

THE UNIFIED UNITY
Matthew 18:18-20

Jesus is calling the church to fulfill its responsibility to the sinning brothers. We have the responsibility of our brother placed in our hands. All of the resources and all of the power we need, to accomplish the task, are ours! Jesus has given the resource of the unified union. Jesus now turns to the subject of unity. He says that what we cannot do on our own, we can do together in unity. It is important to start with the **IMPERATIVE.** *"Assuredly, I say to you, whatever you bind on earth will be bound in heaven, and whatever you loose on earth will be loosed in heaven,"* (18:18). Jesus stated the identical words in chapter sixteen, verse nineteen. The context of discussion is the church. This statement has something to do with the unified body of Christ called the church.

In the translation quoted above, the verb used twice is *will be.* What we do here on earth in terms of binding or loosing, heaven is obligated to do. This is a frightening statement. Does that mean that heaven is like us? Is heaven following our pattern? No, the verb in the original language is a future, perfect passive, verb. This means a better translation is "will have been." This changes the direction of the binding and loosing, which gives us the correct view of what Jesus is telling us.

So it would read like this. *"Assuredly, I say to you, whatever you bind on earth will have been bound in heaven, and whatever you loose on earth will have been loosed in heaven,"* (18:18 corrected). This tells us that whatever we do down here will have already taken place in heaven. This becomes the reason for our doing. We are to get into the flow of what is taking place in the heavenly realms. Jesus' pattern prayer was *"Our Father in heaven, Hallowed be Your name. Your kingdom come. Your will be done on earth as it is in heaven,"* (6:9-10). Our actions on earth are to reflect the actions of heaven. Heaven will spill through you and me, here on earth, all of its attitudes, motives, love, purposes, and powers. We are a demonstration of the Divine activities of the heavens.

This is the resource we have at our disposal to win our world - the sinning brother. We are to link arms together as the church. In the combined unity of our love, God will enable us to reach into the heavenly realms. Unity with each other is unity with the Father, and unity with the Father brings unity with each other. Flowing love to each other is like flowing love to the Father, and flowing love to the Father enables our flowing love to each other. We are now in unity with each other and heaven.

What is taking place in heaven that should be taking place down here? This is the picture Jesus gave His disciples of the Father's concentration (18:10-14). The cry of one little one has interrupted the entire business of heaven. Heaven has concentrated its entire attention, action, and aggression on the needs of the little ones. *"Even so it is not the will of your Father who is in heaven that one of these little ones should perish,"* (18:14). The Father's great delight and excitement comes in rescuing the little ones. Now all of this is going to take place, through us, in the unity of the church. We are a reflection of this concentration!

Jesus calls self-centered disciples out of their self-focus into the focus of the heavens. Jesus calls us out of self-seeking to spill out our lives for others. We are going to stop wrapping our righteous robes around us, only being responsible for number one. Now we are going to spill out our lives in love passion for others, just as it is done in the heavenly realms. It is the style of the cross.

We must see the **IMPACT** of this. *"Again I say to you that if two of you agree on earth concerning anything that they ask, it will be done for them by My Father in heaven,"* (18:19). The key to the verse is the word *agree.* It is a dynamic word. It is the root word for "symphony." It means a chorus of harmony. All the instruments are making their own individual sounds as the musicians are tuning them. The director steps forth, and produces beautiful music through that harmony. The context of the word *agree* in this verse is prayer. Jesus presents the idea of symphonic prayer. It is a prayer of overwhelming harmony. You and I are to link together in the harmony of love, and reach into the heavens. Harmony flows through the heavens into us, and through us into the heavens. This kind of harmony brings the entire power of God to bear upon our needy world.

Is there a Biblical example of this? Yes, it is Pentecost day. One hundred and twenty disciples have pushed aside their personal agendas and prejudices. They have seen the competition and self-seeking for what it is. They have pushed aside the question, *"Who then is greatest in the kingdom of heaven?"* (18:1). They have come to terms with the cross - death and resurrection. Dying to themselves, they are open to harmonious agreement - symphonic prayer. In this upper room, God has enabled them to reach into heaven. There is a moving of the power of God. A sound, as a rushing mighty wind, sweeps through. They hit the streets in that kind of agreement and three thousand people come to the altar at the close of the first sermon.

The **IMPLICATIONS** are startling. ***"For where two or three are gathered together in My name, I am there in the midst of them,"*** (18:20). We have missed the truth of this verse. All my life I have heard this verse used as a promise from Jesus. He is promising to appear when two Christians get together. Can you imagine this? God in heaven sees two Christians visiting and He says, "Well, I've got to go, after all I promised." How many times have you heard this verse quoted when the prayer meeting group is small? The leader says, "There aren't many of us here, but be encouraged. Jesus promised to come even if there were only two or three." The promise from Jesus is not that He will appear each time we get together.

In verses eighteen and nineteen, Jesus describes the reality of what takes place when we get into harmony. He is giving a definition of the church. (1) There are two Christians. The church is always community. We are not isolated from each other, but we are a working body. (2) It is two Christians who are in symphonic harmony. They have set aside all the petty things that would divide them. They have died to themselves and the issue has become bigger. (3) They are agreeing on what is "in His name." Their harmony is in Jesus and His heartbeat. This is all implied in the Father's shepherd's heart. The outpour through these Christians can only be explained in the terms of Jesus Himself, and He produces the atmosphere. (4) It is because of this atmosphere that Jesus is seen in the midst of this group. In their symphonic harmony, the flow of the heavens happens in them. They have reached out in oneness to each other, and reached up into oneness with heaven. In that flow of harmony, heaven spills through them and reproduces the life of Jesus among them. That is the church.

Is there a Biblical illustration for this? There were three Hebrew children named Shadrach, Meshach, and Abed-Nego (Daniel 3). They refused to bow to the statue the King had erected. The penalty for disobedience was to be thrown into the fiery furnace. Because the King was mad, he had his men heat the furnace seven times hotter than normal. The King's men threw in the three young men. They reached out to link with each other. They reached up in surrender, linking with heaven. In the harmony of that kind of oneness something began to flow between them. The King noticed they were not burning and exclaimed, ***"Look! I see four men loose, walking in the midst of the fire; and they are not hurt, and the form of the fourth is like the Son of God,"*** (Daniel 3:25).

Jesus calls us to this. It is the solution to the problems of our generation. Here is the key to church growth. This is the secret to evangelism. We must die to ourselves. The cross and its style must become reality in our relationships with each other. In unity, with each other and the heavenly realms, Jesus can again pour His life through us. As the world sees Jesus in our midst, it will be drawn to Him.

"Jesus, please make us the church again. It is our only chance to win our world. Our programs and schemes have not brought the needed results. We need You, and we need each other. We submit to You, and we submit to each other. In Jesus' name we pray, Amen."

Matthew 18:21-35

Unforgiveness – The Source

Some years back I went through a life changing experience. It did not take place in a day, but over a period of two years. I made a commitment to read about the lives of the great saints of the Church. The Church has recognized these men and women as people who had special contact with God. These people had literally changed the course of history.

I found myself in unusual book stores buying old books that had long ago lost their popularity. I discovered the names of individuals who were unknown. These people included the monastic movement of the Church. The Desert Fathers challenged me by their commitment. There were men like St. Anthony, who sacrificed great wealth for a greater calling. St. Nicholas, who became our Santa Claus, was among them. The list goes on and on.

It did not take long to discover something common in each of these individuals. They did strange things. Simon, the Stylite, chained himself to the ledge of a great cliff. What could motive a man to do such a strange thing? He stood there, day after day, through the heat and storms. His driving passion said, "I have to know God!" It is a strange way to get to know God. I do not recommend that you do the things that these men and women did, but I do commend them for their deep, internal compassion and hunger. The drive that said "Somehow, someway, I have to know God" consumed them.

In the lives of these saints, hunger for God most often began with a crisis experience, where God would reveal Himself to them. With the revelation, the hunger seemed to grow. Isolation from society was their common practice. Leaving their families, many went to the caves, and others went to the deserts. Nothing but bread and water sustained them for months at a time. They longed to know God.

I recognize that in many areas they were wrong. The abandonment of family is not the call of God. Many self-punishment practices they went through are hard to reconcile with getting to know God. Perhaps the greatest place they missed it was the great cause to change their society. It is a tragedy that Christianity has had such a hard time maintaining a balance between a hunger for God and a hunger to win the world. Our balance is off, either way, most of the time. It is easy to become nothing more than a social club doing compassionate ministry. On the other hand, it is easy to focus on God until we lose all perspective of our fellow man.

John Wesley emphasized this in his Methodist movement. He spoke of "a social Gospel." For most of us, that phrase is a complete turn off, but what did he mean by that term? It was a combination of hunger for God and a hunger to change the world. There is no Gospel that does not embrace its present day and spill into the lives of others.

The Gospel is not the Gospel when man wraps his righteous robes about himself, and sits in his sanctuary, simply to glorify God. The Christian is never isolated from the need of his brother.

Jesus gives us the same emphasis. How easy it would have been for Jesus to lead His disciples into a state of glorifying God in stillness. He could have bypassed the evil of His day, especially after the way they treated Him. But Jesus constantly brought His disciples back to others, others, others. In this passage, Jesus presents forgiveness toward others. Forgiveness received from God must flow into forgiveness toward others. God ties His forgiveness of us with our forgiveness to others.

Jesus gives us this teaching in parable form (18:23-35). The context in which He tells this powerful parable is significant. The disciples have been in a heated debate over a question they now propose to Jesus, **"Who then is greatest in the kingdom of heaven?"** (18:1). They want to know who gets to fulfill the role of the number one disciple. Who will get to boss the other disciples and have his own way? Whose name will be in the largest print? Who gets to hold the microphone? What is in this for me? How will I benefit? These questions formed the atmosphere in which Jesus tells this parable.

In the middle of a mission to win a world, the disciples were fighting about the order of their names in the bulletin. Jesus has spent days telling them about the cross and its style. They can see nothing but position and power for themselves. Jesus has called them to die to themselves and lose their lives. They think about how they can gain from being a part of this group. Chapter eighteen shows Jesus dealing a blow to self-centeredness. He will not sidestep the issue, and He is very severe. His eyes are flashing and His chin is set as He leans into their faces to give them a message of death of self-centered carnality.

Jesus delivers this message through teaching. This teaching comes in contrasts, but this is not a new method for Jesus. The proposition of His message is, "Self-centeredness always produces a definite pattern in relationship." Stated another way, we say, "When certain patterns appear in relationships, you immediately know that self-centeredness is present." What are these patterns?

SELF-CENTEREDNESS IS UNFORGIVING
Matthew 18:21-30

The contrast is vivid, and is between the master and the servant. This is the same contrast Jesus shows between the Father and the disciples. In the parable of the forgiven servant, the servant goes and finds a fellow servant who owes him one hundred denarii (18:28). The value of one denarii in our day is $16.67. The forgiven servant grabs his fellow servant by the throat and demands full payment. Was that wrong? Some people are always wanting to get out of what they owe, so there is the necessity of demanding payment. If someone owed you money, you would want it back. This was especially true with servants who had very little. The forgiven servant desperately needed his $16.67! He had to work hard for this money. He lent it in the faith that his fellow servant would pay it back. The forgiven servant was within his rights to make such a demand of his fellow servant.

Then comes the contrast! The master had just forgiven the servant ten thousand talents. In our currency this equals $2,370,000.00. Even though the servant had been forgiven this huge amount, he refused to forgive his fellow servant a mere $16.67. The total picture tells you that the forgiven servant's demand is not right.

This contrast shows us the immensity of Jesus' teaching. When you hear the disciples asking, ***"Who then is greatest in the kingdom of heaven?"*** (18:1), they do not seem to be out of line. They want to get the chain of authority established so there will not be any misunderstandings. Each person has to look out for himself. You cannot let people walk all over you any time they want to. You must have your guard up. Certainly some self-centeredness is necessary in this world, if it is kept under proper control. Everybody is that way. It must be proper!

But when you bring this self-centered scene against the background of the rugged cross of Christ, it changes. Jesus has given up His rights to get you into the Kingdom. Something is desperately wrong. What looked right in the world's setting is horrifying in view of the cross. Jesus cannot tolerate self-centeredness, but the disciples have not grasped this truth. They have heard Jesus teaching the cross style repeatedly. He explained it to them, but the disciples are still thinking in the patterns of the world. Jesus gives the teaching to them again through this parable.

What does this self-centeredness produce? First, it produces **CALCULATION**. ***"Then Peter came to Him and said, 'Lord, how often shall my brother sin against me, and I forgive him? Up to seven times?' "*** (18:21). This is really a generous offer from Peter. Do you realize the kind of world from which Peter came? He lived in a massive world of paganism. Their whole concept was to do unto others before they did it unto you, and do more to them than they do to you. In this great sea of paganism, there is this isolated island of Judaism. The Jews believed you should only do to others what they did to you. It was an eye for an eye and a tooth for a tooth. This was a great improvement over the pagan world. Now Peter is willing to go beyond that. He is so generous. He will wait until it is done to him seven times before he seeks revenge.

Peter expected Jesus to brag on him for his generosity. He was far above paganism, and he was even willing to go beyond Judaism. Does he not show a generous heart? Jesus said, "No! You have missed it again, Peter." Peter's offer sounds great when compared to paganism or Judaism, but when compared to the Kingdom of God, he reveals his calculation. Peter had been keeping a list and counting up the number of times others offended him. Jesus is calling him to throw away his pencil and paper. He is calling us to quit keeping track of what others do. Self-centeredness motivates us to keep lists. Self-centeredness is calculating.

Self-centeredness produces **MANIPULATION**. *"The servant therefore fell down before him, saying, 'Master, have patience with me, and I will pay you all,'"* (18:26). This is difficult to analyze because it comes very close to our personal lives. The master has caught the servant in the act of embezzling his funds. There is no way he cannot admit his guilt. He has stolen $2,370,000.00.

What can he possibly do in a moment like this? What excuse can he offer? He begins conniving. He drops to his knees and he begins weeping. "Oh master, have mercy on me. I will pay you back every penny I owe you. Just give me a little time," he cries. It is a lie. He could not possibly ever pay back that amount. That is the power of the story. The servant is trying to con the master. The master knows it, and the servant knows it. But what is the servant to do? The master has caught him. If he can just talk his way out of this moment, and get more time, he can probably con someone else. Perhaps he can manipulate another situation and satisfy everyone. The answer to the situation is not manipulation or *"Master, have patience with me, and I will pay you all,"* (18:26). The answer is complete and absolute forgiveness from the Master. The truth is, there is no possibility of a pay back.

The holiness message is the cry for this hour. It is the reality of truth. We have been spending much of our time in Christianity, trying to con Jesus. He has caught us. Guilt takes over. Complications have set in, and we desperately need a way out. We try to con the master in an attempt to step beyond the mess we have created. We bargain with God, and ask Him for more time to pay Him back. But we have no chance of paying Him back. It is a con.

When Jesus takes over your life, you will come to the place where manipulation of God is finished. You cry, "I have been wrong!" You confess your self-centered, conning ways before God. You recognize the only possibility. It is the total resource of the Father's forgiveness. You cannot bargain, but plead for mercy. You surrender, allowing God to do in and to you what He wants to do.

Self-centeredness produces a third condition. It is **UNFOR-GIVENESS**. How do we have a right to read this story and call the forgiven servant a manipulator? His actions easily show us. *"But that servant went out and found one of his fellow servants who owed him a hundred denarii; and he laid hands on him and took him by the throat, saying, 'Pay me what you owe!'"* (18:28). The ultimate test of what is deep inside the heart is seen in your response to an offending fellow servant. Unforgiveness reveals the self-centered manipulator. The tendencies to calculation and manipulation are symptoms of self-centeredness. Unforgiveness reveals self-centeredness in our relationships. The servant has just experienced a limitless forgiveness for a debt he could never pay. Now he has his hands around his brother's throat in unforgiveness for a debt that his brother could pay.

It is easy to respond by saying, "OK, I will forgive my fellow servant." We bite our lip and do the right thing. We do an act of forgiveness. Jesus does not call us to accomplish an act of forgiveness. He calls us to deal with what causes our spirit of unforgiveness. Unforgiveness is a symptom of an inside condition. This call is to face our carnal self-centeredness. We must give up and come to the cross and its style. It is the only chance we have, because self-centeredness is unforgiving.

UNFORGIVING IS CANCELLATION
Matthew 18:31-34

Now we move from symptoms to internal disease. This is much harder. We move from the headaches or skin rash to internal cancer. When you expose the internal cause, the stench is sickening. The rot of the self-centered, carnal heart is overwhelming. If you think that your outward deeds of sin (whatever they might have been) are bad, wait until you are deep in the carnal mind. The condition horrifies you when you see it exists within you.

Let us begin with **REVELATION**. *"Then his master, after he had called him, said to him, 'You wicked servant! I forgave you all that debt because you begged me,' "* (18:32). The word **wicked** is literally evil. The order of the words in the original writing is very significant. The words *"all that debt,"* immediately follow the words *"You wicked servant!"* The master connected the evil with all the debt he had forgiven the servant who continued to live in the spirit of unforgiveness. It is important to note that the master did not call this servant evil when he embezzled $2,370,000.00. He called him a wicked servant when his self-centered, carnal spirit was unforgiving toward his brother.

Jesus establishes a pattern here. We understand the outside deeds of sin. We know what they are, and we can easily see them and their results. There is provision in the cross for great forgiveness of these deeds. You can spend your time correcting the outside actions. Reformation brings some sense of satisfaction, but before it is over, God is going to expose what you are deep in your heart. The principle of carnality, which is enmity against God, shows itself here. Wesley wrote that once we see the carnal, it looks worse than all of the sin deeds ever done. You despair, and ask, "How can Jesus save me with such a condition?" How could God love and live within an individual who has this kind of heart?

Then comes a call to repeat - **REPETITION**. The master continues by saying, *"Should you not also have had compassion on your fellow servant, just as I had pity on you?"* (18:33). Do you see the parallel? What the master has done in forgiving the servant, the fellow servant asks the forgiven servant to do for him. The master's activities are the actions of God. Jesus calls us, the forgiven servants, to be like He is. When you see the internal condition of self-centered carnality, and recognize that God has called you to be like He is, the enemy multiplies the despair of your heart. God has called you to forgive as He forgives, to act as He acts, to be holy as He is holy. Who can accomplish such a call? Where can we ever get the resource to bring this great feat to pass?

The result of this whole experience is **UNFORGIVENESS**. You find yourself back to the beginning step of being aware that you are unforgiving. Jesus continues the story by stating, ***"And his master was angry, and delivered him to the torturers until he should pay all that was due to him,"*** (18:34). Self-centered carnality has such a grip on you that you are incapable of forgiving your brother. Therefore, you are not going to be able to maintain the state of forgiveness from God. Our carnal, unforgiving spirit nullifies the very forgiveness that God extends to us.

Let us stop and summarizes what we have learned. The unforgiving spirit is a symptom of the inward, self-centered, carnal heart. This carnal heart grips me and keeps me from forgiving my brother. The inability of forgiving my brother will soon nullify my forgiveness from God. Now we rush into the conclusion!

CANCELLATION IS PUNISHMENT
Matthew 18:34-35

"And his master was angry, and delivered him to the torturers until he should pay all that was due to him. So My heavenly Father also will do to you if each of you, from his heart, does not forgive his brother his trespasses," (18:34-35). This is a horrible scene! The horror is not found in the external deeds done, but the internal, carnal reality. God is going to hold you and I accountable for not only the deeds done in the flesh, but for the source of those deeds. The severity of judgment day may not be because of the evil of our outward deeds, but because of the terrible condition of the inward heart. What if at the Judgment Day God does not reveal deeds done, but simply exposes us from within? Could it be that is the reason people go to hell? It is not because of what they do, but because of what they are. This is the crying message of holiness. It is easy to see the self-centered carnality of the world. They display it in cheating, adultery, and murder. You can bring that same carnality into the church, dress it up in a nice suit, let it produce some religious deeds, but it is the same carnality. It no longer murders or commits adultery, rather it hates, is bitter, and unforgiving.

Let us now look at the progress! Let us start with **DELIVERED**. *"And his master was angry, and delivered him to the torturers until he should pay all that was due to him,"* (18:34). There is a contrast between verses twenty-five and thirty-four. The master discovers a servant who owes him ten thousand talents. I would have responded with rage. An evil servant stole $2,370,000.00 from me. After all I have done for him, and he treats me like this. I would have screamed at him about his wickedness. But the master does not respond that way. It is simply money. He shows no emotion of anger. The logical business practice is to sell the servant and all of his family. You get the servant's possessions and put them on the market. The master attempts to get back as much of the loss as possible (18:25). Matthew contrasts this with verse thirty-four. *"And his master was angry!"* What got to the heart of the master? It is not the embezzling of funds that really angered the master. The expression of self-centered carnality, which expressed itself in unforgiveness, is what angered the master.

It is easy to see this in the life of Jesus. What got to the heart of Jesus? Some men pulled a woman by her hair to the feet of Jesus. They had caught her in the act of adultery. Jesus did not condemn her, but told her to go and sin no more. Jesus told Matthew, the evil tax collector, to push his books and follow Him. He made no offer of judgment or condemnation. Jesus looked at the sinners of His day and told them He was a physician and a redeemer. He had come to heal them. When did Jesus' eyes flash and His shoulders straighten? It was at the temple where men, filled with self-centered carnality, were in control. They were using God and His temple for their own self-centered benefits. It was then that He put together a whip and cleaned house. When did Jesus look people in the eye and call them a brood of snakes? It was to self-centered Pharisees who used their religion for their own selfish ends. Self-centered carnality got to the heart of Jesus. Now Jesus tells this parable to the disciples, who are expressing their own self-centered carnality.

Is this not a strong message for our consideration? What is it about our lives that gets to the heart of God? Is it telling a lie? Is it the deeds of sin that I do? He so quickly forgives us when we confess our outward deeds! Self-centered carnality, which seeks its own way, enrages the heart of God. Self-centered carnality wants to manipulate God for its own ends, and does not live in the spirit of forgiveness.

How much does this carnality disturb God? The word **TORItURED** tells us. ***"And his master was angry, and delivered him to the torturers until he should pay all that was due to him,"*** (18:34). The word ***torturers*** is a very significant word. This is the only time anyone uses it in the New Testament. It refers to individuals, appointed or hired by the court, to beat people who have committed terrible crimes. Jesus is relating "terrible crimes" with self-centered carnality expressing itself in unforgiveness.

What is the result of this progression of *delivered* and *tortured*? It is **UNFORGIVENESS**. *"So My heavenly Father also will do to you if each of you, from his heart, does not forgive his brother his trespasses,"* (18:35). The one who cannot forgive because of his internal self-centered carnality, Jesus cannot forgive. The one who demands total payment because of carnality, has to pay totally.

Jesus is referring to eternal damnation. He is not referring to the terrible sinners of the streets, but to one who walks in forgiveness. He tells this parable to twelve disciples, who have left all to follow Him. The only thing they have done wrong is to ask, *"Who then is greatest in the kingdom of heaven?"* (18:1). Jesus is very strong on this truth, and makes definite statements concerning the conclusion to self-centered carnality. Jesus' death on the cross was not to slap our hands and make us better. He died to redeem us from all sin - self-centered carnality. We are to lose our lives and be a flow of His life. He has called us to the cross and its style.

"Jesus, You are going to have to express Your deep concern to each of our individual hearts. We offer ourselves to You! Please do not let us get by. We are committed to honesty and truth. Do what You need to do in us. Do not allow us to sidestep the issue of this chapter. We must go beyond the disciples. We are not asking You for more time. We are not going to con You. We want You to do what You need to do to make us like You. We place ourselves totally at Your disposal! In Your name, we pray. Amen."

PART FIVE

Matthew 19

Living the Cross

Configuration of the Cross Style

Matthew 19

Introduction

Does It Work?

Matthew, Mark, Luke and John did not write the Gospels as a biography of Jesus Christ. The Gospels were not meant to be a daily diary of His miracles and preaching. Matthew's purpose was evangelism. He desperately wanted to convert the Jews. If he could convince the Jews that Jesus was the Kingly Messiah they had been expecting all this time, he would have fulfilled his life's dream! He never lets up on this evangelistic emphasis throughout the entirety of his account.

Repeatedly he uses the argument of the authority of Christ. Jesus is presented as the authoritative King of the Kingdom. Matthew reaches into the life events of Jesus and selects those that he believes will make the greatest impact on the Jews. Do not forget that the Holy Spirit was guiding him. The Holy Spirit knew the events that would act as the cutting knife for the Word.

These facts must shape our view of chapter nineteen. This chapter is not a fresh start of new material, but a flow of what he has already presented. He is acting as a lawyer building a great case. Chapter nineteen will be another great container of evidence linked with all that has already gripped us. Bible scholars have labeled chapters nineteen and twenty "The Perean Ministry." Jesus has moved into a new geographical location to minister. He began His ministry in Galilee, moved into Gentile territory and now has come to the region of Perea. Matthew has intimately connected chapters eighteen and nineteen.

Jesus is traveling again. He has gone from His ministry in Galilee into Gentile territory. Jesus wants to be alone with His disciples. He wants to communicate the style of the cross to them. He forcibly presents the reality of the cross in a call to lose their lives. Three great events have taken place - the confession of Peter (16:13-16), the teaching about the church (16:17-19), and the Mount of Transfiguration (17:1-8). Now He is on the move again (17:22). With His disciples He returns to Galilee, but not for ministry. It is a brief stay with several groups of people getting together. We see later that the women joined Him at this time (27:55). As a group, they head south to Jerusalem to celebrate the Feast of the Passover. This will be the last week of Jesus' life. In chapter nineteen they have arrived in the Perean area.

They are just a few weeks from the cross. This event is heavy upon the mind of Christ. Has He really gotten through to His disciples? He has been spending hours trying to clarify the content of His Messiahship. He is a bleeding, suffering Messiah. The disciples have argued with Him to the point of a rebuke (chapter 16). There was plenty of verification that He was telling them the truth (chapter 17). Moses,

Elijah, and the Heavenly Father all gave convincing testimony of the cross style. Surely the disciples have understood this is the style of the Kingdom. However, they are found arguing over positions and power. The great question they ask is *"Who then is greatest in the kingdom of heaven?"* (18:1). The cross style has just struck the inner heart of the disciples' self-centered carnality.

Jesus spends an entire chapter (18) giving these arguing disciples the theology of the cross. He vividly describes the impact that the cross will have on the heart of man as it spills into his relationships. Jesus clearly outlines the concepts and principles for all to see.

The theology is exciting. One walks away from chapter eighteen marveling at the knowledge of the truth. But the theology is dead and meaningless unless we apply it. What difference does it make? We get out a flip chart and diagram great Biblical truths before the Sunday School class. It is marvelous teaching! However, it is a total waste of time unless it is seen acting through my life in my world. Matthew, inspired by the Holy Spirit, knew this well. He is not going to leave the theology of chapter eighteen without adequate application. Chapter nineteen is going to be the practical, everyday living of the concepts. Die to yourself, lose your life, take up your cross, live the cross style - how does this work at my job, home, and school? We state the proposition of this great chapter as follows. **The cross produces death to self-centered carnality, which must affect our daily lives.** How does it affect our daily lives?

Marriage and Divorce
Matthew 19:3-12

It is interesting to note that divorce was as much a debated issue then as it is now. It was a major, controversial social issue. This is the setting of the scene we are discussing. The Jews were hoping to drag Jesus into the middle of this debate and cause Him embarrassment. So the question they are asking is a trick question. The question proposed was *"Is it lawful for a man to divorce his wife for just any reason?"* (19:3). In Jesus' culture, the issue was not over the properness of divorce. It was an accepted cultural norm. The controversial debate was over the cause of divorce. There were two schools of thought that dominated the debate. One was the school of Hillel, and they were liberal in the application of the Scriptures. The other was the school of Schmai, and they were very conservative. The major Scripture under consideration was found in the book of Deuteronomy. Moses said, *"When a man takes a wife and marries her, and it happens that she finds no favor in his eyes because he has found some uncleanness in her, and he writes her a certificate of divorce, puts it in her hand, and sends her out of his house"* (Deuteronomy 24:1). The debate between the two schools centered on the phrase *some uncleanness in her.*

What is the element of uncleanness in her? The liberal school of Hillel said that this was anything that displeases the husband. This could be burnt toast in the morning, bad breath, or improper relationships. The divorce process was very simple. The husband took a piece of paper and wrote on it, "I divorce you!" He signed his name and handed it to her. He then led her to the door and sent her out of his house. Most of the male population loved this concept.

The more conservative school of Schmai stood against this liberal approach. They interpreted the phrase *some uncleanness in her* to relate only to sexual impurity. Thus, the only proper ground for divorce was adultery. In fact, the courts demanded divorce if immorality took place. Here is the raging social controversy. The Pharisees see a great opportunity to draw Jesus into this debate. They ask their question in the midst of a large crowd. They no doubt folded their arms, stood back, and said, "Gotcha!" They believed that Jesus would discredit His ministry with many in that crowd, because the issue had divided the crowd. Matthew states, *"The Pharisees also came to Him, testing Him,"* (19:3). The word *testing* means to tempt or back against the wall. The Pharisees are not searching for truth, or Divine revelation. They are simply using the circumstances to their own best interests.

It is very significant to remember the location where the Pharisees decided to ask this question. It is in the region of Judea, beyond the Jordan River (19:2) or the Perean region. The reason for this significance is that Herod Antipas, who beheads John the Baptist, rules over this area. John lost his head because he made some key statements about marriage and divorce. The Pharisees were hoping that Jesus would do something of the same and experience the same consequence.

Be sure you understand the scene. The Pharisees are folding their arms and grinning in great confidence over their question. The disciples are tense and afraid Jesus will say the wrong thing. The crowds are scratching themselves wondering what is taking place. Jesus stands in the middle of it all with the wisdom of God within Him! Jesus quickly moves past both liberal and conservative schools and brings every one to the penetrating Word of God. The Word of God reveals that the question is not about marriage and divorce, but about internal self-centered carnality.

He begins with **THE DIVINE PLAN** (19:4-6). He presents the Pharisees with the proposal that they did not go back far enough. They wanted to stop with the words of Moses in Deuteronomy, but Jesus takes them back to God's Word at the beginning. ***"Have you not read that He who made them at the beginning 'made them male and female?"*** (19:4). This was a quotation from the book of Genesis chapter one verse twenty-seven and chapter five verse two. This book is their authority, and what they profess to live by. The design of God from the beginning was to establish opposite sexual beings. It was a result of the creative activity of God. The sexual drive is as natural and normal as the hunger drive. God has stamped into the human being an attraction for the opposite sex. It is right, proper, and good, according to the statement of God.

We should also note from this quotation in Genesis that God made male (singular) and female (singular). He did not make male (singular) and females (plural). God did not make female (singular) and males (plural). In God's Divine plan, as seen at creation there was no place for polygamy and their was no place for divorce.

Jesus is not through quoting the Old Testament, which the Pharisees say they follow. ***"For this reason a man shall leave his father and mother and be joined to his wife, and the two shall become one flesh"*** (19:5). This is a quotation from the book of Genesis chapter two verse twenty-four. God, in His original plan, expected the sexual attraction between one male and one female to take precedence over all other affections. It would take precedence even over the natural affection one feels for his or her parents. Thus, one male and one female would cleave to each other establishing a new home called one flesh. This was the Divine plan!

Jesus has quoted to the Pharisees from their own book and now calls them to a conclusion. ***"So then, they are no longer two but one flesh. Therefore what God has joined together, let not man separate"*** (19:6). The Divine plan from creation was one male and one female (verse 4). There was no room in God's plan for polygamy or for divorce. This sexual attraction takes precedence over affection for parents so that the two come together in love relationship (verse 5). The obvious conclusion to this is *one flesh.* God glues, cleaves, and welds the two together into one flesh. By God's Divine plan a man can no more separate himself from his wife than he can separate himself from himself. Written into God's plan, desire, design, creation, and will is the absolute indissolubility of the marriage union.

Immediately there is a reaction from the Pharisees. What Jesus said may have been fine in the Garden of Eden, at creation, where there was an ideal situation. That may have worked when there were only one male and one female present. But we live in a cursed world, full of sin. Ungodly situations are constantly intersecting our lives. There is adultery, homosexuality, and abuse, both mental and physical. Since this is true, surely there has to be some kind of adjustment and compromise in all of this. It is not right to say this is the way it is, with no exceptions, even in God's plan. Jesus went on to show that this was most right. It is **THE DIVINE PROVISION.** The Pharisees must have relaxed a bit, realizing that God has provided for this sinful world. What is the great provision of God for the sinful world and the marriage relationship? It is forgiveness. They must have yelled, "No! No! God's provision is not forgiveness. It is divorce. Moses said so!" So they ask Jesus another question, *"Why then did Moses command to give a certificate of divorce, and to put her away?"*(19:7). Their faces must have held a doubtful grin at this time. For with Jesus taking this kind of stand on marriage and divorce, He was contradicting Moses. Moses was the law giver. For Jesus to criticize him is to say the law of God is wrong.

The wisdom of God fills Jesus again. He says to them, *"Moses, because of the hardness of your hearts, permitted you to divorce your wives, but from the beginning it was not so"* (19:8). There is a big difference between the Pharisees' interpretation of what Moses said and Jesus' interpretation. The difference is between the words *command* and *permitted.* It was not the Divine plan, but *because of the hardness of your hearts* Moses provided a way for you to do what you had already decided. *Hardness of your hearts* means an attitude that will not forgive. Moses permitted them to give a certificate of divorce because they were self-centered and refused to forgive.

The provision of God was not divorce but forgiveness. God knew that the only thing that redeems sin is forgiveness, not another sin. This is the cross style. It was God's answer to sin in Himself - forgiveness. This is why He died on the cross to make such a provision possible. It is forgiveness that is redemptive.

However, this does not finish the truth of this passage. There is **THE HUMAN PROBLEM.** The Pharisees go stumbling off into the darkness of their own making. The crowds begin to separate and the disciples get alone with Jesus. Their reaction to all of this is very revealing. They scream out, "This is impossible." We can identify with this reaction also. What Jesus is proposing is very hard, too hard. The world just is not like that. The disciples said to Him, **"If such is the case of the man with his wife, it is better not to marry"** (19:10). The cross style calls me to lose my life to my wife. The disciples' self-centered reaction says that it would be useless to marry if you cannot use your wife for your own benefits. Losing your life to one flesh relationship is too permanent. There are a multitude of circumstances and situations that come, which no one planned. The call to forgive through them all is just too great. If we have to apply the cross and its style to marriage, it is better not to marry.

The reason all of this is so difficult for us is because of "the human problem." We are seeing again that the great blockade to the cross style is self-centered carnality. The reaction of the disciples in chapter nineteen, verse ten, is a parallel to their question in chapter eighteen, verse one. They are seeking position and are hungry for power. Their self-centeredness wants to control. Every time we apply the cross, to any situation, this human problem raises its head. Self-centeredness wars against the cross style in every scene. Self-centeredness asks, "What can I get out of marriage?" Cross style asks, "What can I give to marriage?" Self-centeredness wants to use someone else for selfish benefits. Cross style avails itself for the benefit of others. Self-centeredness views relationships as stepping stones to arrive at higher levels of position. The cross style views relationships through redemption.

This is a call to the practical spilling out of the death of self. Holiness theology is great. But it is past time to take our brilliant theology out of the class room discussion and bring it into the middle of our home living. It is time for the cross to be something more than a theme for our songs. The cross must be the style of our home living. We must see it in the misunderstandings that occur in relationships. Our communities are waiting for holiness to be lived rather than just talked. Would you be willing to examine your marriage relationship? Might it be time for you to present yourself to God in confession? It is so easy to point a finger at each other; we easily blame circumstances for our problems. All the time our basic problem has been self-centeredness. It is time to come to the cross that one flesh relationship may be reality. Marriage is the beauty of the visible expression of Christ, Who loved the Church and gave His life for her.

Mothers and Dependents
Matthew 19:13-15

Practical application is very difficult. We now approach the second area in which we must see the cross style. ***"Then little children were brought to Him that He might put His hands on them. . . ."*** (19:13). Can you blame those mothers? They had seen the powerful hands of Jesus in the action of miracles. The touch of His hands made the lepers whole. He multiplied bread and fish with the touch of those dynamic hands. They had watched Jesus place His hands on blinded eyes until they could see. They had even watched those hands touch the ruler's dead daughter. Those hands restored life. Every mother wanted to see the powerful hands of Jesus placed upon her child. They came bringing their children. We do not know the number, but it must have been a multitude.

The inward desire of these mothers bespeaks **THE DIVINE PLAN.** Jesus turned to the disciples and said, *"Let the little children come to Me, and do not forbid them,"* (19:14). This is the heart of the Divine plan. The theology expressed in chapter eighteen settled it. Why did the disciples not comprehend the truth of this theology? Jesus was making a theological statement when He set a boy on His lap (18:2). Jesus made a child the symbol of the Kingdom of God (18:3-4). He called the disciples to experience the status of a child without rights and demands (18:3). Jesus strongly warned the disciples about offending little ones (18:6). He even crouched this warning in the framework of hell fire (18:8-9). He called them to receive the children like they would receive Him (18:5). His dream for all of us is that we might become His little children. This is His plan.

God always includes **THE DIVINE PROVISION** in His plan, *"for of such is the kingdom of heaven,"* (19:14). God has provided an inheritance for those without status. Those who cannot accomplish and have no way to purchase or merit, will inherit the Kingdom of God. It is the poor in spirit who own the Kingdom of Heaven (5:3). The provision is that those who lose their lives will find it in the middle of the Kingdom. Those who die to themselves, Jesus will raise in the middle of Kingdom life. Those who will forgive will also know forgiveness. It is the way to live in the flowing heart of the Kingdom of God. God's provision is that those who will set aside their rights will receive the inheritance as a son of God.

All of this sounds tremendous, but there is **THE HUMAN PROBLEM.** The problem here begins with *"but the disciples rebuked them"* (19:13). A major thrust of chapter eighteen was to receive and protect little ones. Now there are twelve disciples blocking the door way and telling the children to leave. Did the disciples sleep through Jesus' sermon? Did they not grasp even a little of the great theology He just gave them?

We know what the problem is! It is self-centered carnality. They are still operating from the perspective of their main question, **"Who then is greatest in the kingdom of heaven?"** (18:1). If you are attempting to be elected to the number one place in the Kingdom, then kids do not matter. They cannot vote. They do not help pay the budgets at the church. Children get gum on the carpet. Kids will cost you something! Kids are incapable of repaying. There is little benefit from them. It is harder to use kids for your own benefit.

God, please forgive the church that has problems getting workers for junior church. Please, God, forgive the church that cannot keep a staff for the nursery. The theology of chapter eighteen is great for a discussion in Sunday School. But theology turns to ashes if I do not apply it. I must act out my theology by pouring my life out for those who cannot give back to me. It is time to take up my cross and live its style. It is time to die to myself, and let the Holy Spirit fill me with His style.

Materialism and the Depressed
Matthew 19:16-30

Contained within this section is the story of the Rich Young Ruler. There are strong elements of truth given in this encounter. This story has been kept before the church regularly. It is very practical in its application for it deals, not with a group of disciples, but it is one man encountered by his God. As I read the story I get the feeling that I am this man.

THE DIVINE PLAN is the beginning. *"Now behold, one came and said to Him, 'Good Teacher, what good thing shall I do that I may have eternal life?"* (19:16). God's dream is eternal life for every individual. Embedded into the nature and character of every individual is a bleating cry for life! This cry does not simply come from the senior adult who realizes life is almost over. It is the young who are possessed with this great desire for life. They find themselves aching for fulfillment, righteousness, and life. It is not simply the depressed, homeless, and economically deprived who are restless and desire life. It comes from the young and rich who have everything going their way. They cry for a meaning and a purpose. The cries do not come from those who have no prestige or self-esteem. The loudest cries come from the rich young rulers with position and prestige. It is the Divine plan. God has stamped into the very soul of every individual a restlessness and this cry for life.

But God never makes a plan without **THE DIVINE PROVISION**. Jesus said to the Rich Young Ruler, *"If you want to be perfect, go, sell what you have and give to the poor, and you will have treasure in heaven; and come follow me"* (19:21). The heart of the Divine provision is in following Him. The Rich Young Ruler thought *things* contained the provision of God. His question to Jesus was, *"Good Teacher, what good thing shall I do that I may have eternal life?"* (19:16). This was his perspective because it fed his ego. If there was some *good thing* he could do, then he could brag about what he had done. He could feel good about his own activity and fulfill his self-centeredness. If the **good things** he could hold, contained the answer, then he could brag about what he had accumulated. This would help fulfill his self-centered value system. Jesus confronts him with the proposition that life is not found in his self-centered activities, but in surrendering to Christ centered activities. Life comes in not what you do for Him, but what you allow Him to do through you. It is not in you, doing the will of God, but in you, being the will of God, that you find life. You derive life from Him alone. Jesus was the very provision of God for the Rich Young Ruler. The provision was so close he could have reached out and touched Him. Eternal life was his, if only he would respond to Christ!

THE HUMAN PROBLEM now presents itself. *"But when the young man heard that saying, he went away sorrowful, for he had great possessions"* (19:22). The problem is the same here as it is in all of the other applications. It is our own self-centered carnality. The question to answer is always the same. Am I going to love myself or am I going to fall in love with the Christ of the cross? Is my life going to revolve around myself or around the Christ who has the style of the cross? Will my life be possessed with temporary things, or will it flow with eternal values found only in the cross?

What is the good in our theology or holiness teaching, if we do not bring it into the practical application of daily living? In "Marriage and Divorce" we must die to ourselves until we live for each other. In "Mothers and Dependents" we must lose our lives until we never use those who are less than we are for our own ends. In "Materialism and the Depressed" we must cease to accumulate for ourselves and become an avenue for the cross to spill its value through us.

"Jesus, bring us to death. Thank you for not leaving us alone. You keep coming back to the same basic truth. In some areas of our lives we feel very good about it, but You keep coming back to those areas that bother us. Do not leave us alone! Continue to speak to us until we find the cross and its style applied in every area of our lives. In Your name, I pray, Amen."

Matthew 19:1-10

Marriage - One Flesh or Two

"Dear Jesus, we do not know all of the answers; but we believe You do! We do not know what is the proper action; but we believe You do! There are things hidden that we do not see; but we know that You see it all! We are not resting on what we have to say. We are listening to what You have to say to each of us. Deal with our deepest heart problem. In Jesus' name, we pray, Amen."

The most difficult aspect of Christianity is the practical application of truth. How do we take that which is high and bring it into the lowliness of the routine? How do we take that which is absolutely holy and bring it into an unholy world without contaminating it? Can you take that which is ideal, bring into a society that is not ideal, and make it work? How do you take that which is heavenly, bring it into the earthly, and expect it to remain heavenly? Can that which is sincere, be brought into a dishonest and insincere world, and maintain its high standard? This is the most difficult aspect of Christianity.

However, as great as the problem might be, there is an entire group of us who are absolutely dedicated to living the holy life in our unholy world. If we cannot maintain holiness in our unholy world, then it is a waste of our time. If we are preaching an impractical Gospel, then let us cease our preaching. If what God says in His Word is just high principle to be considered in the classroom, then let us dismiss the class and seek more practical answers. I am a part of the group determined to live this ideal, holy principle in our unholy world. We are committed to experiencing it daily on our streets. We believe that a powerful God can make us adequate in an inadequate world to be what He has called us to be.

The beginning of chapter nineteen is significant. **"Now it came to pass when Jesus had finished all of these sayings, that He departed from Galilee and came to the region of Judea beyond the Jordan"** (19:1). Matthew is establishing a definite connection between chapters eighteen and nineteen. The connection is in the flow of the material. There is a geographical connection between the two chapters. Jesus is moving from the scene of chapter eighteen, Galilee, into the area of Perea. Jesus and His disciples had come from Gentile territory into Capernaum (17:22). They came to meet with several other groups and make the journey south to Jerusalem for the Feast of the Passover. Evidently, the selfish question of the disciples (18:1), and the great theological statement given as its answer (chapter 18), takes place in Galilee just before they left. Now they have arrived in Perea where Jesus will minister for a brief time as they are moving toward a cross.

However, the connection between chapters eighteen and nineteen is much more than just a geographical flow. There is a definite similarity in the style of teaching. Jesus has been teaching through contrast in chapter eighteen; He is now going to continue with that style into chapter nineteen.

The opening statement of chapter eighteen is a question asked by the disciples. *"Who then is greatest in the kingdom of heaven?"* (18:1). The high priority issue of their board meeting is who of them is going to get to be number one. It was self-centered carnality expressed! Jesus has placed the mission of winning the world in their hands, but they could think of nothing but themselves. They have not caught the greatness of their task. Jesus presents a contrast that focuses the issue. He places a child upon His knee (18:2), contrasting the self-centered demands of the disciples with a child who has no rights (18:3-5). The only desire of the child is to set on His lap in love. This is the symbol of what is at the heart of the Kingdom.

Jesus continues by contrasting the disciples self-centered focus with the Father's shepherd's heart (18:10-14). One sheep from His one hundred has gone astray. Anxiety fills Him immediately. It so possesses Him that He has no joy over the ninety-nine sheep safely in the fold. He must risk His very life for the one. This is the pattern Jesus is challenging His disciples to follow. Jesus also contrasts the unforgiving self-centeredness of the disciples with the redemptive forgiveness that forgives seventy times seven (18:22). This forgiveness does not keep an account, but meets each hurt or wrong with the spirit of forgiveness.

Now as we come into chapter nineteen, the contrast is continued. We have selected for our consideration in this chapter the section on "Marriage and Divorce" (19:1-12). At the very beginning of this section there is an obvious contrast (19:2-3). *"And great multitudes followed*

Him, and He healed them there," (19:2). The trial and crucifixion of Jesus will take place in just a few weeks. Some members of this multitude may be present. They might mingle their voices with the cries of the crowd and scream for the blood of Jesus. Jesus knows exactly where He is going and what is going to take place. He knows He is in the shadow of the cross this moment. Yet, Jesus pushes this knowledge aside and pours His life out to a multitude that desperately needs Him. He does not focus on the hurts and the pain He will receive from them in the future, but gives Himself to selfless ministry.

It is the Pharisees who produce the contrast in this scene. ***"The Pharisees also came to Him, testing Him,"*** (19:3). They are not seekers after the truth. This is a temptation, a trick, or a trap. They are attempting to force His hand by dragging Him into a controversial social issue. The motivation for this is their own self-centeredness. They want to protect their own political position. They have a multimillion dollar business going on at the temple, and will allow no one to disturb it. They must remove any threat to their control. The need of the multitude does not seem to move them. Jesus sets aside all the hurt and pain in which some will participate and ministers selflessly to them. This is the contrast.

Another vivid contrast is presented in the rest of this section (19:4-9). Jesus is presenting marriage as a selfless experience. The question of marriage is not "What can I get out of it?" The only proper question is "What can I give to it?" Marriage is not about personal benefit, but a relationship within which the style of the cross can be lived. The contrast to this approach is found in the disciples. ***"His disciples said to Him, 'If such is the case of the man with his wife, it is***

better not to marry" (19:10). The disciples say that if the regulating attitude of marriage is losing your life, then there would be little personal benefit from it. It would not be worth the sacrifice. The disciples are back to their same old self-centered carnal approach. They are wanting to use someone for their own personal benefit. Jesus is continually calling them to the cross style. This is the great contrast.

The conclusion is obvious. Jesus is discussing marriage and divorce with those gathered around Him. Self-centered carnality sets the tone of the discussion for all others involved. The Pharisees are self-centered in their expression (19:3). The disciples are here again with more of the same (19:10). The multitudes that followed Him were wanting to use Him for their own selfish ends (19:2). The entire culture of Jesus' day smelled of self-centered carnality in its approach to marriage. Right in the middle of this self-centered atmosphere Jesus stands tall and confronts everyone. He calls them to the cross and death to self-centeredness. The proposition of these verses (1-13) is as follows. **The greatest deterrent to one flesh marriage is self-centeredness.** Why is it such a great deterrent?

The Foundation Of Marriage
Matthew 19:4-6

Self-centered carnality literally destroys the foundation of marriage. It is easy to see the cultural differences between the day of Jesus and our present world. In the area of transportation and communication there are such vivid changes, it is startling. In the area of science and medicine, the amount of knowledge known now, compared to Jesus' day, is too large to contrast. The dress, educational level, economy, and other key areas have all changed drastically. However, while the cultural settings are vastly different, both societies produced the same basic view concerning marriage and divorce. We have blamed the rise of divorce upon the fast pace of our society. In Jesus' day the pace was much slower, yet divorce was a major problem for them also. Our families seldom sit together around a meal and just talk; thus there is the break down of family communication that creates the atmosphere for divorce. In Jesus' day, they constantly ate together as families and had evenings free for communication, yet still they had a problem with divorce. Does not all of this tell you that the problem goes deeper than the cultural practices? The problem is deep within the heart of people. What did the people of Jesus' day have in common with the modern person of this hour? It is self-centered carnality. This is the root of the problem.

Let me share with you some insight into the cultural setting of Jesus' day. In the eyes of the Jewish law, as interpreted by the Pharisees, a woman was a mere possession. A child was owned and possessed by his father. The female child would never grow out of that position. The father of each female could establish her future marriage when she was just a child. The future husband had to provide a dowry to compensate the father for his loss. When the young lady was married she became a possession of her new husband as she had been of her father.

You can see how divorce could become very easy. The Pharisees interpreted this out of Deuteronomy, chapter twenty-four, verse one. It was here that Moses provided a means for divorce through a certificate. It was nothing more than a piece of paper on which the husband wrote,

"I divorce you." He then signed his name and put her out of his house. There was no provision in this for the wife to divorce the husband.

There were two occasions when the Jewish law, as interpreted by the Pharisees, demanded that the husband divorce his wife. One was when the act of adultery had been committed. Understand that the husband could commit adultery and the wife could not divorce him, but if the wife committed adultery, the law commanded her husband to divorce her. There was a second occasion demanding divorce. If after ten years of marriage no male child had been born to their relationship, divorce was permissible.

There were great arguments over these issues. There was a liberal school that proposed divorce for just about any reason. There was the conservative school that limited divorce to adultery. This issue was debated long and loud throughout every level of society. The Pharisees tried to use this controversial atmosphere to set a trap for Jesus. They asked the question, ***"Is it lawful for a man to divorce his wife for just any reason?"*** (19:3). They thought that Jesus' answer would join Him to one of the schools, thus bringing division to His ministry. But Jesus is so wise.

He confronts the Pharisees with three powerful statements that answer three great questions. The first question is **WHO CREATED MARRIAGE?** ***"Have you not read that He who made them at the beginning made them male and female?"*** (19:4). The Pharisees claimed to live by the direct quotation from the Holy Scriptures. The one who created marriage was not Moses, so why should we listen only to him. The One who created marriage was God. This was His ordained plan. God made them male (singular) and female (singular); He did not make them male (singular) and females (plural). So in God's original plan there was no room for polygamy, nor for divorce. God created the marriage institution.

However, there is a second question Jesus asks. It is **WHO INSTRUCTED CLEAVING IN MARRIAGE**? Jesus continued, *"For this reason a man shall leave his father and mother and be joined to his wife, and the two shall become one flesh"* (19:5). Again this is a quotation from the Old Testament Scriptures to which the Pharisees had committed themselves. The verb tense of this Old Testament statement is very significant. It uses the word *shall* twice. It connects with the two main parts of the truth. *"A man shall leave his father and mother"* and *"the two shall become one flesh."* The thrust of this is the future emphasis of the word. The Pharisees dared not suggest that this was a commandment of God for days of old, but it did not apply now. This was true in the Garden of Eden, but it is not true now because things have changed so much. However, this commandment was not about what was, but it is about what is! God said it then, and it still holds true today. This was God's desire for marriage in the Garden of Eden, and it is still His great desire for your marriage now.

The phrase *be joined to* is the word "cleave." This literally means glued. God is speaking about one male and one female being glued together. They become inseparable. The idea is that of welding. When a piece of metal is broken, it is welded back together. It will never break at the weld, because that has become the strongest part of the metal. The sexual attraction between a man and woman takes precedence over the natural affections either may have for their parents. They are to come together and be welded into one flesh. What a beautiful picture of the marriage relationship!

The question Jesus proposes in verse four is. "Who Created Marriage?" The answer is, God did! The question He proposes in verse five is "Who Instructed Cleaving in Marriage?" The answer is, God did! Now He asks **WHO CONFIRMED MARRIAGE**? *"So then, they are no longer two but one flesh. Therefore what God has joined together, let not man separate"* (19:6). The confirmation in marriage is *one flesh*. God does the confirming. It was God who made this great union possible in the first place (Genesis 1:27). It was God who issued the command that the first couple should go, be fruitful and multiply (Genesis 1:28). God came and said, *"It is not good that man should be alone"* (Genesis 2:18). God made Eve out of Adam's rib, and He presented her to him as a helper comparable to him (Genesis 2:12). It was God who established marriage. It was God who glued man and woman together. God has been doing the confirming from the beginning.

Again the concept of glued, welded, cleaved, or be joined together is the heart of being *one flesh*. In this passage (19:5-6), Matthew uses this word concerning the relationship within marriage. This word "cleave" appears in Paul's writings. *"Or do you not know that he who is joined to a harlot is one body with her? For 'the two,' He says, 'shall become one flesh"* (1 Corinthians 6:16). Paul is saying that the same thing that happens between a husband and wife in marriage also takes place between and man and a harlot. They become one flesh through the gluing process.

The undercurrent of this whole discussion is the creativity of the **one flesh** relationship. It has to do with a child being brought into being. The being of the male and the being of the female are intertwined into a brand new creation. It is the intermixing of the two into **one flesh**. The child born to this relationship is the physical evidence of the spiritual reality of the **one flesh**. The **one flesh** is so inseparable that no one can divide it. Let the husband take half of the child and go his own way. Let the wife take the other half of the child and live to herself. It cannot be done. Jesus is saying that God has done a marvelous thing in the creation of the marriage institution. The two have intermixed themselves in the **one flesh** and a child is born. God's plan screams at us. You cannot separate yourself from your wife or husband any more than you can separate yourself from yourself. It is impossible. By God's order the marriage relationship is an indissoluble union.

We all agree that this sounds wonderful. We would nod in agreement that this is probably the way it should be. Perhaps it was possible in the Garden of Eden, but there is a fly in the ointment. Something has happened that has destroyed the process. What is the fly? It is self-centered carnality. That is the whole point of the passage. When we apply the reality of the cross style to marriage relationship, what raises its ugly head? Self-centeredness exposes itself for what it really is. This passage is not a teaching on marriage and divorce, but on the deep heart need of each of us. It is self-centeredness that divides our homes. Self-centeredness splits us apart. It will not forgive, and it is demands its rights. This passage is a call to the cross. We must die to ourselves. Crucifixion is our only chance. It is time we get flat on our face before God and repent of the selfishness that shakes its fist in the face of God and His plan. We must come to death.

The Flow Of Marriage
Matthew 19:7-9

Self-centered carnality literally destroys the flow of marriage. The central purpose of the Kingdom of God is relationship. The deep desire within the Father for each of us is relationship. God is not asking us for brilliant performance of our duty; He is calling for intimate relationship. From a theological perspective we understand that the entrance into this relationship is through two crisis experiences of initial sanctification and entire sanctification. The major emphasis in Christianity is not experience. It is flowing Jesus into our relationships on a daily basis. God does not want your birth certificate; He wants to live with you on a moment by moment basis. This truth parallels the marriage relationship. Marriage is not simply a ceremony held on a certain day for us to remember every year. It is not a preacher saying some nice words and the bride and groom exchanging some vows. While the moment is significant, the heart of marriage is the continual, constant flow of relationship. What is it that disrupts this flowing relationship in marriage? There is only one element that destroys this flow; it is self-centeredness.

Through some key statements Jesus is asking the Pharisees and us some important questions. Question number one is **WHO COMMANDED DIVORCE?** *"They said to Him, 'Why then did Moses command to give a certificate of divorce, and to put her away?' He said to them, 'Moses, because of the hardness of your hearts, permitted you to divorce your wives, but from the* *beginning it was not so"* (19:7-8). The Pharisees were confident as they asked their first question (19:3). They were sure Jesus would embarrass Himself, because His statements were so powerful. Now they think they see a way to take care of Him for sure. Jesus has just said that in God's plan there was no divorce, yet Moses commanded that they get a divorce. Is Jesus saying that Moses contradicted God's plan?

Jesus clearly says that the problem was not in Moses, but in the interpretation the Pharisees had of what Moses said. There is a strong contrast that highlights this. The Pharisees stated, ***"Why then did Moses command. . .?"*** (19:7). Jesus answered, ***"Moses . . . permitted you . . . ."*** (19:8). The Pharisees were attempting to blame Moses for their divorces. It was as if they did not really want to do it, but due to the command of Moses, they were forced into it. All the time the cause of their divorces was ***the hardness of your hearts.*** Moses simply let them do what he knew they were going to do anyway. The Pharisees and their forefathers were stuck on themselves. Their decision to have their own way and live for themselves led Moses to give them a legal way to do what they had already decided. "Who Commanded Divorce?" It was not Moses, but their self-centered carnal hearts.

The second question is **WHO CONCEIVED DIVORCE?** Who first had the thought of such an idea as divorce? What is the source of this idea? Jesus gave a powerful answer to this question. ***"Because of the hardness of your hearts, . . ."*** (19:8). Jesus was accusing the Pharisees and their forefathers of being hard in their hearts. It literally means an unforgiving attitude. It is an individual who is so filled with himself that he cannot extend forgiveness to someone else. Thus, he refuses God's provision for loving relationships through forgiveness.

It is easy to think that this only applies to an ideal world, with ideal situations, involving ideal people. No one would want to promote divorce as good and proper, but in some circumstances it is an answer to the problem. Jesus boldly says, "NO! It is not an answer!" God's answer is not divorce but forgiveness. The reason God's answer is forgiveness is that it keeps the relationship flowing. Divorce cuts off relationship. Self-centeredness builds walls and blockades communication. Forgiveness tears down walls and promotes communication. Forgiveness reaches out and builds bridges. Forgiveness is God's answer. What keeps us from forgiving? It is self-centered carnality. It is self-centered carnality that conceived divorce.

If self-centered carnality commanded divorce, self-centered carnality conceived divorce, then **WHO COMPREHENDS THE EFFECTS OF DIVORCE?** *"And I say to you, whoever divorces his wife, except sexual immorality, and marries another, commits adultery; and whoever marries her who is divorced commits adultery"* (19:9). Self-centeredness concentrates on the immediate hurt it is experiencing. It cannot go beyond the conflict of the moment. The focus is on how it affects me, how much I hurt right now, and what they did to me! Self-centeredness is short sighted and is focused on now.

The contrast to this is the cross and its style. The cross enables us to have a long range view. Satan easily sucks us into a quick fix for our problems. Later we discover that the immediate fix has created greater problems. Death to self-centeredness gives us eye sight into the future. It enables us to look beyond our immediate hurt, and it gives us the ability to hear the voice of God. His voice guides proper decisions for our lives. Where are we going to be fifty years from this moment? What are our dreams, or what are God's dreams for the future? When self-centeredness is in control, we only care about the immediate moment.

We must never give in to correcting one sin by creating another sin. Can you see the foolishness in God correcting your sin by sinning Himself? If you sin against God, He rises in self-centered anger and smashes you. He ends up sinning to correct your sin. My sin causes God to sin. Sin perpetuates sin that perpetuates more sin. Sin seems to beget sin, which begets more sin. How did God handle sin? When you sinned against God, He decided to stop sin forever. How did He do it? He died on the cross, lost His life, and forgave you. Forgiveness is the only chance we have to stop sin. In self-centeredness you hurt me, so I hurt you, which causes you to hurt me again. Sin goes on and on. In the midst of this process someone must lose his or her life and come to the cross. It is here that forgiveness takes place and stops sin. Who will lose his or her life?

Who comprehends the effects of divorce? Self-centered is the blinder that will not allow us to see the long range effect of divorce. It never comprehends the effects of divorce, but only looks at the immediate hurt. Jesus is calling us to the view of the cross.

The Focus Of Marriage
Matthew 19:10

Self-centered carnality literally destroys the focus of marriage. *"His disciples said to Him, 'If such is the case of the man with his wife, it is better not to marry"* (19:10). Again there are three major questions answered in this verse. Question number one is, **IS THIS THE CASE?** The disciples are wondering if this is the way it really is.

Did they really understand what Jesus said? When a small group discusses this truth, there is a normal, common reaction from most people. They look at all that Jesus has stated and say "This is too hard." They go on to question whether He really did say it. How do we know this is the truth? This is an impossible truth. They will continue by giving a long list of marriage and divorce situations. Is Jesus saying we should simply forgive them and go on? This is an impossible truth.

There is one convincing fact that tells me we have discovered the heart truth of this passage. This is exactly what Jesus is saying. It is the fact that the disciples responded this way. This is too hard. It would be better never to get married if this is the truth. But notice that their reaction came from the basic motivation revealed in the question they ask earlier, ***"Who then is greatest in the kingdom of heaven?"*** (18:1). Self-centered carnality filled them. If they approached their relationships within the disciple group this way, would they not approach marriage the same way? They want to know how they will benefit from marriage. If you approach marriage from this self-centered view, what Jesus is saying is impossible. This is why we must come to the cross. The call is to die to self-centered carnality. The focus of marriage is not you, but others. It is not how you are going to benefit, but others. It is not what is going to come to you, but what you can give to others. Yes, disciple, this is the case of a man with his wife, so lose your life and live the cross style in your marriage.

The second question being answered in this verse is, **IS THIS THE CONFINEMENT?** The reaction of the disciples in verse ten is that the kind of marriage relationship Jesus has presented is to confining. This kind of one flesh marriage, where each person loses his life to the other, would completely box in those persons. When marriage is presented in terms of cleave, glued, welded, it is so confining and binding that no one will want to enter it.

However, this is all decided by your viewpoint. Self-centeredness views this **one flesh** marriage as too confining; but the cross style looks at marriage as refining. In the hard moments of relationships when I cannot run away, God can refine my person through my marriage partner. Self-centeredness sees this kind of marriage as putting me in a box. The cross that is the loss of my life sees it as an opportunity to give myself. Self-centeredness says this kind of confinement will destroy me; the style of the cross finds growth in it. Marriage is an investment of two people into each other, which refines each of you into something you never could be without giving yourselves to each other. The heart of divorce is the attitude that refuses to let God refine you through your mate. It resists the shaping and molding of the Holy Spirit through relationship. It refuses to lose its life. Self-centered carnality will never submit to your mate. That is why it has to die. A cross is necessary if this style is to be lived through the marriage.

This brings us to the last question. **IS THIS THE CONCLUSION?** The conclusion of the disciples was *"it is better not to get married"* (19:10). Is this the proper conclusion? The answer is NO! The conclusion is that it is better to lose your life. Jesus is inviting us to the death of self-centeredness. He wants us to live on the cross. True life comes in the midst of death. It is easy to deal constantly with surface problems and never face the undercurrent, depth cause. Jesus is calling us back to the root of the real problem. Whether it arises in a desire to be number one in the disciple group, or arises in the issue of marriage, the source is still self-centered carnality. It is time to throw your life away and embrace the cross.

"Jesus, You are the love of my life. You have come to give us the truth. Do not let us get distracted from the heart issue. You are not hard or mean, but You are loving and caring. This is what motivates You to bring us to truth. We will accept You as truth and come to Your cross. In Jesus' name, we respond, Amen."

Matthew 19:13-15

Children - Of Such

In Matthew's Gospel, chapter eighteen thunders into chapter nineteen. You must visualize all that is taking place in chapter eighteen, before you can understand chapter nineteen. Jesus presents the theology of the cross style in chapter eighteen. Now in chapter nineteen, the application of that theology confronts us. If we do not apply the theology to our lives individually, it is a theology without sense. Jesus has given us great mind boggling concepts in chapter eighteen. In chapter nineteen we see those great spiritual principles brought to the practical meaning. In chapter eighteen Jesus teaches a marvelous truth, but He presses to change the style of our normal lives in chapter nineteen.

The cross style theology of chapter eighteen is death to self-centeredness. It calls me to release what I can accomplish, or my sufficiency. It is a change from seeking position to seeking ministry. The manipulation of others for self-promotion must stop. But how does this apply in the normal situations of my life? In verses one through twelve, Matthew applies it to *Marriage and Divorce*. When two individuals, male and female, lose their lives to God and to each other, they become **one flesh**. Marriage produces a new unit that the male and female could never be alone. This is a unit that no one can dissolve.

The second application of the theology of chapter eighteen brings us to the issue of this chapter. How does death to self-centeredness apply to my relationship with children? This passage (19:13-15) presents a mirror in which we see our reflection. The disciples had personal confrontations with Jesus, and yet, comprehended so little of what He shared. We discover the evidence of this in the practical application. Perhaps the disciples were asleep in the theological class room. Time after time it appears they were there, yet not actually present.

Jesus was seated in the living room of a home where He and the disciples had come for a visit. Mothers had brought their children to this home to receive the blessing of Jesus. The disciples stand at the doorway and refuse the children entrance into the presence of Christ. They are physically blocking the way, and they are verbally rebuking the children for coming. Their actions and words make a statement to the children. "Children do not come in here. You are not welcome into the presence of Jesus. You are a bother, and you are not important enough for Him to give His attention to you."

Jesus' response is immediate. ***"Let the little children come to Me, and do not forbid them;"*** (19:14). A literal translation of these words is very strong. It might read like this; "Get out of the way of the children. Stop hindering them from coming to Me." It is a message to us all. Dad, get out of the way of your children. You cannot let one moment of your influence be a blockade between your child and Christ. Your lukewarmness could build a barrier between your child and Jesus.

You are responsible, Dad. There is a message here for you too, Mother. Get out of the way of the children. Do not let your vanity and self-centeredness build walls that keeps your child from Jesus. These messages also apply to grandparents. It goes beyond the immediate family relationships. Board members must get out of the way of the children. It is easy to attend the board meeting in self-centeredness. Our self-agendas become blockades to the moving of the Spirit of God that would reach to the children. It is a very strong truth to consider.

In chapter eighteen, Jesus sat a child on His lap. The boy snuggled down against the chest of Christ in love and contentment (18:2). Everything Jesus is proposing in His theology, we see as He sets the boy on His lap. Jesus calls the disciples to become like this little child, if they want to make entrance into the Kingdom of God (18:3). It would mean a reversal in focus or concentration for the disciples. The self-seeking, wanting position, and superiority over others, would now give way to servanthood, selflessness, and ministry. However, this is not just a call to *become,* but it is a call to *befriend.* Jesus says that the evidence of a reversal taking place is seen when you can receive a little one like you receive Him (18:5). Then Jesus expands the idea to include anyone who is less than you are. The test of death to self-centeredness is how you receive those considered beneath you.

Jesus continues by calling us to *be careful* (18:6). Satan will use self-centered carnality to offend a little one, which is sin. If you cling to your self-centeredness, it becomes a handle for demonic use, and you are in danger of everlasting, hell fire (18:8-9). Jesus' severity is impossible to miss.

If there is any confusion, Jesus quickly clears it. He calls us to *behold* (18:10-14). We are to see the little ones exactly the way the Father beholds them. The Father focuses all of His attention on a crying little one (18:10). He has a shepherd's heart. A driving anxiety fills His heart at the thought of one straying sheep. It overshadows any joy He feels for the safe sheep in the fold. This anxiety drives Him to risk His life in order to rescue the one. That distressed one is His priority.

Step from the impact of this great theology (chapter 18) into the scene of our present study. After all of this strong teaching, what are the disciples doing? They are standing in the door way, refusing the children entrance to Christ. They are rebuking them because the children are not important enough to demand the attention of Jesus. You can see the forcefulness of Jesus when He answers them! "Get out of the way of the children and stop hindering them from coming to Me!"

Jesus gives His reason for allowing the children to enter when He says, ***"for of such is the kingdom of heaven"*** (19:14). This statement is the pivot point of the entire passage. Everything in the scene revolves around this phrase. These children represent the proposition of the passage. **The little children are symbols of the essence of the Kingdom of God.**

Their Position - What They Derived
Matthew 19:14

Jesus gives this truth to the disciples, who have experienced the theology of chapter eighteen. They are not the shy type, who sit in the corner and suck their thumbs. The disciples are aggressive. They do not cry over the slightest hurt, and they are far from the category of sissy.

Peter has defended himself more than once. No one pushes him around. He is a leader. The Scripture does not call James and John the "Sons of Thunder" without reason. They are always wanting to call down fire from heaven and burn up the city who rejects them. This passage presents us with some pretty strong characters.

Do you see how radical the call of Jesus was for this group? They left their families to follow Jesus. They desperately wanted to be a part of the Kingdom of God. They had waited for the Messiah all of their lives. Now, in Jesus, they see the fulfillment of their dreams. Could the Kingdom of God be present now? Jesus tells them that the center point of the Kingdom of God is a child. What a shock! Society has taught them to stand up, do not cry, and always demand your rights. Suddenly Jesus confronts these disciples with the reality of the Kingdom, which is the symbol of a child. This was a symbol of weakness for them. Jesus was not proposing that the Kingdom of God is weak. It has great strength, but the basis of the strength is vastly different from the perception of the disciples. They thought the basis of the strength would be in them. It would be their ability, their self-sufficiency, their training that would support the Kingdom. Jesus presents another basis for the strength of the Kingdom. It has to do with the *Position* of the child.

This position begins with **DEMOTION - COMPLETE**. This must have been radical to the disciples. Jesus said, "I want you to demote yourselves." How else could the disciples have interpreted Jesus' call to be as a child? They were competing for the number one spot in the Kingdom of God (18:1). They all wanted to sit in the big chair. The disciples loved power! If Jesus had spoken of promotion, it would have been more reasonable to them. Whoever did the most miracles, or won the most converts, or attended the most services would receive the biggest rewards.

Jesus called them to demotion. He refers to the status of a child. In Jesus' day a child had no status. He or she was a possession of their father. He could sell his child into slavery. A Roman father could abuse his child. It was within his rights. The child had no rights. That is why the child is a symbol of the essence of the Kingdom.

The disciples had the basic perspective of the world. The world decides your greatness by the number who serve you. You are very important if many people clamor after you. Great people get their feet washed. Now Jesus presents this radical concept of the Kingdom. The more you serve, the greater you are. Your position is highest when you pour out your life for others. The measure of your greatness is how much you love others. It was a call for demotion to the lowest status.

There is a second element in this position. It is **DEMANDS - NONE**. This was the position of the child who had no basis for any demands. He had no rights. This is contrary to the thought process of our world. The world offers help for those who think their rights have been violated. The focus of our world is on making personal demands and getting them. Indeed this is a radical call to a new position!

While this is true, we need to understand the atmosphere of the cross style. Let us look at what giving up my personal rights is not. It does not parallel surrendering my right to eat cake while on a diet. Imagine yourself sitting at the dinner table after a wonderful meal, and you are still hungry. The host passes a plate full of delicious, moist, rich, luscious, chocolate cake. Everyone else is taking large portions and remarking about how wonderful it tastes. You sit there drooling at the corners of your mouth. You have surrendered your rights to dessert, showing self-control and discipline, but you have not given up your personal rights.

Jesus is talking about the position of dying to self-centered carnality, making your rights immaterial. They simply do not matter. A greater desire supersedes your rights. You do not drool at the mouth or grit your teeth because you must do this to be in the Kingdom of God. This is not about keeping your rights under control. You have lost the basis for your rights. They are gone.

The exciting part of this is the concluding concept. It is **DERIVE - EVERYTHING**. The child of Jesus' day had no basis to make any demands. He was of the lowest status, but as a son, he derived everything from his father. He was the legal heir to the entire resource. The family name and its prestige are his, because he is the son. The wealth of the family is his. It is not what the son has earned or merited on his own, but he derives his wealth from his father. He does not get it from his ability or cleverness, but because of relationship to his father.

The Parable of the Prodigal Son is a vivid picture of this. The youngest son demands his rights from his father. He felt he had a right to spend his inheritance when he wanted and on what he wanted. So the Father gave him his rights, which always result in pig pen living. The same is true for us today. When I finally get what I want, I find I do not want what I get. When I do what I like, I do not like what I do. When I finally demand my rights, I discover I do not want them. They always bring me to pig pen living. My rights are self-destructive. That is what happened to the Prodigal Son. When he realized this, he decided he did not want his rights. He went to his father with no basis for demands. He had demoted himself by demanding his rights. He now realized he had no right to call himself a son, but sought for mercy, hoping for the position of a slave. From that position he received a ring for his finger, a robe on his shoulders, and a celebration party. From that position he derived the benefits of a son. Do you see why Jesus used a child as a symbol of the essence of the Kingdom? In the demoted position, we derive everything.

Their Proposition - What They Desired
Matthew 19:13

"Then little children were brought to Him that He might put His hands on them and pray," (19:13). What is it that a child desires? Let us go back to the beginning scene of chapter eighteen. Jesus is in a home. Evidently the family has children acquainted with Him. The children love Jesus. The disciples gather around Jesus in the living room. They are demanding an answer to the question, *"Who then is greatest in the kingdom of heaven?"* (18:1). In response to their question, Jesus turns His attention to the boy of the home. By extending His arms, He calls the child to come to Him. The boy runs across the room, leaps into the arms of Jesus, and snuggles in a warm embrace. Can you see Jesus grinning as if this was the answer to the question?

What does a child want from Jesus? He wants the warmth of relationship expressed in a hug. What do the disciples want from Jesus? They want position. They want to use Jesus to get it. Let us take a closer look at what the child wants from Jesus. He wants **CHRIST'S ATTENTION** (19:13). The children have come to Jesus. There is no mention of healing, or counseling, or miracles. They have simply come that Jesus might notice them. This is characteristic of a child. A child does not plot to con his father out of a new car. He does not plot to overthrow the structure of the home and become head of the house. No! A child gets up at the crack of dawn, runs into the father's bedroom, jumps into the middle of the bed, and yells, "I am here!" That is what the children were doing. They had come to say, "Jesus, I am here, and I want You."

This is the depth of the holiness experience. It is death to self-centered carnality until we want nothing but His attention. It seems we constantly want something from Jesus. We are so busy using God for our personal ends. We are real con artists. Jesus calls us out of this. He wants us as a child with a heart beat for Him alone. The children also wanted **CHRIST'S AFFECTION.** *"Then little children were brought to Him that He might put his hands on them"* (19:13). To see the full impact of this truth, we must understand the verse in its context. At the beginning of this chapter Jesus had come to the region of Perea (19:2). There were great crowds following Him. What did they want from Jesus? They wanted healing; they wanted to use Him. No doubt some of this crowd will be at the cross three months from now. They will be crying for His blood. It all shows that they are simply using each moment for their own benefit.

The Pharisees also make an appearance at the beginning of this chapter (19:3). Jesus has been undermining their political power with His great popularity. They see a great opportunity to use the situation for their own benefit, and they offer a question, which they have designed as a trap. Their desire is not to know truth. They, along with the multitudes, operate out of their own self-centeredness. The disciples fit this pattern

(19:10). Their self-centeredness twists its way through every aspect of their lives. Now it is presenting itself in their view of marriage. They can see no motivation in getting married unless you would gain great personal benefit. The whole concept of losing your life to your wife and becoming *one flesh* is foreign to their thinking.

The chapter continues with the story of the Rich Young Ruler (19:16+). The fundamental of his life is his materialism. He has been pulling to himself for his entire life. Yet, he still has a strong desire for life. Jesus confronts him with the proposition that it will cost him everything he has, even a cross. With his concentration on himself, he turns away sorrowfully. He fits in well with the environment of the context. The multitudes, the Pharisees, the disciples, and now the Rich Young Ruler are all filled with themselves. In the middle of this self-centered scene is this passage about the child who has come wanting nothing but the love of Christ. Why does this seem so hard for us? Why can we not come to Jesus with our minds only focused on Him? His call is not to use Him, but He calls us to be available for Him to use us. That is the style of the cross.

The third element in the child's desire is for **CHRIST'S ACKNOWLEDGEMENT.** *"Then little children were brought to Him that He might put His hands on them and pray,"* (19:13). The parents were bringing their children that they might have the blessings of the Lord, the approval of Jesus. In studying the lives of the great saints, I discovered Saint Theresa. Sickness and suffering filled her life. Death took her in her early twenties, but she left behind some writings. She expressed her deep desire to be a rag doll for Jesus. A child will play with a rag doll for some moments, lose interest and leave it abandoned in the corner. Later, the child discovers the doll for a brief time, and then leaves it under the bed in the darkness. The rag doll exists for the pleasure of the child. Saint Theresa had found the style of the cross. Oh, to abandon our lives to Jesus until He can use us when and how He wants. We have no demands or expectations. Our one supreme desire is to be His pleasure. Do you see why Jesus used the child as the symbol of the Kingdom?

Their Provision - How They Are Defended
Matthew 19:15

"And He laid His hands on them, and departed from there" (19:15). The Old Testament customs give us real insight into this passage. The court of each Jewish city was held by the city gates. Any who had grievances would tell them to the elders who were in charge of hearing and rendering fair judgments. There were two groups of people, the widows and the orphans, who had no representation in the Jewish courts. There was no protection for them. They could not receive justice, but were at the mercy of the injustice of all men. In their helplessness, the Lord God Jehovah made a provision for them. He declared, in the Old Testament, that since these two groups had no protection, God, Himself, would be their Protector. Anyone who treated a widow or orphan unjustly would have to deal with the sovereign Lord.

That is something of what is taking place in this passage. In their self-centeredness, the disciples are seeking to protect themselves, guarding their positions and what they think they have. They are free to express their own demands, but Jesus is calling them to take on the status of a child, who has no voice in the courts. He wants them to become poor in spirit so He can give them the Kingdom. If they will come in helplessness, He can give them His great resource. He is their provision.

How is He their provision? He is their **DELIVERER** (19:15). *"And He laid His hands on them and departed from there"* (19:15). The last phrase of this verse is very significant. Jesus is on a journey. He comes into Galilee to meet with several groups of people (17:22), to begin the journey to Jerusalem. They are going there to celebrate the Feast of the Passover. The scene in this passage is only one incident on the journey. Jesus is just a few weeks from the cross. The children do not know what is happening. The hands that are now blessing them are the hands that the Roman soldiers will nail to the cross in just a few weeks. Jesus gathers the children on His lap. They are not aware that this Jesus was on His way to make provision for them. He will not bring redemption for the self-centered who could take care of themselves, but for the helpless children who cannot redeem themselves. Many have their own plans and careers, and do not see the need for a deliverer. But the poor in spirit, who have no righteousness of their own, will derive His righteousness. He will be their Deliverer.

He was also their **DECLARATION**. The children do not realize that the one who is blessing them is flowing the Word of God to them. The Word of God has come from the pages of the Old Testament and has taken on flesh, now touching them. How can the children know the Word if this does not happen? You can place a scroll in their hands, but they cannot read or understand it. The only chance they have of comprehending and embracing the Word of God is in Jesus. He is now extending His arms to them. In Him they can know the living Word. The Law of God would no longer come to them from Mt. Sinai, but it has taken on flesh and is hugging them in love. The children do not realize all of this, but surely we do! We have not simply read great ideas about servanthood, but we have seen the One who actually is a servant. He is not One who simply wrote about losing your life, but lost His life on a cross. We have seen the literal declaration of the heartbeat of God among us.

How was Christ to defend the little ones? He was their provision as their Deliverer and Declaration. This provision went beyond this to the **DISCIPLES**. They were a part of the provision for the little ones. They were to be the body of Christ. Because their focus was on themselves, they did not see it. Personal position, and what was good for them, made up their argument. The poor in spirit were their responsibility, and they did not realize it. God had put them here for others. We pray for those who are outside the church and never realize that we are the very provision of God for them. We pray for those who are less than we are, and do not realize that we are the provision of God for ministry to them. You and I are the provision of God for those who do not have our possessions.

Jesus had taken the power He contained within Himself and granted it to His disciples (Matthew 10). He sent them out to minister through this power. These chosen men duplicated the ministry and miracles of Jesus to their world. Demons had come under their control. It was time for them to give some kind of report to Jesus about their ministry. Jesus has been detained, so the disciples spend their time bragging to each other. When Jesus arrives, he hears their bragging. He asks them to be seated. He picks up a child and sets him on His knee. Turning to the disciples, he tells them that any one who cares for a child like the one on His knee, is taking care of Him. He says that anyone who cares for Him, is caring for the One who sent Him. Their care for others is the measure of their greatness. Jesus calls the disciples to be the provision for the little ones.

It is inconceivable to me that a church, living close to the heart of God, would have a difficult time getting people to work in Junior Church. It is hard to imagine that a church, loving Christ, would be unable to find people to staff the nursery. How could anyone say, "I am stuck in the nursery this Sunday?" That would be like saying, "I am stuck with Jesus, again." Our purpose is to be the provision for the little ones. Keep in mind that it is not just those who are children in age, but anyone who is helpless or less than we are. What could possibly keep us from being the provision God intends us to be? The only hindrance is self-centered carnality. The disciples displayed that for us.

"Jesus, bring us to death! The truth of the cross is as strong to our generation as it was to the disciples. We are having as difficult a time accepting it as they did. The world has trained us in self-centered styles. Bring us to the cross and its style. You are our total strength. We will then be the flow of Your power to our world. We will be the provision for the little ones. We have built our churches, given our money, taught our Sunday School classes, but we have failed to become the provision to our hurting next door neighbor. Please forgive us and change us. In Your name we pray, Amen."

Matthew 19:16-22

A Cry For Perfection

Chapter nineteen is a study in the application of the cross style. Jesus has just finished giving the disciples the great theological statements of the style of the cross. But our theology is less than worthless until we live it out in everyday life. What does the cross have to do with our materialism? The reaction of the Rich Young Ruler to the call of Christ is a part of the vivid application. Perhaps we will see ourselves as we begin the study of the cross style application to **Materialism and the Depressed.**

"Jesus, we are people of great possessions. The greatest symbol of our self-centeredness may be our materialism, which we see evidenced by our extreme comfortableness. It is difficult to speak about this because it probes at us all, but we are honest people, and we are committed to Your will. Speak to us! In Your name we pray, Amen."

One word, above all others, constantly drew John Wesley into arguments. He used it in his preaching and theological writings, and it constantly brought negative responses. It is the word *perfect* or *perfection*. This word has continued to cause arguments throughout the holiness movement. The major problem was not just the use of the word, but the insistence of linking it with *Christian*, and the introduction of the subject of *Christian Perfection*. If the words and phrases *supposed to* or *endeavor to, someday maybe* or *work harder at* could proceed the words *Christian Perfection*, people might have tolerated the idea better. However, Mr. Wesley constantly spoke of *Christian Perfection* as if one should have it right now. He proposed that God could do something deep in the inner heart that would bring us to a status of perfection before God. Another part of the problem was that many who were listening to Wesley's message did not listen to the entirety of his presentation. They simply heard the words *Christian Perfection* and erupted into anger. Communication and understanding ceased. Wesley's definition was clear. *Christian Perfection* did not mean *perfect in action*. Everyone should understand this. There are too many human limitations for us to be perfect in action. We are learning patience, which means there are degrees of impatience within all of us. This effects our service to God, which means we are probably never perfect in our service. *Christian Perfection* is not human perfection. Every time I view myself in the mirror, I am deeply aware that I am not perfect. This idea does not include being perfect in our knowledge. God alone has the quality of omniscience. Lack of knowledge means I am prone to misjudgments that produce wrong actions. I am without perfection in these areas.

Christian Perfection, according to John Wesley, was only connected with the heart. The heart is the one area where we must have perfection, and we must not neglect it. There is no excuse we can use here. God calls each of us to deal with the heart. It is not only possible to be perfect in the heart, but it is absolutely necessary. God can cleanse everything in the heart that is anti love, thus, anti God. Man can have *perfect love* with a *perfect heart*. This perfection centers in the motive of the heart, and every individual's heart can flow with perfect love. The perfect motive has to flow through the imperfect body, emotions, and actions of the human life. How can this be?

In chapter eighteen of Matthew, we saw the self-centered carnality of the disciples. They gave us the evidence of the need for death to self-motive. Jesus wanted to save the disciples from their own destruction. The style of the cross would become the style of His life from within. This was not optional, but it was absolutely necessary. It was a call to a *perfect heart*. In His instructions to a young man who is seeking life, Jesus uses the word *perfect*. Jesus said to him, **"If you want to be perfect . . ."** (19:21). Eternal life, in a present state, is intimately connected with being perfect in your heart. It is *Christian Perfection*.

It is amazing that this young man would even come to Jesus, and Jesus' response to him is even more amazing! If the Rich Young Ruler had come to the evangelical church of our day, we would have assured him that he was all right. After all, he had all the characteristics that make up a blessed, respectable, evangelical church member. Obviously God was pouring His blessings upon the young man, because he wore expensive clothing. He could expect to make it to heaven because he had kept all the commandments. This young man did the will of God because he went to church regularly and voted yes on all of the proposals. Why would he seek life from Jesus when he already had it all in abundance?

While we can rationalize our thoughts and cover our feelings, our hearts will not stop pounding the truth. In the midst of all that we have accumulated, the heart knows that the keen edge of life is missing. The completeness of life has slipped us by. There is a burning ache and a driving hunger, deep within, which screams "something is missing." This drove a young man with everything to ask of the Christ, "What is it I am missing?"

You can relate to this, can you not? In the middle of our goodness, miracles, sermons, churches, programs, and offerings, there is still this internal awareness that we lack something. We need to be whole in Jesus. We need *Christian Perfection*. This brings us to the proposition of this passage. **The fullness of life is found in Christian perfection.**

What are the elements of Christian perfection?

The Ultimate Good
Matthew 19:16-17

In our quest to be right with God, we become concerned with the details, forgetting from Whom the details come. We can become so involved in the crisis of religious experience that we lose site of intimate relationship with Christ. We focus on good deeds until we forget that a deed is not good in itself. Ultimate goodness comes from the person of God. This is the same concern from which Jesus speaks to the Rich Young Ruler.

Jesus begins with **THE FACT**. The fact is that there is an *Ultimate Good,* and He is God. At the center of the universe is the throbbing heart of God, and He is good. At the start of all things, there is an aggressive force, Who is a person, and He is good. One Who is good is permeating the atmosphere around you, pressing upon you daily, and surrounding you with *Prevenient Grace.* He is caressing you with tenderness and great care. Hear the fact! There is an Ultimate Good, and He is God. Jesus turns to the Rich Young Ruler and says, ***"Why do you call Me good? No one is good but One, that is, God"*** (19:17). There is only one source of goodness. Outside that single source, there is no goodness. God is the ultimate good from which all goodness comes. The world is not out of control. God has everything under His dictates and every dictate is good. You can rest easy in surrender to this good God.

There is an obvious question that we need to propose! If God is so good, why is there such great suffering in our world? Those who have never done anything to deserve such suffering seem to have the most. Child abuse, starvation, and disease are all evidence that something is wrong. How can the deep hurts that you and I experience in our personal lives be explained in terms of a God who is good? Does this not call into question any goodness in our universe?

The answer is found in the reality of *non good.* No one wants to hide this fact. While there is the Ultimate Good, there is also the non good. This non good does not exist on its own. Everything that we consider non good is traceable beyond the actual deed or circumstance. We know that ultimately every evil thing in the universe has its attachment to the source of all evil, who is a person we call Satan. There are no isolated acts of evil as if they exist alone. Every evil deed is attached to something far beyond the actual deed. While this is true of evil, it is much more true of good. There is not a good deed that is good within itself. It finds its goodness from a source beyond its own existence. This source is the Ultimate Good, who is God. Holiness (goodness) is all derived from the Person who is Holy. Holiness is never my own. Apart from Him there is no possibility of ever possessing even the slightest trace of holiness. Holiness is never what I can be; it is always Who He is. It is never what I will do; it is always Who He is. In the Old Testament, a bush was burning due to the presence of God (Exodus 3). The voice of God told Moses to take off his shoes because he was standing on holy ground. The ground was not holy in itself, but derived its holiness from the God who stood upon it. The Ark of the Covenant was holy because it was the dwelling place of God. When God was dwelling within the Ark, you dare not touch the Ark lest you die. Men cannot be holy within themselves apart from the Ultimate Holiness. The only possibility for holiness is for God to fall upon us. When God is upon and within the person, he or she will be holy. I must not talk about holy deeds, but must speak of a Holy God who flows through me and makes everything I do, holy. There is an *Ultimate Good.* The focus of our life should not be upon the deeds that we can do, but upon the God who possesses us from within.

This great fact allows us to also see **THE FALLACY.** *"Now behold, one came and said to Him, 'Good Teacher, what good thing shall I do that I may have eternal life?"* (19:16). Be sure you understand the question he is asking! This young man has everything he needs, except the *Ultimate Good.* He has self-discipline, proper heritage, religious ceremonies, and knowledge of the law. He is lacking in nothing except intimate contact with the *Ultimate Good*, and every deed he does lacks this plus factor.

He is aware of this lack, and it has brought him to search for reform. Yet, in the reform he wants to maintain himself as the heart of his universe. Every deed he does has the touch of self-centeredness about it instead of the *Ultimate Good*. His question to Jesus reeks of the expression of self! If he would only come under the control of the *Ultimate Good*, there would flow through him the goodness he wants. He is looking for one good deed his self-centeredness can produce to merit life. It is the greatest of all fallacies. We cannot produce goodness without the *Ultimate Good*. The Rich Young Ruler is seeking holiness that he can produce without embracing the God who is Holy.

Without hesitation, Jesus calls the young man back to **THE FUNDAMENTAL.** Jesus said, *"If you want to be perfect . . . follow Me"* (19:21). It is a call to come to the *Ultimate Good*. If he could die to himself, the theology of chapter eighteen would become the quality of life experience. The *Ultimate Good* would produce a quality of goodness through him that he can never know on his own. He must cease to be at the heart of his own universe. The cross and its style must become his experience. He would cease to be the producer of his own living, and he would become the vessel for the *Ultimate Good*.

The Unleashed Law
Matthew 19:18-19

The conversation between Jesus and the Rich Young Ruler progresses to the discussion of the law. The transitional statement of

Jesus, which leads into this discussion, is ***"But if you want to enter into life, keep the commandments"*** (19:17). The Rich Young Ruler immediately asks, ***"Which ones?"*** (19:18). Jesus boldly says, ***"You shall not murder, You shall not commit adultery, You shall not steal, You shall not bear false witness, Honor your father and your mother, and, You shall love your neighbor as yourself"*** (19:18-19). My experience with the law has been extremely negative, giving me a negative perspective of the law. Some of this I derived from a study in the Book of Hebrews. The author uses the word *nullify* regarding the law. He says that Jesus sat the law aside. The law did not accomplish righteousness; it was a failure. The law was lacking, thus, my negative approach to the law.

Now I think I see another approach here. It is a balanced picture of the law. It is **THE FACT** of the *Unleashed Law*. At the heart of every law is an unleashed law. We will call it *the spirit of the law*. The purpose of the law is not that we do a particular deed. Our performance of good deeds was not God's plan in giving us the law. His desire was that we would manifest, from our hearts, the *spirit of the law* in our obedience to the law. The law is never a deed done, or an activity accomplished, as if it were all sufficient and contained within itself. There is always an undercurrent in the law. The law, as a deed, is simply a means by which we release the undercurrent, or *spirit of the law*.

The Ten Commandments display this for us (Exodus 20). The first commandment is ***"You shall have no other gods before Me"*** (Exodus 20:3). It is a command to pull down all the carved images and break up all our idols. We go through our homes and render them clean of all false gods. Now we can say that we have kept the law. But the first commandment is not just about having graven images! You could cease to possess idols and still not fulfill the commandment. The spirit of this law is that each individual is convinced of the reality of only one God - Jehovah. We will push aside all other loyalties for commitment and concentration on the only true God. Even our own self-sovereignty must cease, by an act of our will, to let God be God in our life. In the first of the Ten Commandments we see a physical demonstration of God's desire for a deep, internal loyalty from us.

The second commandment deals with the name of God. ***"You shall not take the name of the Lord your God in vain,"*** (Exodus 20:7). We are to cleanse our language until no swear words escape from our lips. We can proudly say we have kept the second law of God. However, God's intention goes beyond this simple refraining. There is the deep spirit of the law, which is the real desire of God. If man could only grasp the majesty of God, and allow God to grip him with overwhelming respect for the Divine, that would result in a person who would not swear or degrade the Person of God. The realization that we are His representatives, His body, tells us that we must eliminate every attitude that is not like Him, lest we bring reproach upon Him. The letter of the law may be carefully kept, but the spirit of the law is God's heart's desire.

The third commandment concerns the Sabbath Day. ***"Remember the Sabbath day, to keep it holy"*** (Exodus 20:8). The letter of the law may view this commandment as simply physical. We must have no actions on the Sabbath Day that are not religious. Often, we have reduced it to not watching television or playing ball on Sunday. But the heart of this commandment is far beyond physical actions.

There is an undercurrent, a spirit of the law. The call is for an inward spirit that cries out in worship to God. While many may refrain from physical actions, and think they have kept the law, they may have forsaken worship experience. It is this spirit of worship that is the real intent of God's heart; it is the unleashed law.

Now we come to **THE FALLACY**. ***"The young man said to Him, 'All these things I have kept from my youth,"*** (19:20). That is a startling claim for anyone to make. This young man says that he thinks that he obeys all of the commandments that Jesus has listed. These commandments included murder, adultery, stealing, or bearing false witness, honor of father and mother, and loving your neighbor as yourself (19:18-19). Yet, the young man sensed a great lack, and he knew he did not have life. What was his problem? He may have kept the letter of the law, which Jesus proposed, but he had not grasped the spirit of those laws. God designed the law so that we might be gripped by the heart of God. The young man in this scene had never gone beyond physical accomplishments into the matter of the heart. That is the fallacy.

I confess to you that this truth startles me. It is difficult to know how to apply it and respond truthfully to it. It is amazing that every commandment Jesus listed has to do with relationships (19:18-19). The spirit focus of each of these laws is others. While we can boast that we have not murdered anyone or committed adultery, have we missed the undercurrent of the law? I have done the duties of the church, tithed my money, kept the special rules of the church; yet, there is still the spirit of the law that screams for my attention. Has *the spirit of the law* captured my heart? One can parade his goodness and never know the *Ultimate Good,* and one can parade his law keeping and never embrace the *Unleashed Law*. This was the conflict that Jesus had with the Pharisees. Repeatedly they degraded Jesus because He focused on the spirit of the law instead of the letter of the law. It is no wonder that Jesus constantly kept talking to them about their hearts.

At this point, Jesus brings the young man back to **THE FUNDAMENTAL.** Jesus said, ***"If you want to be perfect, go, sell what you have, and give to the poor, and you will have treasure in heaven; and come and follow Me"*** (19:21). It is a call to the cross style. Death to self-centeredness is the fundamental. The young man must come from the letter of the law and let his heart be gripped with the Spirit of the cross. That is at the root of all the commandments. His self-centered carnality has taken the expression of his own law keeping. Often, the standards that we establish for ourselves are an expression of our own carnality. It gives us a false sense of rightness and superiority. It is a product of our own discipline or self-control, which is motivated by our self-centeredness. The heart of the law is to bring us to death, allowing the Spirit of the law to flow through our lives.

Would it not be tragic to develop some respectable people who keep respectable laws, but do not have the plus factor of His life? That was the conflict between Jesus and the Pharisees. He was constantly calling them to deal with their hearts. My outside actions may keep the letter of the law, but I must ask if my heart is filled with the Spirit of the law? The issue is not how many laws do I keep, but does my heart burn for the God who is the heart of the laws?

The Unlimited Relationship
Matthew 19:21-22

"Jesus said to him, 'If you want to be perfect, go, sell what you have and give to the poor, and you will have treasure in heaven; and come and follow Me.' But when the young man heard that saying, he went away sorrowful, for he had great possessions" (19:21-22). A person can do good deeds and miss the *Ultimate Good.* Also, a person can keep the letter of the law, but miss the *Spirit of the law.* But the greatest tragedy is to seek God, and miss the *Unlimited Relationship.*

One day I stood in a Buddhist temple in a land far away. From the shadows I was watching the various people make their way to the shrine. There were hundreds of them. They had worthless paper money they had bought at a little store outside the temple. In an act of worship to their god, Buddha, they would set the money on the table with some food products. I watched as these people picked up incense sticks and lit them. They would point them toward their god and wave them for several minutes. From another table, these worshipers would pick up a bundle of sticks, rub these sticks together, and drop them. It was an attempt to predict the future and help them in decision making. The look on their faces gripped me deeply. They looked so empty. I saw the frustration that they could not express aloud. The hollowness of their actions screamed that there had to be something more than this. I wanted to grab them by the shoulders and ask, "Do you know your god, Buddha? Do you know what it is to live in the resource of his power? Can you lean your head on his chest and know the warmth of his love? Does he bring peace to your heart and wipe away your tears? When you are in the midst of a trial, is your god experiencing it with you in intimate companionship?" What they were missing was unlimited relationship.

While the scene I witnessed that day did something in my heart, it was only the beginning. What really disturbed me was a thought concerning our church and its people. I thought of how we use our morning devotions like incense sticks to wave in the face of our God. We use those moments to make sure we have the edge on a good day. We treat the Bible as a rabbit's foot, rubbing it to bring good luck. We bow our heads and pray before a long journey. It is a magic ceremony we go through to bring us safety. Of course, we believe in prayer and in Bible reading, but what a tragedy if in our attempt to reach God, we miss unlimited relationship with Him. The unlimited relationship slips by because our doing distracts us.

It may help us to look at **THE FACT**. At the heart of the universe there is a God who wants intimate relationship with you. Everything that has, and is, taking place in the world points to God, Who wants to know you personally. Observe the stars and imagine the immense resource that keeps things operating, and know that this resource has one purpose. That purpose is for you to know God. God has a plan designed for your benefit, not His. He longs for the generation when you arrive, so He can indwell you. There is a second part to this great fact. You have a heart that screams for relationship with God. You can cover, hide, resist. and bury it in substitutes, but it still screams that you were built to know God. God has built into you a craving for relationship with Him. Why do you think a young man with wealth, rulership, and popularity would come seeking life from Jesus? You will not be satisfied until you are living in the unlimited relationship. Self-righteousness, ceremonies, rules, standards, and good deeds will not satisfy this hunger. Neither theology, philosophy, nor a detailed knowledge of the end times will be enough. This cry for God comes from within you every moment of your life. As there is a God at the heart of the universe who wants to know you, so at the heart of your universe there is a deep desire to know God. Jesus is calling the Rich Young Ruler to be perfect in relationship with Him. Christian perfection is contained in this perfect love. This fact brings us to the reality of **THE FALLACY.** What a disaster to live in the correctness of doing all the right things and never deal with the fallacy. The one thing that breaks relationship with God is our own self-centeredness. The only thing that stands between you and a perfect relationship with God is the stench of your own self-will. Adultery, stealing, and dishonesty are merely symptoms of this inner condition. Self-centered carnality is the fallacy.

In our generation this self-centeredness often shows itself as materialism. It is a part of our comfort zone. We do not mind giving our leftovers, but we carefully guard our main supply. We do not mind giving some of our interest, but we are determined to save the principle for ourselves. The complication of the problem is that we live in a materialistic culture. The world is constantly elevating materialism. We breathe it in and breathe it out. But note, materialism has the stench of self-centeredness about it. It is an expression of our carnality. I can control it; I can derive self-value from it. As strong as this might be, I desperately want to respond to Jesus. The Rich Young Ruler refused the cross; I want to embrace it.

We must keep in view the progression of chapter nineteen. Chapter eighteen is a theological discourse of the cross and its effect on self-centeredness. It is a call to death. Now in chapter nineteen, we are to apply this powerful truth to three areas. Marriage and divorce are discussed in verses one through twelve. The number one problem in marriage is self-centered carnality. Unless the cross comes to the heart of marriage, it will not succeed. The second application, in relationship to children, is found in verses thirteen through fifteen. The disciples rebuke the children when they come to Jesus. Self-centeredness is the major problem between adults and children. The source of abortion is self-centered carnality. Now, in verses sixteen through nineteen, we discover the same major problem exists regarding materialism. Having materialism is not the problem; the problem is in the materialism having us. Self-centeredness stands opposed to the cross and its style.

This brings us to **THE FUNDAMENTAL**. *"If you want to be perfect, go, sell what you have . . ."* (19:21). Did you notice the emphasis on selling *what you have?* What do you consider to be your possessions? This is a call to give up, surrender, or yield what you have. This is a problem that affects the evangelical church of our day. We highlight the amount we give in tithing. We give 10 percent, which is considered our fair share. Our emphasis is on - how much do you give? The emphasis of the New Testament is - how much do you keep? Jesus is standing behind a large pillar in the temple. His disciples are with Him. He anticipates something wonderful taking place. An aged lady walks with difficulty through the front door of the temple. She has her robes wrapped tightly around her. Stopping in front of the offering box, she looks from side to side. When she is convinced no one is watching her, she takes out her coin purse and dumps its entire contents in the offering. She gives all she has. After she leaves, Jesus explains to the disciples the greatness of what she did. The disciples look confused. How could two coins be great when the Pharisees give hundreds of dollars? It is not great in terms of how much she gave, but the greatness is in how much she kept. If an individual makes ten thousand dollars and tithes one thousand of it to the church, nine thousand dollars remain for the raising of his or her family. Another individual makes one hundred thousand dollars, and he or she tithes ten thousand to the church, retaining ninety thousand dollars for personal needs. Either amount violates the principle of the cross and its style. The cross style is a call to go and sell what you have. You are not your own. Your schedule, energy, and money do not belong to you. Jesus bought and paid for you with a great price, and you are called to give up your rights to Him.

"Jesus, what is our focus? Perhaps it is not materialism, but something else. What are we tightly holding? Would You call us to release it to you so that we might be perfect? Call us to Yourself. Save us from ourselves! Call us beyond our goodness, law keeping, and materialism. Thank You for the call of the cross. In Jesus' name, we pray, Amen."

Matthew 19:16-21

Back to the Beginning

The difficulty with chapter nineteen of Matthew's account is its application. Matthew designed the entire chapter to take the theology of the cross and expose it through everyday life. Its closeness to our personal life is what makes it a difficult application. While the application is different for each individual, there are some common elements. Matthew divides this great chapter into three areas, **Marriage and Divorce** (19:1-12), **Mothers and Dependents** (19:13-15), and **Materialism and the Depressed** (19:16-30).

"Jesus, I believe that You are speaking to us as certainly as You were talking with those people two thousand years ago. May we listen and heed as we have never done before? Take us back to the beginning! In Your name, I pray, Amen."

Even the casual reader of the Book of Ecclesiastes is familiar with the constant phrase used to bring home truth. It is a negative statement. It verifies what most of us have experienced in daily life.

"Vanity of vanities, all is vanity" (Ecclesiastes 1:2). This is a depressing reality. The author, known as the preacher, has investigated every area of life and has discovered there is nothing new under the sun. His search included sexual pleasure, materialism, knowledge, power, and prestige. His conclusion was *"vanity of vanities, all is vanity."*

While this may be a negative statement, it has a positive side. If there is nothing new under the sun, then there are no new problems and there are no new solutions. There are only old questions that already have answers. Every trial that confronts you has confronted hundreds of people in the past. Those before you have already blazed the trail and found the answers.

The Rich Young Ruler proposed to Jesus, what he thought was, a brand new question. *"Good Teacher, what good thing shall I do that I may have eternal life?"* (19:16). He thought Jesus would have a new answer for his new question, but it was not a new question. God has no new answers, for there are no new questions. He has answered all of the great questions of the heart, even before the heart asked. Before man sinned, God knew the solution. He had already dreamed of the death of Jesus Christ. Problems never catch God off balance. He has attached an automatic answer to every problem. The Father has revealed all light. Do you know who stands at the beginning of light? Do you know who is the fountain from which all answers flow? His name is Jesus! He is the Alpha and the Omega, the Beginning and the End. All revelation flows from Him. He sees all of life from the beginning, and the perspective comes from the Divine purpose. When man proposes the great questions of life, God simply takes us back to the beginning. It is from the beginning perspective that we discover the right answers.

How Do I Find Life?
Matthew 19:16-22

Would you have to return to the beginning of time to discover life? We have all asked the question proposed by the Rich Young Ruler. We may not have used his exact words, but we asked in our own language. Each of us screams for the meaning of life. Every human, of every generation, has had the same question. God gave the answer to life at the beginning. If you want it, you must return to the beginning.

The beginning of life is **CHARACTER**. *"So He said to him, 'Why do you call Me good? No one is good but One, that is God. But if you want to enter into life, keep the commandments"* (19:17). The Rich Young Ruler revealed his confusion with the very question he asked. It revealed that he had a basic problem. He asked, *"What good thing shall I do that I may have eternal life?"* (19:16). Could the Rich Young Ruler possibly produce eternal life by any thing that he did? While character flows into activity, there is a fiber of character completely beyond the activity. One cannot start with the activity unless he possesses the character. The Rich Young Ruler was lacking.

The question of the Rich Young Ruler also revealed his confusion about the content of eternal life? He was asking to inherit eternal life, as if he did not have it. His view of eternal life led him to believe God would extend his days, and he did not realize that everyone has life without end. Everyone will live forever. Physical death ends life on earth as we know it, but we will all live on in eternity. The damned in hell live forever. If he wanted an extension of days, it was already his. The difference between life in heaven and hell is not length, but it is the quality. The search of the Rich Young Ruler should be for the quality of life that comes from character. The character of life that produces quality is none other than God. **"No one is good but One, that is, God"** (19:17). At the beginning of life is the One who has the highest quality of character - God. At the heart of the universe, there is a good God. Throbbing at the heart of the universe is a God of love. His whole character flows with the essence of love that produces a quality life. If you want a quality life, you must be in contact with this source.

The beginning of life is *Character*, and the beginning of character is **LAW**. **"He said to him, 'Why do you call Me good? No one is good but One, that is, God. But if you want to enter into life, keep the commandments.' And he said to Him, 'Which ones?' Jesus said, 'You shall not murder, You shall not commit adultery, You shall not steal, You shall not bear false witness, Honor your father and your mother, and, You shall love your neighbor as yourself"** (19:17-19). This is difficult for many of us to accept, because we despise legalism. Legalism kills the spirit of man, damns the soul, and distracts us from Jesus. If the beginning of character is law, then God could crack His whip over our heads until we begin to do what He demands. But that would be a forced law, which does not produce quality of life; it produces restlessness, judgmental attitudes, whitewashed sepulchers that are full of the stench of death.

The beginning of character may be law, but it is not a forced law. Did you notice the commandments listed are each focused on love for others? The beginning of life is character, and the beginning of character is law. It is not a forced law (legalism), but it is the law of love. The law of love loses itself for others. When you care more for others than for yourself you have reached the law of love. Paul summarized the entirety of the law in one word - *love*. Jesus spoke of loving the Lord your God with all of your being, and your neighbor as yourself. He captured the essence of the law with those words. John Wesley summarized the holiness by calling it perfect love.

This should not be hard for us to grasp. It is only when we allow God to remove everything alien to love that we build character. Character builds a whole life. Quality life comes from character that flows with selfless love. We must experience a cleansing of the heart, where God removes everything alien to love. The Holy Spirit must spread His love abroad in our hearts. That would make love the motivating force of our lives. We would find ourselves filled and saturated with love, and incapable of doing anything but loving. Some people look upon love as a high ideal. It is not! A thousand times I must repeat, "It is not!" This is not a goal that we are working toward. This love is absolutely necessary now. Love is not our hope of achievement some day, but love is the bear minimum of life, which God requires now.

How do you find life? The beginning of life is *Character*. The beginning of character is *Law*, and the beginning of law is **RELATIONSHIP**. Jesus said to him, ***"If you want to be perfect, go, sell what you have and give to the poor, and you will have treasure in heaven, and come, and follow Me,"*** (19:21). We are not seeking some remote philosophy that stimulates our thought process and causes us to meditate on the meaning of life. We want the practical essence of life. Man discovers relationship in the embracing of Jesus Christ. He is the flow of perfect love through us.

Jesus is very practical with the Rich Young Ruler. There is only one thing standing in this young man's way. It is his materialism - his stuff. He must escape the grip of materialism to enter relationship with Jesus. It is impossible to serve God and mammon - meaning materialism (Matthew 6:24). You cannot maintain proper relationship with Jesus while you grip materialism. Love for things and love for Christ cannot abide in the same being, because each is destructive to the other. A love for things will destroy you, and life will not flow through you. Your personal comfort will pamper you into death. Self-protection will hinder sacrifice, and that hinders the Kingdom. When we are busy guarding our valuables, we find it difficult to risk our lives for Christ. Jesus is calling the Rich Young Ruler to lose his life and come to a cross. We must fear for this present evangelical generation. Have we become so soft that we cannot make the sacrifices necessary to serve God with our whole hearts? If the answer is yes, we will never know life!

This is a strong and tough application. How do you find life? The beginning of life is character; it is the character of God. The beginning of character is law, not legalism, but the law of love flowing through the character. The beginning of love is relationship through intimacy with Him. It is death to self and all that has a grip on you, allowing you to know Him and Him alone. That is life!

How Do I Find Life With Others?
Matthew 19:3-10

I have been on a search for life for me. How do others fit into this? It is significant that the Rich Young Ruler used the same approach as the Pharisees. The young man thought that he could grasp eternal life by doing. Until now, he had obtained everything in his life by grasping. The foundational philosophy of life for the Pharisee was legalistic doing.

That was his approach to marriage and divorce. He was interested in how to get out of marriage, but Jesus' focus was on how to get into marriage - **one flesh.** The Pharisee was seeking a way to legally break his marriage vows, but Jesus was interested in how to abundantly keep the sacred vows. Jesus takes the Pharisees back to the beginning.

How can I find life with others? The beginning of marriage is LOVE. ***"And He answered and said to them, 'Have you not read that He who made them at the beginning made them male and female?"*** (19:4). You would expect me to emphasize love as the foundation of all that makes marriage the *one flesh* experience that Jesus presents. Husbands must love their wives as Christ loved the Church. Wives must love their husbands. Parents are to raise the children in the atmosphere of this love. There is no way to have a home without the foundation of love. There is only a house present when love is absent.

While this is true, it is not what Jesus is highlighting in this passage. Love is the beginning of marriage, but it is not love between husband and wife. It is God's love! God formed the idea for marriage from His beating and compassionate heart. He made marriage out of His flowing love for man. God created man, but saw a need in his life. Out of love God intervened in that need. He took a rib from Adam's side and created ***"bone of my bone and flesh of my flesh"*** (Genesis 2:23). God created women as an acting love for man.

We pride ourselves on being the *now* generation. We see everything as in the present. The excuse we use for our behavior is that we are consenting adults. However, marriage did not come into being from consenting adults. It flowed from the loving heart of God. He included Himself in the marriage relationship, a triangle - male, female, and God. Marriage is saturated with the love involvement of God.

The beginning of love is **LAW**. *"So then, they are no longer two but one flesh. Therefore what God has joined together, let not man separate"* (19:6). At the heart of the love, between husband and wife, is the law produced by the love of God. The mind of God dreamed the marriage relationship, not man. Marriage has the creative finger prints of God on it. It is His Divine plan, and He built it to work His way. Marriage only works when it follows the Divine plan, will, or law.

A fundamental principle of life is that you do not break the laws of God. The laws of God break you. You cannot see the law of gravity. What if you challenge it? Suppose you gather a crowd at the base of a tall building, and notify them that you do not believe in the law of gravity. Tell them that you are going to ascend to the top of the building and defy the law. At the conclusion of your jump, the result will be that you did not break the law of gravity. It will break you! In a like manner, you can defy the law of God. In marriage you can live for yourself, but do not think you will not pay the consequences of breaking His law.

Jesus takes us back to the beginning. The beginning of marriage is *love*. The beginning of love is *law*. Now you need to understand that the beginning of law is **RELATIONSHIP**. God's purpose in building the triangle of marriage was for His intimate involvement through relationship. He calls us to join Him in the cross style. I am to die to my self-life in my marriage! If I cannot submit to my mate, I can never submit to His Lordship. The very act of losing my life to my mate is the act of losing my life to Jesus. I find life when I lose my life. In the loss of my life I find Him, and in the loss of my life to others, again I find Him.

How Do I Find Life With Others In The Kingdom?
Matthew 19:13-15

Every individual has a deep internal need for the Kingdom! Our lungs scream for air, and our lives scream for the Kingdom. God created us for the Kingdom. If we are going to understand the Kingdom, we must go back to the beginning. Jesus presents the children as the essence of the Kingdom. The beginning for the Kingdom is childhood.

The beginning of children is **LOVE**. *"Then little children were brought to Him that He might put His hands on them and pray,"* (19:13). This returns us to the picture of marriage as Jesus presented it. God, out of His love, created woman for man. Now man and woman, out of love, cleave to each other and become *one flesh*. The product of this flowing love is a child, and since life comes from God, this child is a product of the love of God.

God's heart breaks over the act of abortion. It is the murder of the love of God within the mother's womb. Everyone involved in abortion is going to have to deal with the Creator who loves the little ones. He has intimately attached Himself to every unborn little one.

The beginning of the Kingdom (children) is *Love*, and the beginning of love is **LAW**. *"But Jesus said, 'Let the little children come to Me, and do not forbid them; for of such is the kingdom of heaven"* (19:14). The law of the Kingdom is *a child*. The life of a child represents the essence of the Kingdom! Childlikeness is the emphasis of the Kingdom. The heart of the Kingdom is living without rights, status, or demands. It is the style of the cross. Lose your life! Give yourself away! Do not protect yourself! The heart of the Kingdom is giving up yourself and trusting in Him. The loss of your life is the law.

The beginning of the Kingdom (children) is *love*, the beginning of love is *law*, but the beginning of law is **RELATIONSHIP** with the least. Now Jesus strikes at the heart of self-centered carnality. ***"Let the little children come to Me, and do not forbid them; for of such is the kingdom of heaven"*** (19:14). The children were considered the least, and the disciples were using them for their own self-centered ends. But the Kingdom of God calls the disciples to a new relationship. It is a relationship with the least. This would require death to selfishness. The disciples could no longer manipulate for self-centered desires. Jesus is calling them to the cross.

In each of these sections, Jesus has taken us back to the beginning. The cross is to be lived out in our relationships. (1) The Rich Young Ruler was called to die to his own doing as symbolized in his materialism. He must die to find life. (2) The marriage partners are called to lose their lives to each other. All domination must cease, as each submits to other, and to God. Competition has no place in this submission. As each loses his or her life, each finds God in the middle of the *one flesh* relationship. (3) The least (children) are the symbol of the Kingdom of God. If you want to find life, you cannot live for yourself. Who wants to find life?

"Jesus, You continually bring us back to one need. We need to die to our self-centeredness. Let the Holy Spirit guide us in our yielding. Let each area of our lives be revealed to us so others can see the cross style in us. Could our biggest problem be that we are stuck on ourselves? There is no life without death. There is no life with each other unless we lose our lives to You, and then to each other. There is no life in the Kingdom without the death of the cross being lived in us. Call us to death again. In Your name we pray, Amen."

Matthew 19:23-26

How to be Saved in a Materialistic World

"Dear Jesus, we believe what You have say in Your Word. You tell us that with God, all things are possible. Is it possible for You to speak directly to us? As You astonished your disciples, would you also astonish us? Would you focus us on what You want to do? It is a distinct miracle of God when You convict us about our materialism and we release it to You. We ask You to do a miracle in our lives. In Jesus' Name, we pray, Amen."

Have you witnessed a street preacher passing out Gospel tracts? "Are you saved?" he shouts in the evangelical jargon of our day. The disciples used the same jargon in Jesus' day. ***"When His disciples heard it, they were greatly astonished, saying, 'Who then can be saved?"*** (19:25). Evidently this phrase has been around for a long time.

It seems that the disciples were relating this phrase to the idea of making entrance into the Kingdom of Heaven. Jesus has just given a brief discourse about the difficulty of a rich man making it into heaven.

Twice He refers to the Kingdom of God or Kingdom of Heaven (19:23-24). The disciples equate *being saved* with entrance into the Kingdom of God. They understand that there are two Kingdoms. There is the Kingdom of Satan and the Kingdom of God. To exit the Kingdom of Satan and to enter the Kingdom of God is explained by *being saved.*

This is basic or fundamental information. It is beginning knowledge for every Christian. In giving this beginning information, Jesus speaks about materialism. This is not an unimportant issue. It is fundamental. It is not a subject that comes to the Christian after several years of growth; it is not an optional matter. Jesus treats it as a very important matter in *being saved.*

Materialism is not an issue of good or bad, an issue that requires growth or improvement. Jesus does not call the Christian to grow in understanding before surrendering his or her materialism. The grip of materialism on the life is not an issue of better and best. We want the best for our lives, but we do not believe that a release of materialism is necessary to be in the Kingdom. If we hold on to our materialism, perhaps God will reduce our rewards, but our destination will remain the same. No! Jesus' emphasis made the grip of materialism an issue of heaven and hell. Materialism has a direct baring on salvation.

The progression of the events, between Jesus and the disciples, usually has a certain order. The present scene has taken an unusual turn. Normally the disciples come to Jesus with a question. Peter is often the bold one in letting Jesus know that he did not understand what happened. The usual pattern is that one or more of the disciples will ask a question, and Jesus answers that question. However, in this passage,

Jesus takes the initiative. He has just come from an encounter with the Rich Young Ruler (19:16-22). The subject was materialism, and He wants to give the disciples additional information (19:23-30). He knows that this information (19:23-24) is essential for the disciples. This makes these verses extremely important for us.

The proposition of these verses is the same as the title of this chapter. **How can we be saved in a materialistic world?** We will strive to formulate the questions that Jesus answers in these verses. May God help us to grasp His truth!

Is Materialism A Sign Of God's Blessing?
Matthew 19:23

"Then Jesus said to His disciples, 'Assuredly, I say to you that it is hard for a rich man to enter the kingdom of heaven" (19:23). I want you to consider carefully what you believe is the touchable and tangible evidence that God is blessing your life. The external and visual evidence that God is blessing your life is a strong part of your assurance of salvation. This physical evidence is high priority to you. When you have moments of discouragement or depression, you will rely on it. What is the external evidence of God's blessing?

If you believe that materialism is an external sign of God's blessing upon your life, then prosperity is very important to you. Since you are prosperous, you know God is blessing you. If you believe that speaking in an unknown tongue is an external sign of an internal blessing, you will seek such an experience. You are not satisfied until you speak in this unknown tongue. It becomes the way you know you are right with God. Healing is often another of the touchable and knowable evidence of God's blessing. Some believe that when you are right with God, you will not be sick. Those who believe this are always talking about healing. It becomes a central part of their belief system. Because this issue is very important, I need to propose the question to you again. What do you consider to be the touchable, tangible and knowable evidence of God's blessing on your life?

The Holiness Movement has grown from the heart of the cross. Based on the Word of God, this movement believes that the external evidence of God's blessing and presence is holiness. When you are holy, God is in your life. When you are not holy, He cannot be found. You cannot equate holiness with the observation of rules. You can keep a list of things to do and things not to do, and not be holy. Holiness is not maintaining ceremonies. You can have a perfect attendance record at church and still not be holy. Holiness is a quality of God's life. God, in His Word, states, *"Be holy, for I am holy"* (1 Peter 1:16). It is the essence of the nature of God. When you live in His presence or His presence lives in you, you are holy. It is derived holiness. Holiness is not what you do; it is Who He is! Holiness is the evidence of His indwelt presence within you.

Perfect love describes holiness. Perfect love is shed abroad in our hearts by the indwelt presence of God. The world sees the tangible and physical evidence of holiness, or perfect love, in the way I treat my fellow man. When we see you acting in perfect love toward your brother, we know the blessings of God's presence is all over you. When your life displays hatred, bitterness, and strife, we know that you have missed His presence. The physical and tangible evidence of God's blessing on your life is not materialism, or speaking in an unknown tongue, or healing. It is perfect love.

Let us look at the **PAST AND PRESENT**. *"When His disciples heard it, they were greatly astonished, saying, 'Who then can be saved?"* (19:25). I have been extremely curious about this question. How could the disciples respond to Jesus' teaching with this question (19:23-24)? Jesus said, *"It is hard for a rich man to enter the kingdom of heaven"* (19:23). He made it stronger by saying, *"It is easier for a camel to go through the eye of a needle than for a rich man to enter the kingdom of God"* (19:24). I would have asked, "What rich man can be saved?" Not being wealthy, I do not think this statement applies to me. The disciples respond with the question, "Which one of us can get saved?" Surely they do not think of themselves as wealthy. They left their fishing business to travel with Jesus, making no money in the process. How can they consider themselves rich? But the disciples are bothered by the hindrance of materialism to the salvation of those who are rich! How could this be?

This information called me to begin an investigation into the religious background of the disciples. What had their religious upbringing, as Jews, taught them? I was amazed to discover that the emphasis of today was also the emphasis of the past. Their religion had taught them the "health and wealth gospel!" It was the basic philosophy of the Pharisees' teaching.

The disciples were traveling with Jesus when they met a man who had been born blind. Their immediate response was a question. They asked, *"Rabbi, who sinned, this man or his parents, that he was born blind?"* (John 9:2). It seemed obvious to them that God was not blessing this man, so there must be sin connected to his life. The Pharisees believed that certain physical disabilities or illnesses were caused by certain sins. They equated blindness with the sin of immorality. Evidently the disciples believed that when God blesses you, you are physically whole. Jesus' correction of the disciples is strong.

The Pharisees also taught a gospel of wealth. When God blesses you, you prosper. They often quoted Old Testament passages. The first Psalm describes a man who delights in the law of God.

> *"He shall be like a tree Planted by the rivers of water.*
> *That brings forth its fruit in its season,*
> *Whose leaf also shall not wither;*
> *And whatever he does shall prosper. "* (Psalms 1:3)

They concluded that you can tell how spiritual you are by the size of your bank account. Did not God promise we will prosper in whatever we do?

That gives you some background for this scene. When Jesus tells the disciples that a rich man will have a difficult time getting into heaven, they are extremely troubled. If a person who has the blessings of God (evidenced by his riches) has a difficult time getting into the Kingdom, how could poor disciples (evidenced by their lack of wealth) ever make it? Thus, they ask the question, "Which one of us can be saved?"

It is easy for us to say that we do not believe in a health and wealth gospel. Without the background of the disciples, we reject this teaching. Be very careful. This health and wealth gospel is very cunning. It finds its way into the heart and influences the mind. Imagine yourself driving down the highway, and you nearly have a wreck. At the moment of crisis you pray, and the wreck does not happen. You go on your way with great rejoicing. God has blessed you with deliverance. Further down the road you see an accident with injured persons. Do you conclude that you are blessed by God and they are not? If God was blessing them, would He not have delivered them also?

Let us suppose that I come to your house for a visit. I admire your beautiful home. The draperies are magnificent; the carpet is plush; the light fixtures are expensive. You turn to me with a bit of pride and say, "Yes, God is blessing us." I see the evidence of those blessings in your fine house. Is this how you know? If someone takes your fine house from you, would that mean that God has ceased to be bless you. Do you see how easy it is to fall into this trap?

What do you do with your failures? How do you reconcile the negative circumstances with your spiritual relationship with God? When things do not work out the way you plan, does it reflect in your spirituality? What do you do with your failures? Is your sickness a result of spiritual failure? Jesus went to Nazareth to hold an evangelistic campaign. After just a few services, the Nazarenes asked Him to leave. His ministry was a complete failure in that town (Matthew 13:54-58). Was He not walking in the blessings of God? Had Jesus stepped out of God's will? Is success the evidence of God's blessing? If so, how do you live with your failures? If suffering is a sign of spiritual failure, how do you explain the triumph of the men and women who suffered for their faith? (Hebrews 11).

Here is the question again. "Is materialism a sign of God's blessing upon our lives?" The Pharisees said, "Yes!" The disciples said, "Yes!" But we must receive the mind of Christ. In the **STRONG AND**

STRONGER, Jesus talks of the mind of God. ***"Then Jesus said to His disciples, 'Assuredly, I say to you that it is hard for a rich man to enter the kingdom of heaven"*** (19:23). The word **hard** means *will have great difficulty*. A rich man can enter the Kingdom of God only after overcoming great and difficult obstacles. The obstacles are his riches or materialism. However, Jesus continues by drawing a more difficult picture. ***"And again I say to you, it is easier for a camel to go through the eye of a needle than for a rich man to enter the kingdom of God"*** (19:24). It is impossible for a camel to go through the eye of a needle. Is Jesus saying that it is easier to do the impossible than for a rich man to enter the Kingdom of God? Jesus' second statement is stronger than His first! Materialism is not a sign of God's blessing, but it is an obstacle that hinders an individual from being saved. You must deal with the key issue of materialism, if you want to enter the Kingdom of Heaven. If materialism is a sign of God's blessing, Jesus was not blessed. Jesus said to a scribe who was thinking of following Him, ***"Foxes have holes and birds of the air have nests, but the Son of Man has nowhere to lay His head"*** (Matthew 8:20). "Is materialism a sign of God's blessing?" The Pharisees say, "Yes!" The disciples say, "Yes." Jesus says, "NO!"

In Jesus' value system, the focus is on the **INWARD AND OUTWARD**. The central issue of difference, between the Pharisees and Jesus, is very apparent. Every conflict exposes the focus of the Pharisees, which is on the outward. They are concerned with the external laws, ceremonies, and appearances. Jesus consistently calls them back to the inward heart. He wants them to go past what they are doing to what they are being. It is not an issue of a deed done, but expression of an attitude.

That explains why the Pharisees teach that materialism is a sign of God's blessing. Jesus teaches that materialism has no value in spiritual life, instead it is a hindrance to spiritual values.

Is Materialism An Impossible Obstacle To Salvation?
Matthew 19:25

Materialism is not a sign of God's blessing, and it can even be a hindrance to salvation. Materialism, as a hindrance to salvation, becomes a part of the discussion that emerges from the question the disciples have asked Jesus. ***"Who then can be saved?"*** (19:25). The answer has a progression. Can materialism hinder salvation? Jesus' answer is, **POSSIBLY**, and He gives the context for what He wants the disciples to understand. ***"Assuredly, I say to you that it is hard for a rich man to enter the kingdom of heaven"*** (19:23). The word ***hard*** means *with great difficulty*. A rich man must overcome his materialism, a great and difficult obstacle, before salvation. Wealth and comfort have huge binding fingers. Entry into the Kingdom of God requires sacrifice, and those who have great materialism find sacrifice very difficult, and nearly impossible. We have grown so accustomed to the power of our materialistic world that we do not realize its trap. In many years of Christian ministry, I know of only a few instances where people have lowered their standard of living to be free for Christian service. Do you know anyone who has turned down a job promotion to remain in the ministry he or she has established at their present job?

Is materialism an impossible obstacle to salvation? Jesus begins the progression with *Possibly* (19:23), and continues with **POSITIVELY.** ***"And again I say to you, it is easier for a camel to go through the***

eye of a needle than for a rich man to enter the kingdom of God" (19:24). The translation for **And again** is i*n fac*t. The grammar structure of this verse uses a double empathic. Matthew attempts to state the truth twice. Jesus gives the truth of verse twenty-three, and then repeats it forcibly in verse twenty-four.

In verse twenty-four, Jesus restates and intensifies the truth He has spoken in verse twenty-three. He gives the picture of a camel going through the eye of a needle. Bible scholars have attempted to explain the truth of this illustration. Some have thought that the word **camel** should really be *cable*. When the scribe was copying the Scriptures by hand, perhaps he made a wrong mark and changed the word. The Greek word for *cable* is similar to the one for **camel**, but if we switch the words, would that change the truth? The cable was the one used on a sailing ship in Jesus' day. It was huge in comparison to the needle used for tent making. Pulling this cable through the eye of a needle would be as impossible as a camel walking through. Other scholars have said **the eye of a needle** refers to the small gate beside the main entrance of the city. At night, the main gate was closed, and only the small gate was used for access. In order for the camel to go through the small gate, someone would have to remove the burden from his back, and then the camel would have to kneel down. Preachers like this interpretation because it makes a great sermon illustration. But who has the right to adjust what Jesus is saying in this verse? The camel was the largest animal known to the Jews, and they also were familiar with the size of the household darning needle. The problem with allowing Jesus' illustration to stand, is that it makes it impossible for a rich man to be saved. But that is exactly what He is saying!

Jesus does, however, give us the **PLUS FACTOR**. *"But Jesus looked at them and said to them, 'With men this is impossible but with God all things are possible"* (19:26). When Jesus told the disciples that a rich man cannot possibly enter the Kingdom of God (19:24), they respond by asking, *"Who then can be saved?"* (19:25). Now Jesus explains that what man cannot accomplish through his own resources, he can receive through the resources of a redeeming God. Look at the evangelical church of our day. Many of these congregations are made up of the upper-middle class who are controlled by their materialism. They love the comfort of their padded pews, and they have spent millions of dollars building magnificent church building as monuments to themselves. God has the power and the resources to break the heart of one of these church members and bring him or her into the Kingdom. It is impossible for man, but it is possible for God. It is a miracle when one humbles himself, takes up the cross style, and gives his life to the Kingdom. If a church member, who thinks that his materialism is a sign of God's blessing, kneels at the cross and abandons himself, that is a miracle. Our congregations are full of people who think about the ball game during the sermon. It is very hard for a board member, who has everything he wants in materialism, to give up his comfort, fall on a cross, and die. How can he risk losing everything he loves? If it ever happens, it is indeed a miracle! Is materialism an impossible obstacle to salvation? Humanism says, "Yes." A redeeming God says, "NO!"

Is Materialism a Necessary Sacrifice For God?
Matthew 19:21

This question brings us back to the context of this presentation. A young man comes to Christ seeking life. The expensive clothes tell us that he has life in abundance. He appears to have everything that marks the blessings of God, but he knows that something is missing. Jesus concludes. *"If you want to be perfect, go, sell what you have and give to the poor, and you will have treasure in heaven; and come, follow Me"* (19:21).

Jesus demands the total sacrifice of wealth. This is a difficult command for the Rich Young Ruler. It involves **A RE-EVALUATION OF OWNERSHIP**. The command of Jesus was for him to *sell what YOU HAVE*. The sin of materialism is not the physical items. Objects are not sinful. You cannot point to an expensive house and say, "Look at that sin!" The issue is the priority, or ownership, of that object. The problem facing the Rich Young Ruler is not wealth or materialism, but his ownership. Ownership bespeaks control. When an individual owns something, he protects, uses, and controls it. The amount of value is not the issue. *You having* the ownership IS the issue.

A RECOGNITION OF OBLIGATION makes ownership an issue. Jesus' command involved the Rich Young Ruler's materialism and his obligation to others. He needed to deal with his possessiveness. *"If you want to be perfect, go, sell what you have and GIVE TO THE POOR"* (19:21). When we have ownership, we miss the purpose of our possessions. We think that we earned the money. The Old Testament asks, "Who gave you the ability to make money?" Everything we have is a gift from God. The ability to think, the energies to move, and a healthy life, all come from Him. Since He has so blessed us, there must be an important reason. I must discover that reason. When I claim ownership of my materialism, then I do not need to know God's purpose for giving it to me. The focus of Jesus is on the poor - others, others, others. When I own my materialism, I focus it on me. When I see it as a gift from God, it becomes an instrument to aid others.

The issue of materialism is not tithing. When the evangelical church member tithes, he feels like he has accomplished his obligation. He believes he owns everything, and he gives God 10 per cent. His focus is on himself, and to him, this is generous. When you realize that God owns everything, and He has lent some of it to you, your view changes. God, in his generosity, gives me materialism to help others, others, others. When we have not dealt with ownership, we excuse the selfish, stingy, qualities of the evangelical church.

Jesus quickly brings the Rich Young Ruler to **A RE-EMPHASIS OF OBEDIENCE.** His command was ***"and come, follow Me"*** (19:21). Where is Jesus going? The cross is only two and one half months away. Jesus is on the journey from Galilee to Jerusalem to embrace the cross, when he encounters the Rich Young Ruler. He calls this young man to a sacrificial life. He calls him to experience the cross and its style. What would keep the young man from responding to this call? It is his materialism. What could possibly keep us from responding? Will it be our materialism?

"Jesus, it would be awful and go to hell over what will not matter one hundred years from now. While we may not be millionaires, it is easy to be filled with our own need to be comfortable. We are so busy accumulating stuff. Oh, God, please save us from ourselves! You alone can accomplish that miracle. Do whatever you need to do to bring it to pass. We hear Your command to bring all that WE HAVE, sacrifice it to You, and live the style of the cross. In Your name we pray, Amen."

Matthew 19:27-30

Principles of Surrender

"Jesus, You know how inadequate we are in our communication. Only the Holy Spirit can help us grasp the truth on the heart level. If anyone can make the Gospel clear for us, it is You. Yet, the disciples who walked with You in the flesh, consistently missed what You said. We have had two thousand years of the grace of God, and the flow of Your presence in our churches. Pentecost, with the fullness of the Holy Spirit, came before us. Surely, You can speak to us through Your Spirit. You bring us to a choice, after we understand. We are listening to You Jesus. In Your name, we pray, Amen."

We can see a common characteristic in all disciples, both past and present. The characteristic is their ability to talk, talk, talk. The twelve, original disciples, set the tempo for all of us. They spent most of their time in conversation. We could excuse their actions, except for the fact that they belittled every situation by what they said. They whined and complained about nearly every situation. They were a vivid contrast to Jesus.

Jesus gave a powerful message on marriage (19:4-9), taking things back to creation. He wanted all to see God's plan for marriage in its fullness. God would glue the husband and wife together, creating *one flesh*. A strong unit is created when both the male and the female lose their lives to each other. This *one flesh* union is stronger than either individual can be separately. The excitement of that possibility grips the heart and gives new direction. But listen closely. Can you hear the whining and complaining of the disciples? ***"His disciples said to Him, 'If such is the case of the man with his wife, it is better not to marry"*** (19:10).

On another grand occasion, the little children are coming to Jesus (19:13-15). An army of boys and girls is hungry to know Christ personally. Parents want Jesus to place His hands on their children. The selfish expressions of the crowds wanting the miracles of Jesus is not found here. These parents are expressing pure love. But listen again. You can hear the whining and complaining of the disciples. They have barred the door and they are rebuking the children. Are we as forbidding as they were? Do we repel instead of attract? Somehow we act as if we have joined the Trinity and have the right to veto.

The Rich Young Ruler came running to Jesus. He was searching for life (19:16-22). He will do any good thing that will enable him to possess it. The end of the story is tragic. He wonders off in emptiness and sorrow, for he has great possessions. Jesus called him to forsake all and follow Him. The disciples are spectators to this scene. Listen to what they have to say. ***"Then Peter answered and said to Him, 'See,***

we have left all and followed You. Therefore what shall we have?" (19:27). Can you hear them as they whine and complain? Peter claims they have left all, but what had they left? They had set aside some fishing nets that needed to be repaired. Their fishing business barely fed their families, and they really needed to put their boat into dry dock for rebuilding. They are coming along behind Jesus, but in reality, they spend most of their time rebuking everything He says. They especially do not like what He says about the life of being the Messiah. Jesus has set aside the attributes He possessed as God to become a man. He is heading straight for the cross. They are a part of the need for His death, and they have the nerve to come to Him and say, **"we have left all and followed You."** Did they think they have earned some rights for benefits? Their voices are saturated with their self-centeredness.

Peter and the other disciples have missed the truth again. Jesus has been teaching them with great patience. How can they be so blind? In chapter sixteen, He gives them the very core of truth. In chapter seventeen, He takes them to the Mount of Transfiguration where heaven verifies the truth with Divine confirmation. The theology of the cross is so clear in chapter eighteen. Now in chapter nineteen there is a display of the practical application of this truth. The disciples still do not get it. Continuing in patience, Jesus summarizes it for them one more time. He gives them the *Principles of Surrender.*

Principle Of Following
Matthew 19:28

"So Jesus said to them, 'Assuredly I say to you, that in the regeneration, when the Son of Man sits on the throne of His glory,

you who have followed Me will also sit on twelve thrones, judging the twelve tribes of Israel" (19:27). *"You who have followed Me* are very important words. Jesus brings the Old Testament law down to blinding simplicity. He clarifies the ethical issues of the Gospel in two words, *follow Me.* These words are the pulse beat of Christianity. The climax of all Jesus said to the Rich Young Ruler is found in the closing phrase *"come, follow Me,"* (19:21). Peter restates it when he said, *"See, we have left all and followed You,"* (19:27). When Jesus responds to Peter, He says, *"You who have followed Me will also sit on twelve thrones"* (19:28). It is the *principle of following.*

If we are to grasp this principle, we must understand the **CROSS CONTENT.** *Following Jesus* has become a part of our evangelical jargon. We put it on bumper stickers, sing it in our songs. It has become something of a religious ditty. We have not yet discovered the seriousness of what we are saying. There is significant content to this *following.*

Jesus ends His Galilean ministry with the miracle of feeding the five thousand. He then moves into Gentile territory with His disciples. They enter the region of Tyre and Sidon (15:21), and continue around the eastern coast of the Sea of Galilee, to the region of Decapolis. The happenings of chapters fifteen, sixteen and seventeen take place in Gentile territory. Then Jesus makes a distinct change in direction (17:22). Jesus and His disciples cross the Sea of Galilee and enter the city of Capernaum. His purpose for returning to Galilee is not to minister. There were several groups of disciples meeting here, and the purpose of their gathering was to journey as a group to Jerusalem for the Feast of the Passover. Jesus knows that He is headed for the cross. He plans to spend the entire journey talking to His disciples about it. This is not just a theological discussion about the cross; He is taking actual steps toward the cross. Chapter nineteen is a part of His journey. When Jesus pleads with the Rich Young Ruler to follow Him, He is talking about the cross. There can be no question in any one's mind about the destination of this journey. It is the cross. The content of following Jesus is always the cross and its style.

The principle of following also has **FUTURE FOCUS**. Many people in our generation have difficulty with a focus on the future. We pride ourselves on being the *now* generation. It is hard for this group to come out of the immediate pleasures and focus on something bigger. You can see the same problem in Peter's statement to Jesus. ***"See, we have left all and followed You. Therefore what shall we have?"*** (19:27). Peter wanted to know what they would receive. Though the intent of his question does have future involvement, his main concern is his future on this earth. He really wants to overthrow Rome and establish earthly rulership. Peter, and the other disciples, are looking for a military Messiah. They want political freedom for Judea. In just a few days, these disciples will be arguing over the right-hand and left-hand positions in this coming Kingdom.

Tax reformation is not the focus of Jesus. He is not concerned about Roman domination. Jesus is going to shake the foundation of Hell, for the sake of what will matter forever. He is going to spill His blood for something bigger than political gain. Jesus has His eyes set on eternity, and He is calling his disciples to live big. Sometimes our eyesight is so narrow, all we can see is the solution to our immediate problem. Due to the smallness of our living, a few physical accomplishments make us feel worth while. Burnt toast is not worth the shedding of one tear. What will really matter one hundred years from now? The focus of following has a view of the eternal. It is bigger than the present events.

The principle of following is a **SHARING SERVANTHOOD**. Jesus clearly illustrates this to His disciples. ***"Assuredly I say to you, that in the regeneration, when the Son of Man sits on the throne of His glory, you who have followed Me will also sit on twelve thrones, judging the twelve tribes of Israel"*** (19:28). There is much controversy concerning this verse. Much of it misses the truth Jesus is speaking. Some have concerned themselves with the meaning of the twelve tribes. Are they the twelve tribes of Israel, or are they symbols of the church? Are the thrones, actual thrones in the halls of judgment? Will we have to go and bow down to the disciples who are sitting on these thrones? None of this has anything to do with the truth Jesus is presenting.

Jesus says that in the future there will be ***judging.*** This excites us, because it gives us a very important picture. But clearly understand that what Jesus did, He does. What Jesus was, He is! The author of the Book of Hebrews states, ***"Jesus Christ is the same yesterday, today, and forever"*** (13:8). Jesus had a style while He was here on this earth. He will have the same style in eternity. We believe that Jesus is the invisible God, made visible to us. We see what God is really like in the person of Jesus. The eternal God, in His forever dwelling place, has made Himself known to us in the person of Jesus. What is He like? He washes dirty feet, pours His life out for the poor, and gets involved with lepers. He lives the cross style. The heart of the eternal God is always the same. When God decided to judge sin, He did it from the cross.

Was this a temporary thing for God? Did He do this for three years on earth and then set it aside? Is He washing feet now? On earth, He had a crown of thrones, but in eternity will He wear the gold crown of a ruling King? His throne was a cross on earth, but perhaps He will have a gold plated throne in heaven. If He flowed with mercy and love here, will He rule with an iron fist there? Will He exercise a selfish will in eternity, though He denied Himself here on earth? What a false truth! The style of Jesus here on earth is the same style He will have in eternity. Washing feet, selflessness, and the style of the cross, He will continue in eternity. He has not changed. The style of the cross is the style of the Kingdom of God. Jesus will remain the servant King.

He promises His disciples that they will get to judge (19:28). However, they are to judge in the same manner that Jesus judges. He judges in the style of the cross. The call continues to be a call to service. If that sounds undesirable to you, then you do not want to go to heaven. The cross style is the only acceptable style there. If you find serving even a little hard here on earth, then heaven will not be comfortable for you. We are merely in training here for a life of serving there. If losing your life is a hard message for you here, I assure you, it will be the only message heard in heaven. The cross, and its style, is the heart of the coming Kingdom. We will share in the life of serving with Jesus forever.

The Principle Of Forsaking

Matthew 19:29

"And everyone who has left houses or brothers or sisters or father or mother or wife or children or lands, for My name's sake, shall receive a hundredfold, and inherit eternal life" (19:29). It is

very important that we understand *forsaking*. It is the **CONCERNED CONTENT.** *Forsaking* means little unless it is something I care deeply about. I have no problem surrendering what I do not have, and I take great delight in giving up what you have. It is not difficult for me to surrender the "unknown bundle" to Jesus. If I do not have knowledge of what is in the bundle, giving it up is not a problem. It is when the "unknown bundle" becomes known that I have difficulty. I do not think I would have a problem giving Jesus the million dollars I do not have. However, the thought of giving Him the five dollars in my pocket disturbs me. Forsaking what I care about is where the problem lies for me.

There are two areas of concern for Jesus. One is the area of belonging. Notice the words He uses, **"And everyone who has left . . . brothers or sisters or father or mother or wife or children . . . ."** (19:29) This is the "herd instinct." We all have the need to belong. The family unit was the strongest unit of belonging in Jesus' day. Today it might be a gang, your peers, or your buddies on the job. Everyone has the need to fit in or be accepted. How could Jesus expect me to give up this need to belong? Perhaps we can better understand giving up the "herd instinct" when we understand the second area. It is the area of security. Jesus continues, **"And everyone who has left houses . . . lands. . . ."** (19:29). We dream of paying off the mortgage on our house, as if that will make us secure. We spend our days working, scraping, and planning for our own security. How could we possibly surrender this drive we have for security? Belonging and security are proper needs. Why would He mention these two specific needs? The reason is that they are important to us. Jesus calls us to *forsake* what we care about the most.

Does this mean it is wrong for me to plan for my retirement? Is it evil for me to want to provide for my family? Before making a judgment on this, you must see the complete truth of His presentation.

We must see the **FAITHFUL FOCUS.** *"And everyone who has left houses or brothers or sisters or father or mother or wife or children or lands, for My name's sake, shall receive a hundredfold, and inherit eternal life"* (19:29). The heart of this verse is *"for My name's sake."* Jesus does not force us to yield. He did not have to die on the cross to make us do anything. God does not have His whip out, and He does not use the scare techniques of a hell centered Gospel. He calls us from the heart! Our voluntary focus is what He wants from us. He wants to captivate us until all other belonging fades into the background, and all we see is the light of His face. Christianity is choosing what we will set aside for Jesus. The call is to passionate love, not to struggling and trying. When you find everything fulfilled in Him, you will not struggle to give up your securities and relationships.

What is the result of this kind of focus? It is **SUPERIOR SERVANTHOOD.** *"And anyone who has left. . ., shall receive a hundredfold, and inherit eternal life"* (19:29). Do not think that if you surrender these securities and relationships, then you will reap the benefits of prosperity. You cannot view this through selfish eyes. Matthew has written about Jesus and the message of death to self-centered carnality. He is not proposing that if we are selfless here, we can then be selfish in heaven. The call is not to yield our lives on earth, so we can grab what we want in heaven. Christianity is not the denial of my needs on earth, so I will not have to deny myself in heaven. If I give up my materialism on earth, then I can have a mansion with a golden street in front of it. I serve in my life on earth, but when I get to heaven, I will be served. NO! NO! NO! Jesus calls us to the style of the cross, which is to deny myself, die to self-centered carnality, and forsake all for Him. We must focus on Jesus until we see nothing else. His style becomes our style, both here and in heaven. Heaven will be an expanded opportunity to pour my life out for others. Here, I only have a small amount to give Jesus, but in heaven I will have an abundance to give. We have such a brief time to serve here, but eternity will expand our time for service. Heaven is going to be an extension of the cross style that Jesus has given us on earth. If you have any reservations about living this style on earth, you need to forget heaven. You will be miserable there.

Principle of the First
Matthew 19:30

"But many who are first will be last, and the last first" (19:30). We can only have a proper understanding of this verse when we see it in light of chapter twenty, verses one through sixteen. Verse thirty summarizes the parable Jesus tells at the beginning of chapter twenty. In fact, verse sixteen of chapter twenty is a repeat of verse thirty. *"So the last will be first, and the first last. For many are called, but few chosen"* (20:16). You can easily see the connection between these two verses. Jesus begins and ends the parable with the same statement. It must have been an important statement to Jesus.

If we are to understand this principle, we must understand the **CAUSING CONTENT.** Motive is the concern here. If we have the first place position, what will we have (19:30)? Does it mean we will have the biggest car? Perhaps it means to be superior in muscle strength, or money and power. This may be what being first means here in this world, but Jesus is speaking of the Kingdom. In the Kingdom it means to be like Him - the cross style. I must die to myself. It is the motive of perfect love toward God and others. The call is to lose my life, give myself away, and cease to live for myself. In the eyes of the world, only one person can be number one. Only one person can have the most money or be elected to the position. In the eyes of the Kingdom, if motive is perfect love, then every one can have it.

This brings us to the recognition of our **FALSE FOCUS**. The disciples are consumed by their personal ratings. They have the world's view of being number one, but that is a false focus. The Kingdom of God calls us to focus on others. When a person is first in the world, he or she has the position to lord it over others. But when a person is first in the Kingdom, he or she serves everyone. The world's standard for number one means to be smarter than others and take advantage of them. Helping your brother is the focus of the Kingdom. Wealth makes you number one in the world, but the Kingdom sees sharing your resources as the measure of being first. The Kingdom and the world are total opposites. What is first in the world is last in the Kingdom, and what is first in the Kingdom is last in this world.

This brings us to the conclusion, which is **SURPRISE SERVANTHOOD**. *"But many who are first will be last, and the last first"* (19:30). Who would have guessed this? There is no way we can discover this in philosophy class. The mind of humanity can never dream up this. The wisdom of the world cannot produce this. Christianity is the call to spill your life out in aggressive service for others, now and in eternity. Who would have thought it? Heaven is going to be the continuation of the cross and its style - the life style of Jesus. If you don't want to die to yourself here, don't go to heaven. If you don't want to roll up your sleeves and get involved in the hurting lives of others, don't go to heaven. You are going to spend all eternity living out the blood process of the cross for others.

"Jesus, save us from our desire for comfortableness. Can You give us the focus of the Kingdom until it becomes our life? Show us Your face. Capture us with your love. We embrace the cross and its style, for now and forever. In Your name, we pray, Amen."

PART SIX

Matthew 20

Reviewing the Cross

Conclusions of the Cross Style

Matthew 19:30-20:16

Principles of First

"This is a strange truth, Jesus! Yet, it should not be strange to us, because we have found it to be the heart of the Kingdom of God. This world operates on an opposite standard of the Kingdom. The Kingdom of Satan thinks with one thought pattern while the Kingdom of God processes with another. Why should we be surprised that what is first in the world is last in the Kingdom, or what is last in the Kingdom is first in the world? Adjust our thinking and make us Kingdom people. In Your name, we pray, Amen."

The thought process of the Kingdom is unique. Kingdom thinking includes principles the world has not realized. It calculates facts, knows insights, and sees truths that the world cannot grasp. The world is dead in its trespasses and sin. It has no way of thinking the thoughts of the Kingdom of God. Kingdom thinking is strangely different, and its basis is the reason. The thought process of the Kingdom and the thought process of the world have different starting points, which result in a different value system, with radically different priorities. The Kingdom of God operates on a standard the world views as ridiculous. Those who live by Kingdom principles are viewed as quite unreasonable. There are hidden factors that the man of the world cannot understand. If he understood, he would radically change his life style, but he is dead to these principles.

Self-centered carnality is the basis of the world's thought process. What am I going to get out of it? How will it benefit me? I must constantly look out for number one, and I must fight for myself. Words like me, my, and mine are the basis of the world's thinking. It is a self-centered focus. The thought process of the world comes from this focus.

The basis of Kingdom thinking is radically different. Self-centeredness has to die and the cross style must be established. The focus is not on self and what I can get, but on Christ and what I can give. This creates a whole new style of living, with a new philosophy and a different thought process. It calls for the loss of your life.

The disciples have not adjusted to this Kingdom thinking. They have been struggling with the basis. Cross style living is a new approach. They are stuck on their own patterns. Jesus is patient with them and keeps bringing them back to the fundamental of the Kingdom of God.

Jesus told the disciples that His Messiahship would lead to a cross and the loss of His life (16:21). He was trying to establish a new thought process. The essence of the Kingdom would be death to self-centeredness, through the cross. Peter and the other disciples argued with Jesus for six days about this truth (16:22). Then a living example of Kingdom thinking presented itself. A father comes with his demon-possessed son (17:16). Nine of the disciples are present, but they are unable to cast out the demon. They have had victory over demons before, but are powerless now. Their unbelief is the explanation for their defeat (17:20). They could not accept the thought process of the Kingdom of God. They wanted to cling to their old basis, traditions, and patterns. But no ministry would flow through them without the Kingdom thinking, which comes from the Kingdom basis. Ministry flows when self-centeredness dies. The style is that of depending and learning.

Don't you think the disciples would learn their lesson? Not so, for they are arguing over which one of them will get to be number one in the Kingdom of God (18:1). They are focused on themselves; it is the thinking of the world. Jesus spent the entirety of chapter eighteen explaining again the new fundamental of the Kingdom of God. It is not just a presentation of a theological discourse, but He gives a practical application. **Marriage and Divorce** is the principle of the cross style applied to our homes (19:1-12). **Mothers and Dependents** applies to the way we treat those who are less than we are in social status (19:13-15). **Materialism and the Depressed** gives application to our daily lives as we live in a materialistic world (19:16-30).

The disciples fail in each of these applications. They tell Jesus that it would probably be better not to get married than to have to lose your life to your mate (19:10). If marriage is not for self-benefit, why would you want to be married? The disciples stand in the doorway of a home, blockading the children's entrance to Jesus (19:13). The children have no social status, thus, the disciples cannot be bothered with them. After all, these children cannot help them build their position as number one. In another illustration, a young man runs to Jesus, only to find himself running away from Jesus (19:16). Jesus called him to give up his elements?

The Sovereignty of the Land Owner
Matthew 20:15

Do not lose sight of the fact that this discussion is stimulated by Peter. His question is the reason for this parable. ***Then Peter answered and said to Him, "See, we have left all and followed You. Therefore what shall we have?"*** (19:27). The church has given strong teachings on rewards. We sing of a heaven with streets of gold and big mansions. If we work hard for Jesus here on earth, what will we get in heaven as our reward? That is the identical question Peter asks Jesus. He has just witnessed the Rich Young Ruler's refusal to give up his materialism and follow Jesus (19:22). Jesus told the Rich Young Ruler that if he would sell all he had and give to the poor, he would have treasure in heaven (19:21). Peter and the other disciples had done what the Rich Young Ruler refused to do. They had given up everything to follow Jesus. Peter wanted to know how he would benefit.

Peter reverted to the world's thought process, which is self-centered carnal focus. The focus is on doing. If we would do more, we could get more. If we give enough money to the church, invest enough time in Kingdom work, we build up a deposit in heaven. Heaven's construction crews will build our mansion from this deposit. Our reward in heaven will parallel our hard work for Christ here on earth. Do you see how wrong this is? It is wrong because it comes from the basis of the world's pattern. It is self-centered carnality, which is a works mentality. The works mentality always springs from the foundation of self-centered carnality. I do; therefore, I merit a reward. I have done; therefore, I should get. I have sacrificed; therefore, I am deserving. Peter has missed the truth.

One of the most exciting truths about *The Sovereignty of the Landowner* is found in the beginning of the parable. **"For the kingdom of heaven is like a landowner who went out early in the morning to hire laborers for his vineyard"** (20:1). This verse teaches us that the sovereign landowner needs laborers. The sovereign God is self-sufficient, independent, and creative. He can sit on His throne and think worlds into existence. Be assured that One who can think and it is, does not lack resource to get things done. This sovereign God, pictured in the parable, is going to the marketplace to hire laborers to work in His vineyard. I cannot get over the fact that a sovereign God, who can do anything He wants to, any time He wants to, has tapped me on the shoulder and asked for my help. A sovereign God has placed Himself in the position of needing me. If that makes sense to you, you are much smarter than I am.

There is a clear motive behind God putting Himself in this position. It is His love. God is sovereign, thus, He does not have needs. But God decided to love, and that has created this need. God does not love me because He needs me; He needs me because He loves me. Except in a sovereign God and His influence, there is no love like this. It is Kingdom love, and is our new base.

Chapter nineteen applies this great theology. In our teenage years, we discover we have a need. We call it love. Out of this need, we seek to get married. But this need, which we call love, is filled with self-desires. How does the Kingdom of God affect this need? Marriage, in

Kingdom love, does not mean we love our mate because he or she satisfies our needs, but we desperately need our mate because we love him or her. That is Kingdom love, God's love. His love has no angles or conditions. The need God has for you comes from His sovereign love for you. The sovereign God is pictured as a landowner who comes to the marketplace looking for me, because He needs me.

"Is it not lawful for me to do what I wish with my own things?" (20:15). The sovereign landowner is answering a rebuke. Those who worked all day do not think those who worked a few hours should receive the same wages. Doesn't a sovereign God have the right to do as He wishes? If God had asked for my advice, I would have discouraged Him from putting Himself in the position of needing laborers. It is not economically sound; they are too expensive. It is not practical because they are not dependable. In the long run, God will certainly not receive benefits that will match His expenses. But God does not operate on the economy of this world - what do I get out of it? God operates on the economy of the cross style Kingdom - how much can I give?

So when evening had come, the owner of the vineyard said to his steward, "Call the laborers and give them their wages, beginning with the last to the first," (20:8). The source of their wages is the sovereign landowner. Everything they will receive is found in the landowner. Jesus is teaching us that the source of every blessing, every good thing, and every benefit is our sovereign God. It is not a matter of our earning or meriting it. In fact, there is no possible way to ever earn a blessing from Him. If we ever receive anything from His hand, it is because the sovereign God has decided to give it to us. In our theology, it is called **GRACE**. Grace is not experienced in a moment of repentance; He pours it out upon us for a lifetime. Grace is a heavenly experience. Every moment we are privileged to spend in heaven comes from a sovereign God giving from His resources. If there is a mansion, or a speck of gold on any street, it won't be because we deserve it. We can never earn or deserve it! Every blessing from Him will be because He decided to love us. His love delights and finds pleasure in giving us grace. So we must not fall into the trap of asking the question Peter asked, *"See, we have left all and followed You. Therefore what shall we have?"* (19:27). This question does not fit the Kingdom thought process; it is the wrong basis.

Spirit of Competition - None
Matthew 20:1-12

Against the back ground of the sovereignty of the landowner, we need to look at competition. Self-centered carnal thinking always concludes itself in competition. The Kingdom of God knows nothing about competition. The Kingdom of God never asks the question, *"Who then is greatest in the kingdom of heaven?"* (18:1). I earn more than you, and I work harder than you. My sacrifice is bigger than yours, and I attend church more often than you. My Sunday School Class is larger than yours, therefore, I deserve more than you. NO! Not in the Kingdom of God! This kind of competition comes from the thought process of self-centeredness.

In the parable, the laborers hired at six o'clock in the morning are saying, *"These last men have worked only one hour, and you made them equal to us who have borne the burden and the heat of the day"* (20:12). It is true that this does not appear fair. The complaining laborers worked twelve long hours through the heat of the day, while the other laborers only worked one hour. They did not even break into a sweat. Yet, the landowner is giving both groups the same wage. How could this be fair? They began to compare, and comparison always comes from a self-centered perspective. We compare ourselves with ourselves. When this happens, categories are established. What you have experienced is compared to what others have experienced. This becomes your basis to judge your own activities and establish your personal rights. Each of us thinks that our circumstances are much harder than all others.

Let me declare that this is a wrong comparison. You can always find someone who has not sacrificed as much as you, or is worse than you are. If you want to compare yourself with someone, let it be Jesus. Peter tells Jesus, ***"See, we have left all and followed You. Therefore what shall we have?"*** (19:27). This question comes because he compares himself with the Rich Young Ruler. This young man, who was seeking life, was confronted with selling all that he had and giving it to the poor. He heard the call from Jesus to follow Him (19:21). But as quickly as he ran into Jesus' presence, now, equally as fast, he runs from His presence. Peter says that he is not like the Rich Young Ruler. He has sacrificed; he left his fishing business to follow Jesus. This comparison concludes that Peter should receive great rewards. Peter's problem is that he compares himself with the wrong person. He should see himself in light of Christ. Jesus left His God position to take on flesh. He who is equal with God, because He is God, set it all aside for the sake of a cross (Philippians 2:5-8). If you think your circumstances are hard, come to the cross and see bleeding hands and a world screaming for blood. It is the self-centered focus that compares us with ourselves. But the Kingdom thought process of death to self eliminates this comparison.

The laborers who worked twelve long hours were paid by the landowner. ***And when they had received it, they complained against the landowner,*** (20:11). There is a progression. Self-centered carnality not only compares itself with itself, but also begins to complain. Complaining is always a result of comparison. There is always someone who hasn't done as well as you have, and yet, gets bigger blessings. Why did God allow this to happen to me? Notice that the laborers did not complain about each other, but they complained against the landowner. Self-centeredness always shakes a finger in the face of God and complains against Him. The landowner responds to them by saying, ***"Friend, I am doing you no wrong,"*** (20:13). The laborers accuse the landowner of wronging them. Self-centered comparing will always result in accusing God of not giving fair treatment. Look at a man who is, or has been, dead in trespasses and sin. He deserves nothing but eternal hell. Does it not amaze you that he has the nerve to stand in the face of God and condemn Him for unfair treatment?

This is a call to flee from the self-centered basis. We must die to ourselves. We must release ourselves totally to Christ. Our lives must become the style of the cross. Comparison and complaining must cease. God is sovereign; He has a right to do exactly what He wants to with what belongs to Him. We have no right to demand anything, as if we could earn or merit one blessing from Him. Our righteousness is as filthy rags in His sight and can produce no rewards. We are without merit; competition is dead.

Surprise of Rightness
Matthew 20:15

The Principle of the First is the basis of the Kingdom thought process. The foundation is the sovereignty of God. Man has no chance of earning or meriting anything. He is without rights, therefore, the spirit of competition is dead. This brings us to the *Surprise of Rightness*. Jesus surprises us with another parable of explanation. Jesus is always full of surprises. It is a goal of my life to know Him so intimately, that there will be a minimum of surprise for me on His return.

So when evening had come, the owner of the vineyard said to his steward, "Call the laborers and give them their wages, beginning with the last to the first," (20:8). The landowner restructured the system of the world. The world's method of payment was to start with those hired first. They are paid, and they leave not knowing what the other laborers will receive. But the sovereign landowner reversed the process. The laborer who worked one hour received a denarius (20:9). Seeing this, those who had worked twelve hours supposed they would receive twelve denarii. **But when the first came, they supposed that they would receive more; and they likewise received each a denarius,** (20:10). Why would the landowner allow each to see what the other received? That is the spiritual principle being revealed. The landowner wants the laborers to recognize the depth of their self-centeredness.

Our sovereign God is consistently doing that in our lives. He restructures our circumstances to reveal our self-centered carnality. He allows the trials and pressures we experience to reveal our spiritual selfishness. Are we learning the lesson? Are we comparing and complaining, or are we confessing and surrendering? Speaking to the laborers he hired first, the landowner says, *"Is it not lawful for me to do what I wish with my own things? Or is your eye evil because I am good?"* (20:15).

There is something more to learn from this parable. God not only restructures the circumstances to reveal self-centered carnality, but He reveals Himself that we might we see ourselves in light of His presence. The landowner was asking the laborers, "Do you not see how evil you are in light of my generosity?" The goodness of the landowner exposes the evil of the laborers. When I compare myself to street people, I am high quality. On the job, I appear decent when everyone is fighting. In the huddle where they tell dirty jokes, my morality shines. But when I come into the presence of Jesus, who lives the cross style, I see myself as I really am!

When the King died, Isaiah went to church in search of answers. His entire world and career had been shaken. When he entered the church, he paid attention. That will always change your life. He saw God high and lifted up, which brought an immediate revelation of himself (Isaiah 6:1-5). It is the result of the presence of God. The sovereign God restructures our circumstances to bring revelation. He brings His selfless life style, and the beauty of His denial, to reveal the condition of our hearts. He calls us to die to self-centered carnality.

So the last will be first, and the first last. For many are called, but few chosen, (20:16). This statement introduced the parable (19:30), and now it concludes the parable (20:16). Peter gave expression to the thought process of the world by asking what he would receive for leaving all to follow Jesus (19:27). The first thought of the world is always

"What am I going to get?" But in the Kingdom of God, it is last. What is first in the Kingdom of God? It is death to self - the cross style. Give yourself away; step out of self-centered focus; let Him bring you to crucifixion. First in the Kingdom is to open your hands, deny yourself, and release. Such actions come last in the world. Looking out for self is first in the world, while caring for your brother is first in the Kingdom. What comes first in the world is last in the Kingdom; what is last in the world, comes first in the Kingdom. Are you in the Kingdom?

"Jesus, forgive us when we have joined with Peter in making our demands. Our questions about receiving have revealed our puniness. We cannot merit or earn anything from You. Your Grace is our provision. We are not bad; we are focused on ourselves. We have used You for our own designs. Forgive us! Thank You for this revelation. We see ourselves in light of Your cross style. God, please save us from ourselves, and bring us to crucifixion! In Jesus' name, we pray, Amen."

Matthew 20:17-19

The Third Time

"Jesus, I am broken before You. I am afraid I will be like the disciples. They felt Your presence; they walked with You daily; but they did not grasp the truth. They believed in Your miracles, but did not comprehend the truth. Forgive me for coming to church and engaging in worship, praise, and prayer, without moving to the heart of what You are in the cross style. I must see truth! In Jesus' name, I pray, Amen."

I want to invite you to find empathy and sympathy for Jesus and weep with me over His staggering loneliness. This loneliness is highlighted in page after page of the Book of Matthew. He moves in loneliness with a group of twelve who call Him their leader. Ministering to the crowds, He is lonely. Come to the Garden of Gethsemane. It is a horrible scene. Jesus is stretched over a rock in agonizing prayer. Drops of blood are dripping from His brow. He is in deep internal agony in His heart. He weeps over the need of the world. Wringing His hands, He pleads before the Father, seeking His will. In this most trying hour, He is alone. Hear the loneliness in His voice as He returns to the disciples and finds them asleep. He asks, ***"What! Could you not watch with Me one hour?"*** (26:40).

Weep with me as we step into the scene of the betrayal. Soldiers come with torches lighting the sky. Judas, the betrayer, leads them. He plants a kiss on Jesus' cheek. It is an act of blasphemy. The soldiers drag Him to a mock trial at Caiaphas' palace. Search with Him for a friendly face. Where is the one who will stand by His side in His defense? There is no one. He is alone! Go to the Praetorium where a garrison of soldiers is milling around Him. They are making fun of Him. They place a scarlet robe on His shoulders in mockery of His Kingship. They crown Him with a crown of thorns and placed a reed weed scepter in His hand. They anoint Him with their spit. Hitting Him, they yell out their mockery. Who is there to put ointment on His wounds? There is no one. He is alone!

They drag Him up the hill called Golgotha. He is nailed to a tree in the worst form of human punishment. Who is there to sympathize with Him? The cross is dropped into a hole with a thud. Can you imagine the pain pulsating through His body? Who is there to die with Him? There is a thief on one side and a murderer on the other, but where are those who care for Him? He dies alone! Joseph of Arimathea takes Him down from the cross and buries Him. He is alone in the tomb. If it hadn't been for the women of the Church, the disciples would not have known where to find the empty tomb. He went to His grave alone.

But you do not need to wait until the Garden of Gethsemane to begin your weeping. His aloneness does not begin in Matthew chapters twenty-six and twenty-seven. In this very chapter (20), He is alone. Yes,

His disciples are clustered around Him, but He is still alone. He is alone also in chapters nineteen, eighteen, seventeen, and sixteen. The moment He mentioned the subject of the cross, He began to journey alone. The disciples caught no vision of what He was doing. They did not grasp the cross style as the heart of the Kingdom of God. As He shared with them the reality of His cross, they built walls of resistance. When the crowds moved Him because they desperately needed someone to die for them, the disciples were unable to catch His vision. He was alone. They fought every step He took toward the cross. The disciples rebuked him and argued with Him as He displayed the style of the cross. Gripped by their prejudices and traditions, they could not grasp the heart of God. They were so self-centered; they could see nothing but thrones, rulership, and position. They surrounded Him, but He was alone.

He now tries again (20:17-19) to bring them to the reality of His cross. This is the third prediction of His death and resurrection. It is another attempt to get them ready for the cross. In Matthew 16:21, He gave the first prediction. The grammar structure tells us it was something He started then and continued to do. He came to them in Galilee and gave His second prediction (17:22). But they still did not listen to Him. They looked at Him with wonder in their eyes, as if His statements were religious chants that had no meaning. He seemed to need to say these things, but they had no significance. He was alone! Now He comes the third time (20:17-19) with great urgency. He must prepare His disciples for the coming cross. The Kingdom of God is resting upon their shoulders. The leadership of the future church is at stake in them. They must see the reality of the cross and its style. Listen to His plea as He attempts, one more time, to share His heart with them. Let's consider the elements of His plea.

Element of Preparation
Matthew 20:17

Now Jesus, going up to Jerusalem, took the twelve disciples aside on the road and said to them, (20:17). The occasion came with a desperate urgency. Jesus realizes the entire Kingdom of God will be placed in their hands. He has to get them ready for what will take place. Jesus took them out of Galilee to spend specific time with them (chapters fifteen and sixteen). He wanted to remove Himself, and them, from the pressure of the crowds and the leaders of Israel. He spent nearly six months trying to prepare the disciples for the cross.

If you were in Jesus' sandals, how would you prepare your disciples for the cross? How would you teach them about the cross style? They were on the front row for His great teachings. Three of them saw the manifestation of heavenly beings on the Mount of Transfiguration. The truth came to life in the confrontation of the Rich Young Ruler. Jesus has carefully given them the theology of the cross repeatedly. Now He is going to predict the details of the coming cross. Will the knowledge of the sequence of events help them get ready? They must understand that the cross is not the end. There will be a resurrection. He tries to prepare them.

The disciples are aware that something is wrong. Things are not as they once were. There is tension among them as they struggle over position. They are not only arguing among themselves, but they are arguing with Jesus. Walls have been built between them. They seem bewildered by it all. Jesus is giving physical expression to the pressures. He stands in the very shadow of the cross. It is only a few weeks away. He doesn't laugh as much now. His shoulders are a bit stooped, and a few wrinkles have formed on His brow. How is He going to communicate the cross to His disciples? They seem to lack the ability to comprehend, and yet they must. In some sense, they are all He has. The entire Kingdom of God is at stake here. Mark and Luke give us additional information concerning the context of this third prediction. Mark tells us that Jesus was walking some distance ahead of the disciples. He is wondering how He is going to get through to them. The disciples are leading the multitudes who have joined this spiritual pilgrimage to Jerusalem. They have question marks on their faces. They don't know what to say to Jesus. Mark tells us that Jesus was moved with compassion for them. He desperately wants them to understand. He turns, goes back the distance, grabs His disciples by the elbows, and pulls them aside.

Now Jesus, going up to Jerusalem, took the twelve disciples aside on the road, (20:17). This is the **CLOSENESS OF THE PREPARATION.** A few weeks prior to this, Jesus and His disciples had returned to Galilee (17:22). The indication is that several groups met together to travel with Jesus to Jerusalem. They would pass through several towns on the way. When the news spreads that the miracle worker, Jesus, is coming, the whole town gathers to see Him. Some joined the group as they continued the journey. Jesus uses the travel time to teach the multitudes. Now He walks some distance ahead of the crowd and the disciples. The weight of telling the disciples about the cross and its style is heavy upon Him. He returns to His disciples. He pulls them to the side of the road, and gets them into a close huddle.

The multitude is not His focus now. He must convince the twelve. In this private conversation, He again begins to tell them of the coming cross.

You and I should understand this. Hundreds of times Jesus has pulled us out of the noise and clamor of the multitude to talk to us. He has yanked us out of our routine and stopped us in a desperate attempt to get our attention. He has pushed us into a corner, away from everyone else for a private conversation. He has got to get us ready. Things are not going to be like they have always been. We have to be prepared. In the closeness of preparation, He speaks to us.

This verse also tells us of **THE CONTINUATION OF THE PREPARATION**. *Now Jesus, going up to Jerusalem, took the twelve disciples aside on the road and said to them,* (20:17). This third prediction is not an isolated statement. It started back in chapter sixteen when Jesus gave the first prediction of His death and resurrection. The grammar structure of that prediction tells us that it was only the beginning of what Jesus would continue to show His disciples. He was pulling a plug from which an avalanche of revelation about the cross would come. From that time on Jesus had one purpose in mind for His disciples. He wanted to teach them the fundamental of the Kingdom - the cross style. He has launched a new attempt to get them ready. This new attempt involved some powerful experiences. Moses and Elijah appeared on the Mount of Transfiguration to speak the truth of the cross. God, the Father, overshadowed the mountain with His presence and confirmed the cross and its style. The display of miracles and the telling of parables all pointed to the cross. A child was embraced to illustrate the principle of the cross style. A Rich Young Ruler vividly displayed a rejection to the call of the cross. This continual flow was to reveal the message of the cross to the disciples.

But you and I should understand this. Isn't this the pattern of our lives? This is not an isolated moment of revelation about the cross. The revelation of the cross has been coming for hours, days, months, weeks, and years. It has come with great intensity. Do you have any comprehension of how far God has actually gone to bring revelation to you? He has accumulated His grace for two thousand years of Church history to unfold this revelation to you. In the middle of this unfolding revelation, He has reached out to pull you alongside the road. He desperately wants you to understand. He wants to prepare you. Things are not going be as they always have been. Life is in the midst of a shake up. He is trying to prepare you.

There is also **THE COMMUNICATION OF THE PREPARATION**. *Now Jesus, going up to Jerusalem, took the twelve disciples aside on the road and said to them,* (20:17). Matthew tells us what Jesus actually said to the disciples. There comes a time when demonstration ends. The mountain top experience always ceases. Jesus takes His disciples aside and gives direct communication. It is not in parable form; it is without hesitation. Jesus leans into their faces and speaks directly to them. This is bold, up front, and down to it, communication.

You and I should understand this. Jesus is that way with us. In His revelation He continually uses circumstances to communicate. He uses the lives of Godly men to reveal the cross style to you. The influence of the church, by His choice, constantly affects you. Then He places His hand on your shoulder and pulls you aside. Face to face He speaks to you the truth about His cross. He must get you ready for what is coming. Things are not going to be as they have always been. It is His preparation.

Element of Prediction
Matthew 20:18-19

"Behold, we are going up to Jerusalem, and the Son of Man will be betrayed to the chief priests and to the scribes; and they will condemn Him to death, and deliver Him to the Gentiles to mock and to scourge and to crucify. And the third day He will rise again" (20:18-19). Jesus predicts the events that will take place in the coming days. He does not want the disciples to be surprised. Hoping they will not be caught off guard, He tries to prepare them with predictions.

There is an inclusiveness involved in the predictions. The sufferings of Christ will include every kind of human suffering that can be experienced. When the cross event is complete, no one can say that Jesus did not suffer in every way known to man. He experienced it all in its deepest form.

"Behold, we are going up to Jerusalem, and the Son of Man will be betrayed to the chief priests and to the scribes" (20:18). Here is the suffering of **INSULTS**. The soldiers have some fun with Jesus. An entire garrison of soldiers with nothing to do, milling comfortably in their home barracks, has Jesus for their pleasure. They mock Him. They place an old scarlet robe on His shoulders as they poke fun. One of them conceives the idea He should have a crown. They place a crown of thorns on His head as they bow in mockery. He should

be anointed as King; they do it with their spit. We understand these kinds of insults from the soldiers. They are outsiders with no understanding of who Jesus really is. They have not felt the call of God upon their lives. They did not sit spellbound as He told the secrets of the Kingdom of God. They are just ignorant soldiers. Insults from outsiders can be tolerated.

But Jesus is telling His disciples that the insults will not be hurled from just the outsiders - ***"and the Son of Man will be betrayed"*** (20:18). These words portray the worst of insults. They tell us that one of His own, one He has trusted, and chosen Himself, will betray Him. One He has loved, and depended on, and into which He invested three years of ministry will be His betrayer. That is the highest of insults. You cannot go beyond this. This cuts to the very depth of the heart. I confess to you I could enjoy this a bit more, if I had not been the one. I have betrayed Him!

Included in the suffering of Jesus is **INJUSTICE**, - ***"and they will condemn Him to death,"*** (20:18). Every step of the way, as you travel the trail from the Garden of Gethsemane to the crucifixion, there is a voice that screams "This is not right!" Jesus should be digging in His heels and protesting against the injustice. Every moment of the scourging, He should have declared His rights. The trial was a mock trial because it was illegal. It was against the Jewish law to conduct a trial at night that involved the death penalty. They had to pay witnesses to lie about the activities of Jesus. Even then, the witnesses could not get their stories to agree. Nothing about this mock trial was fair. When Pilate began to investigate all of this, he reported that he found no fault in this Man. Pilate knew there was no justice in what was happening, thus he attempted to wash his hands of all the responsibility. The only One who did not deserve to die, was going to die!

The prediction continues to declare the suffering of **INFLICTED PAIN**, *"and they delivered Him to the Gentiles to mock and to scourge and to crucify"* (20:19). The worst torture known in Jesus' day was the Roman scourging. They bound the prisoner's hands to a high pole, stretching the muscles of the chest, back, and arms. The man was stripped from the waist up. The whip had a handle two to three feet long. Nine leather throngs extended from this handle. Each throng had sharp metal or stone placed on the end. Every time the scourge came down there were nine cuts in the flesh of the man. The Romans became very skilled with this type of whipping. They learned to flip their wrist at just the right time, causing the scourge to strike the man's back and rake his flesh. Historians tell us that often the flesh would hang like ribbons, and the inner organs would hang out. They discovered that bringing the scourge down upon a man's back forty times would kill him, so they would stop at thirty-nine. Jesus experienced this scourging before He was even declared guilty. It was inflicted pain.

Jesus tells His disciples that they need to be prepared for what is coming. Do they think life is just going to continue as always? He is attempting to get them ready by His prediction. Will they listen?

Element of Principle
Matthew 20:17

Now Jesus, going up to Jerusalem, took the twelve disciples aside on the road and said to them, (20:17). There is something in this verse that goes much deeper than Jesus' attempt to prepare the disciples for an event in the future. It goes further than a prediction to eliminate the element of surprise. Jesus wants them to live at the heart of the Kingdom of God. He wants them to learn a style. He is again declaring the style of the cross. This is much bigger than just getting them to do certain acts, keep certain rules, or accomplish certain duties. That was the style of the Pharisees. Jesus wants His disciples to grasp in their hearts what is fundamental in the Kingdom.

The disciples have learned what to say and what not to say. They tithe from their possessions and sing the songs of the church. But they do not feel about things the way Jesus feels about them. That is what Jesus wants. If the disciples can only see like Jesus sees. He wants them to grasp His cross style. That is what He is attempting to tell them in these verses.

Obviously that is not happening. The disciples come to Jesus in the midst of a squabble. They have been fighting for hours. Jesus is the only one who can settle the argument. The great issue causing their upset is, **"Who then is greatest in the kingdom of heaven?"** (18:1). I can see Jesus take the palm of His hand and strike Himself on the forehead. The disciples have just exposed how they think. Jesus must have said, "You don't feel the way I feel. You don't see things the way I see them. If you did, you would be washing each others feet instead of seeking position over each other." Jesus does not want the disciples to merely do some acts of service. He wants them to grasp the heart of the Kingdom of God. He wants them to be where He is and share His heartbeat. They live in competition with each other; He lives to serve everyone. They live to get what they can get; He lives to give Himself away. They simply do not feel like He feels.

Clearly they have missed the style of the cross. In the Garden of Gethsemane, the soldiers, led by the betrayer, come to get Jesus in the middle of the night. Peter, James, and John are sound asleep. Startled from his sleep by the noise of the soldiers, Peter jumps to His feet. Out of his natural pattern, he reaches for his sword to defend himself. He attempts to cut off a servant's head, but misses and cuts off his ear. Jesus tells Peter to put his sword away and heals the man's ear. Again Peter has displayed that he does not think like Jesus thinks. He does not feel about things the way Jesus feels. Peter cuts people down; Jesus builds them up. Peter causes arguments and fights for himself; Jesus brings peace and fights for others. The insides of Jesus and the insides of Peter do not match. Peter does not have the cross style.

They simply do not understand. Just prior to this third prediction of His death and resurrection, Jesus tells a parable to His disciples (20:1-16). The landowner hired several men to work in his vineyard, and he hired them at different times during the day. Some men worked a full twelve hours, while others worked only a few hours, and some worked only one hour. Yet, the landowner paid them all the same. Those who had worked an entire day were upset with their pay. Surely Jesus must have grinned as he told this parable. It was a story of how the disciples felt about things. Jesus was calling them to the heart of the Kingdom of God. He wants them to feel like He feels, and see like He sees. They want to know how much they can get; Jesus wants to know how much He can give. They want to compare themselves with others; Jesus wants to pour His life out for others. They live the self style; Jesus lives the cross style. It is bigger than just doing some right activities. He wants them to grasp the principle of the Kingdom - the style of the cross.

Jesus' style is **AGGRESSIVE** (20:17), - *Now Jesus, going up to Jerusalem. . .* (20:17). This is a strong statement. Jesus is doing this on purpose. Matthew has declared this about Jesus repeatedly. *From that time Jesus began to show to His disciples that He must go to Jerusalem,* (16:21). What He is doing is a "must." As Jesus gives the disciples this cross information, He is actually walking to Jerusalem where He will be crucified (17:22). He could easily avoid the cross by not going to Jerusalem, but He is aggressively pursuing it. He is determined, in spite of the tricks of the Devil and the rebuke of His disciples, to go to the cross. This is His style.

The cross and its style have not been grasped by the disciples. I think about us! We are so relaxed, laid back, and lukewarm about the cross style. We yawn Sunday morning and comment about the small crowd at the church. It doesn't seem to bother us that our town is going to hell. We aren't pushy. We cause so few problems for our world. The cross was inevitable for Jesus because He was causing problems in His world. He was pushy about the heart of the Kingdom. He was calling His disciples to join Him!

Jesus' style is **ABASING** (20:18). What was Jesus aggressive about? It was the style of the cross - abasement. He poured out His life for His world. He was aggressive about humility, poor in spirit, dying, denial. Notice how He refers to Himself. *"Behold, we are going up to Jerusalem, and the Son of Man. . . ."* (20:18). This is not what an outsider says about Him. Jesus speaks about Himself. *Son of Man* refers to His taking on flesh and dwelling among us. He lowered Himself. It is the style of the cross. He came for this one purpose, and He was aggressive about this single principle.

The disciples are often aggressive, but the problem is they are not aggressive about the right thing. We, too, get upset, but we get upset over the wrong things. We must grasp the principle of the Kingdom of God. The cross must become our focus. Paul called us to allow the mind that was in Christ Jesus to be also in us (Philippians 2:5). I wish we were as aggressive about the cross style, and death to ourselves, as we are about our materialism. I wish we were as pushy about meeting the needs of others as we are about having our own needs satisfied. We must go beyond our actions and rules to think, feel, and focus like Jesus.

This principle is **ARISING** (20:19), ***"And the third day He will rise again,"*** (20:19). Jesus is going to die! There will be the terrible agony of the cross, but there will be a resurrection! This is the principle. **When you lose, you win. When you die, you live. When you become a slave, you become free.** You can afford to give your life away. You can risk dying. You don't need to hesitate to focus your entire attention on the needs of others. Don't be frightened by the cross style. It is the only way to live.

"Jesus, are we like the disciples, trapped in our patterns and traditions? Are we stuck on ourselves? Are we missing the heart principle of the Kingdom? Pull us aside on the road and tell us again of Your cross and its style. Prepare us! Forgive us. We want to see things as You see them. Change us within! In Jesus' name, we pray, Amen."

Matthew 20:20-24

A Self-Centered Plea

"Jesus, this passage may be difficult for us. I am afraid we will see so much of ourselves in the actions of the disciples. We have come for correction. We want to be changed. Would You frighten us over the severity of our condition? Please show us what we have never seen before. We open ourselves and ask you to speak to us. In Jesus' name, we pray, Amen."

The destructive force of the self-centered carnal nature frightens me, and I know I have not seen the full extent of its destructive power. If you and I realized the depth of its potential, we would shrink from it in horror. We could never excuse ourselves again, and we would not tolerate one speck of the carnal mind within us. We would weep for a complete change by God's cleansing power.

The self-centered carnal nature stands opposed to all love, decency, and relationship. It is complete ruin to all righteousness. The carnal nature is the one thing in your life that wars against any desire you have for the presence of God. It stops you from having victory in temptation, and it is the single cause of marriage problems. At the heart of every sin in our world is the self-centered carnal nature. We enjoy blaming the Devil for the evil of our day when we should point the finger at ourselves. It is true that indirectly Satan is the cause of sin, but he has captured us by our self-centeredness, and it does the work for him.

Might I propose a question? If self-centered carnality is that destructive, why have we not already destroyed ourselves? The answer is that there is a hindrance to its destructive power. You have read about it in the Scriptures. God sent His blessed Holy Spirit into our world. He is standing as a great dike against the forces of this destruction. The prevenient grace of God is flowing from Him. He is holding the destruction at arms length, keeping you in the position where you can hear the voice of God. We believe in a literal place called hell. Hell has an atmosphere, and it is created by the attitude of the unleashed, unrestricted, self-centered carnal nature. The carnal nature causes total destruction. Can you imagine self-centered carnality being turned loose to eat like a cancer in every individual? Can you imagine a place where the truth is never told? Self-love would fill the atmosphere and destroy every relationship. Self-centeredness is total destruction.

What we have described is the atmosphere of hell. A story is told of a man who visited hell to see what it was like. Upon his arrival he was led into the great banquet hall. The tables were laden with food fit for the greatest of kings. This didn't look so bad to him. However, when he looked at those who were seated at the tables, he recognized the symptoms of starvation. In the presence of all of this delicious food, these people were starving to death. Then he noticed that they were tied to their chairs. They could not lean forward and their elbows had become unbending. There was no way they could feed themselves. Each person was desperately trying to design a means by which they could feed themselves. No one even thought of feeding the person sitting opposite him. They could easily have fed each other, but self-centered carnality would not allow it.

Self-centered carnality is not restricted to certain segments of life. It permeates every function of our living. Every relationship, all public and private moments, all thoughts and attitudes, are effected. There is nothing untouched by the self-centered carnal mind. Even religion comes under its control. In this passage of Scripture, we see self-centeredness introduced into the prayer life of the disciples. One would think we should focus our prayers on someone greater than ourselves, or the need of our world. But a mother has come with her two sons (20:20). She is related to Jesus. She is a sister to the mother of Jesus. She is Jesus' aunt and her two sons are His cousins. Apparently her sons have told her that they will each have a throne in the coming Kingdom. Each will reign over one of the twelve tribes of Israel (19:28). That is not enough for this mother and her two sons. They want to be over the other ten disciples. After all, they are family to Jesus. Why shouldn't they sit on the right and left hand of Christ in the coming Kingdom? This seems so innocent. Can you blame this mother for wanting the best for her boys? Isn't this an expression of a mother's heart? Why would this be wrong?

The answer is found in the proposition of the passage. **A self-centered request always results in tragic implications.** What are these implications?

Division in the Body
Matthew 20:24

A self-centered request always results in division within the body. ***And when the ten heard it, they were moved with indignation against the two brothers,*** (20:24). This group represents the core of the first church. They are now divided in argument. There are two disciples on one side and ten disciples on the other side. Two disciples, going behind the backs of the other ten, try to get the two highest positions in the Kingdom. The ten disciples are angry because they did not think of this first. This results in indignation within the church. This word is two words placed together. One word means *very much*, and the other word means *to annoy*. Thus, indignation means *very much to be annoyed*. It can also be translated *seized with anger*.

What is the cause of this division? It is a **SELF-CENTERED PLEA**. ***Then the mother of Zebedee's sons came to Him with her sons, kneeling down and asking something from Him. And He said to her, "What do you wish?" She said to Him, "Grant that these two sons of mine may sit, one on Your right hand and the other on the left, in Your kingdom"*** (20:20-21). Do you see the self-centered plea? The self-centeredness of two disciples has revealed the self-centeredness of the ten disciples. There is now a division within the group. The self-centered plea causes argument, indignation, and annoyance. There is a division of the twelve. We are not surprised, are we? It was the scene of the first church, and it has continued throughout history, even into our own generation.

The same thing was true in the Church of Corinth. They were an immature, carnal church. They were divided over loyalty to their various leaders. One group wanted to follow Paul because of his apostleship. Another group felt that Apollo was more effective in ministry, and they wanted to follow him. Still another group wanted to follow Peter. These divisions came from their self-centeredness. The Apostle Paul said to them, *"For where there are envy, strife, and divisions among you, are you not carnal and behaving like mere men?"* (1 Corinthians 3:3). The presence of self-centered carnality always creates envy, strife, and division.

The central issue of division is always self-centered carnality. We do not divide on issues of good or bad. We do not fight over issues that have eternal significance. We divide over junk - anything that will not matter one hundred years from now. Division comes from political manipulation among us. It is rooted in the power we wish to exert over each other. A focus on ourselves causes division. Division within the body is always caused by self-centered carnality.

This story has a **SIGNAL POINT**. Two disciples have attempted (by means of the mother), to get the most powerful positions in the coming Kingdom. They have come to Jesus in a special meeting. So what? Why does that affect the other ten disciples? What do two carnal disciples, using self-centered methods, have to do with the other ten disciples? Do ten have to be self-centered because two are? Could not the ten disciples have gone right on serving Jesus and pouring their lives out for others? Can you hear the ten disciples? "Well, they went behind our backs; they used their family connections." There is only one reason the ten were upset. They are as self-centered as the two disciples. The self-centeredness of the two brothers did not produce the self-centeredness in the ten disciples; it simply revealed what was already there. Circumstances of life and the actions of others toward me, do not create any thing in me. It simply reveals what is already there. We have often said that others are to blame for our actions or reactions. But that was language we used as children; it is time to grow up. Our selfish response to the actions of others is a sign of our own self-centeredness.

This brings us to a conclusion - **THE STANDARD PRINCIPLE**. Every time religion is the instrument of self-centeredness, it brings division within the body of Christ. Every time you, as a member of the body of Christ, use religion for self-centered benefit, you bring argument and strife to the church. Anytime there is division among the body of Christ, it is because of someone's self-centered plea.

Dethroning of the Sovereign
Matthew 20:23

A self-centered plea always results in dethroning the Sovereign. *So He said to them, "You will indeed drink My cup, and be baptized with the baptism that I am baptized with; but to sit on My right hand and on My left is not Mine to give, but it is for those for whom it is prepared by My Father"* (20:23). This is a very significant verse. It is connected to two other statements by Jesus (16:19 and 18:18). The grammar structure of these verses reveals that these statements relate to the church. *"And I will give you the keys of the kingdom of heaven, and whatever you bind on earth will be bound in heaven, and whatever you loose on earth will be loosed in heaven"* (16:19). *"Assuredly, I say to you, whatever you bind on earth will be bound in heaven, and whatever you loose on earth will be loosed in heaven"* (18:18). The verbs in each of these verses are in the future perfect passive. The proper translation changes the verb from **will be** to **will have been**. Jesus tells us that what we do here on earth should parallel what is being done in heaven. In heaven, as binding and loosing takes place, it effects our actions on earth. The same grammar structure used by Jesus as He speaks to the two disciples, is the same. As binding and loosing takes place in heaven, so the preparing of rewards is done in heaven by the Father. Rewards are not the business of those of us on earth. Our business is to rest, yield, and surrender to all that is being done in heaven. We do not dictate to heaven; heaven dictates to us. This is a renewed call to the cross and its style. We are called to lose our lives to all that the Father is doing.

You can see the effects of making demands on heaven. A self-centered plea always results in **DETHRONING HIS LORDSHIP**. God, forgive us for not seeing the issue at hand. We are prone to think only in terms of good and bad. We see a mother who wants the best for her boys. What could be so bad about that? It is not bad, but that is not the issue. It is easy for holiness people to excuse themselves from being what God wants, because we are not bad. The issue is the cross and its style. It is about His Lordship. Who is going to be in charge? Our self-centered pleas tell God that we think we know better than He does. After all, we live here, and we should know what we need. We only have one life to live, and we just want to make it a little easier on ourselves. What is wrong with that? Prayer has become an expression of our own self-centered desires. We try to manipulate God to get what we want. Our self-centered pleas dethrone God.

Our self-centered requests also result in **ENTHRONING OUR LORDSHIP**. When God is dethroned, someone must take His place.

No one is better qualified than the one who has dethroned Him. Your prayer life reveals much about you. If you want to discover a person's priority, what he really wants, and what really matters to him, where would you look? These issues are revealed in his prayer life. When a person talks to God, revealing his most inward heart, you can see what he is really like. Often we pray for a loved one to be saved so the pressure will be lifted at home. How often we have prayed for our church to grow so we would not have to bear all the burdens of paying the financial indebtedness? It is time to examine our pleas and requests of God. Are they self-centered pleas? If they are, we have dethroned God and enthroned ourselves.

This brings us to **EXCLAIM OUR LIABILITY**. We have only one great liability in our lives. It is our self-centered focus. We boldly exclaim it in our prayer life, our relationships, and in our divisions. We must come to the cross. Death to the focus on ourselves must take place so that His style, the cross style, can be seen. We cannot hide any longer. It is a cry for revival. We don't mean "a gully washer" of high emotions. The need is a radical change at the heart level, which takes place when we are honest about our self-centered carnality.

Declaration of Ignorance
Matthew 20:22

The self-centered plea of the two disciples and their mother not only causes *Division in the Body* and *Dethrones the Sovereign*, but it produces a *Declaration of Ignorance*. **But Jesus answered and said, "You do not know what you ask. Are you able to drink the cup that I am about to drink, and be baptized with the baptism that I am baptized** *with?"* (20:22). Their reply to this question is typical of us. ***They said to Him, "We are able,"*** (20:22). Jesus began by saying, ***"You do not know what you ask."*** No one has a right to say this like Jesus! He has walked with these two disciples for nearly three years. He knew them well. He knew their strengths and their weakness. Jesus also knows my strengths and weaknesses. He has come to my life and said, "You have no idea what you are asking."

The question Jesus asks the two disciples is significant. Its importance is found in the work ***drink***. He asked, ***"Are you able to drink the cup that I am about to drink?"*** The word ***drink,*** concerning the disciples, means something different in reference to Jesus. For the disciples, it means "the beginning of the suffering experience." In reference to Jesus, it means "the complete suffering experience." So a literal translation of the question would be, "Disciples, are you able to take one sip of the cup that I am about to drain to its bitterest dregs?" Jesus wants to know if the two disciples think they can even start this suffering experience.

Notice again their response. ***"We are able"*** (20:22). Our self-centered request always declares our **IGNORANCE OF INCOMPETENCY**. Do you sense the self-sufficiency in their answer? They were incompetent, and they do not realize it. It is worse than the three words in their stated answer. The words they used actually have the idea of continuation. They are saying, "We are always able." They declare they can handle every situation, right now and in the future. That sounds like us! We are so quick to think we are able. We will work it out somehow. We complicate the situation and continually increase its complexity, while we declare, "We are able." Our failures scream of our inadequacy. Our programs have not worked, and we are not winning the lost. We are not adequate. Yes, these two disciples are a pattern of us. They couldn't even stay awake in the Garden of Gethsemane for one hour to pray. How could they go to the cross with Him? The disciples ran in fright at the first sign of a threat, and they hid in fear of the Jews. They were ignorant of their own incompetency.

In their self-centered plea, they declare the **IGNORANCE OF INDEPENDENCE** (20:22). The bold expression of our incompetency shows us how ignorant we are of our own independence. We have taken over in our lives. Our self-sufficiency is only matched by our stupidity. A young man, raised in the church, came to me with startling truth. He had memorized all important Scriptures, won all the church contests, and held perfect attendance records. In doing all this, he discovered that he did not need God for a single thing in his Christian experience. He had developed all the proper disciplines, habits, and worship patterns. Respectability, proper actions, good home relationships had all been achieved. God could disappear and it would not effect his life. I wanted to shake his hand and say, "I always wanted to meet a Pharisee." In describing himself, he gave the perfect picture of the Pharisee of Jesus' day. A Pharisee is one whose whole religious life is dependent upon himself.

We must examine and discover what it is in our lives that can only be explained in terms of Jesus. What is it about us that is supernatural? What is in your life that would totally collapse if God were removed from the world? What is it about your church that is beyond program, talent, good literature, and organization? I fear we are like the two disciples who answered, "*We are able.*" We have a Christianity that

Matthew 20:20-24 – A Self-Centered Plea

is a product of ourselves. The greatest tragedy is that we don't even know it! Those who live around us know. Our actions are like a sign around our neck saying, "We are ignorant." We have an **IGNORANCE OF INFERENCE**. In the bold declaration of our self-centeredness, we have declared our ignorance. By our self-centered pleas we have divided the body, dethroned God and enthroned ourselves. We have declared our own ignorance. We must come to a cross and experience His death.

"Jesus, we only have one problem. It is our self-centered carnal focus. Forgive us for attempting to produce Christianity without You. Please save us from ourselves. Give us a revival of holiness which cleanses us of carnality. We come in dependency upon You. In Your name, we pray, Amen."

Matthew 20:24-28

A Selfless Plea

And when the ten heard it, they were moved with indignation against the two brothers (20:24). What a terrible introduction to this chapter. One part of its tragedy is found in its **SELFISHNESS**. Two brothers have plotted behind the backs of the other ten disciples. They even got their mother to act in their behalf. She is an aunt to Jesus; thus, they are cousins to Christ. Because of this family relationship, they feel confident in asking for the right and left-hand positions in the coming Kingdom. Each of them has already been given a throne over one of the twelve tribes of Israel (19:28). But that is not good enough for these two disciples. They do not want to be one among twelve disciples, but two above ten. Self-centered carnality is never satisfied. I wonder what more they would have asked if Jesus had given them this request. Someone said that some of us are simply waiting for a vacancy in the Trinity, so we can apply.

Another element of sadness in this verse is that it is **SEDUCTIVE**. The self-centeredness of the two disciples has seduced the self-centeredness of the ten disciples. Now the entire group is in division, expressing their selfishness. The self-centeredness of the two disciples did not produce, but simply revealed, the self-centeredness of the ten. I can hear the ten disciples defend themselves by saying, "Well, they started it!" But remember our study in chapter eighteen. They all were demanding that Jesus decide which one of them will be number one (18:1). The key word in verse twenty-four is *indignation*. It is two words placed together. The first word means *very much*, and the second word means *to annoy*. The ten disciples *were very much annoyed*, or *seized with anger*, over what the two brothers were asking. Isn't it interesting how we are greatly annoyed when we see our own faults in others?

These twelve disciples are **SYMBOLIC** of the entire church. They are symbolic of the church which will be established by Christ. In a real sense, they are the first congregation of the evangelical church. They set the style and tempo for the days ahead. This is not the only time we will see this kind of self-centered carnality raise its head in division. It will destroy evangelism repeatedly. We could excuse these arguing disciples because they have not experienced Pentecost Sunday. The cross and resurrection have not taken place yet. But that could be somewhat embarrassing, because we have experienced the cross and resurrection. We gather, year after year, to celebrate the coming of the Holy Spirit on Pentecost Sunday. How do we explain our arguments?

Here are twelve disciples expending their energy, dividing over self-centered issues. Just think what would have happened if that same energy could have been used for the Kingdom's sake. Jesus identifies their attitude immediately. It is distinctly the world's. He says, **"You know that the rulers of the Gentiles lord it over them, and those who are great exercise authority over them"** (20:25). The disciples exhibit the style of the world, not the style of the cross. The Roman governors lord it over their subjects. Pilate is a good example. He does not care about the hurts and difficulties of those under him. He uses his subjects for his own self-centered benefits. Helping his subjects is not his concern. How can his subjects help him? Ruling over Pilate is the Roman Emperor. He is not concerned about the needs of Pilate. The Roman Emperor uses all Roman governors for his own self-centered desires. Each politician uses those beneath him for himself. That is the pattern of the world. Jesus sees the world's style in the disciples. They seek for position themselves. They want to lord it over each other.

Jesus has discussed this time and again, but the disciples simply have not listened. Now Jesus patiently tells them He is going to give the truth again on how to be number one. The proposition of the passage is this. **The unselfish Christ tells His disciples how to be number one in the Kingdom of God!** What is the proper procedure?

Submit to Be a Servant
Matthew 20:26

"Yet it shall not be so among you; but whoever desires to become great among you, let him be your servant" (20:26). Notice the **SEVERITY OF THE SUBMISSION**. It is contained in the opening statement of verse twenty-six. *"Yet it shall not be so among you. . . ."* Jesus identifies the disciples with the world's style. It is the style of lording it over each other and fighting for position. It is the result of self-centered carnality. Jesus now becomes severe as He speaks to His disciples. He raises His voice; His face is stern; His eyes flash. Jesus will

not tolerate this from them. This action and attitude will not take place in the Kingdom of God. It is not the style of the cross.

The verb is in the future tense. He is not just speaking of this immediate moment. His concern is for the future of the Kingdom of God. The verb is also in the imperative sense, so it is a command. The King of the Kingdom is passing down an edict. This will not be voted on at the board meeting. The King decides the style of the Kingdom. It will be the cross style. He leaves no room for adjustment. Jesus gives a parallel line at the end of the verse. It is the phrase *"let him be your servant."* Again the verb tense allows the translation "he shall be your servant." It is the future imperative tense. Jesus clearly says, "It shall not be so" and "it shall be so!" This is to be the normal style of the Kingdom. It is not for a few radical disciples. Every one is to live in this pattern. If we want to be Kingdom people, this must be our style - the style of the cross.

It is necessary to more clearly define the **STYLE OF THE SUBMISSION**. *"But whoever desires to become great among you, let him be your servant"* (20:26). Jesus is obsessed with the idea of servanthood. It is in all of His sermons; it echoes throughout all of His parables. His life consistently displays servanthood. Be careful when you say that you want to be like Jesus. You must be a servant.

In verse twenty-seven, Jesus uses the word *slave*. It is a different word than this word *servant*. It is the contrast between these two words that reveals the impact of the truth. This word *servant* is used several times in the New Testament and has a variety of translations. The Apostle Paul writes about *deacons* (Philippians 1:1). Other places it is translated *minister*. Here, in Jesus' words, it is *servant*. It literally means *one who executes the command of another.* It is an individual who sees a need in one of his social peers. He becomes a servant to meet that need, in service of the one he is equal to. He then returns to equality with this peer. This is not about serving those who are greater than you are, but meeting the need of your peers. This is the style of a servant.

But what does this mean? How does it apply? What is the **SENSE OF THE SUBMISSION**? *"Yet it shall not be so among you"* (20:26). The words *among you*, and *let him be your servant* give us this sense. The important word is *your.* Jesus is not addressing the multitude; He is speaking to twelve argumentative disciples. They are competing for position. Jesus calls them to serve each other, their equals. Will they be willing to come from being equal in the twelve and serve each other? Will they serve the one who argues with them over position?

How does this apply to our lives? Jesus calls us to step from the position of equality and serve those who have needs among us? They may be the ones who vote against us in the board meeting. They may be the ones who constantly want us to do their dirty work. This is not about helping our unsaved, next door neighbor. This means helping those who are equal to us in the disciple group. Jesus calls us to be servants, in submission, meeting the needs of our brother.

Wouldn't it be something if this is what Church membership really means? When I take membership vows, I am saying to the entire congregation. I simply roll up my sleeves to say, "I just became your servant. I am equal with you. However, the moment I see a need in your life, I will forfeit my equality and become your servant." That means we do not tell the pastor who to call on, but we call on them ourselves. We will not be critical when the church is not as clean as we think it should be, but we will get a broom.

Imagine this in the giving and taking of marriage vows! These vows would be taken with the attitude of submission that says "I submit to be your servant. I am going to watch your life carefully. The moment I see a need, I will rush to serve you. My life will be in submission to meeting your needs."

Surrender to Be a Slave
Matthew 20:27

If you want to be great in the Kingdom of God, then you must submit to be a servant. But perhaps that is not what you really want. You would rather be number one. If this is your sincere desire, then listen closely. ***"And whoever desires to be first among you, let him be your slave,"*** (20:27). Notice the **SEVERITY OF THE SURRENDER**. The severity that Jesus introduces into being a servant, now carries into being a slave. The opening word of verse twenty-seven is ***and.*** It is emphatic and can be translated *in fact.* Matthew is summarizing everything Jesus has said about this subject in chapters sixteen through twenty. This is not optional or superficial. Jesus is emphatic!

We must embrace the **STYLE OF THE SURRENDER**. In verse twenty-six, Jesus refers to being ***great.*** ***"But whoever desires to become great among you, let him be your servant."*** Being great has some desirable qualities. Each of the twelve disciples will be given a throne over one of the twelve tribes of Israel. They will be ruling, one, among twelve disciples. But they each prefer to be first in rulership. To be great you must come from among your equals, lower yourself, and service their needs. After the service, you return to being equal with the one you have served. But if your heart is really set on being "first," then the requirement is to become a slave. ***"And whoever desires to be first among you let him be your slave"*** (20:27). It is the picture of the galley ship slave. He sits on a bench in the bottom of a great sailing ship. There are benches behind, in front, and beside him. Two men sit on each bench with the handle of an oar in front of each. Every man wears an ankle brace with a chain hooking them together. In the front of the ship is a drummer beating out the rhythm to which they row. They are mastered and controlled by their owner. They are his property. He has a piece of paper for each man. It was signed, notarized, and recorded at the courthouse. They are slaves without rights. No one can declare he is taking a day off, call in sick, or ask for more vacation time. There can be no complaints about the working conditions or the people he works with. He dare not refuse to work because there are hypocrites in the bottom of the boat. He is a slave. The style of the cross means you have no rights.

In an application of this to our lives, we must grasp the **SENSE OF THE SURRENDER**. ***"And whoever desires to be first among you, let him be your slave"*** (20:27). ***Among you*** and ***your*** does not refer to people of the street, your unsaved, next door neighbor, or people who receive your charity. The twelve disciples were arguing over position. Jesus called them to serve each other. He calls us to be a slave to those with which we argue. The call is to be a slave to the one we do not like, the one who is attempting to take advantage of us.

There is a contrast between a **servant** and a **slave**. It is the key to understanding the perpetual aspect of slavery. Being a servant is assuming a temporary position, lower than equal, to meet a need. When the need is met, you can return to equality with the person you have served. However, in the position of the slave, you assume the slave position, meet their need, and are never again equal with them. You remain in the slave position forever. An awareness of equality is always present in the picture of the servant, but as your slave, I am never equal with you.

I have a vivid imagination. In it, I imagine a new church membership vow. Wouldn't it be wonderful if it were common knowledge, something of an unwritten law, that when you took membership vows in the Church, you were declaring yourself to be a slave? At the altar, you would stand and admit that your status is lower than anyone else in the church. You will become a slave to the entire congregation. Your one focus will be to meet the needs of everyone. You will pour out your energy for others. Appreciation and encouragement are not necessary. You do not have to be understood or even liked. Those are factors that will have nothing to do with your position as a slave. You are giving up your rights to be served in return, and you are becoming a slave.

My imagination also reaches into the marriage vows. Just think of this! Imagine standing at the altar of the church, as a bride or a groom, and declaring yourself to be a slave to your new husband or wife? Our marriage will not be based on 50 percent from me and 50 percent from you. I declare myself to be your slave, and my one focus will be to meet your needs. I will not live for myself, but for you. My first thought will not be for me, but for what is good for you. I surrender all of my rights and submit to be your slave. I am losing my life to you.

Sacrifice to Be a Substitute
Matthew 20:28

Jesus gives us an example of how these two suggestions work in practical life. He carefully shows us that this is not idealistic or impractical. If you want to be great, submit to be a servant. If you want to be first, surrender to be a slave and sacrifice to be a substitute. ***"Just as the Son of Man did not come to be served, but to serve, and to give His life a ransom for many"*** (20:28).

Let's look at the **SEVERITY OF THE SACRIFICE**. Verse twenty-eight begins with ***just as,*** and means *even as, in the exact same manner as.* Jesus is referring to Himself. He is not a top sergeant barking out orders. He does not sit in the shade of a tree as his troops march in the hot sun. Jesus is not giving instructions on something He has never done. God is speaking here. He is the Creator, and He is superior to creation. This superior One leaped off His throne and took on flesh. He became our slave, but not for a temporary time. It was not a thirty-three-year sacrifice from the eternal time of God. He became your eternal slave. If you get to heaven, you will find Christ with nail prints in His hands. Those mark His attachment to mankind as He sits at the right hand of the Father still serving in intercession for you. He is not Lord of the Kingdom because He is God; He is Lord because He became the slave of the Kingdom.

It is essential that you understand the **STYLE OF THE SACRIFICE**. ***"Just as the Son of Man did not come to be served,*** *but to serve. . . ."* (20:28). **Served** and **serve** relate to verse twenty-seven, not verse twenty-six. Jesus' reference is not to being a servant (20:26), but to being a slave (20:27). The servant is one, equal with others, but who has voluntarily taken on the role of a servant. He will return to equality with his peers when the act of service is complete. The *slave* of verse twenty-seven is a perpetual slave, who will never again will be equal to you. In fact, this has a purpose clause - **but to serve.** Jesus came to serve. The cross was not a last, desperate attempt. It was always the plan of the Kingdom. It is the fundamental principle that everyone in the Kingdom must possess. It is at the heart of who Jesus is! The cross event was the logical conclusion, or culmination, to the cross style living of Jesus. He gave Himself to the slavery of our needs.

To grasp the full picture of this slave, we need to see the **SENSE OF THE SACRIFICE.** *"Just as the Son of Man did not come to be served, but to serve, and to give His life a ransom for many"* (20:28). We love the theological discussions about this last phrase. It is the ransom theory of the cross. To whom did Jesus pay the ransom? But that misses the point of what Jesus is saying. *Substitute* describes the meaning of ransom. He became the slave substitute. He so identified with your pain, sin, and guilt, that they actually became His. He became what you are. He took your place to serve you.

If I apply this to my life, how far do I push this slave substitute idea? What are the limits of losing my life for others? Where do I draw the line and say that enough is enough? In the Sermon on the Mount, Jesus said that I am to turn the other cheek. But people tend to take advantage of you when you respond that way. You become a sucker. People use you for their own benefit. When do you look them in the eye and say you have had enough? The answer is found in the beginning of verse twenty-eight with the words *just as.* We are to be like He is! We are to go as far as He went? He identified with the needs of others. Their needs became His needs and demanded His life. He called the disciples to identify with the needs of their brothers, until those needs became theirs. He calls us to the same. We help our brother bear his burden as it becomes ours. We become a substitute for his pain. That means we set aside our personal problems for the sake of others. That is the style of the cross.

"Jesus, if only I could be like You. Would you come and be Who You are in me? Could I become Your body, so You can do again what You did two thousand years ago? I want to feel what You feel. I want to see what You see. Bring me to the depth of the cross. Take me beyond myself, my ceremonies, and my self-centered rights. I give myself to You. In Jesus' name, I pray, Amen."

Matthew 20:29-34

Blindness - A Description

The healing of blinded eyes is the most often recorded miracle in the New Testament. There is something about blindness that stirs sympathy within the heart. It appears that Jesus frequently touched blinded eyes. In the traditional teaching of the Pharisees, blindness was equated with sin, generally sexual impurity. One day, when Jesus and His disciples met a blind man, the disciples asked **"Rabbi, who sinned, this man or his parents, that he was born blind?"** (John 9:2). Their question reflected their training under the leadership of Israel.

In the physical environment of Jesus' day, many factors contributed to the numerous cases of blindness. There was little green grass, and the dust and sand were pulverized by the intense heat of the region. The sun would glare off that sand, into the eyes of the people. The days were extremely hot, but the cool sea winds blew on the coastal cities in the evenings. Many would sleep on their roof tops for the cool breeze. The night dew affected the eyes of those who did this. Blindness was a very common infirmity.

Why did Matthew place this story of two blind men at the end of chapter twenty? If he is writing about Jesus' ability to heal blinded eyes, then the inclusion of this story is unnecessary. Matthew has already given several scenes where Jesus performed this miracle (9:27-31 and 12:22). It would have been more profitable for Matthew to tell of other great miracles Jesus did. Perhaps he was fascinated by the healing of blinded eyes and recorded these miracles for his own pleasure. But, Mark and Luke also include this story in the exact sequence of events in their Gospel accounts. Matthew obviously wants to deliver an important message through this story. What is his message?

This story of two blind men sitting by the road, appears to be a bridge or link between the events recorded, and those we are about to embrace. It is a hinge between what Jesus has done and what He will do. It ties the events together, giving impact and understanding to the total message of His gospel account. Chapter twenty is the close of a very special section in the Book of Matthew (chapters sixteen through twenty). Jesus has concentrated on training His disciples in the style of the cross. He gave the three predictions concerning His death and resurrection, spoke to them of His own death, and called them to join Him in this cross style.

Chapter sixteen, *Consideration of the Cross Style*, is Jesus' introduction of this subject to His disciples. Chapter seventeen, *Confirmation of the Cross Style*, is the visual teaching of the style of the cross. Three of the disciples saw Moses and Elijah on The Mount of Transfiguration. The presence of God, the Father, is felt and heard, as He verifies that Jesus is telling the truth about the cross. In the valley, the other disciples see a perfect example of their lack of power, when they cannot cast out one demon. Chapter eighteen, *Confessions of the Cross Style,* is a record of the theological teachings of Jesus about death to self-centered carnality. It is a call to the cross. Chapter nineteen, *Configuration of the Cross Style,* is the practical application of the cross in daily living. And chapter twenty, *Conclusions of the Cross Style,* gives evidence that the disciples do not understand what Jesus is teaching them. The pressure is on Jesus now. The actual event of the cross is very close. He summarizes everything He has said about the cross in this chapter.

Chapters sixteen through twenty hold remarkable truth. They are filled with warmth and compassion. These chapters reveal the heart of Jesus for His disciples. Patiently Jesus goes over the same truth. Repeatedly His disciples fail to embrace it. Chapter twenty is Matthew's record of Jesus' focus on the disciples and His attempt to get them ready for the cross.

What lies ahead in this writing? Chapter twenty-one marks a distinct change. It is as different from the previous chapters as night is from day. Jesus is not focused on His disciples, but has come to embrace all of Judaism. It is a strong confrontation in comparison to the warmth and compassion for the disciples. We see the Triumphant Entry of Jesus, as He presents Himself, King of Israel. He marches to the citadel of Judaism. What an upheaval takes place as He cleanses the temple. He pushes Israel with His claims, and they will push back. Jesus is moving to embrace the cross.

In the middle of the compassion and the confrontation is this powerful story of two blind men. The self-centered disciples stand on one side, while self-centered Judaism stands on the other. Jesus has taught and lived by the cross style, and now the cross event is coming.

Between these two sections we read of two blind men calling to Jesus. This story is a bridge over which we can walk. It spans from the focus on the disciples to the focus on Judaism. These two sections are not as radically different as they might appear at first. The disciples are committed to following Jesus, and the leaders of Israel are committed to crucify Jesus. The spiritual condition of all of them is the same. Both are filled with self-centered, carnal blindness. In this story of two blind men, we will see the solution to the needs of both.

The Condition
Matthew 20:29-30

Now as they departed from Jericho, a great multitude followed Him. And behold, two blind men sitting by the road, when they heard that Jesus was passing by, cried out, saying, "Have mercy on us, O Lord, Son of David!" (20:29-30).

Matthew clearly states the condition as blindness. Let us examine this condition in view of the **DISCIPLES**. It is obvious in the reading of chapters sixteen through twenty, the disciples have one major problem. It is self-centered, carnal focus. It is seen in their six days of rebuke of Jesus. They do not like what is He saying about the style of the cross (16:22). We see it again in their lack of ministry when a father pleads for his son's life (17:16). Their self-centeredness is evident as they fight over the issue of *"Who then is greatest in the kingdom of heaven?"* (18:1). Their approach to marriage (19:10), and their blockade of the children's entrance to see Jesus (19:13), reveals it. Peter even has the nerve to claim that they have left all to follow Jesus. He wants to know exactly what kind of benefits they will get from their great sacrifice, as if they earned something (19:27). Now they are fighting among themselves. The positions of right-hand and left-hand in the coming Kingdom (20:24) is important to them. Their actions flow from the base of extreme self-centeredness. The disciples are filled with carnality.

Each of these situations creates an opportunity for Jesus to teach His disciples about the cross style. He will not give up on them, but patiently and consistently He relates the message of the cross. He gives direct teaching through preaching. There is visual teaching through the Mount of Transfiguration. With all that the Master Teacher gives them, how can they miss the truth? But they do! How can it be? It is because they are blind. They are so focused on themselves that they are blind to everything else. Certainly we see a definition for blindness in these illustrations of the disciples. **Blindness is a focus on self until nothing else can be seen.** The disciples ignore the hurting world around them while they spend six days in argument with Jesus. The heart of spiritual wisdom that Jesus desperately tries to express is lost to them. They are blinded by self-centered, carnal focus.

Let us now compare this with the condition of **JUDAISM**. This has also been made plain to us. We have seen, woven into Matthew's story, the destructive legalism of Judaism. The Jews are focused on their traditions, laws, and institutions. They are consumed with protecting themselves and their institution. When religion exists to protect itself, it ceases to be spiritual and becomes a stench in the nostrils of God. Judaism became unbending, narrow, and blind. Jesus said ***"They are blind leaders of the blind"*** (15:14). What was at the heart of their blindness? They were filled with themselves - self-centered, carnal focus. Even the laws, which they held in high esteem, were a means to build walls and focus on themselves. They would even adjust the law if it would help them. They manipulated the institution to make a comfortable place for themselves. They lived out of their own self-centered ego. They used God and their institution for themselves.

Blindness is the ability to focus on yourself until you can see nothing else. Isn't it amazing that the self-centered, carnal blindness of the disciples and the leaders of Judaism is the same? What is the difference between them? The disciples are focused on using Jesus for their own ends. The leaders of Judaism are focused on using Jehovah and their religion for themselves. Isn't it ironic that those who do not believe that Jesus is the Messiah, and those who do, both are blind in their hearts?

But look at what Matthew places between the disciples and Judaism. It is **TWO BLIND MEN**. *"And behold, two blind men sitting by the road,"* (20:30). Why were they sitting by the road? It was a part of Jesus' culture that blind men would beg to live. These two men have joined for companionship, however, and have stooped to the level of begging. From the view of Judaism, God would never allow a Jew to reach this low. Begging said that God would not take care of you. Begging, blind men were looked upon with disdain.

I have much more admiration for these two blind men than I do for the self-centered disciples and the leaders of Judaism. While they were blind physically, they had spiritual eyesight, which gave them the ability to respond to Jesus. They would not allow the crowd to keep them from Jesus. The physically blinded had spiritual eyesight. The greatest tragedy is when those who have physical eyesight are spiritually blinded. Helen Keller was asked by someone if she could think of anything worse than being blind. Her immediate answer was, "Yes, to be able to see and have no vision. That would be worse!"

The Cure
Matthew 20:34

It is very important that we do not become consumed with *The Condition*. It is easy to criticize for hours, but criticism focuses us on the problem. The early Church talked about their power; we talk about our problems. We must not become problem-centered. Let's focus on *The Cure*.

So Jesus had compassion and touched their eyes. And immediately their eyes received sight, and they followed Him (20:34). Let us look at **TWO BLIND MEN**. A distinct progression takes place in this verse. Compassion comes first. Compassion means *to be emotionally moved deep within your heart*. Matthew relates this event as the heart of the lifestyle of Jesus. It is a great characteristic of the cross style. When Matthew summarizes the Galilean ministry of Jesus, He uses one great quality. *But when He saw the multitudes, He was moved with compassion for them, because they were weary and scattered, like sheep having no shepherd* (9:36). Jesus and His disciples were with four thousand men, beside women and children, on a hillside. Many of that crowd were people with great physical handicaps. Jesus said to His disciples, *"I have compassion on the multitude, because they have now continued with Me three days and have nothing to eat"* (15:32). Matthew shows the quality of compassion coming from Jesus repeatedly.

This compassion is not just sympathetic feeling. This compassion gets involved and touches. Jesus meets the two blind men; He must touch them. In the second step in the progression, the compassion requires touching. Jesus has to get involved with the men and their need. The compassion and touching of Jesus caused the third element. The blind men received His healing. They then began to follow Jesus, which is the fourth part of the progression.

The healed eyes of two blind men now view the wonderful cure. But let's view it through the eyes of the **DISCIPLES**. Do the disciples look confused to you? Jesus has repeated His message of the cross enough that the disciples realize He is going to quit. But they are not getting it. Jesus is not following the rules of a Messiah. If He would just act the way a Messiah is supposed to act, everything would be fine. He talks about dying when He should talk about reigning. His emphasis is on a cross when it should be on a gold plated throne. The Roman Empire needs to be overthrown, but Jesus talks about losing His life. He should be at the temple, expounding the law of God, but He is touching lepers and healing withered hands on the wrong day. This confuses the disciples. They believe that Jesus is the Messiah, but He isn't doing what Messiahs are supposed to do! Are they confused or are they blind?

Why doesn't Jesus have compassion on the confused disciples? He had compassion on two blind men. Why doesn't Jesus touch their confused eyes and help them to see? Doesn't He want the disciples to be cured so they can adequately follow Him? Oh, YES! He has spent nearly six months focused on His disciples. He makes a third attempt to explain it to them (20:17-19). Jesus is not talking to the multitudes, but to the disciples. Jesus has burnt the midnight oil with them, opening the wisdom of God. The same Divine power that flowed to two blind men has been flowing to twelve blind disciples. It is the identical resource!

The Divine power enables two blind men to see, why doesn't it cause twelve blind disciples to see? What is the blockade? How can this be explained? Only one thing stops the power of God; it is self-centered carnality. They cannot see beyond their own wants and needs. They are focused on themselves. We are the same. There is only one reason we remain in our confusion. It is self-centered carnality. The power of God is always touching us, but we do not see it. Our spiritual superiority causes us to shut down the power of God in our lives. We only have one problem; it is self-centered carnality.

JUDAISM is just as tragic. In a Jewish home, the first words spoken every morning were in a question. "Could this be the day?" It was a reference to the coming of the Messiah. Judaism had the Messianic promises contained in Scripture. Every Jew knew the stories and held to the promises. The dream of the coming Messiah, the Deliverer, was kept alive. The more oppressive the Roman domination, the more the vision of a Deliverer burned in their hearts. Their entire religious ceremonies were focused on the coming Messiah. Every lamb offered in sacrifice was a symbol of the coming Messiah. Judaism would recognize the Messiah when He came. No doubt about that! They were constantly on the look out for Him.

Yet, when He came, they missed Him because of their blindness. Didn't Jesus have compassion on Judaism as He did the two blind men? He wept over the city of Jerusalem. He referred to Himself as a mother hen who wants to gather her chicks under her wing (23:37). Didn't Jesus want to reach out and touch Judaism like he did the blind eyes of two men? Every promise in the Old Testament about the Messiah was fulfilled by Jesus. He was the exact match to the Old Testament presentation of the Messiah. The Jews should have recognized Him. Didn't Jesus want Judaism to receive her sight as the two blind men did? Didn't He want Judaism to follow Him? Yes! Yes! The Divine resource that flowed from Jesus to the two blind men was flowing to Judaism in her blindness. Why was Judaism so blind? What was the problem? There is only one problem; it is self-centered carnality. They were so focused on themselves, their traditions, and their power, that they missed His touch.

Is it any different with us? Are we a people who offer all the right sacrifices, do the right things, say the right words and still miss Him? Can we be blind? Are we so filled with self-centered carnality that we miss Him too? The same power that flowed from God to the two blind men was available to the disciples and to Judaism. They missed it. It is available to us. Will we miss it?

The Conclusion
Matthew 20:34

Everything comes to a conclusion. Self-centered, carnal blindness always carries with it the seeds of its own destruction. Perhaps this is the most tragic of all. Let's look at the **DISCIPLES**. Jesus told the disciples about the coming cross. They did not grasp what Jesus was saying. Throughout the Passion Week they are running away. When the soldiers came to the Garden of Gethsemane, the disciples were greatly frightened. They went into hiding during the crucifixion. They boasted that they would follow Him to the death, but they could not even make it through the trials. What caused their fear? It was self-centered carnality. They did not understand, nor embrace, the cross style. Fear is not created by the size of the threat, but it is caused by the smallness of the inner man. The issue of fear is not from without, but from within. Would we dare face our fears to see the underlying cause?

What conclusion do we see in **JUDAISM**? Matthew's account of the next week shows them trying to maintain things as always. On the first Sabbath day, following the crucifixion, they casually talked about the strange weather on Good Friday. "Did you see how dark it became? It was as dark as night around noon. Sure was strange. Oh, well, it cleared up toward evening, so all is well." Judaism went right on with their sacrifices and ceremonies. They gave their offerings and kept their laws. They maintained! The dream of their histories had just taken place, and they went right on as if nothing happened. They maintained! Would we dare examine our own lives? God moves and does something deep in the life of our church. Revival comes and people seek God at the altar of prayer. But the next Sunday, it doesn't seem to matter. We yawn and return to maintaining.

How do you win people to Jesus in a community where there is not a holiness church? The church plant plan is popular in this day. A pastor, with a heart for evangelism, is sent into a community to live. He has very little resources, no staff, and no building. But he begins to develop contacts, make friends, and before very long he has a church. We all applaud. This is wonderful! In another community, not far away, is a church with all of the resources necessary to win the lost. They have a full time pastor, a qualified staff, a lovely building, and plenty of equipment. But they are doing nothing to win their community to Jesus. They have had the same attendance for the last thirty years. What is their problem? It is the same as Judaism - self-centered carnality. They simply maintain.

Let us go back to what ties the scene of the disciples and Judaism together. It is **TWO BLIND MEN**. *So Jesus had compassion and touched their eyes. And immediately their eyes received sight, and they followed Him* (20:34). The conclusion for two blind men was that they began to see. *And immediately their eyes received sight,* is the declaration. Then they began to follow Jesus. Life took on direction and meaning. Jesus wanted the same conclusion for the disciples and for Judaism. It is also meant for us. The same power of God that flowed to the two blind men is flowing to us. Sight has only one barrier. It is our self-centered carnality. We must come to the cross!

"Jesus, it is easy for us to criticize the disciples and Judaism, but we also have one major problem. It is our carnal mind. We confess our self-centeredness openly before You. Bring us to total cleansing. We are deeply aware that there will be no deliverance for us if You do not do it. We cannot bring sight to ourselves. Touch our eyes. In Your name, we pray, Amen."

Matthew 20:29-34

Just Like Me

This is an exciting portion of Scripture. When you get a feel for the Book of Matthew, you see the fluctuation in the atmosphere of Matthew's writings. In chapters eight and nine, there is a sense of hilarity as Jesus conquers every area of life. Having conquered, He reigns over these areas, which is what you would expect from a Kingly Messiah. Chapter fourteen holds great sorrow in the atmosphere. John the Baptist has been beheaded. This causes tremendous pressure for Jesus. He is alone in His journey. In chapter sixteen the atmosphere changes to frustration and anxiousness. The disciples just do not seem to grasp the cross and its style. The One who knows the plan is being rebuked by the ones who do not know it. The finite are rebuking the eternal One. This atmosphere continues to intensify in chapter twenty. We see the strength of Jesus as He presses His disciples with the truth of the cross. He cannot allow them to miss the truth of death to self-centered carnality. We now come to the end of our study of chapter twenty. It is a fitting climax to this section. The atmosphere which has been so pressured has turned to celebration. Jesus is touching the blinded eyes of two men! It is a visible example for the disciples.

"Jesus, we see ourselves in these two blind men. Touch us! In our ignorance and foolishness, arrest us! In the hardness of our hearts, please move us! Please give us vision. We are available. In Your Name, we pray, Amen."

As we study the Gospel accounts, clearly the truth the writers present is a self-revelation. The Holy Spirit's inspiration is to help each of us see ourselves in reality. The Word of God is given to reveal Jesus. Through that revelation we can see ourselves. As you discover the secrets of the Kingdom of God, you see secrets about yourself. The Word of God acts as a mirror, reflecting your image. As you see through the Gospel stories you will see a revelation of yourself. This is true in the story of the two blind men. Are we so much different from them?

The social status of Jesus' culture started with the Sadducees and ended with the lepers. The Sadducees were the wealthy, influential people, while the lepers were the outcasts. They dared not come close. Slightly above the lepers was a group of people who had become beggars. The beggar was a **NATIONAL BLIGHT** upon Israel. It is amazing how few times beggars are mentioned in the Old Testament. Begging was not acceptable. It was a spiritual issue with Israel. How could you be a member of the chosen people of God, destined to bring the Messiah into this world, and beg?

"I have been young, and now am old; Yet I have not seen the righteous forsaken, Nor his descendants begging bread" (Psalms 37:25).

Within the Jewish culture, God had established a welfare system. The poor had provision. When the fields were harvested, grain was left behind for them. No one ever had to beg!

Begging was also a **PERSONAL BELITTLEMENT**. The Pharisees and Sadducees had promoted the health and wealth Gospel. In their teaching, begging was linked with a spiritual need. If you were spiritually right, you would never have to beg. To beg was to admit that you had sinned. When you combine begging and blindness, it gets worse. The Pharisees and Sadducees believed that blindness was caused by the sin of immorality, committed by the blind person or his parents. The Old Testament emphasizes that when the judgment of God comes upon an individual, he will be reduced to begging for bread. So to be a blind beggar meant you had committed, or were connected to immorality, and were now receiving the judgment of God.

The position of a beggar was a **STATUS BENEATH**. Israel had developed, through the sacrifice system, an idea about wholeness. A lamb could not be offered as a sacrifice to God unless it was without spot or blemish. It had to be whole. A priest could not have a handicap. If you were not physically whole, you were defiled, therefore, God could not accept you. Defilement was a very strong issue with the Jews. They were always avoiding anything that, or anyone who, might spread defilement to them. Visible signs were developed which told you who was defiled and what the defilement was. For instance, the leper had to maintain a certain distance between himself and others, and was required to cry out, "Unclean, Unclean." This way no respectable Jew would accidentally come in contact with a leper. The beggar also had a visual symbol. He wore a special coat. Others could identify him, and thus, avoid him.

It is against this background that Matthew tells us the story about Jesus' encounter with two blind men. Is this a story about us? Can we see ourselves in the role of the blind men? As you see the story unfold, perhaps you will want to be in their place and receive His touch!

The Calling
Matthew 20:30-31

And behold, two blind men sitting by the road, when they heard that Jesus was passing by, cried out, saying "Have mercy on us, O Lord, Son of David!" Then the multitude warned them that they should be quiet; but they cried out all the more, saying, "Have mercy on us, O Lord, Son of David!" (20:30-31). Jesus is passing by! Everything that will happen is dependent upon His passing. There would have been no miracle, but Jesus passed by. The two blind men would have remained in their blind condition, except Jesus passed by. The pivot point of the story is Jesus passing by. We call this **PREVENIENT GRACE**. It is a theological term. You will not find this phrase in the New Testament, however, the idea is found on every page of the Scriptures. Love is another word for *grace*. Prevenient means *going before*. Therefore, *prevenient grace* is **the love of God that goes before**. It is the call of God that comes to your life before you receive salvation.

Prevenient grace tells us that God has taken the initiative in our behalf. When we were not seeking Him, He was seeking us. Your desire for Him comes from His desire for you. You were sitting beside the road in your blindness, but Jesus passed by! We have no chance of finding Him, so He finds us. This is our story. We are the two blind men sitting by the road side. Jesus passed by. We did not initiate anything. Jesus passed by. He does it; we respond to it. We simply respond to what God does. There is no requirement of doing; it is a requirement of responding. The summary of Christianity from man's view is response. It never depends on us, but on Him. Will you respond to what He does? You are not required to start anything, continue anything, or merit anything. Will you respond to Him? All other religions require doing. Christianity, alone, knows the reality of God's passing by. Religion is man's search for God, but Christianity is God's search for man.

Do you see your face in verse thirty? You were sitting beside the road. You did not have a chance in your condition of blindness. There was no possibility of doing what needed to be done. But Jesus passed by! It is time to respond to Him. Let us call it a **PROCLAMATION OF FAITH**. Jesus passed by and the blind men cried out, ***"Have mercy on us, O Lord, Son of David!"*** (20:30-31). Jesus' passing by enabled the two blind men to cry out for mercy. How much did they understand when they cried out to Him? Had they studied the Old Testament law and the details of the Messianic promises? Did they know what the disciples knew because of walking with Jesus for several years? No! They had not, but there is good news. Their understanding did not matter. They were responding to what they did know. Jesus was passing by!

Do you see yourself in this picture? How much do you know? Do not be concerned about what you do not understand, but respond to what you do understand. One of our problems in the evangelical church is that we know too much. Understanding is good, if you respond. We are called to walk in all of the light that we have (I John 1:7). Would you respond to what Jesus has spoken to you about? Is that outlandish? Would you dare do anything less than this and think that you were one of His? The level of knowledge is not the issue. The issue is response.

There is another important element in this responding. It is the **PERSISTENCE OF FAITH.** *Then the multitude warned them that they should be quiet: but they cried out all the more, saying, "Have mercy on us, O Lord, Son of David!"* (20:31). The crowds could not keep the two blind men quiet. When a famous rabbi made a spiritual journey to Jerusalem, He passed through a major city like Jericho. The news would have spread of His coming. The people lined the streets to get a view of Him. They hoped to get close, and maybe even touch Him. Jesus used these opportunities to teach those who gathered. Suppose you are there as Jesus is passing by. He is in the middle of preaching a great message. Two blind men demand the attention of Jesus. They cry out and disturb the message of Jesus. The crowd turns on these men and tells them to keep quiet. But they see that they only have one chance. Jesus will not pass by this way again. This is their single opportunity to receive from Jesus. There is no way to keep them quiet now. They are responding to the presence of Jesus.

Everyone who has ever come to Jesus has had to go through extreme obstacles. I do not know if this is God's design or the Devil's plan, but there are always difficulties that hinder our response to Jesus' passing by. If you wait for a time when there are no obstacles, you will never respond. It will never be easier to pray, study the Bible, or witness, than it is right now. These two blind men had one opportunity. They would not allow any obstacle to hinder their response. We blame our past, but soon the present will be our past, and the obstacles will increase by our lack of response now.

The Confrontation
Matthew 20:32

So Jesus stood still and called them, and said, "What do you want Me to do for you?" (20:32). I seldom meet anyone who does not want to experience the call of God. The call of God on our lives is a high moment. We are prone to call upon God. The difficulty comes with the confrontation, but you must understand, the confrontation is inevitable.

The idea of confrontation is negative for us. However, allow me to share good news with you; the confrontation begins with **PREVENIENT GRACE**. *So Jesus stood still and called them,* (20:32). The confrontation of God is filled with a love that goes before. This verse tells us that Jesus had compassion upon these two blind men (20:34). This compassion is the heart of the confrontation.

This scene stands in the shadow of the cross. Chapter twenty-one starts the Passion Week, the last week of Jesus' life. For several weeks, Jesus has pressed toward the cross. The disciples rebuke Him about the very idea of the cross style. Confusion fills the atmosphere. Walls have risen between Jesus and His disciples. The leaders of Israel continue to undermine His ministry. They are a constant threat to Him. With all this pressure, why should Jesus bother with two blind men? They are not His responsibility. What will He gain from this?

Two blind men are very important to the Christ. He came to save the world. Jesus pushes aside the pressure of a world and passes by the blind men. He calls out to them. It is as if the crowd does not exist, and no one else is on the streets. He has come to Jericho for one reason - the two blind men. Do you see yourself in the story? He has done this for you. He confronts you with His *prevenient grace.*

Let's look at this in the light of the **PROBING OF FAITH**. Jesus' question to the two blind men is, ***"What do you want Me to do for you?"***(20:32). While this is a love confrontation, it is not a cheap love. It is not filled with weakness, allowing you to get by. This probing Christ will go to the heart of the issue. A policeman will probe to get at you, but Jesus is a skilled surgeon who wants to heal. A soldier probes to seek and destroy, but Jesus is like the vine dresser who wants to prune for greater growth. He is not probing as a critical professor who is looking for a mistake. He has the desire of an expert chef who is looking for the exact ingredient for the perfect recipe. ***"What do you want Me to do for you?"*** (20:32).

However, understand that there must be the **PRESENTATION OF FAITH**. There is something that must come from you. It is response. ***They said to Him, 'Lord, that our eyes may be open,"*** (20:33). The confrontation is never one sided. Jesus came to Jericho to confront them. They now have the opportunity to respond to the confrontation. In the culture of Jesus' day, every beggar was required to wear a special coat that identified him to the public. A blind beggar had to have a high collar added to the coat. He could wrap it around his face and cover his eyes, because by Jewish law, a blind man was required to hide his eyes in public. It is possible that these two blind men have their eyes covered with these high collars. When they cry out, their voices are muffled by the collars. They cry out the louder. When Jesus asks them what it is they want from Him, they must reach up, pull aside the collar, and expose their blinded eyes.

That is what Jesus is waiting for us to do. We carefully hide those troubled areas in our lives so no one knows. We do not want to risk ridicule. We have learned to put on a religious face; we cover well. It is time to expose ourselves to Jesus. We must allow Him to see us as we really are. We must risk what others may think. Jesus wants us to respond by exposing our need to Him.

The Compassion
Matthew 20:34

So Jesus had compassion and touched their eyes. And immediately their eyes received sight, and they followed Him, (20:34). **PREVENIENT GRACE** flows from the beginning of this story to the end. It is seen in *The Calling, The Confrontation*, and now in *The Compassion*. Jesus is not a Pharisee who thinks blinded eyes will defile Him. A legalist is concerned about how things will look. Jesus only wants to minister. He is a lover who has joined Himself to the need of His brothers. The Book of Hebrews tells us that He is not a stone faced God who cannot be moved by our infirmity. Rather, He is one who is moved by our need. He feels what we feel. He cannot tolerate blinded eyes. Jesus left His throne to get involved with these two blind men in Jericho.

The goodness goes beyond this truth. It is the **POSITION OF OUR FAITH.** Jesus did not just feel compassion for two blind men, but was compelled to touch them. He did not stay in the temple with His lofty ideas about law and religion, but He left it to teach great principles to many people. He was compelled to get involved in the hurts of two blind men. The need of these two men caused Him to leap off His throne and take on flesh. That is the way He is! God is not satisfied with our tithe, or impressed with our gathering on Sunday. Our legalism does not endear us to Him. He wants intimate contact with us. In the midst of our loneliness, He is with us. As the tears run from our eyes, He cries too. In our pain, He is suffering. He struggles with us in our confusion. In the midst of our sin, Jesus died on a cross for us. He has never left us alone.

As compassion flows to your life, a response is needed. It is the **PROGRESSION OF FAITH**. *And immediately their eyes received sight, and they followed Him* (20:34). These blind men moved out and followed Jesus. Does that surprise you? Wouldn't you expect that reaction? It is the natural, normal, acceptable response.

Do you see yourself in this story? Have you taken off your coat and said, "Jesus, see me as I am!" Church service after church service goes by. The conviction of God comes to the inner heart. But some keep covering their need. It is time to completely expose your blind eyes to Jesus. Get honest! Have you allowed Jesus to walk right by and never cry out to him? The opportunities have come repeatedly, but you have never responded. When are you going to crash against the obstacles that hinder you from finding Him? You long for deliverance, and you have seen the vision. Are you not yet willing to go against the crowd that tells you to keep silent? There will never be a better time than right now. It will never get easier. Will you never follow Him?

Or, is the story of the two blind men your story? You have heard His voice and you will respond to Him. You feel His touch, and you can never sit silently in your place again. Your lifestyle has been effected forever, and new vision is yours. Jesus passed by, and you are changed for eternity.

"Jesus, Your confrontation comes with tender compassion. You are calling to us. We hear Your voice. In this moment we cry out to You. We expose our need to You. Please touch us! In Jesus' name, we pray, Amen."

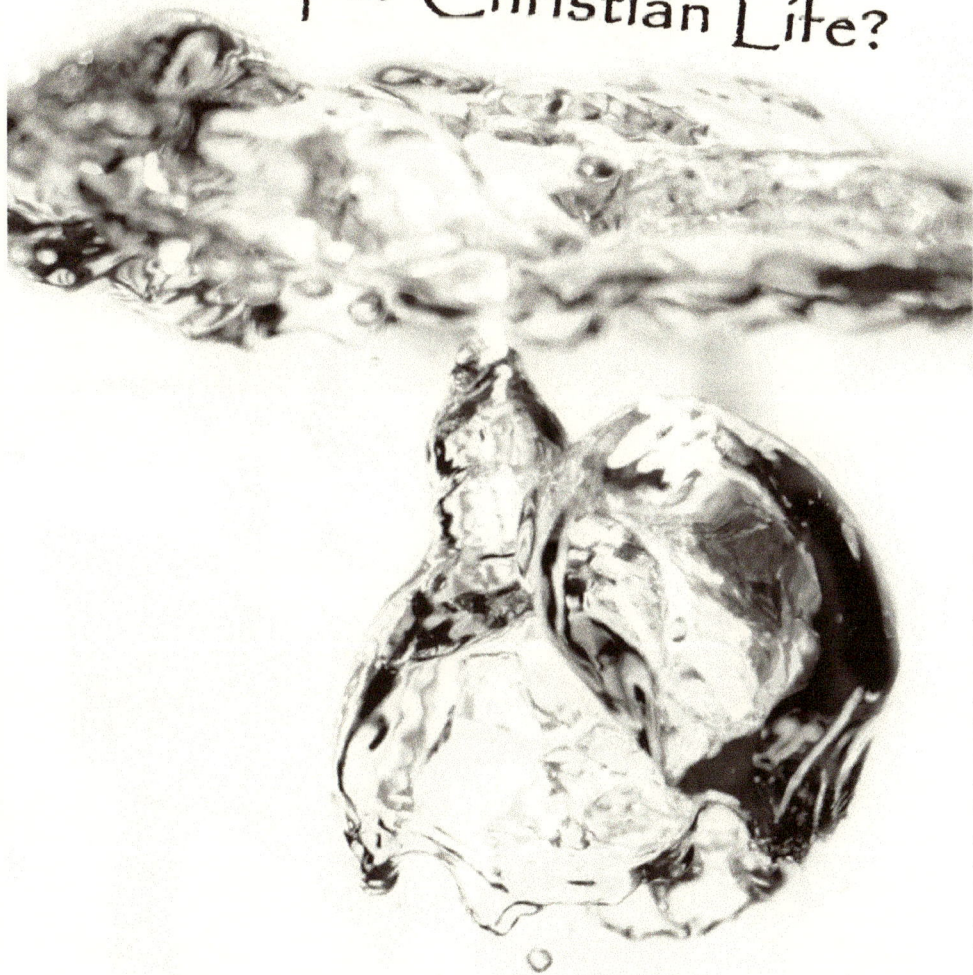

Looking for the Deeper Christian Life?

CrossStyle.org

www.ingramcontent.com/pod-product-compliance
Lightning Source LLC
Chambersburg PA
CBHW030935150426
42812CB00064B/2919/J